EISENHOWER
THE
PRESIDENT

EISENHOWER THE PRESIDENT

CRUCIAL DAYS,
1951-1960

William Bragg Ewald, Jr.

Prentice-Hall, Inc., Englewood Cliffs, New Jersey

Eisenhower the President: Crucial Days, 1951-1960
by William Bragg Ewald, Jr.
Copyright © 1981 by William Bragg Ewald, Jr.

Printed in the United States of America
Prentice-Hall International, Inc., London/Prentice-Hall of Australia, Pty. Ltd., Sydney/ Prentice-Hall of Canada, Ltd., Toronto/Prentice-Hall of India Private Ltd., New Delhi/ Prentice-Hall of Japan, Inc., Tokyo/Prentice-Hall of Southeast Asia Pt. Ltd., Singapore/ Whitehall Books Limited, Wellington, New Zealand
10 9 8 7 6 5 4 3 2 1

Library of Congress Cataloging in Publication Data
Ewald, William Bragg, date
  Eisenhower the President.

  Includes index.
  1. United States—Politics and government—1953-1961. 2. Eisenhower, Dwight David, Pres. U.S., 1890-1969. 3. Presidents—United States—Biography.
  I. Title.
E835.E92   973.921′092′4 [B]   80-22929
ISBN 0-13-246868-9

TO MARY

CONTENTS

..the most glorious of exploits do not always furnish us with the clearest discoveries of virtue or vice in men; sometimes a matter of less moment, an expression or a jest, informs us better of their characters and inclinations, than the most famous sieges, the greatest armaments, or the bloodiest battles whatsoever.

Plutarch, *Alexander*
(Dryden translation)

PROLOGUE

I have lived through the Eisenhower presidency three times. The first, that of a participant, began with my first glimpse of Dwight Eisenhower on the Boston Common at the height of his first presidential campaign in October 1952. He was on a rostrum fifty yards away, earnestly denying his political proficiency and calling for a great crusade to clean up the mess in Harry Truman's Washington; I was in the midst of a noisy enthusiastic crowd that almost wrecked my blue Studebaker coupé by climbing on the hood and roof for a better view of his back. This first living-through ended with my homeward flight, Los Angeles to Washington, D.C., on the campaign plane of the defeated Richard Nixon in November 1960 and the close of the Eisenhower administration in January 1961.

In the years between I served as a member of the Eisenhower White House Staff (1954–56) and assistant to Interior Secretary Fred Seaton (1957–61), with a year off for an Eisenhower Exchange Fellowship trip abroad (1959–60), before joining the Nixon campaign train and plane in the final fall.

Beginning as one of the youngest White House staffers, I often found myself seeing Dwight Eisenhower from a distance: looking across the crowd in Boston; peering out my East Wing office window at the President hitting chip shots across the White House lawn; looking up the long marble White House staircase in horror as eight solemn aides gently carried the President down on a stretcher after his

1

1956 ileitis attack; standing on the Tunisian coast during his triumphant eleven-nation goodwill trip in late 1959 and watching the presidential ship disappear in the distance; looking down from a 707 on a white speck of another presidential ship in the far Pacific after the collapse of his plan to visit Japan in June 1960, following the U-2 fiasco, Nikita Khrushchev's cancellation of the Paris summit conference, and massive Japanese mob protests against renewal of a defense treaty with the United States.

Living through the events of those years, I came to know the principal supporting players—their leanings, their quirks, their eye movements, the tone of their voices. I can never forget the loud "No!" of Jim Hagerty splitting the telephone earpiece when he was asked whether Eisenhower should write congratulations to a carping newspaper publisher who had won a major national award; and the cultivated Boston Brahmin oboe tones of National Security Assistant Bobby Cutler, a wartime aide to General George C. Marshall (who called him "a rose among cabbages"), a superb raconteur, a man like Jonathan Swift in his Anglicanism, fastidiousness with words, and risqué mind. And I can still hear the slow, sage, cautious baritone of Jerry Morgan, joining in a practical joke on gregarious Max Rabb, whose mythical "association" with a "Communist-front group" had just been "discovered": "I can see the headline now, Max: 'Secretary to the Cabinet Denies Red Link'"; and the heavy Alabama accent of congressional liaison chief Jerry Persons, contemplating a nationwide map of rivers and harbors projects: "This map should be entitled 'How to Judge Yo' Sennatuh.'"

Collectively, we were "the nervous men in the White House" because of our constant concern with making a mistake. "We can't have lardheads around here," Kevin McCann once exploded about one staffer's thoughtless answer to an inquiry. Everybody was a threat: the Democrats on the Hill, the ever-prying press, the closet-Democrat holdovers throughout the government, the State Department bureaucrats endlessly endeavoring to put you on the hook, the rich and powerful who could, if turned down, appeal directly to the President, even the man on the street who wrote the White House and stood ready to write his congressman if he didn't like your answer. Every incoming letter or phone call, however seemingly innocuous, might contain a bomb that could blow the unwary to kingdom come.

Always feeling oneself on display, one guarded against any possible slip. Once my wife, Mary, and I entered a restaurant with our

2

two-year-old son Bill, immaculate in his short gray flannels and knee-length socks. When everyone stopped eating to watch him, he realized he was the center of attention and rose to the occasion, proclaiming: "In our house we all say damn." Today we're amused, but then we were horrified.

The stately white ship sailing serenely on the green lawn of 1600 Pennsylvania Avenue was manned by a crew ever anxious. And unswervingly loyal to the President. And hardworking—incredibly hardworking, with too little time for their families. When our first child was about to be born—the one destined to say damn—Mary telephoned me at the office at 1 A.M. to say she thought she should go to the hospital. Bryce Harlow, my boss, having been through all this himself several times and now facing an hours-away deadline, was less sure: "It's probably a false alarm." But when it became obvious my work was not going to be very good, I was permitted to drive home, deliver Mary to the doctor, and then return to work the rest of the night. Early the next morning I dropped by to see my new son, took a shower, and drove back to the East Wing to start a new day.

But none of us ever became wearied. Washington is a glorious city, every inch alive with history and grace. Some say it has Southern efficiency and Northern charm. But in the Eisenhower years we felt it the center of the world, a center neither too precious nor too relaxed. No one could forget the Christmas eggnog parties upstairs in the private quarters of the mansion, or receptions at the National Gallery, or fireworks over the monuments of the city on the Fourth of July, which the staff and the employees and their children watched from the White House lawn, or receptions with dancing in the East Room. Spring comes with ease to the city, one wave of color following another, as cherry blossoms melt to jonquils to magnolias to tulips. It flows into soft summer air.

The beauty of Washington always sustains our public servants, and its simplicity, classical restraint, order, and moderation seemed to reinforce Ike's love of the middle course. What a contrast, for example, to go to a White House reception for the Queen of England, to see her in her jewels, to watch the formality and elegance of her greeting, and to compare it with the informality of Ike's warm grin and quick handshake. Each greeting, of course, was memorable in its own way.

Recent visitors to the White House East and West Wings, with their elaborate furnishings, would have been shocked to see the simplicity of the Eisenhower staff accommodations, usually an old sofa and utilitarian desk. When a carpet wore through, you found a matching (or nearly-matching) piece and patched. The working quarters hummed with the bustle of a large daily newsroom, and each member was free to thumbtack on the sheet-rock walls whatever he wanted. Bob Kieve, for example, had a supply of Spanish dancers, Jose Greco and his dark-eyed partners; and he cultivated on a windowsill a huge sweet-potato plant. He seemed to think his vine lacked something, however, and so he glued onto its infertile leaves one large yellow sunflower blossom.

A man whose deadpan practical jokes masked one of the shrewdest minds in Republican politics, Appointments Secretary Tom Stephens, encouraged members of the administration to paint a picture and donate it to "The Tom Stephens Collection"; this he hung in a West Wing hall. Some of the paintings showed talent, but some officials were reduced to contributing a paint-by-number concoction, like Interior Secretary Doug McKay's horse head.

As shocking as the simple furnishings would be the actual size of the Palace Guard I remember. It had not yet become a muscle-bound bureaucracy. It included a couple of key emissaries to the Hill and a press secretary with one principal assistant. It assembled for lunch in one small oblong room, its walls hung with Navy propaganda photos, since the food was prepared and served by Filipino stewards on leave from sea duty. In this room were two tables for six and four tables for four. That is all, twenty-eight seats. A staff member picked up his napkin ring at a shelf to the right as he entered, and he sat down anyplace except at the one table with a tilted chair, reserved for Staff Chief Sherman Adams and his guests. After lunch one returned the napkin to its ring: it was washed once a week. Most staff members' favorite memento of their White House service is that simple wooden ring bearing one's name and "White House Mess." Everyone wore a business suit except on Saturdays, the day for a sports jacket.

Most mornings the staff met promptly at 8:30 in the Conference Room for a briefing chaired by Governor Adams. This not only assured that everyone heard the agenda of the day; it also meant that all employees were on hand, in person, early, more or less awake—an old Yankee business trick.

A staff member would typically arrive at the White House before the Washington traffic jams, park his car (it had a special sticker) on East Executive Avenue, then enter the White House through a black iron fence and past uniformed White House Police. Guards, in those days of few employees, rarely made mistakes, since they knew everyone by sight. I do remember one unauthorized man who got through the net. He was wearing a white coat and carrying a bucket of black paint; he didn't like the color of the White House.

Working days had a certain rough-and-ready quality, and so did social gatherings. Staff members invited to a reception might be asked to stand on the basement stairs rubbing elbows in their evening clothes until dinner was over upstairs and they could walk grandly into the spaciousness of the chandeliered mansion.

To stand in the center of the White House mansion and look out is to see that it has two vistas, symbolic of the nation. One stretches north up Sixteenth Street to the banks and hotels and businesses, into the nineteenth-century America of money and factories and economic uproar and uplift and Alexander Hamilton. The other vista, opened in a grand imaginative gesture by the clearing of a mile-long alleyway through the trees, stretches south across green lawns to the fields and agriculture and civility of eighteenth-century America, a vista crowned by the rotunda memorial to Thomas Jefferson, standing clear at the farthest point of sight, with its ringing proclamation of the freedom of man's mind.

America is both vistas, and both should be the constant care of all its presidents. During those years in Washington these symbols always seemed a good reminder of the man we were serving.

My second tour through the Eisenhower presidency began with a drive from Washington to nearby Gettysburg, Pennsylvania, to meet with the former President on a Saturday morning in April 1961. (He met that afternoon with President Kennedy to hear what went wrong at the Bay of Pigs.) It ended with the publication of the second volume of Eisenhower's White House memoirs in 1965.

In the years between I served as research assistant to the former President for both volumes of those memoirs—*Mandate for Change* (1963) and *Waging Peace*. I came to know at close range the sensitive personal papers brought to Gettysburg from the White House, and the members of the Eisenhower family. Above all, as I once again lived through the Eisenhower administration day by day, this time I did so in the company of the President himself.

General and Mrs. Eisenhower's home was a farm just outside

Gettysburg, on the edge of the battlefield. Their son, John, his wife, Barbara, and their four children had a small house on the farm grounds about a mile away. But we worked in town in a red brick house on a corner of the Gettysburg College campus, converted into an office for the former President. The General, his personal secretary—first Ann Whitman, then Rusty Brown, both from the White House—and his trusted aide General Robert Schulz had offices—the President preferring the small one—upstairs. (Nothing ever got by the indispensable Schulz, a bulldog in loyalty to Ike and a man of strange gifts. It was Bob Schulz who planned my intricate route to Gettysburg across Washington, D.C., almost completely without traffic lights. And it was Schulz, regarded by many as a martinet, who at Ike's seventy-fifty birthday party at the Drake Hotel in New York came peeping into a nearby room with the women to see our youngest child, just a few weeks old, in his bassinet.) John and I occupied adjoining rooms downstairs. The three of us—the President, John, and I—made up the entire memoirs team.

An individual chapter might originate with a rough top-of-the-head draft from the President himself or with a detailed documented draft from John or me. Then we'd edit and re-edit it—the three of us, the President above all—until in the end it became a Dwight Eisenhower utterance, in both words and content. For late-draft shirtsleeves editorial sessions with John and me and the editors from Doubleday & Company, the President would descend the stairs, and we'd all gather either in my pine-paneled office, once a den, or in a small conference room across the hall, once a dining room. As we worked over the manuscript around the big polished table, Ike would strike out, write in, blow his stack, argue, listen, comment, and decide. Even in midsummer the whole place was cool and quiet, with abundant air-conditioning and deep-piled gray wall-to-wall carpeting.

For me, the fountainhead of the enterprise was none of these rooms, but the glassed-in security-wired back porch, the repository of a dozen or so gray metal filing cases which held the upper cream of the eight-year White House files, nearly all of them kept for the exclusive use of the President by his top secretary, Mrs. Whitman, whom Bill Hopkins called the best he'd ever seen in his forty-plus years on every presidential staff from Hoover to Nixon. This God's plenty included diary entries; correspondence with heads of government, Cabinet officers, and personal friends; records of appointments and phone calls; memoranda of Oval Office conferences with administration colleagues and outside visitors; minutes of Cabinet and National Security Council meetings. These papers, now housed at the Eisenhower Library in Abilene, Kansas, and gradually being opened to students of the period, form the foundation of the Eisenhower memoirs. I combed and recombed them; used them to put together drafts of chapters; questioned the President about them, triggering his reflections; and gradually came to see them as he saw them.

Drawing on these papers and the vast public collections in the Library of Congress, I helped—and at times overhelped—the President with detail. In writing he would often gloss over detail, as he knew. "In these first few chapters I've drafted," he remarked at the outset, "I've described a walk to the center of Gettysburg, as it were. I've said I turned left and right, but haven't described the dogs and cats I met along the way. I agree that these chapters need some anecdotal meat."

So among other things I set out to supply it—that and fidelity to fact. And the going wasn't always easy. I remember one terrible day. How I could have been so insensitive, I do not see. I had been contradicting what he thought was the record. He was tired, bleary-eyed with old papers. Finally we got down to one point dear to his heart. He was absolutely certain he had done one thing, though I had brought him documentary evidence he hadn't. Finally he got red in the face, got up from his chair, and marched out of the room. And I felt small left sitting there at the big table. Imagine, contradicting the General about what was, after all, his own history. Conceivably he could even, though it seemed unlikely, *be* right. Anyway, what did it matter? I was certain *I* was going to be fired, and I felt I deserved it. Ike came back in briskly. "If that's the way the record is," he said, "that's the way it's got to read."

Whatever his foibles, this iron respect for the truth underlay the feeling that I came to have for Dwight Eisenhower. He had begun his days as ex-President with a memorable action. Here was a man who for years had never driven a car; had never had to dial a telephone (he thought you still picked up the receiver and asked for "Central"); who as a young officer had even delegated to an aide the purchase and attachment of properly shiny replacement belt buckles. And suddenly in January 1961 he had found himself approaching the locked gate to his farm. Without hesitation he got out of the car before the driver could, pulled out his keys, fumbled a moment, and opened it up. And before we finished the memoirs, Mrs. Eisenhower, John, and I would find ourselves driving through Palm Desert, California (his winter home), to dinner with the seventy-three-year-old Ike at the wheel. He had both wielded and relinquished great power with realism. As he once remarked to an assistant at the storm center of a major international crisis, "We have to play the cards we've been dealt."

Gettysburg was a happy place, and my years there were happy years. We were in a landscape of Pennsylvania farm folk, apple pan dowdy, Civil War history, and friendly neighbors who never locked their doors. One hierarchy of the office establishment was set by an old farmer-caretaker named John Trostle. If he brought you a half-dozen ears of corn, you were in.

Ike was exceptionally fond of his only child, John: I never heard John's name mentioned without seeing the President's face light up. The relationship of father and son is made exceedingly difficult when the father is as famous as Eisenhower. The offspring of important men have a tension-filled existence even as young children. No one treats them normally; everywhere they are either overpraised or overblamed, given too much by the powerful (who often wish favors in return) or corrected too harshly by underlings (whose job depends on keeping them out of trouble). There is always the added pressure of the son's trying to achieve as much as the father; and how can one measure up to a father who is a five-star general and a president? Eisenhower and John managed all this as well as anyone could, the disagreements fewer than in the average family, the loyalty deep on both sides.

At this time, John was learning to fly, and he insisted that everyone fly with him. I remember one especially hair-raising one-engine trip where he lost North America for a while, and I was more or less stretching my neck through the cloud cover trying to spot dry land. He invited the President to soar with him and me to Berryville, Virginia, and I shall never forget the incredulous expression on Ike's face when he saw the size of the plane. "Is that it?" he demanded. Then he shook his head and said, "Okay. Let's go." John's instructor was the most phlegmatic of characters. He once decided against watching President Kennedy land at the Gettysburg airfield at four o'clock one afternoon because that was his time to eat.

I admired many things about John. He writes with skill and insight, and he has established a particular name for himself in the field of military history. He had an exquisite sensitivity to nuances that didn't fit his father. He grimaced every time he recalled how an editor had slipped in the aside that Eisenhower was "secretly pleased" by Foster Dulles' appointment of Bedell Smith as Undersecretary of State. The coy phrase was out of character.

But the thing I enjoyed most was John's great and perceptive sense of humor. His father would often quote Foster Dulles' observation that the two of them, President and Secretary of State, made a uniquely strong team, given Eisenhower's stature among leaders on the world stage and Dulles' lifelong study of diplomacy. But John saw the humor within. "We ought to start off a chapter with an epigraph like this," he said: " 'With your contacts and my brains, we can't miss—Foster Dulles.' "

Someone for some reason sent Eisenhower a large-as-life equestrian stuffed dummy of Teddy Roosevelt. John detached the Rough Rider from his horse, seated him in a downstairs office, a glass of bourbon in each fist, and left the shades open and the lights on all night. "The Gettysburg people think we're all crazy here anyway," he commented.

John and Barbara were fun to be with and excellent hosts; our children got along well. During the winters I kept my family in Washington, worked at the Library of Congress, and commuted to Gettysburg, but during the summer I brought everyone to a rented house directly on the battlefield. What fun for young boys to play in Devil's Den and reenact the Civil War! The benevolent ghosts of Lincoln, Meade, and Lee were everywhere. The very first day we moved in, John came by to welcome us and invite us to dinner. Mary was upstairs unpacking, and young Bill let him into the living room. John is somewhat shy, and eight-year-old Billy was, too. They looked at each other across the rug until Billy volunteered: "I don't believe in Santa Claus." He thought a minute and said, "And there's no such thing as the Easter Bunny either."

The Eisenhower children were adored by their grandparents, who nonetheless kept them under tight rein. They were unaffected, good children. But their parents did have to worry about having too many tourists about, hoping to glimpse the President's grandchildren. One day I overheard Charles, our second son, ask six-year-old Mary Jean, "Why does everyone want to stare at your house?" And Mary Jean told him: "Because it's the Eisenhower farm, and it's private property!" It was a great help to have the Eisenhower children so normal and good-humored. (Their many pets included a very ugly one-eyed dog named Tuesday.) And Ike was always absolutely insistent upon equal treatment among the kids, rushing to correct any injustice.

At one of his birthday parties, when everyone else was in the living room, I recall Ike was out in the kitchen with the children. Barbara had prepared a banquet of rich good things to eat without strict attention to his diet, only to have him look at the table and observe that the only thing the doctors would let him consume were the tomatoes. He thought a minute and then announced that sliced tomatoes were about as good as anything one could eat. Even a President can't have everything.

The farm was of course a very elegant home, filled with gifts from heads of state, from all over the world. Mrs. Eisenhower had a large collection of Boehm porcelain birds in one room. When Ike got to them, the first time he was showing us around, his comment was "God, wouldn't you hate to have to dust them." He spent hours painting in a small cubbyhole room, and Sergeant Moaney, his longtime black butler and factotum, would retrieve all his discarded canvases from the wastebasket. Ike would blow up, but to no effect. Finally, he took to painting a big X over them, but Moaney's private collection still continued to expand.

Eisenhower and his wife had an excellent marriage, mutually supportive, of the sort prevalent in America at the time, the sort memorialized in the lyric "when men were men and girls were girls." Ike and Mamie found each other different—and amusing. Her concerns were totally home and husband and family. "Ike never brought his troubles home with him," she told me after his death. "People would ask me what he thought about something or other, and I could look them in the eye and say, 'I *don't know.*'"

Once when my wife, John, and I were having dinner at the farm with the President, the four of us alone, John brought up the name of Kay Summersby, Eisenhower's attractive British wartime secretary, whose association with him had for years inspired gossip and speculation. What was she doing now? John asked. Ike handled it perfectly, I thought; a bit hurt, perhaps, he simply told John the little he knew. He was an exceedingly controlled man, able to submit his mind to fact even in this most personal of episodes. Nothing could better illustrate his humility. No defense, no denial, no anger. He was just with himself as with others.

Throughout, Eisenhower was exceedingly protective of his wife. He enjoyed sitting with her on their large glassed-in farmhouse porch, overlooking the green fields, reading, and watching television. And he enjoyed her good sense of humor and her spontaneity. One evening at Palm Desert out of the blue she turned to that earnest young man, me, and asked me to zip up her evening gown. "Ike'll take too long finding his glasses," she laughed.

Incidentally, neither on that occasion nor on any other did I ever see Mrs. Eisenhower do what people who are supposed to have an alcohol problem do: drink too much or drink nothing whatsoever. As I recall, she had a single old-fashioned and was the star of the evening. One more instance of vicious gossip.

"Grief comes out in various ways," she told me after Ike's death. "I've never been much of a crier. My grief comes out through my voice." And as long as she lived at the farm, she felt his presence: "I can still see him coming up the stair, see his hand on the railing."

From the first moment in Gettysburg, of course, I knew I was entering an experience of a lifetime. Yet from the start I recognized, as I feel sure the President did, the inherent irritants in the association we had entered into. I had heard about the General's reticence with praise and about the Eisenhowers' tightness with money—undoubtedly the product of long years on an Army salary. (Once after the President's death, my youngest child came with us to see Mrs. Eisenhower at the farm. On a cocktail table were two little animals on toothpicks, the sort put as decoration into cupcakes, worth under a penny apiece, and it was obvious that he was, to our embarrassment, silently begging for them. Mrs. Eisenhower clearly didn't want to part with them. After a lengthy visit, she got herself together and said that he could have them. He took them up and thanked her, but as he was leaving the house, he carefully put them back on an end table.) Into the bargain this tight-fistedness was, if anything, exceeded by that of Eisenhower's canny Scots publisher and longtime friend Chairman Douglas Black of Doubleday, who negotiated my salary.

I knew all this going in. But I could never totally forget the nagging fact that I had taken a cut in income and was churning out with pencil and paper page after page of a book that would bring both Eisenhower and publisher a great sum—a book that, however generous Eisenhower's acknowledgments, they would pretend was written, every word, by the General himself. And it didn't help to send him regularly Christmas and birthday presents and receive a letter in return.

The President, on his side, must surely have looked at me, as upon any close assistant, as someone who could injure him. What, he must have asked, will this young whippersnapper say about me? What will he do with the information disclosed to him? Does he have sense enough to understand it? Will he tell the truth? I, conversely, had constantly to ask, Am I being bent to someone else's purpose? Will I be fired? It all came down to this: How can anyone give much friendship to an underling who is also in part a spy? And how can an underling like someone who has so much power over him?

These questions remained. But as time went on, answers began to emerge. Objective correlatives, on both sides, began to appear. The President did, with some mild prompting, write generous acknowledgments in both volumes—far more generous, I believe, than for any other assistant on any comparable project. He did give Mary and me, again with some gentle prompting, a signed painting of the Gettysburg autumn woods, which we treasure. And the last gift we ever sent him—a small terra-cotta medallion of Europa and the Bull—he had hanging in his office, almost alone in a wide expanse of wall, on his last day in Gettysburg. And this valuing of my small gift, this time unprompted, I consider the most memorable and touching of all.

The placing of that medallion resulted not from my suggestion and not from my contribution to the memoirs, but from another event— one that ushered in a third reliving of the Eisenhower White House years.

In 1967, the memoirs completed, I began tentative drafting of an account of my own of that presidency. And to get the General's reaction, I sent him a thirty-page summary piece titled "Of Ike and Myths and History," sprung from my outrage at the discrepancy between the President as seen by many journalists and historians— genial, unintelligent, inactive—and the President as I knew him to be.

In this document I was saying things he could not or would not say in his own defense, and his response could not have thrilled me more. It was not only encouraging but humbling and moving to see the gratitude of this monumental man for the fact that someone, anyone, would at long last write a word of outright praise for his performance in office.

From that crucial day until the last time I saw him—late in 1968, on his deathbed at Walter Reed Hospital—we spoke and corresponded about the project, which has resulted in this book. He sent me suggestions and asked friends to help. And the affection and trust on both sides I shall remember the rest of my life.

In this final period I have lived through the Eisenhower presidency for the third time, a historian, looking at both the events and the man himself in retrospect, against swiftly changing backdrops and with the explosion of new sources of information.

One by one, the happenings and revelations of the late sixties and of the seventies have thrown new scenery behind the Eisenhower administration. Vietnam, Merle Miller's publication of Harry Truman's fulminations about Ike and Kay Summersby, Watergate, the Church Committee's allegation of Eisenhower's complicity in an assassination plot, the revolution in Iran, the revelation that the Eisenhower Oval Office contained a secret tape recording system, the nation's experience with ruinous inflation—each of these events, among others, makes us see the Eisenhower presidency in a new light, illuminating or distorting the truth.

Again and again I have recalled that zany moment in *A Night at the Opera* in which Harpo Marx swings on the scene-changing ropes backstage during a production of *Il Trovatore* and gives the old gypsy woman Azucena, singing near the footlights, a non-Verdian succession of backgrounds—fruit pushcart, railroad station, ball park.

In the search for accuracy I have received from these years not only new contexts but new candor. I have supplemented my own experience in Washington and Gettysburg with dozens and dozens of interviews—frequently multiple interviews—of primary sources, the rock-solid people Ike trusted most, who consequently knew most. And they have spoken of him and of his era with warmth, generosity, and abandon: Lucius Clay revealing "the only deal we ever made" in the 1952 convention; Tom Stephens recalling Ike's sudden realization, after the end of a Cabinet meeting: "Jesus Christ, we forgot the prayer!"; Sherman Adams peeling the paint off the walls in remarks on Dulles and Benson; Herbert Brownell revealing the message he carried from Eisenhower to Earl Warren before Warren's appointment as Chief Justice; Arthur Burns recalling his disputes with George Humphrey; Lucius Clay, Bob Schulz, Al Gruenther, Milton Eisenhower, and others speculating freely on the Kay Summersby episode, contributing few new facts and tending to discount most of the tale, which is undermined also by Ike's own letters in 1945; Nelson Rockefeller spinning a theory that Eisenhower's shortfalls as a leader came from an unhappy home life, which prevented his listening to sensitive and knowledgeable Oveta Hobby instead of to the hard-nosed boys like Dulles and Humphrey; Ann Whitman, loyal secretary for years to Rockefeller as well as Eisenhower, labeling this theory "ridiculous"; Richard Bissell, master of CIA dirty tricks, dilating on Eisenhower and assassination; Jackie Cochran describing Ike as her most expensive house guest; Meade Alcorn recalling the "dirtiest job" Eisenhower ever gave a Republican National Chairman.

Finally, these years have yielded up new documents—not only oral histories heretofore closed but above all the voluminous, close-in, unbuttoned diaries of C. D. Jackson, Bernard Shanley, and Jim Hagerty, quoted here extensively for the first time. "I know what you're doing, you sonofabitch," one envious White House staffer told me he used to think to himself as he watched Jim scribble furiously away at meeting after meeting. "You're going to write a book." Well, Jim has never written that book. Instead, he has done something more magnanimous, for which all future students will be forever in his debt: he has opened his journal in its entirety to history. And that history begins here.

So let me end with what this book is not, and what it is. It is not a personal memoir of my own years in the Eisenhower administration. It is not a rehash of the memoirs of the President. Like my old friend, the brilliant journalist Max Freedman, "I will not chew old straw." I have tried to confine myself to facts, verbal comments, and documents hitherto unpublished. Finally, it is not an exercise confined to academic research.

It is a book that draws on all three journeys through the years 1951–61. Others participated in the events—many far more extensively than I. Others have read parts of the Whitman collection of White House papers, those that have been opened, that I read and reread in association with the President at Gettysburg. Others have read oral histories and conducted interviews. But no one else has done—or now can ever do—all three. That fact, I believe, makes the book unique on Eisenhower and perhaps in some measure on the American presidency itself.

Throughout I have tried to answer two related questions. First, what in fact happened: what did Eisenhower do, and how?

When the heat of the day is over, a man wants others to avoid his mistakes and cook by his good recipes. Eisenhower was an excellent chef—many Secret Service men can vouch for his breakfasts—and though sin is more fun in the short run to read about than virtue, it is the "how to" messages that in the end survive. "I saw at first hand the Truman, Johnson, and Nixon Administrations," Ike's Attorney General William Rogers reflects, "and Eisenhower towers over all of them." Since the crash of October 24, 1929, and the Japanese invasion of Manchuria on September 18, 1931, the world has known few years—except the Eisenhower years—free from shooting war, deep depression, or ruinous inflation. What Eisenhower the President did—how he produced eight years of both peace and prosperity—is surely worth our study.

But beyond this I have tried to focus on what Eisenhower the President was. Was he the popular father figure of the 1950s man-in-the-street—the President with the grin, not too bright, but decent, always friendly, somewhat bland, dependent on his staff: the kind of amiable quiet President the country needed in a quiet time?

Was he the hero, bold, spotless, impeccable, of the Republican litany—the leader who restored decency and patriotism to the White House, ended the long night of Democratic decadence, faced down the Communists abroad, cleaned out the subversives in the government at home, restored sound money, and left the office as he had entered it, first in war, first in peace, first in the hearts of his countrymen?

Was he the confirmation of the cyclical theory of Arthur M. Schlesinger, Jr.: one of the hesitant, weak, indecisive presidents—like Harding, Coolidge, and Hoover—who followed such strong, decisive activists as Wilson, Franklin Roosevelt, and Truman, leaders who had made our constitutional system work by unremittingly enlarging the scope of executive power?

Or was he, after all these years of Arthur Schlesinger, exactly the reverse: a leader deserving of the broad label (it stretches from FDR to Hitler) "activist"?

Was Eisenhower the American Neville Chamberlain: the decent, honorable, befuddled President sketched by Emmet Hughes, surrounded by conservative clods and the evil genius of Foster Dulles, a president who, for all his soaring wishes and words, finally failed— failed to reshape the Republican party, failed to come to diplomatic engagement with the Russians, failed to uphold the rights of blacks in 1957, failed to sustain throughout eight years the grand thrust of force with which he had begun in 1953, and thus at the end left his nation slipping toward grave peril, the history of the 1950s a void, an era in which little happened?

Was Eisenhower the American Machiavelli, the devious and deceptive man who succeeded by keeping everybody fooled; the "great tortoise" perceived by revisionist Murray Kempton in 1967, and later by Garry Wills, "upon whose back the world sat for eight years," never knowing "the cunning beneath the shell"? Was Eisenhower the man Kempton saw "coldly measuring the gain or loss from dropping Nixon as his 1952 Vice Presidential candidate," all the while letting Nixon think "it was Tom Dewey's doing"? Was Ike the sneaky man who let Nixon and Adams walk through his mine fields for him, who consciously scrambled his syntax to confuse the press?

In another piece of revisionism in 1974, was Eisenhower the implacable enemy of the Soviet Union seen by Peter Lyon, the pawn of the reactionary golfing rich who paid his bills and composed his economic tenets, the man who summoned his fellow countrymen to war—total war—in his first inaugural address and pursued it for eight years thereafter, relentlessly spurning all Kremlin overtures toward peace? And did Eisenhower, in the words of William V. Shannon of *The New York Times*, thus in effect bring on Vietnam? "As long as the nation pursued the global policies he devised," Shannon wrote, "Vietnam or a war of similar character was inevitable sooner or later."

Or was Eisenhower something even worse, an assassin: a man who, by the "reasonable inference" of Senator Frank Church's Committee on Intelligence in 1975, approved the CIA's plan to murder Patrice Lumumba, Congo Communist, in late 1960?

Some of these descriptions of course contain snatches of the Eisenhower portrait, since Eisenhower the President was a man both complicated and misunderstood. But one need not go so far as Robert Sherwood did when he confessed he never understood what was going on in the "heavily forested interior" of the mind of FDR. Dwight Eisenhower is far more complex than most people have allowed. But he is not a total enigma. In the record of his thought and action a pattern does clearly emerge. This book attempts to set out this pattern.

PROLOGUE

It focuses on a sequence of historical events. Each, I believe, reveals a significant feature of the man and of his presidency—a feature that each chapter analyzes, citing other instances of its appearance during his pursuit and occupancy of the White House. And the events at the outset of the chapters also mark moments when, however slightly, history turned.

Book One

DAYS
OF DAWNING

I

JANUARY 31, 1951

THE GOOD SOLDIER

Five-star General of the Army Dwight D. Eisenhower, Supreme Commander of all the Allied forces in Europe during World War II, had an enormous capacity for getting along with people. He could judge them, he could make them like him, and, rarest of all, he could judge himself. All three abilities he put to the service of a standard, one to which as a good soldier he rigidly disciplined himself. He could, as a result of this control, accomplish great national purposes even with men toward whom he inwardly felt cool or even anti-pathetic—men like Franklin D. Roosevelt during World War II or Lyndon Baines Johnson and Sam Rayburn during the fifties. But the portrayal of this Eisenhower trait, I believe, must begin with an account of his relations not with these men, but with another, one whom Ike came actively and openly to dislike—Harry S Truman. And it must begin at the climax of their postwar association, on January 31, 1951.

The morning of that day, Eisenhower, just named Supreme Allied Commander of the North Atlantic Treaty Organization, flew through a driving sleet storm into Washington's National Airport to effect a rescue. He had come, at President Truman's request, to try to persuade Congress to commit U.S. forces to the defense of Western Europe.

It was a day of darkness and fear. We were fighting a hot war in Korea: Red Chinese forces had launched their first major attack on

21

November 26, 1950, and sent General Douglas MacArthur's troops reeling south. We were scanning the globe wondering where the Communist enemy would strike next: Hong Kong? Japan? Iran? Western Europe itself? Nobody knew: not CIA Director General Walter Bedell ("Beetle") Smith; not Secretary of Defense George C. Marshall; not the National Security Council; not President Truman himself.

From the sidelines Truman had a wondrous variety of advice: pull out of Europe and Korea and scurry home to Fortress America; pull out of Korea and dig in in Europe; abandon Europe and bomb hell out of China; bomb hell out of everybody. (Air-raid tests were beginning in Rockefeller Center; the New York Public Library had posted bomb shelter areas.) *Fortune* magazine summed up the crisis: "Never was America so nearly unanimous on the fact that it has a mortal enemy; never was it in such a quandary about how to proceed." World government now, E. B. White observed, "would resemble a combination of Alcatraz and Brearley."

These were the problems. And nobody thought Harry Truman could cope with them. In those days only a few would have called him, as some historians later would call him, a "great" or "near great" President. A few would have called him a gutsy fighter. But even more would have called him an incompetent—a man not too bright, overwhelmed by his office, saddled with crooks and cronies and grafters all over his administration; plagued by the Communists and fellow travelers and pinkos who honeycombed—or were said by one Joseph R. McCarthy to honeycomb—his whole executive branch.

No, Truman wouldn't do, couldn't do. He was the little man who failed, who reached the exalted World War I rank of captain in the Army, who ran a haberdashery store that went under, who rose in politics on updrafts of the notorious Pendergast machine, whose morals wouldn't allow him to repudiate grafters in his own government, whose social horizon stretched no further than the Main Street of a provincial Missouri backwater, whose high-school-only education trailed far behind Ivy League pennants, leaving him muddled in the boondocks. Even his appearance was typical of the small-town salesman—starched shirt, creased pants, stiff smile, a bit of jewelry showing under the old fedora. One citizen of Dover, New Hampshire—no metropolis—claimed that he knew four hundred men in town who could run the government better than Harry Truman, and he got his comeuppance: "Joe, you underestimate the men of Dover."

Now this beleaguered and unappreciated President was trying to rally congressional and public opinion behind his resolve to commit the United States to team up with our NATO allies to defend Western Europe. Two questions loomed:

1. Did Truman have the constitutional right to dispatch U.S. forces to Europe in peacetime without approval of the Congress? Powerful Republican voices, Senators Robert A. Taft of Ohio and Kenneth Wherry of Nebraska, argued he did not; Truman argued he did.

2. Would the Europeans pull their weight in their own defense? Again, loud voices shouted no: the voice, for example, of former President Herbert Hoover, then a stodgy figure out of a conservative past, who on nationwide radio had called for a cutoff of assistance to Europe until the Europeans themselves summoned enough strength "to erect a sure dam against the Red flood." And surprisingly, the voice of a young congressman from Massachusetts, John F. Kennedy: "If Europe is to be saved, Europe must commence to make sacrifices...."

In this time of darkness and fear an embattled Harry Truman called upon Dwight Eisenhower, at that moment perhaps the most heroic figure in the world; surely the most admired and most trusted of Americans—the Supreme Commander who had led the Allied armies to victory over Hitler. And Ike responded: first with acceptance of the NATO command in late 1950; then with a turn-of-the-year whirlwind tour of the NATO capitals to probe their will to save themselves; and finally with his January 31, 1951, flight to Washington.

As a good soldier, Eisenhower had come for the good of the country, responding to demands of loyalty and duty, overriding all personal sentiments. Over the years he again and again displayed such a capacity to rein in his fiery temper, his quick hot flashes of indignation, in disciplined cooperation for the national good with men about whom he had, at the least, sharp personal reservations. He had done so in suffering the outrages of the insufferable and brilliant British commander Field Marshal Montgomery all through the war. And Eisenhower had done so also with his Commander in Chief in that war, President Franklin Roosevelt.

Why did Ike dislike Roosevelt? The fact that he came, a plain soldier, from Abilene, Kansas, and Roosevelt came, a wily patrician, from Hyde Park, New York, won't explain their divergence (after all, Harry Truman of Independence, Missouri, and Dean Acheson of Groton and Yale got along fine). The answer lies in chemistry: as Eisenhower once remarked to speechwriter Arthur Larson, anent Roosevelt's love of practical jokes on inferiors, "Roosevelt was essentially a cruel man."

This observation, from a man without a trace of cruelty in his nature, suggests the two inhabited different psychological realms. The contrast shows at the famous wartime encounter in Tunisia of these two giants of recent American political history. President Roosevelt, not yet suffering from fatal illness, debonair, determined, courageous, a sage leader of a still young nation before it became dominant in the world, of a fortunate nation struggling to achieve a dream, meets the foursquare General chosen to head the Allied forces, upon whom he depended for the country's safety and doubtless for much of his own position in history. This military alliance would eventually win America's supremacy the globe around, but that was not known.

Roosevelt had come across the sea to meet with Prime Minister Winston Churchill in late 1943 after the victory in North Africa. Ike, returned from inspecting burned-out tanks, finds him sitting at lunch beside the road. The President looks up and asks him what odds, a year previously, he would have demanded that he would see "the President of the United States" eating in that spot.

At every point in the conversation, Roosevelt, ebullient, asserts his dominance: having, in his own mind, taken over the war, he praises that "Old Tory" Churchill, his staunch ally; he says he wishes the African invasion could have come before the elections of 1942. When the Secret Service suggests they move along for security reasons, Roosevelt reminds Ike of his inferior position: "You are lucky you don't have the number of bosses I have," he remarks. He says nothing directly to show he is pleased with Eisenhower's performance, whereas Churchill, always mindful of a subordinate's feelings, had praised it. Roosevelt is Ike's superior, and he is the sort of superior who often rules by keeping men insecure.

In the bright North Africa light one sees the two men silhouetted against the yellow earth: one with his confident smile, his cigarette holder, his sunken eyes, his urbane voice, his crippled body, facing the other, his khaki uniform worn with hat askew, his happy grin, his taut physical strength and alert mental health. The coddled only child, reared to lead, but whose victory has been achieved only after a cruel struggle against disease, faces the confident man of ordinary expectations, the middle child of a large, struggling family of sons, for whom greatness is still unforeseen. The politician *par excellence*, the master of the devious, the man of irony and wit, faces the honest soldier, bluff, straightforward, an average man, the man not of wit so much as of humor. The chemistry was different.

Both men smiled easily, one with open animal good spirits, one with reflective amusement. One enjoyed testing men to learn the parameters of the human condition; one met everyone with the same good feeling and rigid code of behavior, limiting mine and yours: he resisted any intrusion over the barriers, not just his own but anyone else's. Both were optimists, one that the spirit could survive anything, one that the spirit was good. Both knew how to rule men and get exactly what they wanted, though one used balance of power and one used cooperation.

The ends of both were humane, though one saw himself as superior, one as high-average in a superior position. To achieve his goal, one could pretend to be of modest intelligence, the other could pretend to be a god. Roosevelt, using Ike for their mutual good purposes, understood why Ike would obey orders. Ike had a rational ground for obeying his superior, but he reserved his judgment.

One man liked to get up in the morning, one had painfully to pull himself out of bed; one required courage for each movement, one's courage was natural as breath. Both believed in the strength of God. One merely witnessed God's power, one was forced to feel it. Reality was more cruel to one than to the other, his wider experience bought by deeper doubt. Yes, the laughter was different. There was a different chemistry.

When Roosevelt informed Joseph Stalin of his decision to give Eisenhower command of the Normandy invasion—in a message signed December 6, 1943, in Cairo—the words were written down (in a conscious act of presidential cruelty?) by amanuensis General George C. Marshall, Army Chief of Staff, who most probably had hoped for the command himself. With the iron discipline of a great gentleman, Marshall scribbled Roosevelt's conclusion in a backward slanting hand. Then, after the message went, with characteristic magnanimity he sent the original manuscript to his protégé

Eisenhower with a note at the bottom: "I thought you might like to have this as a memento." That faded piece of yellow foolscap, framed, Eisenhower clearly prized among all his trophies.

In public utterances, throughout his life, Eisenhower remained impeccably correct about Roosevelt, the man who had assured his place in history by giving him command. Whenever critics attacked Ike for refusing to drive ahead at the war's end and seize Berlin before the Russians did—as Churchill for one urged—Ike would regularly remind them he was only an agent, a military man following the orders of his Commander in Chief. And though I heard Ike at least once in retrospect speculate privately that "maybe old Churchill was right," he regularly defended his action in holding back from Berlin, in accordance with Roosevelt's political decision.

Never in public and rarely in private did Eisenhower say an unkind word about Roosevelt. In both his book on the war, *Crusade in Europe* (1948), and—much more briefly—in the first volume of the White House memoirs, *Mandate for Change* (1963), Eisenhower told good-humored stories of Roosevelt's visits to wartime Tunisia and its battleground. Both in *Crusade in Europe* and in Gettysburg conversations as we worked on *Mandate for Change* Eisenhower spoke— frequently at the prompting of his liberal editors—of Roosevelt's optimism, of his absolute confidence that the United States and its allies would win in the end. And in *Crusade* Eisenhower set down a summary that has weathered the test of time. "With some of Mr. Roosevelt's political acts I could never possibly agree. But I knew him solely in his capacity as leader of a nation at war—and in that capacity he seemed to me to fulfill all that could possibly be expected of him."

When Republicans rightists attacked Roosevelt for selling us down the river to Stalin at Yalta, Ike refused to join the posse, whatever he may have felt inside. (At Yalta, he told the Legislative Leaders January 25, 1954, "our Commander in Chief didn't have to be so indiscreet and crazy.") As a member of the White House Staff in early 1955, I remember sitting one day in the office of Governor Sherman Adams, Eisenhower's White House Chief of Staff. The phone rang: on the line was Bedell Smith, Eisenhower's Chief of Staff during the war and now John Foster Dulles' Undersecretary of State. The State Department was considering release of the Yalta papers— documents on the secret wartime conference—and some Republican reactionaries were seeing a new chance to clobber the Roosevelt memory.

Not Eisenhower. "Now, Beetle," Adams was saying, "you know how the Boss feels: he doesn't want to throw any rocks at Roosevelt."

But for all this forbearance, Ike remained reserved about Roosevelt, and any sharp-eyed observer could detect his ambivalence. One could see it, for example, in our editorial sessions on early drafts of the memoirs, as the General, his son, John, assorted editors from the publishing house, and I sat around the Gettysburg conference table; Eisenhower would reminisce about the war, suggesting he thought Roosevelt took too lightheartedly the Soviet menace. "You fellows quit worrying," Eisenhower quoted FDR, "after the war I'll take care of Uncle Joe."

Another observer detected this ambivalence in Eisenhower's stag-dinner reminiscences of how, as a relatively young officer, he had once had to help carry FDR off to bed after an evening of too much drinking—a memory that appalled him, in the era of first-strike perils and push-button warfare. "I like a highball or two myself," Ike concluded, "but I'll tell you one thing: nobody's ever going to have to put *me* into bed."

Eisenhower's feeling also came through clearly in the lists of "great men" he was forever compiling, lists that always started with Marshall and Churchill and always ended before including Roosevelt.

And one can see it most clearly of all in a single sentence spoken by Ike December 14, 1961, in his Gettysburg office as he reflected on Roosevelt's willingness to try, through secret wartime agreements, to get some kind of postwar peace in the world. With testy impatience, eyes flashing, Ike summed up his ambivalence: "For those things I don't blame Roosevelt one damn bit, much as I didn't like him." Policy, with Eisenhower, was one thing, personal feeling another. And the fire and self-discipline that lie coiled in his sentence—both had served the winning of the war.

Years later, in the Eisenhower presidency, the same fire and self-discipline would serve another major national purpose—the enactment of Eisenhower's legislation proposals by a Congress controlled by a Democratic opposition under Senate Majority Leader Lyndon Johnson and House Speaker Sam Rayburn.

"That fellow's such a phony," Eisenhower once remarked of Johnson, not without amusement.

Yet, given the Democratic majorities in the Senate and House after the elections of 1954, which became more lopsided in later years, Ike had to work with Johnson, the back-slapping Texas wheeler-dealer forcing himself on history, or let the country face legislative stalemate. Among other things, Eisenhower couldn't stand Johnson's Arab-like habit of pushing his face right into his own during conversation. But on November 6, 1957, a month after the Russians orbited *Sputnik*, Eisenhower invited Johnson to the Oval Office for a detailed history of the United States missile program, and later confided to his diary that Johnson had realized the Democrats under Truman bore much of the blame for U.S. missile delay: "Let's forget partisanship," LBJ had said, "and get the job done." Then with his customary wariness of the Senate's majority leader, Eisenhower confided in his dictation: "I think today he's being honest."

On another day, after Johnson became President, Eisenhower reached a different conclusion. Johnson, embattled during Vietnam, invited Ike to chopper down from Gettysburg for a half-hour top secret conference in the helicopter at a Washington airport. The meeting ended, the chopper took off for Gettysburg, and Ike began scribbling notes on a yellow pad. An aide flicked on the radio, hoping to get the ball game. Instead, he got a news flash: "The President has just met with General Eisenhower...."

"That sonofabitch!" Ike exploded. "He said the meeting would be secret!" And he tore the yellow page to shreds.

Ike didn't wholly trust Rayburn either—a man of whom, as 1956 began, he expected "nothing but politics," whose every utterance he would take "with six grains of salt." "That fellow," he once told me, "would double-cross you." Yet all this suspicion made a counterpoint, over the years, to a genuinely cordial working relationship between Eisenhower and the two Texans. I have no doubt, for example, that Ike meant every word he wrote on July 10, 1956, to his old friend Texas oil zillionaire Sid Richardson, about Johnson't great helpfulness: "Among the things that have been on my mind has been the desire to tell you how wonderful Lyndon was to me while I was ill [with ileitis]. His solicitude really touched me deeply. Also, during the past year when I have had to call on him for help on non-partisan issues, he has always done his best. I just wanted you to know what a great assistance he has been, and how appreciative I am."

Yet I have no doubt that Eisenhower had no regrets whatsoever over leaving this letter out of the memoirs. We had included it in a preliminary draft of one chapter, which in early 1963 we sent for comments to General Wilton B. ("Jerry") Persons, Eisenhower's chief White House legislative assistant. And Persons blew his top: "I suggest that you have a hard look at the potential political consequences of the political endorsement that is given unwittingly to Lyndon on Page 29 of this Chapter. Lyndon is a very active politician who will be running in 1964 and probably in 1968. He can be expected to use anything in the public domain that is to his political advantage and you will see these remarks on many a billboard.... I don't think that Lyndon did anything toward the passage of your program that he did not think to be in his own best political interests." Eisenhower, amused, deleted the letter.

As a result of goodwill on both sides, Eisenhower, Johnson, and Rayburn could join forces, much of the time, on major legislation. ("With Eisenhower as President and Johnson and Rayburn in the Congress," former Defense Secretary Thomas Gates recalls, "you always knew that on defense and foreign policy you'd win, though for political purposes they might give you hell.") And even in disagreement they remained friends. After Kennedy became President, Sam Rayburn once complained about Republican Minority Leader Charles Halleck: "You know, I just can't understand it: Charlie Halleck just *hates* that young man. Why, Lyndon Johnson and I didn't hate Eisenhower; we tried to help him all we could."

And Ike went to extraordinary lengths to placate the Texans, particularly the touchy Johnson. Offhandedly in August 1959, after the Senate Democrats had infuriated Ike by ganging up against the confirmation of Lewis Strauss as Secretary of Commerce, Eisenhower tossed off a list of good Democratic presidential candidates—a list that left the name of Lyndon Johnson out. Word of Johnson't fury got back to the White House, and Ike himself phoned the majority leader to explain: this list, he said, had included no one seriously being considered; it included, for example, only people like Sam Rayburn and Senators Frank Lausche, John Stennis, and Spessard Holland. By no means did it indicate any kind of personal rift between him and Johnson. But Thruston Morton, the Republican National Chairman, Johnson sulkingly replied, had reportedly said that Eisenhower was "burning mad" at him. Again, Ike smoothed the troubled tremors. Personality colors even when it doesn't determine history, but trained minds (and military training helps in this) insulate themselves.

Compromise, conciliation, and persuasion produced results.

Through Eisenhower's eight years we heard again and again from political analysts, most of them Democrats, that the best president was an activist president—a man who kicked the Congress around, went over the heads of the legislative branch to the people, and constantly extended the power of the office, in the manner of Wilson and FDR and, prospectively, Kennedy and Johnson. Yet when one lays the legislative results of various presidents together, one fails to see that the "activist" Democrats accomplished measurably more than "passive and complacent" Republican Eisenhower.

In the analysis of the *Congressional Quarterly*, cataloging the percentage of presidential victories on congressional votes where the President took a clear-cut stand, Eisenhower comes out with a record of 89 percent in 1953 and 82.8 percent in 1954. In contrast, Kennedy comes in with 81 percent in 1961, 85.4 percent in 1962, and 87.1 percent in 1963; Johnson with 88 percent in 1964 and 93 percent in 1965—the best year ever.

But Ike produced his percentages in 1953–54 with a paper-thin Republic majority; Kennedy and Johnson had lopsidedly Democratic Senates and Houses that at times outnumbered the Republicans more than 2 to 1. Neither one ever had to face an opposition Congress, as Eisenhower did in six of his eight years. Yet despite this opposition, Eisenhower produced respectable figures even in 1955 (75 percent), 1956 (70 percent), 1957 (68 percent), and 1958 (76 percent). His record these years stands up successfully against the performance of Lyndon Johnson in 1966 and 1967 (79 percent) and 1968 (75 percent).

So also does the significance of the legislation Eisenhower got through year by year: in 1953 the Refugee Relief Act, which reversed the repressive McCarran–Walter Immigration Act of 1952; in 1954 the ocean-widening St. Lawrence Seaway, the biggest tax cut—$7.4 billion—theretofore in American history, a major extension of Social Security, and a major reversal of agricultural policy; in 1955 the three-year extension of the Trade Agreements Act, HRI; in 1956 the Upper Colorado River Project and the interstate highway program; in 1957 the first civil rights bill since Reconstruction; in 1958 statehoood for Alaska, the National Defense Education Act, the establishment of NASA, and the reorganization of the Pentagon; in 1959 statehood for Hawaii; in 1960 the legislation that reversed the course of United States aid to Latin America and laid the ground for Kennedy's Alliance for Progress. Each of these bills is a milepost.

At times Eisenhower did go over the heads of the Congress to the people, as when he wrote letters to his business friends in 1958 to get the Congress to move on Pentagon reorganization; as he did in 1959 when he took to nationwide TV to explain why he wanted an effective labor reform bill, one that would help clean up the nation's unions—a bill that he got, over the objections of Senator John Kennedy and others. But most of his results he produced through patience and persistence and persuasion, and for his record of results, he owed much to the help of Johnson and Rayburn—help frequently furthered after 1958 by the skill of Eisenhower's chief lieutenants on the Hill, Senate Minority Leader Everett Dirksen and House Minority Leader Charles Halleck.

For all his reservations, Eisenhower recognized these facts. When we got to the last drafts of the second volume of the memoirs, *Waging Peace*, I discovered that in more than five hundred pages he had said not one good word about Lyndon Johnson. And when I mentioned the omission, he did not hesitate; he summoned his secretary and at once dictated several paragraphs of generous remarks, which I have no doubt came from the heart.

For his collaborators on war and on legislation—FDR and LBJ—Eisenhower, despite misgivings, would reveal a measure of esteem as we worked on *Mandate for Change* and *Waging Peace*. He displayed respect and even affection for his great, and too-brief, collaborator in the cause of Republican unity, Senator Robert A. Taft, a man who had more than once questioned Eisenhower's capabilities and decisions and internationalism; who symbolized the bitterness of the battle for the 1952 nomination ("If Taft had won," Henry Cabot Lodge maintains to this day, "our boys would have walked out"); and who thus repeatedly tested Eisenhower's powers of self-restraint, particularly at that memorable meeting of the Legislative Leaders on April 30, 1953, a few months before Taft's untimely death, when he banged the table and excoriated Eisenhower's proposed budget—particularly the Defense part—and received from the five-star Commander in Chief a soft answer that turned away wrath and kept the party together.

But for his great collaborator on NATO, Harry Truman, Ike had no good word whatsoever.

I've seen no evidence that any particular personal warmth or sympathy ever existed mutually between the two men; and abundant evidence that well before the political wars of 1952 Ike privately abhorred Truman's Fair Deal. But whatever cordiality—however formal—Eisenhower may have felt for Truman before 1952, two things above all torpedoed it: (1) Truman's alley-brawl personal attacks on Eisenhower, which at the height of the 1952 campaign brought the rejoinder: "I'll never ride down Pennsylvania Avenue with him! I'll meet him at the Capitol steps. Just how low can you get?"; (2) Truman's charge that in October 1953 he had phoned to make an appointment with President Eisenhower, visiting Kansas City, only to encounter a rebuff, an answer that the President's schedule was full. It didn't matter to Truman that no one in Eisenhower's entourage ever corroborated this allegation. (Once while Ike was at Columbia, his aide Robert Schulz got a phone call purporting to come from Harry Truman. Ordinarily any call from Truman to Eisenhower those days would come to Schulz from the chief White House operator, saying, "My boss would like to talk to your boss." Because this call didn't, Schulz thought it was a phony and refused to put it through to Eisenhower. Something like this *perhaps* happened, with another intermediary, not Schulz, in Kansas City.)

About Truman's political attacks, Eisenhower said nothing as we worked on the memoirs. As always he was following his own prescription: don't see, don't feel, don't admit, and don't answer; just ignore your attacker and keep smiling. Never did he—or could he— descend to the depths of bourbon-laced scurrility and recklessness reached by Truman in his unsubstantiated remarks about Eisenhower—and Kay Summersby—to Merle Miller in 1961, which Miller revealed years later. But the cuts smarted. And when the subject of the Kansas City phone call came up, Ike responded with brimstone: "The man is a congenital liar."

So by the time we worked on the White House memoirs (1961–65), these events had colored and embittered Eisenhower's memory of the great and critical years of the Eisenhower-Truman association, 1945–52.

Eisenhower recalled, for example, his ride through the streets of Potsdam in June 1945 with Truman and General Omar Bradley.

In *Crusade in Europe* (1948) he had recounted the episode with great good humor: "Truman," he said, "suddenly turned toward me and said: 'General, there is nothing that you may want that I won't try to help you get. That definitely and specifically includes the presidency in 1948.'" And Ike had described his own reaction: "I doubt that any soldier of our country was ever so suddenly struck in his emotional vitals by a President with such an apparently sincere and certainly astounding proposition as this.... to have the President suddenly throw this broadside into me left me no recourse except to treat it as a very splendid joke, which I hoped it was. I laughed heartily and said: 'Mr. President, I don't know who will be your opponent for the presidency, but it will not be I.' There was no doubt about *my* seriousness."

In *Mandate for Change* (1963) the account becomes formal and cold, underscoring the cheap politics of a Truman who in 1945 could speak with such adulation and in the 1952 campaign with such disparagement. "While I thanked him for his flattering thought, I had no ambition whatsoever along political lines and would not consider the possibility of seeking a political position. I added that I would never in my lifetime experience a moment of more intense personal satisfaction than that which saw the surrender of Hitler's remaining forces at Reims, France, on May 7, 1945...."

Eisenhower, in our editorial sessions, recalled other instances of Truman's high esteem. In 1946 Truman told Ike, then Army Chief of Staff, "Only two men would be acceptable to me as Secretary of State, you and General Marshall." At that moment Marshall was in China, trying to work out an agreement between Nationalists and Communists. "Fortunately, Mr. President," Ike responded, "I'm going to China in the morning, and I'll tell General Marshall." And the whole thing became a joke, capped by Marshall's response to the news Eisenhower had brought: "Eisenhower, I'd do anything to get out of this place! I'd even enlist in the Army!"

Eisenhower mentioned another memory, tinged with faint contempt: "When I was Chief of Staff at the Pentagon, President Truman always wanted me to come over at about 5:00 in the afternoon for a drink with him and a few of his friends in the White House. I never went, though; I always said I had too much to do."

One final feature of the relationship between Eisenhower and Truman Ike recalled in great detail: their differences over defense policy. This, in fact, was crucial: Ike believed Truman had let our armed forces dwindle after World War II and had thus invited the attack in Korea. As Army Chief of Staff (1945–48) and later as president of Columbia University (1948–53), Eisenhower had frequently sounded the alarm, and because he himself later came under fire for complicity in Truman's defense budgeting, he had had an aide pull all these "defense warning" papers (largely congressional testimony 1945–51) together. In the memoirs we quoted with relish a public warning like this (dated 1947): "In the field of guided missiles, electronics and supersonic aircraft, we have no more than scratched the surface of possibilities which we must explore in order to keep abreast of the rest of the world. Neglect to do so could bring our country to ruin and defeat in an appallingly few hours." Such a quotation came as pure gold after the Russians put up *Sputnik* in 1957 and the Democrats attacked Eisenhower's alleged indifference to missile research.

In our editorial sessions Eisenhower told one other story—which never made it into the book—of Truman's pinch-penny neglect of defense. "He told me in 1949," Ike recalled, "that I could have 110 million dollars to put some military trucks into mothballs. Later, when I was down in Florida, he phoned me long-distance: 'You can't have the money,' he said. 'We're going to try to balance the budget.' 'Mr. President,' I told him, 'you're going to lose a billion dollars' worth of equipment.'"

Their differences over defense came to a peak that year. Eisenhower, then president of Columbia, was serving as an informal chairman of the Joint Chiefs of Staff under hapless Defense Secretary Louis Johnson, and he had been asked to help put together the parsimonious fiscal year 1951 defense budget. Truman submitted it in January 1950. Immediately a dispute began to rage over its adequacy. Secretary Johnson claimed he was trimming the fat; columnist Joe Alsop and others charged he was slicing muscle and bone. On February 24, 1950, Eisenhower went before a House Appropriations Subcommittee to give his judgment.

And he backed that budget. Why? Because Truman was his Commander in Chief, and a good soldier always stands by his Commander in Chief on a major national security decision, whether that Commander in Chief is Roosevelt confronting Berlin or Truman confronting the FY51 budget or Kennedy confronting the Bay of Pigs or LBJ confronting Vietnam.

The needle, as always, pointed true north. And given the popular General's association with this scrawny budget, Louis Johnson gleefully labeled it the "Ike 3," claiming it mirrored Eisenhower's recommendations.

That was too much.

Throughout his informal chairmanship of the Joint Chiefs, and even afterward, Ike cordially backed Louis Johnson's efforts to economize. But their correspondence reveals Eisenhower's growing unhappiness with the continued lowering of the ceiling Truman and Johnson had set on defense spending. On July 14, 1949, on the eve of his departure as chairman, Ike reminded Johnson: "My basic objective has been to develop a peacetime military program and budgetary structure that would be related as closely as possible to an agreed strategic plan. . . . There was . . . achieved a very considerable degree of unanimity in allocating, under the strategic concept, tactical forces to the various strategic areas of the world. . . . [the] so-called 'red brick' process. . . .

"The difficulty next encountered was that the total cost of the 'red bricks' was greater than the maximum we believed, even at that time, would be approved by the President and by the Congress for fiscal 1951. . . .

"Information was next received that the total amounts available in 1951 would be reduced by some one and a half to two billion below the anticipated amount. . . . But this reduction forced even further divergence from the basic purpose—that is, the relating of the military program to the strategic concept. The reason for this is that, as funds go down and down, there is finally reached a point where only the basic inescapable needs of each Service as a mobilization platform can be met, with only a minimum of money provided for the specific emergency of D-Day. . . ." The budget had been cut, not to the bone, but through it.

With Louis Johnson tying the Eisenhower nickname to the Truman-Johnson defense plan, Eisenhower, speaking at Columbia March 23, 1950, went off the reservation: "America has already disarmed to the extent—in some directions even beyond the extent— that I, with deep concern for her present safety, could possibly advise, until we have certain knowledge that all nations, in concerted action, are doing likewise." He was saying in public what he had, diplomatically, said to Secretary Johnson in private.

Johnson replied March 27: The United States had *not* disarmed too much; General Eisenhower knew all about the budget cuts; and he hadn't objected. Two days later, before a Senate Appropriations Subcommittee, Eisenhower smoothed the sharp edges of conflict. When he and the other Chiefs of Staff started to work on the budget, they had a target of $15 billion. Truman and Johnson later cut that back to about $13 billion. Nobody asked Eisenhower whether he agreed: he was a carpenter, not the architect. He felt, he said, that $15 billion should be the ceiling; suggested that $13 billion would be inadequate; and recommended Congress add about a half billion to the budget, hiking it up to about $13.7 billion.

Even in the memoirs Eisenhower would not attack Truman on this issue. But in his own self-defense he wanted a record made public. So he asked me to draft a long appendix for the end of *Mandate for Change:* "Just give the facts. Get every bit of information possible on the expenditure program for the armed forces to fiscal year 1950, the year preceding the outbreak of the Korean War. Don't even mention Truman or Louis Johnson. Don't put the blame on anybody." Only with the later publication of another book of informal reminiscences, *At Ease,* did Eisenhower at last publicly condemn Louis Johnson: he could not bear personal controversy's intrusion into policy, especially into public squabble, even long after the fact. Free discussion, no holds barred before decisions, rigid obedience afterward was his norm: a subordinate was expected to follow or to quit.

Such policy decisions as the one over the military budget did of course matter, and matter significantly, to the relations between Eisenhower and Truman and to the future history of the United States. But far more, it was Truman's personal attacks from 1952 on that colored and edged Ike's memories, in 1961–62, of their postwar association. Given the nature of politics and the men, the result was inevitable, but one could only see it with sadness. For in the years, 1945–52, Truman as President and Eisenhower as successively Army Chief of Staff, president of Columbia University, and Supreme Allied Commander in Europe had together done monumental labors for their common country, their common determination to unite our allies, their common resolution to preserve, against an implacable enemy, freedom of government and freedom of the mind in the world.

"What was the first thing you did when you got home?" the reporters, in Independence,Missouri, asked their still-jaunty former President Harry Truman his first day out of office. "Took the suitcases up to the attic" was his plebeian reply, the answer of the average man who knew himself average and that, damn it, average was good enough. When the Big Three met in regal splendor at Potsdam, it was commoner Truman representing the common man who had the common sense. Plain Harry was like plain Ben Franklin at Versailles, who when he stood up like Joshua, made the sun and the moon, the monarchs and the dictators, stand still. Iran, Greece, and Turkey would be held. Europe, through the Marshall Plan and NATO, would be saved. Because that little clerk put his foot down, America's stock would go up. That is the truth about Harry Truman. But it is a truth that few recognized in 1951.

The collaboration of Truman and Eisenhower came to a climax with Ike's flight to Washington in the dark January of that year. He came at Truman's call. And, in the words of *Time* magazine, he did "for the President what Harry Truman could not do for himself."

Audience by audience, Ike convinced his hearers that the Europeans would rouse themselves; and that America should help—help first and foremost with arms and equipment but also with troops. From the senators and congressmen assembled in the Library of Congress auditorium to the Americans who heard him speak over nationwide radio and TV, Ike won assent for Truman's decision.

Once again, as repeatedly since the war, Ike was demonstrating an unmatched power of persuasiveness. And in the words of a *Life* editorial, he had "once again shown himself to be a foremost symbol of all that is right and good and strong in American policy and purpose"—a splendid policy and splendid purpose, one might add, set by Harry S Truman, and agreed to by both men to the limit.

I like to remember the Truman-Eisenhower association at that kind of summit. And I like to recall two events from their later years that suggest, if not a total reconciliation, at least a step toward it.

The first took place on the day of the funeral of John F. Kennedy in 1963, when the two former Presidents met for lunch at Blair House. Eisenhower reportedly broke the ice with "I think the differences between us have been highly exaggerated." And the two ex-Presidents, with Mamie and Margaret, joined in a great and good-humored round of reminiscences.

The second event took place in Ike's Gettysburg office in 1965 as we were going over a late draft of *Waging Peace*. There, in the final "Afterthoughts" chapter, was another of those lists of the great: a somewhat uneven catalog of "towering governmental figures of the West" including Churchill, Herbert Hoover, Dulles, Marshall, Lewis Strauss, Ernest Bevin, and even, this time, Franklin Roosevelt. But given the expansiveness of this list, I found one name conspicuously missing—Harry Truman's; I pointed out that the omission appeared to glare from the page. The General bridled for the briefest instant. Then he touched pencil to paper: "Oh, hell, go ahead and put Truman's name in there."

II

OCTOBER 14, 1951

CONVICTIONS

On Friday, October 12, 1951, two days before Eisenhower's sixty-first birthday, General Edwin Norman Clark flew from New York to Paris on one of the nineteen transatlantic flights he would make that year to see his friend, the Supreme Allied Commander. For months now, Ike had steadfastly refused to lift a finger to get the Republican presidential nomination, and to Clark the time had come for a showdown.

Ed Clark—a 6-foot-2½, 192-pound football guard graduate of West Point (1922) and the Harvard Law School; first fiancé of Marcia Gluck, who later became Marcia Davenport, best-selling author; a musical neophyte introduced to symphonic mysteries by Boston Symphony conductor Pierre Monteux, a friend of Marcia's mother, famed soprano Alma Gluck; a man raised almost as a son by Gustavus Adolphus Pfeiffer, drug-tycoon uncle of Pauline Pfeiffer, the first wife of Ernest Hemingway, who wrote much of *A Farewell to Arms* in one of the eighteenth-century houses in the Pfeiffers' Easton, Connecticut, enclave, and later dedicated the book to Clark's "Uncle Gus"; connoisseur of French food and wine and raconteur without peer—Ed Clark had served on Ike's SHAEF staff in World War II.

After the war, when Eisenhower became Army Chief of Staff, Clark, now a New York international business consultant, would visit him on business trips to Washington and have sandwiches in Ike's office. When Eisenhower became president of Columbia, their friendship strengthened; Ike would drive up from New York to Easton for trout fishing, and there, on July 13, 1948, the day the news of lightweight champion Ike Williams' TKO of Beau Jack in Philadelphia hit the newspapers—along with the news from Philadelphia of the Democratic convention, then in progress—Eisenhower and Clark talked, as they often did, politics. And then and there, having just turned down nomination feelers by both Republicans and Democrats, Eisenhower admitted to Clark that indeed he might not mind serving in the nation's highest office. From that moment, with Ike's knowledge and concurrence, Clark began tirelessly working to produce this result.

Clark was—and is—a liberal Republican. To him, the 1951 Republican party divided into three parts: the conservatives, headed by Senator Robert Taft of Ohio; the opportunists, headed by Governor Thomas E. Dewey of New York; and the honest liberals, like Congressman Clifford Case of New Jersey and Senators John Sherman Cooper of Kentucky, Ralph Flanders of Vermont, Frank Carlson of Kansas, and Henry Cabot Lodge of Massachusetts. In seeking an ally, Clark turned to Dewey's great enemy, Senator James Duff of Pennsylvania. Duff, like Clark himself, was a maverick— Princeton football player, a hearty, bluff, red-haired, gallused "hit 'em in the guts, kick 'em in the nuts" enthusiast who announced to Clark the first minute of their first meeting: "I'm for Ike all the way. Now let's have a drink."

Together they began looking for islands of strength for Eisenhower in California, in Oregon, and in Washington (under Duff's good friend Governor Arthur Langlie). They got hold of a Beechcraft Bonanza—a four-seater plane that cruised at 180 mph— and sent it flying more than 150,000 miles around the country to test pro-Taft and pro-Ike sentiment.

Knowing what Clark was up to, Eisenhower in 1950 invited him to lunch at Columbia with his good friend Bob Woodruff of the Coca-Cola Company in Atlanta; soon afterward Clark's phone rang: leading Atlanta businessmen on the other end were offering money to the Eisenhower-for-President effort. But the road ran uphill. Not only did Taft have an abundance of backers in the Republican party. Eisenhower himself, before a top secret meeting with Taft at the Pentagon in early 1951—a meeting set up by Clark and Taft enthusiast Cole Younger—wrote out a Sherman, a declaration abjuring any entry into politics, to be revealed if the meeting produced a Taft commitment to the principle of collective security for the defense of Europe. But it didn't. It produced only, as the limousine drove the senator, Clark, and Younger away from the Pentagon, a Taft knee-slapping outburst of admiration for Ike: "By God, that's a man!"

By the early fall of 1951 Duff began to run into static. Eisenhower had never said he would run; never said he would accept if nominated; in fact, had never even declared himself a Republican. Against such a backdrop, Duff was asking Republican convention delegates to sign up; to desert Taft of Ohio or Harold Stassen of Minnesota or Earl Warren of California and join the bandwagon for a man who had never shown a chemical trace of an interest in politics. And the delegates were beginning to balk. How did they know Ike wouldn't pull the rug out from under them all? So Duff huddled with Clark. On October 12 Clark flew to Paris. And the next evening, Saturday, at Ike's residence at Marnes-la-Coquette, after dinner for only four—the Eisenhowers, Clark, and Ambassador Perle Mesta, who had flown in unexpectedly from Luxembourg and who baked the apple pie for dessert—Mrs. Eisenhower, by design, suggested to Perle that the two of them play canasta, and Eisenhower and Clark retired to a private alcove to talk.

"Duff needs assurance from you in writing," Clark told Eisenhower. "If you don't give it to him, here's what's going to happen: Dewey and Taft will fight it out. And Taft will win; the Republicans can't stomach a Dewey candidacy a third time."

Ike understood. "I guess you're right," he said, and the two began to scribble out a letter from Ike to Duff.

But after so many months of stiff-arming politics and politicians, a declaration of political conviction and intent did not come easily to Eisenhower. Finally, he threw down his stub pencil in annoyance: "Can't you just *tell* him?" he demanded.

"No. That wouldn't do it."

"Well, let's let it go overnight."

At six-thirty the next morning Clark's phone rang. "I've been thinking about this all night," Eisenhower told him. "Come on over, I'll give you breakfast."

All that Sunday morning—October 14, 1951, Ike's birthday—the scribbling went on in earnest. And slowly Ike's message emerged: No man who is an American can re´use nomination to the highest office in the land, it said. If it were offered to me, I would accept, and would resign from the Army, because I believe no military officer should seek a place in politics. I consider myself a liberal; I also consider myself a Republican; and through the years whenever I have voted, I have voted Republican. If given the nomination, I will wage an aggressive campaign.

For five hours the two nit-picked the words. They quarreled over the word "aggressive."

"That's Hitler's word," Eisenhower bridled. But the word stayed in.

Finally the draft was done. Eisenhower copied the jumbled mess into a final original in his own penmanship—five closely written pages. His aide, General Al Gruenther, had organized a luncheon for one o'clock, and the guests were being held up outside, without knowing why, while the final holograph was taking shape. (Those guests included Cy Sulzberger of *The New York Times*, a splendid reporter with a talent for getting news behind the news, who never knew why he and the other guests couldn't come in on time that birthday Sunday.) Clark eagerly carried the precious pages from Eisenhower's residence to Eisenhower's office and there, assisted by aide Bob Schulz, made a completely accurate handwritten copy—the only one in existence, given Eisenhower's fear of a leak to the press, a copy that has mysteriously disappeared. For Schulz to this day, the letter marks a critical turn: "That was the first time I thought the Boss might go into politics."

Clark flew back to New York and phoned Duff, who dropped everything and rushed up to meet with Clark; Jock Whitney, millionaire socialite; Jim Brownlee, a partner of J. H. Whitney and Company; and Nelson Rockefeller. They met at Whitney's Manhattan apartment. All read the letter. And when the meeting ended, Clark and Brownlee put it into a special safety deposit box, which could be opened only by those two men; it has been seen by no one else for a quarter century. Duff now had his assurance: for Eisenhower he stood ready to risk his political life. And Ike, too, had turned a corner: two years later he would tell Jim Hagerty that the man who had pressured him hardest to run was James Duff.

In his own hand, to political operatives, Eisenhower had set down, for the first time, an outline of political convictions. Before that moment few people, sworn to secrecy, knew where he stood. What was he? A Democrat who owed his fame to FDR? An Army Neanderthal? Something in between? Or nothing?

Ed Clark of course knew. And so did another man who shared much of Clark and Duff's bluffness and belt: Bill Robinson.

A story told by reporter Marguerite Higgins about William E.

Robinson—an executive of Miss Higgins' paper, the *Herald Tribune*, and later of the Coca-Cola Company—suggests why Ike liked him. After Robinson had joined Coca-Cola, she met him on the street one day. Knowing that while at the *Tribune* he lived and breathed only one thing, hostility toward its great competitor, *The New York Times*, she ventured to ask his opinion of Coca-Cola's great competitor, Pepsi-Cola. Without batting an eye over his outrageous answer, Robinson thundered, gravel-voiced: "Pepsi-Cola causes cancer!"

Robinson was a zealot—loyal, unshakable—and an Eisenhower zealot from the wartime day when the two first met until the day in 1969 when Robinson struggled out of his sickbed (he knew he was dying) in a Florida hospital, overrode the strenuous objections of his doctors ("If it kills me, OK"), called a cab for the airport, and boarded a plane for Washington to attend Ike's funeral. He was indispensable to Eisenhower, who, like all normal men, required friendship. Robinson gave it in abundance. And through the early postwar years, Dwight Eisenhower had confided to him his innermost political secrets, confided them in conversations of frequently volcanic candor.

"The General almost seemed to get on fire with his burning, patriotic feeling to be of helpfulness to the country he loves," Robinson observed in a set of notes he wrote to himself after a wide-ranging discussion at the Pentagon on October 17, 1947. Eisenhower's "high spirit and his great emotional potentiality," Robinson further perceived, "might conceivably develop a highly unbalanced entity in a person of lesser intellectual capacity."

Again and again Ike would "arise from the chair in which he was sitting and stride up and down the office, talking about his limitations at one moment, and in the next outlining the manner in which he would like to be of service, the things he would like to say, the guidance he would like to give to historians in setting forth the facts of his mission in Europe.

"He was completely free, unguarded to the point even of indiscretion. There was no pose, no pretense, no attempt to establish anything for the record, no attempt to build an impression of any kind. He was natural, alive, alert, spirited, and gave the impression of having an intense amount of unloosened energy, both intellectual and physical.

"I came away with the conviction that no public man whom I had ever known, or had ever known about, had such intellectual honesty as Eisenhower. I also had the impression that here was a man who was realistic, practical and disciplined." In a few words, Robinson had caught the character of the man.

In their talks, extending over three years, Ike set forth his political convictions, and on June 21, 1948, on the eve of the Democratic and Republican conventions, Robinson summed them up in a long personal note to *Tribune* owner Helen Rogers Reid.

Eisenhower, Robinson said, believed in the necessity of getting along with the British; unifying the armed forces; and instituting universal military training. He believed in the individual's responsibility for readying himself for some job in the community that would give him independence, self-respect, and "strength of spirit"; but he also believed the individual owed a part of himself to the good of the community and the nation. Though he rejected "rugged individualism in the old-fashioned Republican sense of the word," Eisenhower believed "only the strong can cooperate."

Disclaiming any scientific knowledge of money or taxes, Eisenhower thought any novice could see that taxes in this country reflected either punitive motives or the combined pressures of various groups. He reasoned the country might well gather together a group of experts on money and taxation to recommend an entirely new system with no thought of its political consequences.

Eisenhower believed labor should take upon itself responsibility for more—and more efficient—production instead of trying to hamstring management; management, on the other hand, though it had a right to expect a good profit, also had an obligation for fair and decent treatment of its workers. He thought national legislation ought to flow out of concepts of fairness and equity, not out of the pressures of pressure groups.

On European aid Eisenhower opposed charity. He had no faith whatsoever in acquiring friends through handouts. But the United States *had* to enter into solid, self-respecting partnerships with other countries that were trying to keep their freedom. We simply had to make friends overseas, he argued, before the foes of freedom made slaves with whom they would ultimately encircle and defeat us.

These things Eisenhower was for. And what was he against? Robinson had a forthright answer: the New Deal and Fair Deal, with their endless bureaucracy—a "national disgrace"—and their endless willingness to trade opportunity for the false "security" of dependence upon the state.

Ike saw the Democratic party, absolutely off the record, as in a "terrible state"—a mixture of "extremes on the right, extremes on the left, with political chicanery and expediency shot through the whole business."

And what did all this add up to? To an Eisenhower who "can only describe himself as a Liberal Republican. All his family traditions, his early upbringing, and his experience in recent years convince him that the Republican party is the sound, responsible, middle-of-the-road party." To him, "the middle of the road in America is no narrow white line; it is a broad highway that reaches over to a fanatical fringe on the left and a benighted strip on the right."

To Robinson as to Clark, Eisenhower had labeled himself a liberal Republican. But he was no ideologist. Again and again— before, during, and after his presidency—he would denounce all labels, "especially 'liberal' and 'conservative.'" "On one issue," he claimed, "I find myself siding with the liberals, on another issue with the conservatives. I think all you can do is try to look at the facts, use the sense the good Lord gave you, and forget labels." "The only method," he might have said with T. S. Eliot, "is to be very intelligent."

Repeatedly Eisenhower would remind his "liberal" friends how close he could feel to some archconservatives: "There are certainly far greater areas of intellectual agreement between me and Mr. Hoover, for example, than there are between me and so-called New Dealers," Eisenhower wrote to Robinson March 6, 1951. Of course, Ike added, he could not "accept the views of Mr. Hoover with respect to the wisdom of attempting to make America a military Gibraltar. . . ." But "except on this one issue, I do not recall anything in recent years in which I have found my own views in direct opposition to his." Six years later he would write liberal Republican National Chairman Meade Alcorn much the same thing about the right-wing Republican Senate minority leader, William Knowland.

Time and experience in the White House, of course, would sharpen and refine Eisenhower's convictions and strip away some of their naïveté, though not their idealism. But their thrust would remain fixed.

From First Inaugural to Farewell Address, neither Eisenhower's most crucial beliefs nor his political centrism significantly changed. He passionately sought peace in 1961 as he did in 1953. He upheld the system of America's alliances, building on the rock of NATO, at the end as at the beginning. He stressed the perils of a garrison state in 1953 as in 1961, believing a strong peacetime economy as central to our defenses as a strong arsenal. From start to finish, he valued morale—strength of heart, strength of spirit. And he regularly castigated extremists.

In 1954–55, for example, one hears him condemning, almost back to back, the American Medical Association for attacking his health insurance plan ("how in hell is the American Medical Association going to stop socialized medicine if they oppose such bills as this[?]") and the postal workers for wanting too much of a pay hike ("I understand every postal letter carrier is going around telling his clients that he's underpaid, that his children are starving and... running around in raggedy-assed pants. I wrote a letter saying I was against anything over 7.5% and I am finished trading on this subject....").

Yet despite the power of his political sentiments, throughout 1951 Eisenhower hesitated to initiate his own entry into political partisanship. He would respond to an overwhelming national mandate: but he would not lift a finger to prompt it.

"I am never going to get tangled up in any kind of political activity," he wrote Robinson October 31, 1951, "unless forced to do so as the result of a genuine and deep conviction expressed by a very large segment of our people," adding in late November, "Every passing day confirms and hardens my dislike of all political activity as a personal participant."

It took two people, a woman and a man, of decisive persuasiveness in February 1952 to shake him free, to make him cross the imperceptible line dividing pursued from pursuer.

The woman was Jacqueline Cochran, world-famous aviatrix, world-famous entrepreneur in women's cosmetics, rough and tough amateur in politics. Sometime in December or January she received a telephone call from Jock Whitney: Would she cochair a monster pro-Ike rally in Madison Square Garden? Miss Cochran agreed with enthusiasm. The plan had powerful opponents, however, among the leaders of the Eisenhower movement, including Governor Dewey. If it failed, it could dissuade Eisenhower from running.

But Whitney and Cabot Lodge and Jackie Cochran and her cochairman, publicist John Reagan ("Tex") McCrary—husband of tennis-playing film star Jinx Falkenburg—went ahead. The event would take place February 8 in the Garden after a fight card and thus corral a captive audience. The great hope, of course, was that a mass rally would impress the politicians and above all Eisenhower himself. The great question was: Could such a rally fill the Garden on a February night?

The crucial moment came. The political fans trying to get into the Garden collided with the fight fans trying to get out. And when the smoke lifted and the rally started, the Garden bulged.

A film of the show was rushed to the processor. The next night Jackie Cochran took off for Paris by TWA, sleeping in a hot upper berth with the precious film, the only copy, under her feet. And at five o'clock on the afternoon of Monday, February 11, at the General's elegant residence at Marnes-la-Coquette—the only home Mamie had ever fallen in love with in all their years of roaming from post to post—Miss Cochran joined the General and a scattering of aides in its long salon, where a screen had been set up at one end, and the rough footage began to run.

Miss Cochran was sitting in front of the General, and when the ovation appeared on the screen, she knew it had touched him. The mandate was overwhelming. "He just couldn't believe it," Jackie Cochran said. "As the film went on, I could hear a sniffle once or twice. And then when the film came to an end, I could see one large tear had rolled down his cheek. He was moved in the extreme. He began talking about his boyhood and about his mother. And then he turned to me and said: 'I want you to go back and see four men...'"

The key man of the four was General Lucius Clay—lieutenant to Eisenhower in World War II; hero of the Berlin blockade, whose on-the-ground unilateral decision in reply to Stalin's threat had saved that city; a thin, sharp-eyed, hawklike, keen-minded, steel-trap-memo-ried, soft-spoken, courtly, modest, iron-willed Georgian—in one felicitous phrase, "a civilized Patton," a "no-man" whom nobody ever pushed around, a Galahad who always got what he wanted.

Lucius Clay wanted Dwight D. Eisenhower President. With Dewey, Lodge, and other Ike enthusiasts and moneyed backers, he had been working toward this end for months. And as much as any one man, Lucius Clay would now make him a candidate.

A few days after Jackie Cochran's return from France, Clay himself was flying to London to see Eisenhower, who had come to attend the funeral of King George VI on February 15. The two men met in secrecy at the home of Eisenhower's British wartime aide, Colonel James Gault, and there Ike made his last attempt to resist.

"We have to have a commitment," Clay told him, "a commitment that you will campaign for the nomination, come home before the Republican convention, and run if nominated. If we don't have that commitment, we can't win. We can't hold the delegates who want to back you."

In the presence of two largely silent observers—Texas oil millionaire Sid Richardson and Washington wit George Allen, both of them close Eisenhower friends—the argument raged for hours. Finally Clay headed for the door: "I've got to go."

Eisenhower stopped him: "We can't break up this way. Come into the den for a moment."

And there, in the small adjoining room, Ike gave his answer at last: "I'll do it." Mrs. Eisenhower opposed his running, he said, but eventually he knew she would agree. He asked only that Clay and the others give him time to work things out. And as soon as he could conclude his duties in Europe, he promised, he would return to the United States.

With this commitment, the civilized Patton had crossed his Rhine. The convictions Eisenhower had enunciated to Bill Robinson and Ed Clark, he would now act on in the arena of partisan politics.

III

SEPTEMBER 23, 1952

THE PRIVATE MAN

S hortly before 9:30 on the night of September 23, 1952, some thirty nervous people—intimates and advisers of Republican presidential nominee Dwight Eisenhower—jammed into the crow's-nest-level office of the manager of the Cleveland Public Auditorium to listen to one of the most crucial half hours in American television history—vice-presidential nominee Richard Nixon's "Checkers speech," his defense against charges that through a secret fund he was a man kept and controlled by a cabal of rich backers.

The TV set occupied one corner. Fifteen feet from the screen a sofa, right-angled to the wall, jutted into the twenty-by-twenty-five-foot room. The presidential war-hero candidate, facing the first political crisis of his nearly sixty-two years, sat at the end of the sofa next to the wall; Mrs. Eisenhower sat beside him. Next to her, on a straight chair, sat one of the General's most trusted friends, Bill Robinson, Executive Vice President of the New York *Herald Tribune*, which had just called for Nixon's resignation from the ticket.

As the commercials faded and the scene switched to the Los Angeles studio where the embattled thirty-nine-year-old California senator would make his all-or-nothing stand, everyone in the Cleveland office focused on the flickering screen, except one man. For the next thirty minutes, he told me, he searched and scrutinized Dwight Eisenhower.

The crisis had come with explosive suddenness.

Only five days before, on the morning of September 18, the New York *Post* had broken its sensational story on Nixon's "Secret Rich Men's Trust Fund," which, the story alleged, let him live far beyond his modest means. In the mad and confused world of the whistle-stopping campaign train, Eisenhower had not got the news until late that night, after he finished his major speeches. Years later, as we worked on the memoirs, he recalled what went through his mind:

"What could I say? How much did I know about Nixon when the news of the fund broke? Of course, this kind of problem was not entirely new. During the war, after all, I had had George Patton on my hands.

"But one thing I knew for sure: it would mean defeat either to throw Nixon off the ticket, or to leave some kind of cloud over the whole episode. I therefore had to show that I was taking a judicial attitude, not one of blind partisanship; so I sent word to Nixon telling him to take his time; I'd take care of this."

To my knowledge, no trace of such an Eisenhower-Nixon message exists. I do know that on September 19 in the presence of one of his speechwriters, General Robert Cutler, the Harvard-educated Boston Brahmin head of the Old Colony Trust Company, Ike did scribble out to Nixon a message with a different thrust—a message that, read after Watergate, reverberates with irony: "In the certainty that the whole affair comprises no violation of the highest standards of conduct, a critical question becomes the speed and completeness of your presentation of facts to the public.

"I suggest immediate publication by you ... of all documentary evidence.... Any delay will be interpreted, I think, as reluctance to let the light of day into the case and will arouse additional doubt or suspicion...."

I know also that Sherman Adams (Ike's chief of staff on the train) later recalled that Eisenhower— in an "unfamiliar field" when he heard the news—did remark: "Well, if Nixon has to resign, we can't possibly win." But I could unfortunately never find any trace of a "take your time" message that squared with Eisenhower's recollection. Eisenhower may well have held these views about the dangers of dropping Nixon overboard; but on the evidence the option remained a live one.

As the campaign train rolled through southern Nebraska late that day, Press Secretary Jim Hagerty put out this Eisenhower statement: "I have long admired and applauded Senator Nixon's American faith and determination to drive Communist sympathizers from offices of public trust.

"There has recently been leveled against him a charge of unethical practices. I believe Dick Nixon to be an honest man. I am confident that he will place all the facts before the American people fairly and squarely. I intend to talk with him at the earliest time...."

Eisenhower continued his judicial detachment. To an audience in Kansas City that evening he remarked that though he himself had been unable to talk with Nixon by phone, he had received from Nixon this dictated message: "I have asked the trustees of this fund...to make a full report to the public of this matter...."

"I have read the statement to you," Eisenhower continued, "because I believe it is an honest statement. Knowing Dick Nixon as I do, I believe that when the facts are known to all of us, they will show that Dick Nixon would not compromise with what is right."

Given the Republicans' excoriation of scandals in President Truman's Bureau of Internal Revenue, Reconstruction Finance Corporation, and White House, their outrage at deep freezes and mink coats and tax fixing and bribery and the corrupt head of Justice's Tax Division, T. Lamar Caudle, the fat had hit, indeed, the fire.

Some Republicans saw little wrong. When he first heard the news, for example, Senator Robert Taft had sat down with a yellow legal pad and a pale blue ball-point pen and scribbled off a draft of a defense: "I see no reason why a Senator or Congressman should not accept gifts from members of his family, or his friends, or other constituents to help pay even his personal expenses in Washington. ...The only possible criticism would arise if these donors wanted some legislative or other favors. I know that no such motives inspired the expense payments in the case of Dick Nixon...."

But Eisenhower on Saturday, September 20, still remained judicially at a distance, telling reporters off the record that Nixon would have to prove himself "clean as a hound's tooth"—a standard that, as Elmer Davis remarked, had earlier been used as a measure of the cleanliness of Harding's Interior Secretary, Albert B. Fall.

Hearing of an anti-Nixon editorial in the New York *Herald Tribune*, Ike wrote to Robinson that same day:

"Without a full knowledge of the facts, I am not willing to prejudge any man . . . .

"I have had a sound regard for Dick Nixon, as a member of the United States Navy, as a strong Congressman and Senator, and as a man. I have had reason to believe in his honesty and character. . . .

"I have a feeling that in matters of this kind no one can afford to act on a hair-trigger. But if there is real wrong at stake, there will be prompt and conclusive action by me. . . ."

Amid all the doubters, led by Milton Eisenhower, two men stood unshakably for Nixon—the new chairman of the Republican National Committee, Arthur Summerfield (a short, stocky Chevrolet dealer from Flint, Michigan; a gung-ho, opportunist-conservative, hold-the-party-together-and-biff-the-Democrats partisan), and his principal assistant, Bob Humphreys (a slight, outspoken, twangy-voiced, aggressive former reporter; a shrewd hard-nosed Hoosier idea-man and strategist who secretly knew more about Horowitz and Debussy and Gieseking and Moussorgsky than almost anybody else in Washington, and whose wonder at the magic of their music at times emerged in unforgettable collocations: "Did you hear that perform-ance of 'The Submerged Cathedral'? Sonofabitch!").

From the start, Humphreys back in Washington had just one answer to the question that came from worried Eisenhower staffers across the phone lines from every train stop: "What should we do?" "Don't *do* anything," he barked in his nasal Indiana accent. "Just *be* for Nixon."

Now, on Saturday morning he got up with a brainstorm: put Nixon on nationwide TV. He phoned the idea to the train-riding Summerfield at dawn in Kansas City. Summerfield liked it; they agreed to try it out on Taft, Representative Joe Martin, and other leading Republicans; and half an hour later Summerfield called Humphreys back: Governor Adams says to check the idea out with Bill Robinson also.

Humphreys phoned all day. By nightfall he had enthusiastic agreements from everybody—Taft, Martin, Congressman Charlie Halleck of Indiana, and half a dozen others—except Robinson. Not until late evening could he track Robinson down—to his golf club locker room. His answer came right to the point: "I wouldn't put him on TV, Bob; I'd throw him off the ticket."

On Sunday morning the Eisenhower campaign train rested in

the Union Station rail yards in St. Louis. Summerfield got on the phone to Humphreys in Washington: "Get the next plane out here. We have an appointment with the General late this afternoon."

There wasn't any next plane to St. Louis; only a puddle-jumper that bounced Humphreys all over West Virginia and Ohio before landing him in Louisville, where officials told him he would have to get off: another passenger had his seat for the leg to St. Louis. Humphreys refused to budge, daring the officials to carry him off bodily and thus produce a news story about the airlines' complicity in keeping a Republican official from his meeting with Eisenhower. Finally the plane took off. But by the time he got to St. Louis, Eisenhower and nearly everyone else had gone off to dinner.

"Check the names of the St. Louis people he had dinner with that night," Humphreys told me, "and you'll find that they told him to dump Nixon."

Only one thing remained to do: go out to the train yard, board the stationary train, and beard in his compartment Chief of Staff Sherman Adams, who already had a reputation as the meanest, rudest, most laconic man in the world, a wiry New Hampshire lumberjack with a gruff exterior concealing a heart of stone.

So Humphreys and Summerfield did. And now another problem surfaced. Summerfield suffered from hyperinsulinism, a disease opposite to diabetes; from time to time, he would simply blank out. And at the precise moment when Humphreys and Summerfield entered Adams' compartment, an attack hit the Republican national chairman. "So there I was," Humphreys recalled, "face to face with Sherman Adams—hungry, tired, mad at the delay, biting nails—with Art sitting next to me staring glassy-eyed at the wall, saying nothing. And with the man we most wanted to see gone." It was a rough session. Adams displayed nothing that could be called detachment. In the absence of Ike, he caustically pressed Humphreys to make his case why Nixon should not be kicked off the ticket.

"He may be a sonofabitch," Humphreys yelled, "but he's *our* sonofabitch!"

"General Eisenhower doesn't have sonsofbitches running with him," Adams shouted back.

"Answer me this," Humphreys rejoined. "Do you expect the American people to *believe* that in three days Eisenhower can't find a way to talk to Nixon? Hell, all he has to do is pick up the phone."

At that, instead of jumping for Humphreys' throat, Adams

reached for the phone and told the operator: "Set up a call to Nixon when the General returns from dinner." And at that instant Humphreys' respect for Adams took one enormous leap.*

"Come on," he growled to Summerfield. "Let's get out of here." On his return Eisenhower finally did telephone Nixon, out in Portland, Oregon. They agreed Nixon should go on TV. But from his noncommitment, Eisenhower refused to budge. When Nixon offered to quit the ticket if Eisenhower asked him to, Eisenhower said only that Nixon should make that decision himself. Inside, Nixon boiled.

Sometime in all this furor the train had stopped and Eisenhower had had a phone conversation with Lucius Clay, the man back in New York who had done most to persuade Eisenhower to enter politics in the first place. Clay had one simple piece of advice: "Don't commit yourself one way or the other until you talk with Herb Brownell."

Wall Street lawyer Brownell—the mild-mannered political sharpster who had masterminded the unsuccessful Dewey races in 1944 and 1948 against Roosevelt and Truman, and the brilliant preconvention Eisenhower campaign against Taft—flew out from New York to meet the train, arriving Monday night in Cincinnati. He and Eisenhower and Adams conferred in Eisenhower's car, with curtains drawn. "Don't jump to any hasty conclusions," Brownell urged. "Let Nixon present his case." But he added one opinion of his own: "If you throw Nixon off the ticket, you'll start up the old Taft-Eisenhower fight all over again, and you'll lose the election."

Years later Brownell told me: "And the [Thomas] Eagleton episode in 1972 convinced me I was right." But by refusing to urge Ike to dump Nixon, Brownell infuriated his old boss, Tom Dewey.

That day, Monday, September 22, had brought a report from Gibson, Dunn and Crutcher (a law firm retained by Eisenhower stalwart Paul Hoffman, the esteemed former administrator of the Marshall Plan in Europe) that there was nothing illegal about the Nixon fund. The day brought also the revelation that Democratic nominee Adlai Stevenson, too, had a fund—this one made up of businessmen's contributions to supplement the state salaries of members of his Illinois gubernatorial administration. By Tuesday, September 23, nonetheless, wires coming to Eisenhower were running

*Years later, painfully dying of cancer, Humphreys would write Adams, now a longtime friend, "You've always been able to think of something funny. Write me something funny."

against Nixon about 3 to 1. Worse, Summerfield and Humphreys, now back in Washington, got wind that Bill Robinson had boarded the campaign train in Cincinnati and was riding with the General into Cleveland. So once again they hopped a plane, arriving just as Eisenhower's motorcade reached his Cleveland hotel.

After dinner, before Nixon's broadcast, they all gathered in Eisenhower's suite. The General went around the room, sampling opinion on Nixon: Summerfield violently for, Senator Frank Carlson of Kansas tepidly for, Adams noncommittal, Robert Cutler for an Eisenhower-Nixon meeting before any decision, Robinson violently against. Humphreys watched, and he noticed something.

"I'd never really thought too highly of Eisenhower's intelligence," he recalled later, "much as I admired him as a man. But something Art [Summerfield] said in that room angered him, and I'll never forget his reply. He started off his sentence mad as hell, spitting out the words like a sergeant. And by the time he finished that sentence, he was all smiles and geniality. He had literally gone through a whole spectrum of emotions between the start and finish of one sentence. I'd never seen anything like it."

From that moment one man's respect for Eisenhower's lightning intellect was won. He had witnessed its jagged speed.

They all climbed into cars to go to the Public Auditorium to hear Nixon's broadcast from California before Eisenhower's scheduled speech. Having originated the idea of the broadcast, Humphreys always resented the fact that when he asked Nixon what he should say to reporters about its genesis, Nixon—"the greatest little credit-taker in the world"—had just replied breezily: "Just say *I* thought of it." (Indeed, Humphreys once credited Nixon's success in the Hiss case not to Nixon, but to the hardworking detail man of the House Un-American Affairs Committee, chief investigator Robert Stripling. "If there hadn't been a Stripling, there would never have been a Nixon".)

With only minutes to go before the broadcast, Nixon received a devastating phone call from Governor Dewey in New York saying that he—and by implication Eisenhower—thought that in the broadcast Nixon should announce his resignation.

To my knowledge, Eisenhower knew nothing in advance about Dewey's call to Nixon, either from Dewey himself or through Clay or Brownell. "I once told Nixon point-blank that I hadn't put Dewey up to that call, and I didn't either," Brownell told me years later. "But I don't think he ever believed me."

In the auditorium manager's office Eisenhower and his friends got ready to listen, along with 60 million other Americans, at that time the largest audience in TV history. "Throughout the whole broadcast," Humphreys recalled, "I never once took my eyes off Eisenhower's face. I watched every flicker of reaction. He had a pad of paper and a pencil in his hand that he kept tapping. And when Nixon came to the climax of that speech, Eisenhower brought that pencil down so hard it jabbed right into the pad. Only he and I, of all the people in that room, knew what Nixon was saying, A lot of people think the climax came in the part about his cocker spaniel, Checkers, or his modest house or Pat's good Republican cloth coat. Well, it didn't. It came when Nixon started into the Stevenson fund, then went on to the fact that Senator John Sparkman, the Democratic vice-presidential candidate, had his own wife on his Senate payroll, and then called on Stevenson and Sparkman to make full revelations of their financial history; because, Nixon said, any man who's to be President or Vice-President must have the people's confidence.

"You know what he was doing? He wasn't talking about Stevenson and Sparkman. He was talking straight to Eisenhower. And he was saying, 'Okay, Mr. Eisenhower, if three out of the four of us make disclosures, how long do you think you can avoid putting *your* financial records before the public?'

"And Eisenhower got the point. He was the only man smart enough in that room to get it." Nixon's parting words—words lost on TV because he ran over his allotted half hour—"and remember, folks, Eisenhower is a great man," only covered with syrup the speaker's underlying bitterness.

At this moment of high drama, Eisenhower doubtless had many and varied feelings. His first words after Nixon's conclusion, which I also got from Humphreys and which went into the memoirs ("Well, Arthur, you sure got your money's worth!"), no doubt reflected genuine admiration for a virtuoso performance. And, despite its sentimentality (Clay, listening back in New York, thought it "the corniest thing I ever heard"), it had been. ("I knew I was wrong," Clay said, "when I saw the apartment elevator operator crying.")

Indeed, of all the people in the room, the most enthusiastically pro-Nixon now was William E. Robinson; the tour de force had turned him 180 degrees. Eisenhower himself doubtless recognized that the hazards of rewriting the ticket had now vanished. Yet as Jim Hagerty grabbed a yellow pad and began scribbling down

Eisenhower's dictated message to Nixon, the words—while buoyant and laudatory—still mirrored the detachment that Eisenhower had preserved from the beginning. "Your presentation was magnificent." Though technically no decision rested with him, he continued, the "realities" required that he make a "pronouncement." "To complete the formulation of that personal decision," he continued, "I feel the need for talking to you and would be most appreciative if you could fly to see me at once. Tomorrow evening I shall be at Wheeling, West Virginia. . . . Whatever personal admiration and affection I have for you, and they are very great, are undiminished."

He then went down into the auditorium and made a rousing speech: "When I get in a fight, I would rather have a courageous and honest man by my side than a whole boxcar full of pussyfooters," he said, "I have been a warrior, and I like courage. Tonight I saw an example of courage. . . . I have never seen any come through in such fashion as Senator Nixon did tonight."

He said all this and the crowd whooped it up, and yet he still had not nailed himself down to a flat decision. Not until the next evening, as he and Sherman Adams drove out to the Wheeling Airport in a cold spotty rain for, at last, the meeting with Nixon—with Eisenhower in some tension about the meeting, Adams observed, "though you had to know him pretty well to realize it"—did Adams surmise that Eisenhower had made up his mind after the broadcast to keep Nixon on the ticket. But the detachment Eisenhower felt for Nixon never died.

Nearly twenty years after this episode I asked Eisenhower's eight-year press secretary, Jim Hagerty: "When do you recall seeing Eisenhower angriest?" Jim had come through the whole 1952 campaign, served with Ike from first day to last in the White House, and had conversed with him off and on through eight more years thereafter. And out of this long day-in, day-out association flashed one single instance: "I believe I saw Eisenhower maddest during the 1952 campaign, when reporters asked me whether he would make his finances public." Stevenson and Sparkman had announced that they would release their tax returns extending over the past decade. And as Nixon subliminally implied, Eisenhower now stood alone. "Would he follow Stevenson's example?" reporters asked Hagerty. "I couldn't get to the General," Hagerty told me, "and so I asked his brother, Milton. And Milton said of course Ike would make all those records public. So I told the reporters. And when Eisenhower heard I had committed him, he blew his stack." In fact, Eisenhower later told assembled reporters "off the record" that he didn't care *what* Hagerty had said: he was *not* going to publish his finances. "Why should I dance to someone else's tune?" Eventually Eisenhower relented and put out the record. It contained nothing extraordinary—a summary of his income tax returns for the past ten years which showed earnings of $888,303, including $635,000 for the sale of *Crusade in Europe;* taxes of $217,082, including $158,750 in capital gains taxes (approved in advance by the Treasury Department) on the book. No one raised an eyebrow about anything.

Then why the resistance, the anger? The answer, I believe, lies not in Eisenhower's wish to hide anything, but in his private reserve behind the warmth and the grin and the ebullience: one didn't commit him to partisan politics against his will, as Cabot Lodge had done in a January 1952 press conference; one didn't call Eisenhower's revered General George C. Marshall "a front man for traitors" and then push forward before the photographers to put an arm around him, as reactionary Senator William Jenner of Indiana had done early in the campaign; and one didn't invade Eisenhower's privacy by making him tell the world how much money he'd made and how much he'd paid in taxes. "He don't take shovin'," one of his closest aides once observed. It infuriated him.

The coincidence of Hagerty's recollection, striking over those decades, confirms Humphreys' shrewd insight into Eisenhower's private world that crucial September night. And the event—the moment of Nixon's challenge to Eisenhower on the TV screen— displays as nothing else the complexity of the relationship between the two men, and the complexity of the Eisenhower reaction, which combined adrenal anger, practical good humor, rigid self-disciplined detachment, and quickness of intelligence. Nixon had acquired power, and, Eisenhower was smart enough to understand, Nixon would always use it. Eisenhower's fury, however, never turned to gnawing bitterness. Years later, I asked General Lucius Clay whether he believed Nixon's challenge to Eisenhower in the broadcast had left a permanent scar. Clay discounted it.

"Resentment was totally out of character for Ike," Clay replied. "He was the least vengeful man I ever knew."

IV

OCTOBER 3, 1952

"A FEELING
FOR
ORGANIZATION"

However thin you slice it, it was a mistake—a grievous mistake that I feel certain pained Dwight D. Eisenhower to his last day.

Senator Joseph R. McCarthy of Wisconsin had called General George C. Marshall—Eisenhower's benefactor and idol, a man whom his associates, even the cynics, to this day speak of with hushed veneration; Joe McCarthy—a slipshod, brawling, beefy, headline-grabbing opportunist who cared nothing for the truth—had called this monumental man, a man to whom honor meant everything, part of an infamous conspiracy. Why? Largely because Marshall had selflessly taken on a no-win diplomatic assignment for Harry Truman in China after the war and failed to prevent the alleged "loss" to the Communists of that giant country and its half billion people.

And now on October 3, 1952, McCarthy was running for reelection in Wisconsin, and Eisenhower was whistle-stopping through the state with McCarthy aboard the campaign train.

Long since, Ike had made unmistakably clear his esteem for Marshall. At an August 22 press conference in Denver, when reporters bored in with questions—What did he think of Marshall?

Did he agree with McCarthy that Marshall was a traitor? Would he back a senator who called Marshall a traitor?—Eisenhower shot up, red-faced, from behind his desk.

"George Marshall is one of the patriots of this country. . . . Maybe he has made mistakes. I do not know about that, but from the time I met him on December 14, 1941, until the war was over, if he was not a perfect example of patriotism and loyal servant of the United States, I never saw one. If I could say any more, I would say it, but I have no patience with anyone who can find in his record of service for this country anything to criticize. . . . There was nothing of disloyalty in General Marshall's soul."

Well, then, what about McCarthy?

"I am not going to support anything that smacks to me of un-Americanism."

The needle had pointed true north.* But with the demands of politics, the entreaties of teammates, the advice of men Eisenhower trusted—men who were working their hearts out for him—the needle would at times, almost imperceptibly, jiggle.

The Republican National Committee, for example, had put together a little slide show that went hammer and tongs after the Truman foreign policy, including the China policy. "It was pretty rough on Marshall," Bob Humphreys told me, "and I'll never forget showing it to Eisenhower, sitting there watching him grimace and twist his napkin and wondering what he'd say when the lights went back on. Well, it ended, and everyone sat nervously waiting for the General's reaction, and then suddenly old Doctor Snyder, Eisenhower's physician, piped up, 'Well, I guess that was about the size of it.' I could have hugged him. Nobody criticized a word. And as

*Not once in any of our conversations did I see anything to suggest a resentment over Marshall's alleged anger—if indeed the episode ever happened, outside Harry Truman's happy-hour recollection on Merle Miller's tape recorder—over Eisenhower's alleged intention to divorce Mamie and marry Kay Summersby. Only once did I sense the slightest trace of possible ambivalence: Eisenhower was recounting how, after his departure from Washington for overseas in 1942, Mrs. Eisenhower had abruptly and unceremoniously been forced to vacate their home at Fort Myer. Eisenhower spoke with chagrin. And then he added: "I'm *sure*," and he emphasized the word, "General Marshall never knew anything about this." But he gazed off for a fleeting instant into the distance and one sensed the faintest passing shadow of a doubt. Eisenhower and Marshall both may have wanted the Supreme Command, and personal history always colors public history. But Eisenhower would never, and could never, question Marshall's loyal greatness.

we left the room Eisenhower told me: 'Look, I've never said Marshall never made a mistake. But when these people start calling him a traitor, I'm just not going to go along with it."

On the night of October 2, as the campaign train rolled across the Illinois border into McCarthy's home state, Eisenhower doubtless reflected that only through a foul-up was he going into Wisconsin at all. In later years he always insisted that he had ordered his staff not to schedule him in there after the September 9 primary, which McCarthy easily won. Chief of Staff Sherman Adams, however, never recalled such an order, and neither did his right-hand man, Senator Fred Seaton of Nebraska. Lacking a flat edict, and confronting the implorings of Wisconsin's governor, Eisenhower stalwart Walter Kohler ("It would insult Wisconsin to single it out for a nonappearance"), his aides scheduled Eisenhower into the state against his will.

The afternoon before Eisenhower's train left Illinois for Wisconsin, Kohler, Wisconsin National Committeeman Henry Ringling, and Senator McCarthy flew by private plane from Madison to Peoria. They went directly to the Pere Marquette Hotel, where Ike was stopping for a few hours, and—to keep McCarthy's presence secret—were spirited up in a freight elevator to the room of Arthur Summerfield. ("When I saw him go up in that elevator," speechwriter Gabe Hauge recalls, "I felt sick.") At 5:30 a message came from Eisenhower: he would like to see McCarthy alone. The senator left.

A half hour later McCarthy returned to Summerfield's room. What happened in that half hour alone with the General, McCarthy described to reporters as a "very, very pleasant conversation." But from the hallway outside, speechwriter Kevin McCann couldn't help overhearing something else: Eisenhower's "white-hot anger." It had been building up for days, and now it exploded. "He just took McCarthy apart. I never heard the General so cold-bloodedly skin a man. The air turned blue—so blue in fact that I couldn't sit there listening. McCarthy said damned little. He just grunted and groaned. And when he came out, I really felt sorry for the guy. He'd been in the hospital and had unquestionably flown to Peoria against his doctor's orders. He was no heavyweight anyway. And under the attack he just went into shock."

Eisenhower proceeded to a buffet supper with his staff and

Kohler. McCarthy was not invited. McCann put him on the train, and late that night it pulled out of the station.

Next morning, October 3, McCarthy—a big grease spot on his tie—Kohler, Seaton, and conservative Senator William Knowland of California took over Adams' compartment. Adams had a copy of the speech Eisenhower would deliver that night in Milwaukee—a square-jawed anti-Communist text drafted in large part by young Emmet Hughes of the Time-Life organization, a self-avowed liberal. The speech contained one paragraph in praise of General Marshall; publisher Arthur Sulzberger of *The New York Times* had suggested it to Eisenhower, and Ike had written back that he would use it in Milwaukee. Kohler thought the speech great—all but that Marshall paragraph. It was gratuitous, he told his friend Adams, out of place. Summerfield and Knowland, to no one's surprise, concurred. The day blackened. At the first whistle stop, at Green Bay, Eisenhower told the crowd, in reserved phrases, what he had told McCarthy face to face the night before: He didn't like the senator's methods. And he went on to Appleton and Neenah and Fond du Lac telling crowds, in effect, "You elected him, but I don't agree with him." Somewhere the train took a bad lurch, and Eisenhower banged his head on a steel wall; he felt groggy all day.

The political editors persisted. "Everybody knows how Eisenhower feels about Marshall," Kohler pleaded with Adams. "This line is just out of place in this speech."

Finally Adams succumbed to this argument. He went in to see the General, and in retrospect he feels he made a mistake. "Gabe Hauge is one of the best people I know, and he fought tooth and nail against deleting that paragraph. I should have taken him in with me and said to the General, 'I've given you my recommendation, but you should hear the other side.' But I didn't. And if I had, the question of why we were in Wisconsin in the first place would probably have come up all over again." So Adams made his recommendation. Eisenhower listened. Then he gave an answer Adams will never forget, "as peremptorily as if he were sentencing a man to death."

"Are you telling me that paragraph is out of place?" he asked sharply.

"Yes, sir."

"Then take it out."

Anyone drafting a speech, of course, has the right to make any changes he wants up to the moment of utterance. As the decision was being sealed, Press Secretary Jim Hagerty recalls he was already stenciling the text of the speech for release to reporters, with the Marshall paragraph in. But he had given it to no one.

Who then knew about the paragraph in addition to Eisenhower and his immediate entourage? Two people, for certain: Arthur Sulzberger, though he doubtless knew a lot can happen to a paragraph on its way to a speech; and *The New York Times*'s reporter on the train, Bill Lawrence. Sulzberger had told Lawrence nothing about the paragraph, but Fred Seaton had. That very morning, Lawrence asked about it once again, and Seaton—perhaps trying to hold a veteran liberal reporter (and fellow Nebraskan) in line, perhaps realizing that coming from Sulzberger, the paragraph would eventually surface anyway—kept answering Lawrence: Don't worry about McCarthy's presence on the train; just wait until you hear Eisenhower's defense of Marshall tonight.

When Eisenhower, on Adams' advice, made the key decision, did either man realize that the Marshall paragraph had thus already become public property? The answer seems to be no. Eisenhower, and presumably Adams, knew that the paragraph originated with Sulzberger, and that it might therefore one day come to light. But Bill Lawrence's autobiographical revelation of his part in this episode did not appear until after my conversations on this question with Governor Adams and long after my work on the memoirs with General Eisenhower. Though both Eisenhower and Adams realized in retrospect that the paragraph had leaked out, neither knew how. And as far as I can tell, both men believed that at the moment of deletion they were still editing a privately held draft.

So in fairness one has to remember:

1. Eisenhower had every right to put in or take out anything he wanted. In any speech text, what counts is the end result, not any one or five or twenty-five preceding drafts.

2. Eisenhower and Adams had the right to privacy in this process. As Jim Hagerty said, aside, years later, after he learned of Seaton's role, "Staff people shouldn't go around talking about drafts." Yet in the circumstances Seaton's conversations with Lawrence, as Lawrence reported them, are understandable and defensible.

3. If Eisenhower and Adams had known the paragraph had already gone public, they would *probably* have left it in.

4. The deletion was a mistake. In retrospect, nearly everyone agrees on this fact. Therefore, in working on the memoirs, when we got to this episode, a group of us inserted a carefully worded paragraph saying as much, drafted in large part by Bryce Harlow with embellishments and palliatives from Milton Eisenhower and Gabe Hauge. And when the General saw it, he erupted.

"I don't believe a word of it!"

He struck it out and substituted a defensive paragraph of his own, cleaving to the Adams argument that the Marshall defense intruded. Through later revisions of the manuscript we tried another paragraph, and another and another. Finally, over time, Eisenhower agreed to a carefully worded apology. It was an admission of error—an admission carefully hedged—but an admission.

In the Milwaukee deletion Eisenhower had made a mistake. He had also revealed a significant characteristic of his leadership: Dwight Eisenhower, more than any President in recent memory, was an organization man.

From the Normandy invasion to SHAPE to the White House, he believed in organization. As he said in a little-noticed passage in *Mandate for Change:* "Organization makes more efficient the gathering and analysis of facts, and the arranging of the findings of experts in logical fashion. Therefore organization helps the responsible individual make the necessary decision, and helps assure that it is satisfactorily carried out. . . . There are men and women who seem to be born with a feeling for organization, just as others are born with a talent for art."

From his first day as President, Eisenhower wanted in the White House an efficiently arranged staff; led by a Chief (Sherman Adams); and peopled with experts holding clear-cut responsibilities—for example, Jim Hagerty for press relations, General Wilton B. "Jerry" Persons for congressional liaison, New York lawyer Tom Stephens for appointments, New Jersey lawyer Bernard Shanley for legal questions, Dr. Gabriel Hauge of Harvard for economics, Robert Cutler, also of Harvard, for National Security Council staff work, Emmet Hughes for speeches, and Time-Life executive C. D. Jackson for cold-war planning.

He also wanted in the White House some effective instruments of control. One was the budget process. "Eisenhower was more budget-minded than any other executive I've ever known," one of his Budget Directors Percival Brundage, a senior partner in Price Waterhouse, told me. "He started out as an Army captain responsible for a post facility worth $25 thousand, and he said he'd been budget-minded ever since. He'd have me come in regularly at 8:00 A.M. to tell him the budgetary effect of every proposed policy. He saw the budget as a mirror of the organization's operations, and no man ever served in government who understood it better."

By the summer of 1953 he had established another instrument of control: the office of the Staff Secretary, under Colonel—later General—Paul T. Carroll. This office checked all papers going to the President; routed them around for staff work; made sure Adams and all the other right people saw them; got them to the President on time; kept things from falling through the cracks; and deterred freewheeling. Eisenhower had only contempt for the Kennedy claim that sloppy organization reflected genius at work.

Of all the Presidents he served, from Hoover to Nixon, Executive Clerk Bill Hopkins found none more demanding of his staff than Eisenhower. And, Hopkins and others recalled, Eisenhower didn't want staff people stopping to flatten against the wall as he passed, or hesitating outside his Oval Office waiting for him to get off the phone: they were busy, and they should keep moving.

In the summer of 1954 Eisenhower established a secretariat for the Cabinet to ferret out subjects for discussion—for example, Mission 66, which refurbished the entire National Park system; set agendas for the weekly meetings; and follow up on decisions taken. A comparable, even more elaborate, organization existed for the National Security Council. It oversaw the writing of endless interagency papers specifying U.S. policy on every conceivable subject from missiles to Burma to the Horn of Africa to military dictatorships. It brought these in for discussion and resolution of disagreements at regular NSC meetings chaired by the President—meetings which at times produced outright Donnybrooks between, for example, Foster Dulles and his brother Allen or Admiral Arthur Radford. To be sure, some waffle papers resulted from the process. It was somewhat cumbersome. But it did these things: (1) It forced interagency teams to ask constantly and systematically "What if?" and thus exemplified Ike's often-repeated wartime dictum on readiness: "Plans are worthless, but planning is everything." (2) It helped Eisenhower decide. As his Deputy Assistant Bob Merriam observed, "He wanted to hear the arguments and even more the counter-arguments, and all at the same time." (3) It made decisions stick. After the Kennedy people dismantled much of the NSC mechanism, considering phone calls among friends as more efficient, Eisenhower's Defense Secretary Tom Gates asked Kennedy's NSC Assistant McGeorge Bundy, "How can you ever expect to make a decision stick by phone? It's impossible."

But organization to Ike was not just a virtuoso exercise in controls. He surrounded himself with able advisers, conferred authority on them, and held them accountable.

"It was almost scary how much power he delegated to you," Attorney General Herbert Brownell, a man not easily scared, once recalled. And Brownell never forgot the shiver that went down his spine when once he brought Eisenhower a list of prisoners to be pardoned; Eisenhower approved it, but added ("the only time he ever lectured me"), "If I ever find that any political considerations influence a list like this, it will go hard with you."

In 1960 Brownell's successor Bill Rogers reported the Department's readiness to seek antitrust indictments of leading executives in the electrical equipment industry, including some known personally to Eisenhower.

"Did these men do what you say they did?" Eisenhower asked.

"Yes, Mr. President."

"Can you prove it?"

"Yes."

"It's a sad thing." And then, with no request for a review or a delay or a second thought, "Go ahead and indict them."

Eisenhower listened to his advisers' advice—liberal, conservative, in between. He listened to economic royalist George Humphrey—Cleveland industrialist, Secretary of the Treasury, the skeet-shooting, quail-hunting owner of a Georgia plantation, and the only Cabinet member with whom Ike had a social relationship—and called him in May of 1953 "a man of splendid personality... persuasive in his presentations," with his facts well in hand. Many others considered Humphrey the most effective man in Cabinet discussions and Ike even listened to him with approbation when George in early 1957 did the unthinkable: complained about Eisenhower's already-public proposed budget and warned that continued high taxes could trigger a recession that would "curl your hair." And Eisenhower listened, informally, to his liberal younger brother Milton—who rose in the federal government through FDR's New Deal and ultimately became president of Johns Hopkins—held him in more affection than perhaps anyone in the world, and regularly called him "the most highly qualified man in the United States to be President."

Eisenhower listened to Boston tycoon Sinclair Weeks, Secretary of Commerce (labeling him in one moment of irritation "so completely conservative" that at times he seems illogical); and to Boston Brahmin Cabot Lodge, ambassador to the United Nations, who in 1954 hoped, for Ike's sake, for a Congress controlled by the Democrats instead of the reactionary recalcitrant Republicans.

Eisenhower listened to Jewish cold-war conservative Lewis Strauss, AEC chairman, and stood by him enraged in 1959 as his enemies cut down his confirmation as Secretary of Commerce. And he listened to Jewish civil rights liberal Max Rabb and backed him to the hilt in the summer of 1953 as he walked the corridors of Congress to persuade Eisenhower's rickety one-vote Republican Senate majority (including such less-than-liberal stalwarts as Welker of Idaho, Dirksen of Illinois, and Jenner of Indiana) to override their own inclinations and the poisonous tooth-and-claw enmity of reactionary Democrat Pat McCarran of Nevada, and open the floodgates of the United States to 215,000 European refugees—East Germans, Dutch, Italians, Greeks, and other assorted victims of Europe's high birth rates, glutted labor markets, and inpourings from Iron Curtain satellites.

Eisenhower listened to unwaveringly conservative Agriculture Secretary Ezra Taft Benson and to liberal Staff Secretary Brigadier General Pete Carroll—brilliant young (forty-three) West Point graduate, tie loosened, cigarette holder clenched between his teeth, former personal aide to Ike at SHAPE, a man seemingly destined to become Army Chief of Staff, who would work seventeen hours a day to figure out the right course for the President ("he was just like Al Gruenther; by golly, the right thing was the *only* thing"); who would get red in the face, even pound the President's desk: "Damn it, Mr. President, you can't let them get away with this"; who believed Eisenhower should make Washington the most magnificently beautiful capital in the world, and who, when he learned Eisenhower was planning to make a Montana speech to members of Benson's Forest Service, urged the abandonment of forests as the indicated subject ("Hell, those people out there know all about forests. The President will be speaking on the day he has declared a National Day of Prayer. That's what he should talk about—prayer"); and who a few days later suddenly died of a heart attack, remembered as "one hell of an administration liberal," with the selflessness and devotion Eisenhower prized above all.

Eisenhower tested his advisers' convictions. He didn't like yes-men; he wanted to know what a man *really* thought, off-guard. "He wanted a specific recommendation, not a dozen options," Lucius Clay observed. "And he had a habit which could have been dangerous. When someone came in with a recommendation, he had one instinctive reaction: 'No! Prove your case to me.' He was not being hostile. He was merely trying to test the man's strength of belief and logic. If the assistant backed down, Eisenhower lost confidence in his suggestion."

One day in Ike's first term, Orme Lewis, Assistant Secretary of the Interior, cautiously entered the Oval Office with Secretary Douglas McKay. "What do you want to talk to me about?" the President asked.

"Statehood for Alaska," McKay replied.

"Well, it better be goddamn good," the President shot back, having some sincere and long-held convictions, mostly negative, of his own on the subject. Lewis didn't recover for a full ten minutes. And though he valiantly persevered with his presentation, on Alaskan statehood Eisenhower remained unconvinced.

When his subordinates disagreed, Eisenhower refereed their disputes with decisiveness and sensitivity.

The organization did not always exude sweet harmony. Cabinet and near-Cabinet officers would at times, of course, foul up, and when they did, Jim Hagerty's diary for 1954 would sparkle with sudden rage—always his, often Ike's. Commerce Secretary Weeks, for example, deep in the recession of that year, approved a new technical method of sampling unemployment, which suddenly kicked the total up by 700,000. He was "a damn fool," Hagerty sputtered, to approve the change without knowing what figures would result. When the U.S. Information Agency sent out to all hands around the world an Alsop column blasting AEC Commissioner Lewis Strauss, Hagerty fumed ("a lousy job"). When Assistant Defense Secretary John Hannah unilaterally released a secret document on military manpower, he made the President "sore as the dickens."

And when Ezra Taft Benson and his Agriculture Department did almost anything, Hagerty groaned. "Agriculture Dept. in soup again," he observed wearily on February 9, for continuing to publish a pamphlet on how to wash dishes, a pamphlet that Ike in the 1952 campaign had ridiculed. "[I] told them to lose [the] ten thousand [copies] they still have," Hagerty concluded, with the afterthought, "What dopes over in Agric[ulture]."

But early in 1955 Agriculture was at it again. "Benson and his administrative assistant, Smith, have really fouled up the Ladejinsky case," Hagerty wrote. Benson, he went on, had made "ridiculous charges" against former Agriculture land-reform expert Wolf Ladejinsky, cleared for security by the FBI and recently hired by Harold Stassen's foreign aid agency. Hagerty pleaded with the stubborn Benson, but with no effect. "Why doesn't Benson admit he made a mistake and let it go at that [?]" an incredulous Eisenhower asked. When Benson persisted in his accusations, the time came when Hagerty thought Ike should give the Secretary a direct order to shut up. But Ike refused, chuckling to his apoplectic press secretary: "O.K., work it out the best you can with Ezra."

Differences did come to a head—and to Ike for decision—between Dr. Arthur Burns, former Columbia professor and then chairman of the Council of Economic Advisers, and Treasury Secretary Humphrey.

As 1954 ended, Burns had been working late into the night drafting Eisenhower's annual Economic Report, due to go to Congress in January. ("I've never outgrown the habit," Burns told me, "of doing my own writing.") After several weeks, he had entered the "nononsense stage," his nerves on edge, and he had produced a draft which he sent around for comments.

The phone rang: the Secretary of the Treasury was calling.

"Arthur, I've been reading your report."

"Good, George, I'm glad you're interested in it."

"I *am* interested, Arthur. But the report's no good. It's too socialistic. We're going to have to start all over again."

"George," Burns replied in the measured tones of W. C. Fields, "I'm not changing one comma. If you don't like it, you tell the President. But right now you're wasting *my time*." Click.

A few hours later Burns's phone rang again: his friend and fellow economist Gabe Hauge was calling, *agitato*:

"Arthur, do you know what's happening? George Humphrey is organizing a campaign against your report. We have to get people organized for it."

"Gabe," Burns replied, "I don't want anybody organizing anything. This is *my* fight."

("Now why did I say that?" Burns asked reflectively as I interviewed him years later. "Because I wanted to take on Humphrey and his big tycoons all by myself? Perhaps. But I really said it because I had confidence in the end in the President—in his making the fair and right decision.")

Humphrey went to Eisenhower and told him of his objections. So when the day arrived for Burns to present a summary of the report to the whole Cabinet, Eisenhower knew of the dispute between two of his most trusted lieutenants.

"Arthur," Eisenhower quipped as Burns entered the Cabinet Room, "I see you have a pipe in each hand."

"Mr. President," Burns chuckled, "I'm well prepared!"

Burns gave the highlights of the long report. Instantaneously, when he finished, Nixon, Labor Secretary Jim Mitchell, Postmaster General Arthur Summerfield, and Health, Education, and Welfare Secretary Oveta Hobby burst into spontaneous verbal applause.

And Humphrey's organized tycoons? "They didn't say a word," Burns recalled with glee. "Only one of them, Sinclair Weeks, asked one or two timid questions. And that was all."

"Arthur, that's a brilliant effort," Eisenhower remarked at the end. Then and there he might have given Burns's report his blessing. But, Burns recalls with admiration, he didn't. Instead, Eisenhower asked Burns to give him the report in its entirety; he would read it alone and make up his own mind.

"If I had been found wrong," Burns reflected afterward, "well, it's not too bad at times to know you're wrong. And I knew where my hat was." But Burns was not wrong. By late that same afternoon he had on his desk a letter from Eisenhower:

"While naturally I have not been able to give to each sentence the attention that such a report as yours deserves, I assure you that I find no parts that are 'troubling' me. I repeat that I have every conviction that it is going to be a magnificent document—even if some of our radical liberals will unquestionably call it a reactionary treatise, while the real reactionaries will call it a 'blueprint for socialism.'

"All of which probably proves that you are just about right.

"You know I am grateful to you for the tremendous burden you are carrying."

"Nothing ever made me prouder," Burns declared. "And you

know why Eisenhower read through that whole long report that same afternoon? Because he knew I was concerned; he didn't want me to sit there worrying."

Differences between Burns and Humphrey persisted. Late in 1955 Humphrey began agitating for a tax cut. Burns demurred, thinking the timing bad, with a new threat of inflation emerging. "Arthur," Humphrey countered, "the President can't have two advisers on taxes. He'll just have to choose between us."

The two set up an appointment and entered the Oval Office. Eisenhower greeted them with explosive warmth. "Boy, am I glad to see you fellows: I've just had a damn fool businessman in here, and you know what he wants? He wants me to *cut taxes!* And with inflation starting up again!"

Burns almost choked with repressed laughter. And on taxes Humphrey said not one word.

Trouble erupted also, in 1958, between the Republican National Committee and the State Department. Early in 1958 Republican National Chairman Meade Alcorn got an anonymous phone call: "I have absolutely reliable information that the State Department is getting ready to appoint Henry Labouisse, a Democrat, to a major job, from your home state of Connecticut." The caller hung up.

Alcorn, knowing Labouisse not only as a Democrat but as a possible Senate candidate in the forthcoming 1958 election, went immediately to Christian Herter and Douglas Dillon at State, and at once ran into a stone wall. "We're going to appoint him anyway," Dillon announced. Alcorn, determined to block the move, made an appointment with Eisenhower, and all three appeared in the Oval Office. The argument raged. Finally Eisenhower spoke: "Chris, I brought you and Doug down here to run the State Department. I brought Meade here to tell me what makes sense politically. This sounds like a political decision to me, and that's the way we're going to decide it."

To this day Alcorn recalls the relish and admiration with which he heard those decisive words. "When Ike looked you straight in the eye and said, 'Meade, this is the way it's going to be,' you didn't need a confirmation in writing." And once Ike decided, Percy Brundage recalled, you didn't reopen the subject the next day, either.

Finally, as in the Milwaukee speech, Eisenhower at times would accept his advisers' conclusions over his own.

The process was central to Eisenhower's way of working. The men about the President were extensions of his mind, and he looked to them to serve a crucial function. As his cold-war strategy adviser C. D. Jackson perceptively observed in his diary for July 8, 1953, in response to a complaint that Eisenhower was supplying less foreign policy than Truman and Acheson: "Key to the problem is basic misconception of the kind of leadership the President is accustomed to exercise. He does not initiate leadership, but he wants energetic, alert staff to bat things up to him, and when he approves he will then lead. [Undersecretary of State] Beetle Smith, Bobby Cutler and I understand this. Foster Dulles hasn't got the faintest conception—and that is where everything gets off the rails and nothing gets done."

But Eisenhower devised the organization, and in the end it served him, not he it. Using it, while seeming to hold a loose rein, he kept on top of major decisions. "You know how the Boss worked," his longtime aide General Robert Schulz once insightfully observed when I asked him exactly what single individual, of all the contending "kingmakers," had finally persuaded Eisenhower to run in 1952: "All the little pieces came in to him, and he put them together."

Should he have relied on a different process? Did his leaning on his organization betray weak leadership? Nelson Rockefeller, for one, citing instances where the group's conclusion overshadowed Ike's own better instincts, believes so: Like Lincoln, Rockefeller told me, Eisenhower should far more frequently have announced, with his one "aye" confronting his subordinates' eight "nays," "The ayes have it."

But consider what Eisenhower's reliance on a collegial process reflects. It reflects above all his perception of one clear fact—that all wisdom on all major decisions, particularly decisions on national security, war and peace, life and death, does not, indeed *cannot*, reside within one mind.

And recall the contrast: the self-contained self-sufficient hermetic world-in-a-single-skull presidencies of Lyndon Johnson and Richard Nixon. Eisenhower was no Nixon, sitting in isolation at Camp David, scribbling on a yellow legal pad, thinking his own thoughts. And the characteristic man in Eisenhower's organization was not a mindless H. R. Haldeman, who in 1978 could write from prison: "I was a robot....I was a good machine. I was efficient, I didn't require a lot of 'oiling.'"

To self-reliance one can perhaps credit much of the creativity in Johnson's Great Society and in Nixon's sweeping schemes for government reorganization, a guaranteed annual income, wage and price controls, and the opening into Communist China. But to their infatuated self-sufficiency one must surely credit their far more overwhelming disasters—Vietnam and Watergate.

Ironically, the same theoreticians who wondered beforehand whether, as a soldier, Eisenhower as President would be too authoritarian, in hindsight proceeded to criticize him as too indecisive in his handling of the office. Perhaps the very disagreement in their conclusions supports the probability that he, in this respect as in so many others, was actually a moderate. His staff system, like democracy itself, represented no hard thin line, but a broad central road, between the extremes of tyranny and anarchy. Not the least of the merits of the system was its providing elaborate records and checks and balances for executive decisions. Ike's method also assured that one agency could not make a decision without knowing how it affected another; at the presidential level, all decisions were coordinated.

In any discussion of policy, Eisenhower encouraged everyone to speak out. Challenging, and urging the others to challenge, he wanted to hear all sides. At the end of the process, and only then, did he decide, exercising his power, but on the information received, on data as objective as he could obtain. After he made his decision, he expected everyone to support it. For Eisenhower demanded both loyalty and selflessness. Associate Special Counsel Roemer McPhee recalls Ike's fury when told of one Air Force officer's achievement in his "spare time." "When you're a military officer," the President exploded, "there's no such thing as spare time. Your time is a hundred percent your duty. I worked for Black Jack Pershing to two or three A.M., and nobody ever mentioned *my* spare time." And he stabbed his pen through the heavy paper he was signing.

The leadership process, however, did not depend on coercion. "Eisenhower never said, '*I order* you to do this,'" Robert Anderson recalls. And it thus underlay the President's greatest achievement in the judgment of Jim Hagerty—his "getting people to compromise divergent views without anyone's surrender of principle."

Eisenhower's organization did not produce answers unfailingly correct and it did not guarantee the final rightness of every final leap (intellectual, emotional, imaginative) of the leader: what system can? But in retrospect Eisenhower's method of leadership—leadership through a devoted, intelligent, loyal organization, leadership that recognizes the fallibility of all men, and of any one man—that leadership appears not as a defect, but as a signal strength.

At least those who had a part in the process so remember it. A quarter century after Eisenhower's inauguration, a large group of the members of his White House staff met for a warm and nostalgic reunion—the first in Washington memory. And when a reporter asked the reason for the historic gathering, she got a sufficient answer: "Perhaps because it's the first time the members of a White House staff ever *wanted* to see each other again!"

The camaraderie that filled the room was an arresting tribute to the man they had served. I found myself recalling a story I had heard from Meade Alcorn: Early in 1976 President Gerald Ford invited him and the other former Republican national chairmen to the White House for breakfast. As the guests were waiting for the President to arrive, Bill Miller turned to Alcorn with a question: "Do you know the difference between Gerry Ford and Ike?" Several answers flashed through Alcorn's mind, but before he had time to reply, Miller continued: "With Gerry Ford, you won't know he's in the room until you see him; with Ike, you always knew he was in the room even before you saw him."

Book Two

DAYS OF SUN

V

SEPTEMBER 27, 1953

CONSTITUTION-ALIST

If Earl Warren had followed Dwight Eisenhower's advice on Sunday, September 27, 1953, he would not a few days later have been named Chief Justice of the United States. And if Warren had not become Chief Justice in 1953, not only would the history of subsequent years have altered but historians would never have had to pore over the puzzle of the relationship of the monumental Chief Justice to Eisenhower—a relationship that reveals a principle central to Eisenhower's presidency.

The choice came to Warren that September Sunday at McClellan Air Force Base near Sacramento in a meeting of several hours, shrouded in secrecy, with Eisenhower's emissary, Attorney General Herbert Brownell. Much has been written about that meeting: by Warren biographers who assert that he stubbornly insisted that Eisenhower keep an earlier promise and appoint him Chief Justice or nothing; by Warren's longtime gubernatorial assistant Merrill F. ("Pop") Small, who to this day wonders why Brownell had to fly coast to coast for a lengthy face-to-face conference unless some disagreement existed; by Eisenhower, who in *Mandate for Change* guardedly says only that Brownell went to Sacramento to explore Warren's record in the law; and by Warren himself, who in his memoirs (1977) heatedly denies demanding the position of Chief Justice, but who omits one crucial fact. One man heretofore has remained largely silent—Herbert Brownell. But now with his addition to the earlier accounts and speculations, the pieces at last fall into place.

To understand what happened that Sunday, one must go back to the beginning, to the 1952 Republican convention. As Taft and Eisenhower came down to the wire in a neck-and-neck race for delegate votes, Warren, California's progressive and popular governor, and Tom Dewey's running mate in 1948, headed the seventy-vote California delegation as its favorite-son candidate. By bolting to Taft on the second ballot (as conservative Senator Bill Knowland, who nominated Warren, would have done with alacrity), Warren could have dumped Eisenhower's whole applecart.

So Lucius Clay and Ike's chief delegate-seeker Brownell wanted from Warren two things. The first was those seventy California votes on the crucial Fair Play Amendment. This change in convention rules, devised by Brownell out of a reading of the Republican convention of 1912, blocked Taft's delegates with contested credentials from voting themselves, from their temporary convention seats, into permanent seats. Brownell got those California votes, and when the amendment passed, it demonstrated what Brownell wanted it to demonstrate: that Taft lacked a majority in the convention. Thus Warren and his delegation helped foreshadow Ike's victory.

Second, Brownell and Clay wanted Warren's agreement to hang in there to the end: not to throw his votes to Taft. And Warren again cooperated: even after Ike had gone over the top, Warren refused to switch.

In return, Clay told me years later, Warren got a commitment—"the only commitment we ever made": if Warren stayed in the race to the finish and Eisenhower won, Warren had Clay's assurance, through an intermediary, that Eisenhower would offer Warren a position of his own choice in the new administration. The commitment was Clay's alone, not Eisenhower's. No deal was struck, no quid pro quo. Brownell does not recall it; Clay didn't even tell the General about it until "days later," and Eisenhower always denied that he owed Warren anything.

Moreover, Warren himself, as Brownell later observed, throughout was working "for Warren," not Eisenhower: Warren knew, Brownell said, that defeat of the Fair Play Amendment would probably assure the nomination of Taft; when he came out for "Fair Play" at the Republican governors conference in early July, he didn't foresee that passage of the amendment would go far to assure the nomination of Eisenhower (he was simply "outmaneuvered"). Warren's agreeing to stay in the race permitted him to do what he planned from the start—hope for a deadlock and his own later-ballot emergence as the Republican nominee.

Nonetheless, Warren did his part. And now he had a claim, however tenuous, on an Eisenhower appointment.

Not that Eisenhower had to be pushed. During the campaigning in California, an episode took place that stuck in Eisenhower's memory for years. A write-in movement for General Douglas MacArthur got started, and anxious strategists worried that this might dilute the Ike vote and throw the state to Stevenson. Eisenhower always admired the way Warren had appeared, listened, and calmed things down: "All this worry is ridiculous. In fact it's so ridiculous that I'm not going to campaign any more for Eisenhower in California. He'll carry the state without any trouble." Eisenhower told this story again and again for years, even after leaving the White House. As the campaign continued in California, Brownell recalled later, Eisenhower "saw Warren as a big man; and his respect turned into a real crush."

The election won, Clay put out a feeler to test Warren's interest (none) in becoming Secretary of the Interior. Then one late November morning Eisenhower walked into Brownell's office at the Commodore Hotel headquarters.

"Say, Herb," the General said, "I want to put in a call to Earl Warren and tell him that I'd like to think of him for the first vacancy on the Supreme Court. What do you think?" Brownell concurred.

Months later Brownell entered Eisenhower's office in the White House. "I'm having a hell of a time finding a Solicitor General. I've asked and already been turned down once."

Eisenhower reflected: "You know, Earl Warren's been away from the law for a while. Why not ask him to take this post? It would give him a chance to brush up on his law in preparation for going on to the Court."

Brownell made the offer to Warren, who was heading for Europe. Within a few days Warren cabled back his acceptance in code: "Looking forward to return to my work." Then suddenly on September 8, Chief Justice Fred Vinson died of a heart attack.

Clay had given Warren an assurance. Eisenhower himself had specified the Supreme Court. But neither guessed the first vacancy would turn out to be Vinson's. And now Eisenhower hesitated. Despite the promises, despite his persistent feeling, as Clay said, that "we had committed him," he did not believe himself bound hand and foot to send Warren's nomination to the Senate.

So Eisenhower ruminated. He wrote his brother Milton outlining his criteria for a Chief Justice (integrity, experience in government, competence in the law, national stature). He considered the necessity to balance the court between Republicans and Democrats (at the moment the Court had only one Republican, Harold Burton). He seriously thought of appointing Foster Dulles. He listened to recommendations (his old friend Kenneth Royall, Truman's Secretary of the Army, called; they discussed Judges John J. Parker, Orie Phillips, and Arthur T. Vanderbilt; and Ike assured Royall, "I'm not going to make any mistakes in a hurry"). And at last he came to a tentative conclusion: Warren should go onto the Court; but preferably not at once. Given Warren's ten-year absence from the legal profession, Eisenhower wanted him to consider this course: Become Solicitor General, as planned, and take the next vacancy.

As Brownell flew to McClellan Air Force Base with this advice, neither he nor the President knew how binding Warren considered Eisenhower's commitment. But as the two men talked, two things became immediately apparent: 1. Warren believed Eisenhower had promised him the first vacancy. He recognized the President's right, of course, to elevate any present Associate Justice to Chief Justice, and appoint Warren to the Associate's seat. But he would regard the appointment of an outsider—for example, Vanderbilt or Dulles—as a breach of faith. 2. Warren rejected Eisenhower's plan for reentry through the office of Solicitor General.

"He was quite cocky about the whole thing," Brownell recalled. "There was a vacancy on the Court, and he was ready to step into it." Warren assured Brownell he had no philosophical differences with the administration and told him he could leave for Washington immediately.

So the meeting ended, with Warren as he emerged, his driver observed, "beaming broadly." As Brownell returned to Washington, no one knew what Eisenhower would do—whether, for example, he would exercise the option to appoint a sitting Associate Justice Chief Justice. In her keen-eyed diary, Eisenhower's personal secretary, Ann Whitman, observed that the President had considered naming Republican Burton to the top position, but concluded he fell short as an administrator.

So in the end Eisenhower appointed Warren. And he appointed him with enthusiasm. He had had no secret preference waiting in the wings, ready to be unveiled if Warren had agreed to become Solicitor General. He had had no misgivings about Warren's qualifications for the Court, only about a too-rapid reentry into the law. And those misgivings Warren had triumphantly overridden.

Against all comers, left and right, Eisenhower defended the appointment. In response to an old Office of War Information friend of his brother Milton's who believed—actually believed—that Warren was a cat's paw for reactionaries, Eisenhower wrote Milton:

"I believe that we need statesmanship on the Supreme Court. ...Warren has had seventeen years of practice in *public* law, during which his record was one of remarkable accomplishment and success. ...He has been very definitely a liberal-conservative; he represents the kind of political, economic, and social thinking that I believe we need on the Supreme Court...."

And in response to conservative expectorations, Ike on October 8 wrote in his secret diary: If the "Republicans as a body should try to repudiate him, I shall leave the Republican Party and try to organize an intelligent group of independents, however small."

After a delay ("Is Senator [William] Langer dragging his feet on this? Damn it, he's casting grave doubts on one of the greatest statesmen given to the Supreme Court in our time"), the Senate confirmed the appointee. And then on May 17, 1954, the new Chief Justice took a shattering historic action: he announced the Court's unanimous decision in *Brown* v. *Board of Education*—the decision that declared segregated schools unconstitutional.

To Warren, that decision not only climaxed a lifetime of public accomplishment, it marked the end of his cordial relationship with Eisenhower. With bitterness in his memoirs he alleges that Eisenhower resented the decision. He excoriates the President's refusal, while in office, publicly to affirm its rightness. And he implies what he privately charged directly, livid, to his immediate family and to Brownell: that Eisenhower had improperly attempted to forestall the decision by inviting Warren to an informal White House stag dinner in early 1954 while *Brown* was still *sub judice;* seating him near the lawyer for the segregationist states, John W. Davis; praising Davis to Warren's face; and rehearsing to the Chief Justice an old segregationist argument: Don't put our sweet little white girls next to those big sexually advanced black boys.

The bitterness overflows into other comments on Eisenhower

in the book: Warren's implication that the President-elect told Warren, in the phone call from Columbia, that Warren would have become Attorney General if Brownell hadn't got there first; his condescending portrayal of ex-President Eisenhower as a legal knucklehead who advocated killing all those communist SOB's; his snide comments on the Dixon-Yates imbroglio.

"Warren was always jealous of Eisenhower," former Attorney General William Rogers observes. To Rogers' predecessor, Brownell, who had known Warren since the presidential campaign of 1948, Warren's virulence reflects other less-then-lovely features of his personality: his capacity for pettiness; for holding a grudge ("Warren never would have had dinner with anyone who opposed the *Brown* decision"); and for suspiciousness ("He was a stubborn Scandinavian," Brownell once noted with a shudder. "And he always thought somebody was out to get him"). But even worse, that virulence betrays a misreading of Eisenhower—of his incapacity for sneakiness and guile; his generous enthusiasm for a wide range of opinions and friendships, including southern opinions and southern friendships; and above all the rigorousness of his constitutionalism. Not to mention the sturdiness of his respect for Warren himself.

Eisenhower did not, repeat not, I am convinced, invite Earl Warren to the White House to undermine the *Brown* decision. I have no doubt that in a moment of thoughtless candor Eisenhower did relay to the Chief Justice the southern horror of adolescent miscegenation: I heard him say the identical words a decade later in his Gettysburg office. But the leap from this regional concern—which in the circumstances not only Eisenhower but Warren, given the positions they held, should have at least noticed—the leap to the conclusion that Eisenhower was nefariously lobbying against desegregation—that leap is unthinkable.

Consider several facts, all of which Warren's account omits: On civil rights, as on many other subjects large and small, Eisenhower listened to his southern friends, including southern Democrats in the Senate and House; but within his organization, that extension of his own mind, he had one central civil rights adviser, his liberal New York Attorney General, Herbert Brownell. In late 1953 Brownell had convinced Eisenhower—over the President's pronounced reluctance—that the Justice Department should file with the Supreme Court an *amicus curiae* brief against the constitutionality of school segregation, a brief to which, in the end, Eisenhower contributed his own handwritten editings, some of which appeared in the text of the Court's decision. Before, during, and after *Brown*, on civil rights Brownell had more of Eisenhower's confidence than any other living man. To believe Warren's account is to believe Eisenhower had abandoned this known liberal, in order to shill for nameless reactionaries.

It is also to misread the composition and probable thrust of this particular stag dinner. Brownell was there. So was Cabot Lodge, Eisenhower's U.N. ambassador, who had long urged upon Eisenhower—without success—the establishment of a federal Fair Employment Practices Commission to assure equal job opportunity for blacks. Two of the other guests were, like Warren, Brownell, and Davis, distinguished authorities on the law: Professor Edward S. Corwin, and Dean Erwin Griswold of the Harvard Law School. But if any single problem of juridical immediacy dictated the guest list, it was not, I believe, school desegregation, but a piece of legislation that these men (of course excluding Warren) and at least one other guest (Lucius Clay) were at that moment opposing tooth and claw, with John W. Davis earning Eisenhower's particular admiration: a constitutional amendment proposed by conservative Republican Senator John Bricker of Ohio to restrict the President's treaty-making powers.

The dinner took place February 8, just two weeks before the amendment came to a climactic cliff-hanging series of Senate votes. Surely the Bricker Amendment formed a major focus of the informal gathering for Eisenhower, not some shady scheme to pour poison into Warren's ear.

Next, the *Brown* decision did not, as Warren claims, destroy Eisenhower's esteem for the Chief Justice. From the start, Eisenhower had concerns about the decision's practical ramifications, but none whatsoever about the wisdom of the man who had enunciated it.

To Jim Hagerty the day after the decision Eisenhower confided his uneasiness: "The President is considerably concerned, as are all of us," Hagerty wrote in his diary, "on the effect of the ruling. There is a strong possibility that some of the southern states will take steps to virtually cancel out their public education system and through legislative devices within their states place most of their schools on a 'private' school basis, giving state aid to such 'private' institutions. The President expressed the fear that such a plan if it were followed through would not only handicap Negro children but would work to the detriment of the so-called 'poor whites' in the South. The state we are particularly afraid of in this instance is Georgia under Governor Talmadge."

To Hagerty a month later, on June 16, Eisenhower reaffirmed his admiration for Warren. He had considered, he said, "only two men as Chief Justice. One of them was Earl Warren and the other was Foster Dulles. If Foster had been younger and therefore able to serve as Chief Justice for many years, I think I would have appointed him. However, I wanted a man to serve as Chief Justice who felt the way we do and who would be on the court for a long time. Therefore, I chose Warren."

To his most intimate confidant, his Abilene boyhood friend, Navy Captain Everett E. ("Swede") Hazlett, in a letter hitherto unpublished, Eisenhower wrote on October 23, 1954, five months after the decision, that he thought it might work:

"The segregation issue will, I think become acute or tend to die out according to the character of the procedure orders that the Court will probably issue this winter. My own guess is that they will be very moderate and accord a maximum of initiative to local courts. [italics added]" And his praise for Warren remains undiminished: "Your implications seem to be that Governor Warren was a 'political' appointment. It was most emphatically not. . . . A Chief Justice . . . must be a statesman and, in my opinion (since I have my share of egotism), I could not do my duty unless I appointed a man whose philosophy of government was somewhat along the lines of my own. All this finally brought me down to Warren. . . ."

Finally, in December 1955, more than a year and a half after *Brown*, when Jim Hagerty asked about Warren as a possible Republican nominee if Eisenhower's heart attack precluded his running again, Eisenhower snapped back: "Not a chance, and I'll tell you why. I know that the Chief Justice is very happy right where he is. He wants to go down in history as a great Chief Justice, and he certainly is becoming one. He is dedicated to the Court and is getting the Court back on its feet and back in respectable standing again. . . ."

Without question, Eisenhower did from time to time voice frustration over the *Brown* decision, primarily because of the "peremptory process" (Sherman Adams' phrase) that resulted from it. Like Brownell himself—whom some Southerners saw as a radical Rasputin of desegregation—Eisenhower blew off steam more than once at the administrative headaches the Court's judgment brought on. And at times, as to Arthur Larson in the fall of 1957, just after Little Rock, Eisenhower would call the decision flatly wrong.

Without question, also, Eisenhower from time to time would blow off steam about Earl Warren. I myself once, and once only, heard him say in Gettysburg in 1961, "The two worst appointments I ever made came out of recommendations from the Justice Department: that fellow who headed the Antitrust Division, Bicks, and Earl Warren."

But on the evidence, Dwight Eisenhower did not, on May 17, 1954, become at one decisive stroke an implacable dissenter from the *Brown* decision and an implacable scorner of its architect.

My own view is that when all the arguments were in, Eisenhower would have come down exactly where he came down in his memoirs: on the side of Earl Warren, the *Brown* decision, and desegregation. Eisenhower was a man who understood, liked, and sympathized with Southerners. He was a man capable of seeing the problems the decision would cause, given the fears and customs of a great region of the country. He was a man capable of questioning the redemption of society by force. He was a man capable of quick and unreflective reactions. And he was also a man capable of holding in suspension a variety of answers to vexatious questions, and talking about them out loud to people with frankness and without an eye to how his remarks would sit with future generations. But the one thing I find him absolutely incapable of is making up an answer in which he did not believe and setting it down in a book to burnish his image. In the end, though not without qualms, I believe he would have voted with Earl Warren.

Finally, Eisenhower's refusal to affirm the *Brown* decision stemmed not from his unconcern for civil rights, as Warren implied, but, ironically, from a quality both President and Chief Justice shared in abundance—a rigid awareness of a role imposed by the Constitution.

"Both Eisenhower and Warren," Brownell noted, "were very reserved men. If you'd try to put your arm around either of them, he'd remember it for sixty days." For more than seven years they sat, each on his eminence, at opposite ends of Pennsylvania Avenue, by far the two most towering figures in Washington, each playing out a noble role, in tragic inevitable estrangement. To Eisenhower, what

Eisenhower thought about the *Brown* decision—or indeed about Earl Warren—was not the point. The central point, as Herbert Brownell defined it years later, is this: Eisenhower was a constitutionalist. He believed in the separation of powers, as he had learned at West Point. He never saw himself as a moral dictator. As President, he had a role to play, a role with prescribed powers he would not evade, prescribed restrictions he would not exceed.

For this reason, throughout his career as General, Army Chief of Staff, and President, he regularly tried to help black people advance, within the limits of the various roles he held. For this reason in 1953 he desegregated the Navy depots in the South and the public places of the District of Columbia. For this reason he had questioned Justice's filing an *amicus* opinion in the *Brown* case, approving only when he learned that the Attorney General, in *his role as an officer of the Court,* had an obligation to express his legal judgment.

For this reason, the day after the Supreme Court decision, Eisenhower conferred with the commissioners of the District of Columbia to make the Capital city a model in the changeover to integration.

For this reason, he told reporters the next day, "The Supreme Court has spoken, and I am sworn to uphold the constitutional processes in this country; and I will obey."

For this reason, in 1957, Eisenhower used the ultimate power of his office—the dispatch of the 101st Airborne to Little Rock's Central High School—to enforce the judgment of the Court.

He had a role imposed by the Constitution, a role that demanded not that he pick and choose among the laws of the land, declaring personal preferences, but that he enforce all with an even hand. And for this role he knew the overriding reason: to hold the country together through times, like this, of deep division; and to uphold "the binding effect," as he wrote his friend Hazlett in deepest privacy on July 22, 1957, "that Supreme Court decisions must have on all of us if our form of government is to survive and prosper....

"I hold to the basic purpose. There must be respect for the Constitution—which means the Supreme Court's interpretation of the Constitution—or we shall have chaos....This I believe with all my heart—and shall always act accordingly."

VI

NOVEMBER 11, 1953

HISTORY'S RECORDERS

In Theodore White's *Breach of Faith*, Vice-President Richard Nixon in 1954 remarks "wistfully" to Jim Basset "that he'd love to slip a secret recording gadget in the President's office, to capture some of those warm, offhand, great-hearted things the Man says, play 'em back, then get them press-released." Thus, as White observes, "the idea of taping was there, then, nearly twenty years before." So was the equipment, concealed in a "huge, ugly-looking piece of furniture" in Ann Whitman's office.

On the morning of Saturday, November 7, 1953, shortly after nine, Ike threw a switch in his Oval Office and what Ann (like Nixon) called a "gadget" went into effective action for the first time. It worked without a hitch, and she wrote in her diary: "A complete verbatim report of the conversation could be made—but the work!" She didn't transcribe every word of Ike's talk that morning with the doubtless unsuspecting Sinclair Weeks, Secretary of Commerce, about the need for a presidential troubleshooter (a man like Milton Eisenhower or Cabot Lodge, who could compose disagreements among Cabinet members) and about the need to change the Taft-Hartley labor law, which had triggered just such disagreements between Commerce and Labor. Instead, she listened to the record and wrote a third-person synopsis ("President asked," "Weeks suggested")—a practice she would thereafter follow.

Thus Ann Whitman became the third, unseen, person in the Oval Office just as she became the third, unheard, person on the presidential telephone line, monitoring phone calls and producing records of varying sorts: a mere log ("10:42 A.M., President called Dulles"); or a skimpy one-liner ("Mrs. Eisenhower called from farm about mice"); or a more extensive replay of the words that flashed between Ike and his old friend British Prime Minister Anthony Eden on a meeting to patch up differences after the disastrous British-French-Israeli invasion of Egypt in 1956, which the United States had condemned (the timing is bad; we'll have to postpone the visit).

After Watergate and Nixon's deployment of tape technology, it may surprise readers—even former staff members—to hear that Eisenhower used it too. So let me enter these caveats:

1. He wasn't the first. During the press conferences of FDR, two staff men would sit in a little dugout ("it was too small to be called a room," Executive Clerk Bill Hopkins remembers) right under the Oval Office and make old Victrola-type platter records of every question and every answer, all unseen by the reporters crowded around the President inches overhead.

2. Eisenhower didn't use the apparatus often. It didn't run night and day, holidays and weekends. He switched it on only sporadically, and the recording of Oval Office conversations makes up only a minute fraction of the eight-year record.

Out of the thousands of presidential conferences through Eisenhower's eight years, the archivists of the Eisenhower Library have identified transcripts of exactly twenty-six containing internal evidence (e.g., "monitoring began after interview started") of a taping process. Another fifty transcripts or so, by rough estimate, appear obviously to have come from a tape but lack any internal corroboration. The twenty-six, which cluster primarily in the years 1953–55, form no discernible pattern. They include one-on-one meetings with Cabinet officers (Nixon, Brownell, Weeks); a meeting with Foster Dulles and other advisers; meetings with Republican politicians one-on-one (John Taber, Eva Bowring, Frances Bolton) and two-on-one (Joseph Meek and Everett Dirksen); interviews with writers (Bela Kornitzer, with Murray Snyder present, and Merriman Smith); one-on-one conversations with trusted outside confidants (Lucius Clay, Paul Hoffman); meetings with leaders of foreign countries (the Emperor of Ethiopia and his entourage, and Queen Frederika of Greece) and with representatives of foreign governments (V. K.

Krishna Menon). These transcripts, taken together, give no indication: (a) that the President asked anyone's permission to make a recording; and (b) that he had any encompassing reason—for example, the meetings' contents or participants or sensitivity—for using the equipment. He used it for subjects mundane and significant, foreign and domestic; with government insiders and outsiders; with men he trusted not at all, like Krishna Menon, and men he would have trusted with his life, like Lucius Clay.

The transcripts are a tiny part of a large whole. More voluminous, though still sketchy and haphazard, are Ann Whitman's jottings on the President's phone conversations. When, during the Army-McCarthy fracas, the Cabinet on July 16, 1954, focused on the too-widespread habit of telephone monitoring throughout the executive branch, Eisenhower recognized at once the central invasion of privacy problem and the merit of letting the person on the other end of the line know he was being overheard. The Army, he said, should announce the immediate establishment of this practice. But, as with the taped recordings, I have seen no evidence that the same guideline was followed in the Oval Office. Governor Adams' policy memorandum, which the Cabinet agreed to, enunciated only the "general practice" of informing callers of monitoring, and left specific methods of preventing "abuses" to each agency head. And the President himself concluded with a chuckle: "You know, boys, it's a good thing when you're talking to someone you don't trust to get a record made of it. There are some guys I just don't trust in Washington, and I want to have myself protected so that they can't later report that I said something else."

Like Foster Dulles' secretary, Phyllis Bernau, who monitored the calls of the Secretary of State—including conversations with Eisenhower—her close friend Ann Whitman did not confine herself to the untrustworthy. Within the limits of her time she tried to transfer at least some part of these ephemeral exchanges with all varieties of callers from utterance to paper. For she realized that while Eisenhower was no string-saver (he told her, without effect, that he wanted his scribbles and doodles destroyed), for the conduct of the presidency, he did want a written record of discussions conducted, agreements arrived at, directives given. Writing maketh the exact man. Records refresh memory, prevent misunderstanding. And in his years in office they took many forms.

First, the minutes of meetings of the Cabinet and the legislative leaders. The terse, accurate, and somewhat dry official record was set down for nearly eight years by Assistant Staff Secretary Arthur Minnich (a shrewd, circumspect Cornell Ph.D. in history) with a series of "Supplementary Notes" that included some—but not much—more juice. (Minnich, at Adams' instance, slipped this whole file [1953–56] to reporter Bob Donovan, who sprinkled it liberally through his book, *Eisenhower: The Inside Story.* When Adams left Washington in 1958 he took copies of the cabinet records [1953–58] with him, and scattered them liberally through his 1961 book *First-hand Report.* Ergo, some similarities between the Donovan *Inside* and the Adams *First-hand.*)

The notes are seldom funny, even when they try. In 1954, after the passage of the St. Lawrence Seaway bill, Foster Dulles commented to his colleagues on the merits of improving harbors as well as constructing the waterway itself. "Duck Island [Dulles' Lake Ontario retreat] must need a new harbor!" Eisenhower wisecracked. Laughter ensued. But few episodes more amusing than this emerge from these pages.

At least once as I worked on the memoirs these notes reminded me of the clay feet sometimes beneath solid-seeming historical monuments. Straight out of the Minnich text and into an early draft of the book I transferred these presidential words to his Cabinet associates: "[There was] lots of patronage in the New Deal days. I was in charge of a CCC camp in Pennsylvania, [and I] called a major to active duty from the Reserves to serve at [that] camp. Washington rebuke[d] me for recalling this Republican instead of a Democrat!"

When the President read this direct quotation, he angrily crossed it out. "I never said anything like that! Somebody's garbled it all up. Here's how it happened." Then he called his secretary and dictated a different recollection, which appeared in *Mandate for Change.*

But for this emendation, future historians would have had an easy time: they would have had no choice but to follow Minnich, who after all was there. Now, however, they have a problem: could it be that Ike was right the first time in his recollection—and accurately reported by his rigorous recorder—and wrong the second, when he changed the book?

Faithful as the Cabinet and Legislative Leaders minutes (usually stamped "Confidential") are, those for the meetings of the National Security Council (usually "Eyes Only") are even better—

compendious, detailed, accurate, taken by a succession of scribes, including historian S. Everett Gleason and Dr. Marion Boggs. But even notes as scrupulous as these can, like a verbatim transcript, mislead if one mistakes the pacing or the tone of voice of the speaker. For example, at one NSC meeting the participants fell into a jocular, boisterous exchange on troublemakers around the world who should forthwith and summarily be knocked off. After a few minutes of this, they got back to business. But as one observer quipped to the notetaker on the way out, "I sure hope you didn't record any of that!" The notetaker hadn't. For he knew how the silent blue typescript on white paper, evoking no levity, could convey to a future scholar a totally false message about the formal planning of multiple assassinations around the world.

In reporting comments that were made in all seriousness, however, he and the other amanuenses were meticulous to a fault. When Senator Frank Church and his Select Committee on Intelligence in 1975 began to disclose darkly that it had found evidence that Eisenhower had ordered a political assassination in an NSC meeting, I knew, having read all the minutes in their entirety, that they contained not one scintilla of corroborating evidence. Not one scintilla. And when the committee finally reported, it produced no evidence from this source, leaning instead on the vague and uncertain recollections of a single witness at a single meeting, uncorroborated by anyone else at that meeting, including notetaker Boggs.

Of conferences in the Oval Office, the record was kept in a variety of ways.

During Pete Carroll's tenure as staff secretary (1953–54) it was, mostly, kept not at all. Pete lived always in the future, sometimes in the present, never in the past. He left no trail of paper behind him. And when his assistant Minnich would conscientiously disappear to write a record, on his return he might well find Carroll looking for him, some red-hot crisis in hand: "Where the hell've you been? We've got to get this done by five o'clock!"

All that changed during the tenure of Pete's equally brilliant successor, Colonel (later General) Andrew J. Goodpaster, a Princeton Ph.D. who later became Supreme Allied Commander in Europe; under him, the records were kept with painstaking accuracy. At meetings on national security questions, when one, two, or three would go in to see the President, Andy himself would also go, yellow pad in hand, to scribble out rough notes for yet another Memorandum of Conference with the President. At meetings on congressional subjects staff members with liaison responsibilities—Jerry Persons or Bryce Harlow or Ed McCabe—would do the same. To Goodpaster historians will forever owe thanks for the volume and detail and regularity of these minute-by-minute records of the Eisenhower presidency. He went far toward assuring that almost nobody would go in to talk with Eisenhower unless accompanied by a White House notetaker.

To this practice of course, there were exceptions, one particularly glaring: John Foster Dulles. He would see the President alone. And on returning to his State Department office, he would at once dictate a memorandum of conference which would remain in his files. Ike had no problem with this process. But the White House Staff, left outside in the dark, didn't like it. And when Dulles' successor, Christian Herter, began meeting with Eisenhower, Goodpaster, with yellow pad, would pull up a chair too.

For Eisenhower, handwritten notes were the preferred method. The presence of a third person—as notetaker only, not participant—also kept the record from becoming self-serving. As Dean Acheson once observed, "I never knew a participant to write up an argument and come out second best."

Whatever the event—Cabinet meeting, Oval Office conference, colloquy with foreign leaders—its shape and content for future history inevitably reflect the personality and angle of vision of the notetaker.

Nothing better illustrates this fact than the notes written up by three Americans in March 1957, when, after the Suez crisis, Eisenhower sailed to Bermuda to restore the fractured Anglo-American alliance by meeting with his old wartime friend Harold Macmillan, who had succeeded the hapless Anthony Eden as Britain's Prime Minister.

Eisenhower's own dictated memorandum, *inter alia*, candidly records some initial Anglo-American differences:

"Very early in the conversation, the Foreign Minister, Mr. [Selwyn] Lloyd, delivered a tirade against Nasser, saying that he was not only an evil, unpredictable and untrustworthy man, but was ambitious to become a second Mussolini....This was followed by a presentation by the British of the need of obtaining promptly a satisfactory arrangement for the use of the [Suez] Canal. They felt the matter of tolls was probably the most important single consideration in such an agreement....

"I immediately pointed out to them the inconsistencies in their approach to these two problems. If we were at this moment to begin an attack on Nasser...then the hope of getting an early and satisfactory settlement on the Canal would be completely futile.

"They quickly saw the point of this...."

Goodpaster recorded for posterity the crucial meetings on missiles—our agreement to give to the British IRBMs, while continuing to hold custody of their nuclear warheads. And he caught Eisenhower's overarching observation: "The weapon is one of tremendous psychological importance, although I am still inclined to discount its military significance. In fact I believe that when the two sides come to the point of waging war with such weapons, all sense and logic will have disappeared."

Unlike either Eisenhower or Goodpaster, Ann Whitman composed grace notes—acute observations of tiny, often bizarre details framing the solemn secret sessions in Bermuda.

"I arrived at the Mid-Ocean [Club] 24 hours before the President and the rest of the party. I battled a nice little field mouse (captured, finally, by the Secret Service and buried with a seven gun salute), a fly in my coffee, and ants in the bathroom. I felt like a creature from a Charles Addams cartoon—still do—sleeping in the narrowest of beds and sort of riding out the gale....

"The President got a longhand letter from the King of Greece, which asked him to discuss with Mr. Macmillan the solution of the Cyprus problem. (I do not know how this letter got to the President; it was written in a large, flowing, almost incomprehensible hand....) It said that the only personality who could negotiate with the British on behalf of the Cyprus people is the Archbishop [Makarios] of Cyprus, now exiled by the British in the Seychelle[s] Islands..." The three notetakers, Eisenhower, Goodpaster, and Ann Whitman, observe differently.

To Ann Whitman's facility with words, her shrewd and humorous observation, future historians will owe floodlighted snapshots of presidential life not only in Bermuda in 1957 but at other moments throughout Ike's eight years—moments of frenzy or ludicrousness or quiet rumination.

On May 13, 1958, for example, she captured a day of problems, problems, problems: two libraries burned in Lebanon; the United States blamed for French troubles in Algeria; anti-U.S. demonstrations erupting in Burma; Nixon attacked by mobs in

Venezuela; a thousand troops flown to Cuba and Puerto Rico to help rescue him if necessary; Ike finally declaring, "I'm about ready to go put my uniform on."

On June 4, 1958, she captured trivia: "white dinner jacket day. ...With invitations to a dinner for visiting President Heuss of Germany a card had been enclosed saying, 'white dinner jacket.' ... Today of course was a fairly cool day and a white dinner jacket seemed a little conspicuous and out of place. When the President learned about it, he literally blew his top. He was going to wear his black coat, despite everything. Then we discovered that poor President Heuss was having a white coat made—rushed by the tailor—and to be safe had also bought a black one. So the President had to wear a white one, which did not please him. This matter was discussed in detail with the President, Mrs. Eisenhower, the Secretary of State, [Tom Stephens,] etc., and thousands of State employees....

"At 8:00 the dinner—white dinner jacket—for President Heuss. The guests included a lot of dowager ladies including Mrs. Gifford Pinchot who wore a deep purple dress, a green scarf, and carried an orange ostrich fan that (according to the newspaper) perfectly matched the color of her hair. This made my day."

In the eight years of Eisenhower's presidency, Ann Whitman saw him more than anybody. She heard him talk in unguarded moments. She heard him confess his lack of interest in the theater (he always felt conscious it was make-believe, and always wondered what was going on behind the scenes) and his enthusiasm for Charles Laughton ("No actor can compare with him").

She heard him discourse on painting. He pointed out to her the differences in the shades of the grass, the dead-looking shrubs, and the magnolias outside the Oval Office. "All amateurs," he said, "should go back to using only three primary colors, or at most 6 or 7, and blend them as the early artists did."

She heard him recall his mother's last words, spoken to her nurse: "You better get back to bed, it's cold."

And in the diary that she kept for the President's own files, she preserved these moments, whenever she could, from oblivion. Ann Whitman deserves our thanks.

The best, liveliest, and most candid notes, of course, fell outside the formal system, indeed outside Eisenhower's awareness: notes written for the closet of the author, not for the Boss or the beady eye of Sherman Adams. The takers of these notes include fallen disciple Emmet Hughes (largely in 1953 and 1956), with his slurs against Foster Dulles; they include exasperated cold-warrior C. D. Jackson, with his explosions against Foster Dulles and his occasional disappointments with Eisenhower (largely in 1953); they include generous, gentlemanly Bernard Shanley, with, among other things, his unique observations on the 1952 campaign. And above all, the notetakers include hot-tempered Jim Hagerty, with his always aggressive loyalty to the President.

Hagerty's voluminous detailed diary runs for hundreds of thousands of words, unhappily only for parts of the years 1954–56. Variously waspish ("I don't think Shanley has any idea of the hard work that the office [of Appointments Secretary] entails"); liberally partisan against the more conservative Republicans on the Hill ("no guts, our guys"); intolerant of critics of the President ("to hell with slanted reporters"); honest ("always best, when you make a mistake, to admit it"); derisive ("Senator Carlson said Conrad Hilton fell on his knees in prayer when he opened his new hotel; what a laugh!"); and blunt ("Cabot Lodge messed up the President's text with $2 words"), Jim had an eye for detail, a style of clarity and force, and above all, an ear for the exact words Ike uttered, pounding the table, pacing the floor, arguing with recalcitrant Republicans of the Right.

The best press secretary in memory, Jim captured an Ike the President in swift instants of candor and humanity: an Eisenhower of magnanimous common sense telling Foster Dulles that if a Russian boy who fled to the West now wants to return home, we should "give him a bicycle and let him pedal across the border"; of outrage at a pluperfect foul-up in the Commodity Credit Corporation, telling the Legislative Leaders, "Let's fire some of the bastards"; and of fatalistic impatience, advising the nervous Secret Service, "If they're going to shoot me, they're going to shoot me—so what!"

Fortunately when Churchill and Eden came to Washington in June 1954 for a meeting they wanted—and Ike and Foster didn't—to talk over manifold family disputes between the U.S. and U.K., Jim hovered nearby, writing. He began with the Eisenhower-Dulles preparations for this frank and affectionate visit:

June 23: "Winston," the President said, "has a wonderful way of turning conversations at some later time into ironclad agreements. We surely want to avoid that." "The way you have to work with Winston," Ike added, "is to get him thinking it's his own idea."

June 24: "Dulles said he was sure . . . the British were going to make a plea for a differentiation between French Colonialism and British Colonialism. The President interrupted to say, 'Sure, the British always think their Colonialism is different and better. Actually, what they want us to do is go along to help keep their empire.' Dulles then said that [British Ambassador Sir Roger] Makins had reminded him that on Sunday Churchill, unlike the Americans, always ate a 'huge luncheon.' The President was a little amused at this and said, 'I suppose we have enough food in the White House to give Churchill his huge luncheon, but I'll be damned if I'm going to change my habits for the Prime Minister—I'll have a light luncheon.'"

This is Hagerty on England's policy on Latin America:

"*Guatemala*. . . . Dulles. . . . said that he had received a cable from Lodge asking whether he should break openly with the British and use the veto for the first time in . . . the United Nations to vote against the British. Dulles said that . . . Guatemala was entirely a problem for the American states and within the purview of the UN Charter which holds that such problems should be handled through the regional organization. The President interrupted to say that he thought we were 'being too damned nice to the British on this' and said that as far as he was concerned to go ahead and use the veto and show the British that they have no right to stick their nose into matters which concern this hemisphere entirely. 'The British expect us to give them a free ride and side with them on Cyprus and yet they won't even support us on Guatemala. Let's give them a lesson.'"

"*Southeast Asia*. . . . Dulles said that the settlement at Geneva would be something we would have to gag about—'I don't think we'll like the settlement.' The President said he agreed and said that both he and Foster would look at any British proposals with a jaundiced eye. . . . 'I'll tell you what we'll do, Foster. Let's you and I listen and refuse to be committed and look bored at some times.'"

"*Atomic Weapons*. . . . 'If we ever get into trouble when we need these bombs,' the President remarked, 'it is our duty to provide them as quickly as possible to the British Air Force. I don't want to see American crews and American crews alone take the punishment they will have to take to deliver those bombs.'"

During the Washington conference with the British, Hagerty recorded on June 26:

"My own personal observations are that Churchill is considerably physically weaker than he was when I saw him in Bermuda which of course is due to the fact that since Bermuda he has had two strokes. He is almost in the dotage period and gives the appearances at least of losing connection with the conversation that is going on in the room. However, when he speaks he still retains the forcefulness of delivery, the beautiful, ordered and intelligent command of the English language although he doesn't seem to be able to stay on a point very long. He seems to get on one subject and repeat it many times. An example of this is the several talks that he has already given on the complexities of a central form of government, the advantages we have here with our 48 states taking much of the local load off our government and his thoughts on the restoration of the heptarchy. He said this to the staff in the President's office on Friday; he repeated it at the Congressional luncheon today; and he stopped me in the hall on the second floor of the White House to give me a private speech on the subject. That was when the electric storm broke and the Prime Minister, like a little boy, rushed from the President's study to go to the solarium to watch the rain...." Hagerty's notes are priceless, preserving the flavor like the meat of history.

Most of the forms of the record which have been mentioned required the presence of a third person in the Oval Office. In the absence of a third person—in conferences confined to Eisenhower and someone else—there were these possible outcomes: (1) no record at all; (2) a record—like Hagerty's or Jackson's or Hughes's—retained as the private property of its author; (3) a record—like Dulles'—kept for himself and Eisenhower; (4) a record—like those of Ann Whitman—for the presidential files; (5) a record dictated by Eisenhower himself; (6) last and least, a tape.

If transcribed verbatim, tapes have a conspicuous merit. They relay the exact words spoken, in jest, in reflection, or (as on one May morning in 1957) in wrath.

Through the spring of 1957 both Republicans and Democrats on the Hill had been making life hard for Ike, now a lame duck, by bellowing for cuts in his allegedly spendthrift budget and by denouncing foreign "giveaways." They would not see that the military defense of the free world depends upon the economic health of the free world. Senator Styles Bridges of New Hampshire, a crusty conservative, had made a speech calling foreign aid advocates "do-gooders." Jim Hagerty read the ticker and scribbled in ink on yellow pad a red-hot memo to Eisenhower recommending a woodshed hiding: a reminder to Bridges that "if anyone is getting sick of 'do-gooders' it's you—political do-gooders who can't or won't see the full picture and fulfill the obligations we have as a leader of the free world." The President, like Hagerty, also had had it up to here, and next morning, after the Legislative Leaders meeting, Ike called Bridges in on the carpet, switched on the gadget, and left historians with the only extended verbatim record extant of an Ike chewing-out.

"I am convinced that the only way to avoid war," the President told the Senator, "the only way to save America in the long run from destruction, is through the development of a true collective system of defense.

"It is pretty hard when I have to bear the burdens not only of the Presidency, but of the titular head of the party, to have said by one of the principal people in the party that this is nothing but a do-gooder act.... I think nothing could be further from the truth. I realize that as of this moment it is a very popular thing to talk about saving a dollar. Frankly, I would rather see the Congress cut a billion off ... defense [than off foreign aid]—as much as I think it would be a mistake.... If we depend exclusively on our own arms, we are headed for a war; there is going to be no other answer....

"If I knew a cheap way out of this one, I certainly would take it.... If Mr. Truman (and, unfortunately, a Republican Congress in 1946 and 1948) had given us what the Chiefs of Staff authorized me to request—which was 15 billion dollars a year over and above stockpiling and pay increases—I believe there never would have been a Korean War.

"I begged them for 110 million dollars, but never could make them see the need for it. (I think you were among the group I went down to talk to.) I am not blaming anybody, but I want to say this is just another incident in a long lifetime of work on this.

"Finally, I think my party ought to trust me a little bit more when I put not only my life's work, but my reputation and everything else, on the line in favor of this...."

Bridges, shaken, asked to see the ticker story. Then he started to explain: "What I meant by that statement was Yugoslavia, Indonesia, India and others—where I thought they in turn would contribute nothing to the mutual security, and therefore the money that you put into those countries was advocated particularly by do-gooders."

The President shot back: "Take some countries, like India for example. India has 350 million people. Suppose India said 'we take our stand with the West'—consider where we are, right up against an 1800 mile border against China.

"How much have we got to put into India to make it

reasonably safe for them to even exist? Frankly, this is the one country I had in mind when I said that there are one or two countries in the world that I would want to be neutral. Now we have no obligation to defend them, and if the other fellow attacks them, they violate a world treaty because they are jumping on a neutral country. I had a long talk with Nehru about this, and he is up against the matter of 350 million people practically starving. You could put all the defenses in the world in there, and they will go Communistic...."

Bridges backed and shuffled: "I don't blame you for being disturbed about that little statement given to you. That in effect is what I said, but it was only *part* of what I said."

Typically, once Eisenhower had his apology, he moved toward conciliation:

"You are the United States Republican Senator who has been in the longest. You're respected. You're intelligent and can look these problems in the face....

"I do not object to arguments over detail or procedures or practices; rather, I am pleased, because this shows we are not dependent upon anyone else's brain or thinking. But if we don't find a common ground for attacking these problems of the day, we deserve to be forgotten by posterity.... Did you ever see one of the Net Evaluation Studies given to me every year?"

"No."

"I will give you just one figure I remember from the last one. In a single attack we figured something like 25 million were killed, 60 million had to go to the hospital and there were not enough hospitals. When you begin to think of things like that, you know there must not be war.

"We must convince the Russians that if they attack, they will suffer the same thing or worse and therefore deter it. Once you get the deterrent established, how do you keep the rest of the world from going Communistic?..."

"It is that simple with me. And I want to wage the cold war in a militant, but reasonable style whereby we appeal to the people of the world as a better group to hang with than the Communists."

Bridges then tactfully switched to a congenial target: "I'm just as concerned and worried as you about this party split. I am not a candidate for anything; I have no ambitions in the world. But how could we alleviate misinterpretations through the press? When anything is said, they pick up only the pieces."

"They do it all the time," the President agreed, with equal

tactfulness, and the conversation soon ended, with friendly plans for the future. The gadget caught them all that day, exactly as uttered, exemplifying what a tape can do at its best.

Other days it demonstrated what it could do at its worst: catch nothing at all.

On December 16, 1956, in the President's own plane, the *Columbine*, flown by the President's personal pilot, Colonel William G. Draper, Prime Minister Nehru of India arrived in Washington.

"If only we could get the Old Man and Nehru together," Bern Shanley had mused a year earlier, voicing the hope of countless people that such a meeting of two strong men from the ends of the earth would produce a great push toward peace.

Eisenhower, however, never fully trusted Nehru; he particularly disliked India's ambassador to the United Nations, the wily serpentine leftist V. K. Krishna Menon, labeling him a "menace and a boor"; and Eisenhower resented Nehru's double standard on aggression—harsh censure of Israel, the U. K., and France for their invasion of Egypt; tolerant understanding of the U.S.S.R. for its simultaneous invasion of Hungary.

Nehru was of course engaging in the typical game of the third world, siding with Russia instead of the United States, playing off the two largest nations against each other. Heads of even petty countries constantly asked Washington to give them more, more, more, or they would go Communist. Eisenhower had a right to be angry with Nehru. Such men invite danger when they fail to stand up for international morality, and formal alliances play no necessary part in this process. Ultimately, the weaker have even more interest in upholding law than the strong, and law is always the last and best protection of nations or men. Might makes right only when the righteous give themselves up, a lesson that Gandhi blazoned on twentieth-century history: Gandhi will be famous among men when Hitler and Stalin are footnotes.

But Nehru's surface weavings, I believe, never touched or distorted the spirituality underneath. Once when my wife and I were visiting him in his office, he suddenly turned, took down a small iron lockbox from a shelf behind him, opened it, and produced its entire contents, a moving letter he had just received from Gandhi's most saintly disciple, Vinoba Bhave.

Nehru and Eisenhower met alone for long talks in Washington in 1956, and these produced long records.

One memorandum preserves for the future historian an illuminating array of Nehru opinions: on the Middle East (Arab speakers always seem to get excited when addressing a crowd); Hungary ("It spelled the death knell of international Communism"); India's neutrality ("any definite alignment by India with the free world would serve only to weaken ... the combination"); socialism (the public sector in India is necessarily larger than in the United States, though both countries have a mixed economy); American political noisemakers (he paid little attention to them). This was the record—fourteen pages of it—Eisenhower himself dictated after their first session December 17-18.

The second record reads almost like an Eisenhower monologue: on a voluntary neutral belt across Europe starting with Poland, Czechoslovakia, Romania, Bulgaria, and Hungary ("that idea would begin to make some sense when approved by free elections. ... If Germany chose to join such a pact, we could have nothing to say"); on Eisenhower's Suez crisis correspondence with Anthony Eden (someday if he and Nehru both were retired old gentlemen, he would like to show him the letters); Communist China ("he would like to get our people over their currently very adverse attitude toward Red China." Most of the hostility stems from American resentment over China's holding ten Americans prisoners, plus the memory of our casualties in Korea. "With those things straightened out, we would of course naturally do something with our public opinion here; secondly, we could do something about sending newspapermen over there who would begin to find out what they are thinking. There would then be a flow of news coming back that would tend to ameliorate this uneasy state of pandemonium. And there could, out of such a small achievement as this, spring something very fine." But at this moment "it is impossible for us to take the first step"); armaments ("If any nation uses aggressively any arms ever given to them by the United States, they are going to be in trouble with us. ... We have always been very careful not to give great stocks of ammunition, so that no one can go too far astray"); Eisenhower's own future ("I have no ambition left in the world except to leave a record—not a personal record, but a knowledge that something has been advanced to help the cause of peace in the world").

In this second record, the taped record, Nehru leaves future historians hardly anything at all. The mysterious East had unwittingly outwitted the technology of the West. For this second record is the record produced by the gadget; and Nehru had murmured so quiety it couldn't catch a thing.

Record-making is replete with hazards. Raconteurs self-serve, and even write fictions, as the Frenchman did, *"pour l'histoire."* No principal, as minute-keeper, ever comes out second best. Frazzled secretaries forget to write down the tiny passsing events of the day that, like each point of color in a Seurat, make history leap alive. Cold transcripts often convey no pace, no tone of voice. And gadgets when soft voices die, lie. Surveying all these possible pitfalls, one despairs of history *wie es eigentlich gewesen* and appreciates the wisdom of that definitive pronouncement of Henry Ford: "History is bunk."

Yet withal the written word, for all its frailties, is the best reliance we have. To Francis Bacon the written word was the maker of the exact man. To Winston Churchill it was the only instrument by which he would run the war. And to Dwight Eisenhower the written word was in the conduct of government, a means to order and efficiency. Furthermore, in the command of an organization, it was, as an avenue to knowledge, power.

Only Eisenhower himself had access to all the written words of his White House and to the reality they reflected. Sherman Adams never saw the notes of the NSC and never knew the taping system existed. General Goodpaster never saw the phone log or the synopses of recordings. Foster Dulles never saw memoranda on politics or economics or agriculture. Ann Whitman, though many files crossed her desk, never saw the NSC minutes, and remained outside the closed-door Oval Office conferences themselves, conjecturing.

Assistant Staff Secretary Arthur Minnich had come into the White House on Inauguration Day of 1953 understanding he was to see all, know all, preserve all—to record history as it happened. Within a week he knew he couldn't. His colleagues wouldn't let him: "If I'd had access to every meeting, every scrap of paper, only one man in the White House would have had more power than I—the President himself." So Minnich confined himself to the Cabinet and Legislative Leaders minutes.

Knowledge permits rule. Eisenhower, the most powerful, was the most knowledgeable. All the little pieces came in to him, and he put them together.

Finally, in the fashioning of history, to Eisenhower the written word was the final arbiter. As we re-created the history of his presidential years, that stubborn fact pained him at times. It made him bridle. But in the end he respected it.

Two instances:

For years Ike had been telling friends with irritation that in August 1952 the leaders of the Republican National Committee had come out to Denver to urge him to run on his own personal popularity "like a goldarned matinee idol," and he had refused. "They didn't think I had a brain in my head!" As I worked on the memoirs I would see Bob Humphreys frequently for lunch on Capitol Hill, and when I casually mentioned Eisenhower's comment, he exploded. "We made no such suggestion!" He let me see a copy of his presentation—one of only three in existence—and it proved him right. Though it mentioned that both Republican candidates had "warm and winning personalities," it said nothing about victory through popularity; instead, it focused on eight central issues. I told the President this text failed to verify his recollection. He deleted his original wording.

Second: in writing up the Geneva summit conference in July 1955, Eisenhower himself did an early draft recounting how he thought up the Open Skies plan for U.S. /U.S.S.R. aerial inspection of each other's territories, consulted with Foster Dulles, got the approval of Nelson Rockefeller (C. D. Jackson's successor as special assistant for cold-war policy), and then sprang the plan on the Russians. The draft chapter went to Rockefeller in New York for comment.

Weeks passed. Finally a letter arrived from the governor explaining with apologies why he had delayed so long in answering: his recollection departed so sharply from that of the President that he just had not known how to point out the discrepancy. So he was sending along some documents written in 1955 that showed a far different chronology: that more than a month before the Geneva conference, a secret panel chaired by Rockefeller at the Marine Corps Base at Quantico, Virginia, had recommended the plan for Soviet and American overflights; that weeks of study by State and Defense followed; and that Eisenhower did not decide to accept it until July 20, when at the President's request Rockefeller came to confer with him in Geneva.

With these Rockefeller papers in hand, I revised the President's original recollection and sent it along to him, plus the documentation. I never heard another word on the subject. Eisenhower incorporated every change verbatim, recognizing that his memory had simply played a trick on him. The realization that he himself had not authored one of the most arresting international initiatives of his presidency undoubtedly hurt, but he accepted it. I never saw anything more convincing on his humility, honesty, and fidelity to fact.

Years later, I asked Colonel F. W. Deakin, a distinguished Oxford don, and Winston Churchill's historical research assistant, whether he had ever had a similar experience with the Prime Minister. Deakin said he had. He would frequently ask Churchill to recall a specific event and would then confront him with a document that refuted the recollection. The result invariably made Churchill furious.

This anecdote, I believe, suggests a difference between Ike and his great friend Winston. For Eisenhower, that that is, is. Ike was not only, like Churchill, a superlative leader; he was a superlative leader who customarily could submit his own ego.

Yet he was not perfrect. From the beginning of this chapter, from that morning on November 11, 1953, when Eisenhower threw the switch, one key question has hung unanswered: Should Eisenhower have recorded the words of his guests without their knowledge? No matter how many qualifiers one enters (he wasn't the first; he didn't do it often; he did it only when he had no other means; he did it at times as a defense against people he didn't trust; he did it for the national good; it produced no transcripts that, like the Nixon tapes, could damage anyone), still, in retrospect I believe one can come to only one answer: no. With the advantage of hindsight—after the 1960s fear of the naked society, after Watergate—it appears, and appears rightly, as an invasion of the individual's right to privacy, as a wart, however understandable, however benign, on the portrait of the Eisenhower presidency.

VII

APRIL 26, 1954

ALLY

On the morning of April 26, 1954, the Republican Legislative Leaders and the President were facing head-on the imminence of French defeat in Indochina. Eisenhower did not advocate that the United States send in combat troops, becoming a single partner of the French. But his words mirrored the agony of the moment: We "must keep up pressure for collective security and show [the] determination of [the] free world to oppose chipping away of any part of the free world. Where in the hell can you let the Communists chip away any more? We just can't stand it."

Senator Eugene Millikin of Colorado broke in: "If our allies desert us, we'll have to go back to fortress America."

At that precise moment Jim Hagerty's diary captured Ike's explosion: "Listen, Gene, if we ever come back to fortress America, then the word 'fortress' will be entirely wrong.... Dien Bien Phu is a perfect example of a fortress. The Reds are surrounding it and crowding back the French into a position where they have to surrender or die. If we ever came back to the fortress idea for America, we would have...one simple, dreadful alternative—we would have to explode an attack with everything we have. What a terrible decision that would be to make."

The outburst, fleetingly caught by Hagerty's camera shutter, illuminates the key reason behind one of Eisenhower's signal achievements as President—keeping us out of a Southeast Asian war.

As his writhing that April morning showed, staying out was a torment. Ike was a soldier, a five-star man of war. "I am a sword," he had once told a visitor during the quieter days of his presidency of Columbia University, "and the sword is in the closet, and the door is shut."

He was no peace-in-our-time appeaser. If the Communists should renew the war in Korea, he had told the bipartisan congressional leaders on January 5, 1954, we'd "hit them"—even their Manchurian factories— "with everything we've got." He believed in massive retaliation: "[We] have the weapons and the planes to do it."

It wasn't easy for such a man to sit by and watch the slow strangulation of those brave French soldiers under the heroic command of General Christian de Castries at Dien Bien Phu—in that long narrow roadless valley 180 miles northwest of French-held Hanoi, deep in the Communist-held hinterland on the Laotian border— seized by the French in November 1953; ringed with fortifications and strung with barbed wire; manned with more than ten thousand of their best troops; supplied by planes—the only way—first to a landing strip and then, after the Vietminh took that, by airdrop; and, from March 14, 1954, onward, pummeled and pounded and beaten and carved down, by artillery in the hills and infantry on the ground, until on May 7 it collapsed, a garrison no bigger than a baseball field.

It wasn't easy, as that tragedy loomed, with Foster Dulles cabling on April 26, "France is almost visibly collapsing under our eyes," and with French Foreign Minister Georges Bidault almost physically collapsing; it wasn't easy for Ike to have to tell his old friend from the wartime French Resistance, no, the United States would not come to France's rescue, would not unilaterally dispatch our B-29s in force in a desperate attempt to save Dien Bien Phu.

And it wasn't easy for Ike to do nothing when the first domino fell. Like Roosevelt and Truman, Eisenhower believed in the domino theory: "You have a row of dominoes set up," he told reporters in early April, "you knock over the first one, and what will happen to the last one is the certainty that it will go over very quickly." (If you give Hitler Sudeten Czechoslovakia at Munich, he won't stop until he takes England.) Eisenhower believed Indochina a lead domino of "incalculable" significance. And so did many others. In fact, the most extreme advocacy of the domino theory that season in the Senate came not from reactionaries Joe McCarthy or Bill Knowland or Mollie Malone, but from two certified liberal Democrats: Hubert Humphrey (the loss of Indochina would mean the loss of all Asia) and Paul Douglas (it would mean the loss of all Asia, the Middle East, "Africa, and so on"). And no one in the Senate or House spoke up to disagree.

Yet Ike refused to go in. Why? There were many reasons. Some were tactical.

1. He didn't want to fight *on* the ground.

He said so in private on January 8, 1954, to the National Security Council: with the one possible exception of Malaysia, which we'd have to help defend as a bulwark of our offshore island chain, he could not imagine putting American ground forces anywhere on Southeast Asian soil.

He said so in public to reporters on February 10. The Pentagon had announced that we were sending in (until June 12 only) two hundred Air Force mechanics to repair American-made planes.

Senator John Stennis of Mississippi had attacked: "First we send them planes, then we send them men. . . . We are going to war, inch by inch. . . ." And Eisenhower answered him: *"No one could be more bitterly opposed to ever getting the United States involved in a hot war in that region than I am; consequently, every move that I authorize is calculated, so far as humans can do it, to make certain that that does not happen."* [italics added].

In saltier words he told the Legislative Leaders February 8 that he was "frightened about getting ground forces tied up in Indochina" and that we had therefore put them in back areas, where they could train the French and Vietnamese but not get into a fight. "Don't think I like to send them there," Eisenhower continued, "but after all, we can go into Iran, Korea, Formosa, and Indochina with these technicians and not run a little bit of a risk. But we can't get anywhere in Asia by just sitting here in Washington and doing nothing. My God, we must not lose Asia. We've got to look the thing right in the face."

Through the succeeding agonizing months, Ike's visceral response to an American bog-down in the Vietnamese jungles remained fixed.

At times this concern reflected his days in the Philippines, his awareness of the perils of jungle and rain. To the Cabinet on March 26, he reflected on the problems of supply lines: "You know, in rainy weather, a pack train will eat up all its food in sixty days." He wanted no part of such an American action in such a place.

"Repeatedly the President said to me," Robert Anderson, then Secretary of the Navy, later recalled, " 'The United States just can't throw its forces, out of a limited population, against the teeming millions of Asia.'

"On that he was unshakable," Anderson declared.

2. Eisenhower did not want to fight *against* Ho.

Not because he secretly admired the Vietminh leader. One sentence, often quoted from Eisenhower's memoirs, has indeed pleased Ho's partisans: "I have never talked or corresponded with a person knowledgeable in Indochinese affairs who did not agree that had elections been held as of the time of the fighting, possibly 80 percent of the population would have voted for the communist Ho Chi Minh as their leader rather than Chief of State Bao Dai." By later extrapolation, in an honest election, Ho could have beaten Ngo Dinh Diem. But the extrapolators have taken the sentence out of context: Ike wasn't talking about Diem, after 1954. He was talking about fat, decadent, absentee Emperor Bao Dai, during 1954. Of course Ho could have beaten him, and so probably could anybody else.

The real reason Ike didn't want to fight Ho is that he shunned entanglement, in draining wars, against surrogate enemies. One could never hear Ike boasting, as LBJ reportedly boasted, that any day now he would have Ho's pecker in his pocket. If you have to have a fight, Eisenhower believed, fight the root enemy—Stalin or Malenkov or Mao; as Charlie Wilson said once at an NSC meeting, "When I go after a rattlesnake, I like to go after his head, not after his rattles."

Ike had ended the Korean War by letting the Red Chinese know that if they didn't come to terms he would widen the war: end their privileged sanctuary beyond the Yalu and end our ban on the use of atomic weapons. In a limited war, the United States is the underdog.

And so, at the April 29 meeting of the National Security Council, when talk got around once again to the possibility of unilateral American intervention with ground forces, Ike had an arresting answer: If the United States were to let its troops get into scattered conflicts around the world, the end result would be the undermining of all our defenses. Before he would decide to go into Indochina unilaterally, he said, he would look first at a direct attack on the Soviet Union. It would be better, he said, to hit the head of the snake than to play the enemy's game and all by ourselves fight satellites all over the globe.

Without question these tactical reasons counted. But another, crucial, reason transcended them—the one reflected in Eisenhower's explosion at Millikin: Eisenhower was not a loner in character; he did not see the presidency as a loner in the conduct of government; and he did not see the United States as a loner in the world. Knowing the limits and self-limits to power, and submitting to them, Eisenhower was what he had been since he first burst onto the world scene in 1942—a man trusting other men; a public servant bound by the law and the Constitution; a generous, loyal, and understanding ally.

From the start he laid down cold his iron refusal to go to war without the Congress.

"Step by step and day by day," Senator Stennis declared March 9, "we are coming nearer to a fighting part in the war in Indochina."

"What will we do if one of [our technicians] is captured or killed?" James Patterson of the New York *Daily News* asked the President the next day.

"I will say this," the President answered: "There is going to be no involvement of America in war unless it is a result of the constitutional process that is placed upon Congress to declare it. Now, let us have that clear; and that is the answer."

It remained the answer. On Saturday, April 3, for example, Dulles and the chairman of the Joint Chiefs of Staff, Arthur W. Radford, convened a secret meeting at the State Department with Knowland, Lyndon Johnson, Richard Russell, Joe Martin, John McCormack, and other congressional leaders of both parties, to consider possible courses of action. As one participant, Robert Anderson recalls the meeting, it was exploratory only—*one more tentative working of the gray area between the extremes of unilateral ground-troop intervention and capitulation.*

"The Air Force," Anderson says, "was arguing that with air support, the United States could buttress the French ground forces at Dien Bien Phu. We knew that without help, because of the incompetent way they had been running the war, they were facing disaster." (Indeed, two days earlier Eisenhower himself had speculated to Hagerty and some luncheon guests that surreptitiously "the U.S.

might have to ... send in squadrons from two aircraft carriers... to bomb [the] Reds at Dien Bien Phu.") "What could we do to save them? That was the question. The President wasn't asking for anything. He hadn't arrived at any fixed conclusion except one: he would not send United States ground forces into Asia."

When the meeting ended, Phyllis Bernau's monitoring notes reveal, Dulles reported the upshot to Eisenhower by phone: The Congress would go along with "vigorous action if we were not doing it alone. They want to be sure the people in the area are involved too." Both President and Secretary concurred: "The stakes," they recognized, "concern others more than us." "You can't go in and win," Eisenhower said, "unless the people want you. The French could win in six months if the people were with them." It would be "unconstitutional and indefensible," he agreed with Dulles two days later, to neglect the right political prelude, intervene, suffer defeat, and lose the United States' prestige.

Through the month of April, however, as the pursuit of an alliance proceeded, the option of an air strike to save Dien Bien Phu also remained alive. ("Staff on an hour's call to return to Washington because of Indochina," Hagerty noted in his diary Saturday, April 24. "Situation getting very grave, and it may be necessary to support French troops at Dienbienphu with two carrier aircraft we have off the coast. French would like us to send in these planes for a quick strike. Of course, if we do use them, we probably will never admit it, but decision to assist the French by use of American planes will be a very calculated risk and could lead to war.") Two days later, on April 26, Ike told the Legislative Leaders that the French "are weary as hell" and that it didn't look as though Dien Bien Phu could hold out for more than a week. Nonetheless, he insisted that if we were to put one combat soldier into Indochina, our entire prestige would be at stake, not only there but throughout the world. Three days later, when the NSC met on April 29, Vice-President Nixon still argued for air strikes, for their psychological value; they would show the Communists we had drawn a line beyond which they could not go; and show the British they couldn't veto American action. But the three service chiefs opposed them. And so did Ike: before thus intervening unilaterally, he'd want to consider hitting the head of the snake.

So despite the provocation, American intervention—in any form—never came off. The Congress did not sanction it. And

Eisenhower did not, in Noam Chomsky's trenchant phrase, launch an "Executive war."

Contrast this iron respect for legal and constitutional groundings with the freewheeling of Lyndon Johnson after he in turn became President. I can best illustrate this by an almost ludicrous bit of personal history.

In the summer of 1965—long after I had left Washington, and after President Johnson had sent more than a hundred thousand American troops into Vietnam—the phone rang on a warm Saturday afternoon at my home in Greenwich, Connecticut.

"I'm calling from Washington at the request of the Assistant Secretary of State for Far Eastern Affairs, William Bundy," a voice said. And he had what I thought an excellent question: "What legal grounds do we have for being in Vietnam? Specifically, what binding commitment did President Eisenhower make to President Diem?"

He was asking, he said, because he knew I had read through all the Eisenhower presidential papers.

I was dumbfounded. Could the caller and his superiors really be so ignorant? Or did he know all about the published documents on the subject, and was he calling to find out whether I might have come across some agreement—a personal letter of commitment from Eisenhower to Diem, say—so secret that not even the State Department would have a copy? I could only assure him that, to my knowledge, no "secret commitment" whatsoever existed.

So in the absence of any new secret letter, the Johnson administration proceeded to try to hang their troubles on an old public letter—Eisenhower's message to Ngo Dinh Diem, the new President of South Vietnam, released October 25, 1954, three months after the cease-fire agreement and the North-South division of the country. The letter, the Johnson men contended, bound the United States hand and foot in a "commitment" to South Vietnam, a commitment that, in the end, forced us to put more than a half million American troops into that country. Even Eisenhower, who congenitally and constitutionally *always* backed *any* president on foreign policy, couldn't stomach this distortion, and (albeit respectfully) said so.

For this letter committed nobody to anything. Its key paragraphs, with key words underscored, simply said:

"We have been exploring ways and means to permit our aid to Viet Nam to be more effective and to make a greater contribution to the welfare and stability of the Government of Viet Nam. I am, accordingly, instructing the American Ambassador to Viet Nam to examine with you...how an intelligent program of American aid given directly to your Government can serve to assist Viet Nam *in its present hour of trial, provided that your Government is prepared to give assurances as to the standards of performance it would be able to maintain in the event such aid were supplied.*

"The purpose of this offer is to assist the Government of Viet Nam in developing and maintaining *a strong, viable state, capable of resisting attempted subversion or aggression through military means.* The Government of the United States expects that this aid will be met by performance on the part of the Government of Viet Nam in *undertaking needed reforms.* It hopes that such aid, combined with your own continuing efforts, will contribute effectively toward an independent Viet Nam endowed with a strong government...."

I have quoted five of the letter's central sentences, and they commit nothing. The other four commit even less. "Frankly, Collins," Foster Dulles told General J. Lawton Collins, our first emissary, as he left for Saigon that fall, "I think the chances of our saving the situation there are not more than one in ten." One does not make a "commitment"on those odds. Lyndon Johnson went to war in Vietnam without being forced by an Eisenhower pledge, and without his action's being legitimized by an Eisenhower *sine qua non*, a congressional declaration.

Eisenhower, of course, never himself asked Congress for such a declaration. Because he would not go it alone. He had to have an alliance. And the kind of alliance he believed in, he could never put together.

For weeks during that spring of 1954 he tried hard. Even with allies he would not have gone into Asia with ground troops (as he wrote Gruenther April 26, "Additional ground forces should come from Asiatic and European troops already in the region"). But given adequate allies, Ike *might* have gone to war. And, *pace* the Pentagon Papers, he did not keep that danger a secret from the American people.

On March 29, four days before the meeting with the congressional leaders, Foster Dulles delivered a crucial speech at New York's Overseas Press Club. The speech did two things: It stressed allied action, and it forecast possible peril. The imposition on Southeast

Asia of the political system of Communist Russia and Red China, "'by whatever means,'" he warned, "would be a grave threat to the *whole free community*. The United States feels that that possibility should not be passively accepted, but should be met by *united action*. This might have serious risks, but these risks are far less than would face us a few years from now if we dare not be resolute today....The danger of general war seems to have receded....If it is so, it is because *the free nations saw the danger and moved unitedly* with courage and decision to meet it....The United States is a member of a *goodly company* who in the past have *stood together* in the face of great peril [all italics added]...and who have overcome the peril."

On April 5 Dulles was cabling Ambassador C. Douglas Dillon in Paris that although the United States would not intervene unilaterally at Dien Bien Phu, and although any coalition would have to include "active British Commonwealth participation," "the United States is doing everything possible...to prepare public, Congressional and Constitutional basis for united action in Indochina."

On April 16, in an "off-the-record" address before the American Society of Newspaper Editors, Vice-President Nixon got off his much quoted remark—which did not long remain off limits—that if the French withdrew from Indochina, the United States might have to send in "our boys."

Was this a trial balloon, a deliberate Eisenhower test of America's stomach for unilateral intervention with ground troops? Not only Nixon's memoirs but Hagerty's diary indicates it was not, that Nixon had stepped off the reservation: "In afternoon started to get queries on off-the-record talk Nixon made to newspaper editors in Washington. Nixon, in answer to hypothetical questions said that he did not believe French would fold up in Indochina, but if they did, we would have to hold Indochina because of its vital importance to free world...Checked with Nixon to see if this were right, and he said it was but that he was answering hypothetical questions. Played dumb on this in answer to all queries. Think it was foolish for Dick to answer as he did but will make the best of it."

The next day Hagerty "talked to President in the morning about Nixon speech, and he asked me to get in touch with Bedell Smith and have State Department put out statement on hypothetical question without cutting ground from under Nixon." Accordingly, the department agreed that Nixon's words reflected American policy, but declared the dispatch of American troops "unlikely." On April 19 Dulles himself said the same thing.

On May 7, before Dulles made a major nationwide television speech on the fall of Dien Bien Phu, Eisenhower went over the draft word for word, penciling in at least one easy-to-understand slogan: "the United States will never start a war. . . ." But once again Dulles stressed the seriousness of the loss of Indochina: "This common defense may involve serious commitments by us all. But free people will never remain free if they are not willing, if need be, to fight for their vital interests." If the forthcoming peace conference in Geneva should lead to a Communist take-over in Indochina, he went on, "or if hostilities continue, then the need will be more urgent to create the condition for a united action in defense of the area."

But the alliance effort failed, largely because of France and Britain. From the start, Ike made it clear that he didn't want to fight to save the French empire. In the 1952 campaign, talking about the Korean War, he had said, "Let it be Asians against Asians," and had returned from the battlefield with a new awareness of the value of training the South Korean soldier. Now, looking at Indochina, he wanted no part of a "white man's party" to save French colonialism.

To him, an alliance was not just a military partnership. It was a military partnership with a cause worth fighting and dying for. The British-Israeli-French invasion of Egypt was not such a cause in 1956. And French imperialism was not such a cause in 1954. And despite Eisenhower's urging again and again, the French steadfastly refused to see this fact.

Nothing comes through with more acidity during these months than Ike's utter exasperation with French weaseling and hedging about what they were fighting *for*. We sanitized some of this exasperation out of the memoirs. But it emerges in Ike's remarks to the Cabinet on March 26: "If we could only sit down and talk to them man to man [as] we can with the British when things get tough. But not the French. It sure takes a lot of patience." The exasperation surfaces in Ike's offhand remark to Hagerty as he signed a declaration on April 15 that the United States would not pull its troops out of Europe: "I suppose this is necessary to give our French friends some guts."

And the exasperation breaks forth with full force in Ike's correspondence with military friends.

To Al Gruenther on April 26 (just after Bidault had implored us to send the B-29s into crumbling Dien Bien Phu) Ike let himself go: "While I had some secondhand reports of your feeling that the French leaders had practically abdicated, I had not before known of your personal views with respect to the astonishing proposal for unilateral American intervention in Indochina. Your adverse opinion exactly parallels mine.

"As you know, you and I started more than three years ago trying to convince the French that they could *not* win the Indochina war and particularly could not get real American support in that region unless they would unequivocally pledge...independence to the Associated States upon the achievement of military victory. Along with this ... this Administration has been arguing that no Western power can go to Asia militarily, except as one of a concert of powers, which concert must include local Asiatic peoples.

"To contemplate anything else is to lay ourselves open to the charge of imperialism and colonialism or—at the very least—of objectionable paternalism. *Even, therefore, if we could by some sudden stroke assure the saving of the Dienbienphu garrison, I think that under the conditions proposed by the French the free world would lose more than it would gain* [italics added].

"One of the great difficulties that the French seem to have these days is the inability of its government to make up its mind as to what to do in any given set of circumstances. Ever since 1945 France has been unable to decide whether she most fears Russia or Germany. As a consequence, her policies in Europe have been nothing but confusion; starts and stops; advances and retreats!... It is all very frustrating and discouraging...."

On April 27, Ike was amplifying on this theme to his boyhood friend from Abilene, Captain E. E. ("Swede") Hazlett, USN, in a hitherto unpublished letter:

"For more than three years I have been urging upon successive French governments the advisability of finding some way of 'internationalizing' the war; such action would be proof to all the world and particularly to the Vietnamese that France's purpose is not colonial in character but is to defeat Communism in the region and to give the natives their freedom. The reply has always been vague, containing references to national prestige, Constitutional limitations, inevitable effects upon the Moroccan and Tunisian peoples, and [digressions] on plain political difficulties and battles within the French Parliament. The result has been that the French have failed entirely to produce any enthusiasm on the part of the Vietnamese for participation in the war. (Incidentally, did you ever stop to think that if the British had, in our War of the Revolution, treated as equals the Americans who favored them—whom they called Loyalists and we called Tories—the job of Washington would have been much more difficult, if not impossible? I have read that when the entire colonial forces in the field numbered not more than twenty-five thousand, that there were fifty thousand Americans serving in some capacity with and for the British. Yet no really effective service was rendered by these people because the British persisted in treating them as 'colonials and inferiors.')

"In any event, *any nation that intervenes in a civil war can scarcely expect to win unless the side in whose favor it intervenes possesses a high morale based upon a war purpose or cause in which it believes* [italics added]. The French have used weasel words in promising independence and through this one reason as much as anything else, have suffered reverses that have been really inexcusable...."

Into the bargain, Ike's infuriation with the French over goals was compounded by other things: their incomprehensible tactics (putting that garrison into Dien Bien Phu in the first place, for example) and their hand-wringing.

"Bedell," Ike scribbled angrily in the margin of a March 12 memo from Smith (then Undersecretary of State) to the President which mentioned that the French *doubted* of a satisfactory military solution, "If the first sentence of the second paragraph is final French conclusion, why don't they withdraw request for military aid? Might be well to ask!!!"

As possible allies the French were hopeless. And so were the British: despite Eisenhower's pleas, they—Churchill himself—steadfastly refused to do anything to help.

"The British are frightened, I *think* by two things," Ike wrote Hazlett in his April 27 letter. "First, they have a morbid obsession that any positive move on the part of the free world may bring upon us World War III. Secondly, they are desperately concerned about the safety of Hong Kong. For the moment the Chinese Communists are not molesting Hong Kong and the British are fearful that if they should be identified as opponents of the Communists in the Indochina affair, they might suffer the loss of Hong Kong at any moment. All this is conjecture, but in respect to this particular point, my own view is in almost direct opposition. I personally feel that if the Communists would take a good smacking in Indochina, they would be more likely to leave Hong Kong severely alone for a long time. Moreover, if a 'concert of nations' should undertake to protect Western interests in this critical section of the globe, it would appear that Hong Kong would almost automatically fall within the protected zone. Just what the outcome will be, of course, is still largely a guess...."

In his personal diary that same day Eisenhower went even further in his frustration with British intransigence against a coalition:

"The attitude of Britain in this respect is bitterly resented by Australia and New Zealand. It is entirely possible that these two countries will approach the United States separately to request that in company with them—and possibly with the Philippines, Thailand, France, and Indochina—we form a coalition to the complete exclusion of the British. This would be a very tough one for us, but I think that I would go along with the idea because I believe that the British government is showing a woeful unawareness of the risks we run in that region."

Even in late May and June, when the threat of massive undisguised Chinese intervention increased the provocation for the United States to enter the conflict, Eisenhower did not abandon his insistence on alliance. On May 27 Admiral Robert Carney, Chief of Naval Operations, declared in a major foreign policy speech—uncleared by State—that the United States was "approaching a fork in the road.... Do we want to turn into the smooth dead-end or take the rougher road that offers us a good destination if we have got the guts and strength to manage it?" Asked about this at his news conference June 2, the President kept his options open. He had not decided whether to ask Congress for authority for American intervention. But at a top secret meeting of his advisers the following day he made sure Carney and everybody else understood his stand: The United States could not and would not carry the entire security burden of the entire free world. Though he believed the United States should intervene if the Red Chinese did, the United States would even so want a commitment—and Eisenhower asked Dulles to get it—from Australia, New Zealand, and the Philippines that in such circumstances they too would request intervention authority from their parliaments.

"I am even yet spending days and hours," Ike wrote Gruenther June 8, "trying to get a political climate established among the interested powers that would make it politically feasible within the United States to render the kind of help that our own interests and those of the free world would seem to require. But because we insist on treating everybody concerned as sovereign *equals*, it is extremely difficult to bring about the meeting of minds that is now so necessary."

He would not go it alone. That was out of the question. As Dulles told the Legislative Leaders on June 28: "We have got to find a line which other people will be prepared to defend. We cannot carry, unwanted or unasked, the entire burden."

For this reason above all Ike kept us out of Vietnam in 1954. Nine years later, in 1963, as the fall publication date of *Mandate for Change* approached, the chapter on Indochina seemed to be getting longer and longer. And so Eisenhower did what he usually did: impatiently chopped away at the ending—his retrospective analysis of that tragedy. The analysis that ultimately survived in the book looks better and better as time goes on. But even better appears the more detailed summing-up, hitherto unpublished, that in large part wound up on the cutting-room floor in a late draft dated February 13, 1963— more than two years before the massive Johnson troop buildup that ended in disaster: "I am convinced that the French could not win the war because the internal political situation in Viet Nam, weak and confused, badly weakened their military position. . . . Indeed, the lack of leadership and drive on the part of the Emperor [Bao Dai] was a factor in the feeling prevalent among Viet Namese that they had nothing to fight for. . . .

"It is exasperating and depressing to stand by and watch a free world nation losing a battle to slavery without being able to commit all your resources, including combat troops, to its aid. Willingness to fight for freedom, no matter where the battle may be, has always been a characteristic of our people. The conditions which prevented American intervention with military force on behalf of the French Union were surely frustrating to me.

"One measure, however, advocated by some, I felt to be completely unfeasible, and I still do: the use of large formations of United States ground troops. Public opinion in our own country would not have supported such a move. The concern of Members of Congress, and the reaction to the Vice-President's speech in April, were convincing evidence that Americans felt deeply about getting sizable ground forces involved once again in Asia.

"But this factor in itself was not overriding. Had the circumstances lent themselves to a reasonable chance for a victory or a chance to avert a defeat for freedom, then the task of explaining to the American public the necessity for sacrifice would have been an acceptable one. The jungles of Indochina, however, would have swallowed up division after division of United States troops, who, unaccustomed to this kind of warfare, would have sustained heavy casualties until they had learned to live in a new environment. Furthermore, *the presence of ever more numbers of white men in uniform probably would have aggravated rather than assuaged Asiatic resentments* [italics added]. Thus, even had all of Indochina been physically occupied by United States troops, their eventual removal would have resulted only in a reversion to the situation which had existed before.

"In the matter of massive air strikes in support of Dienbienphu, I have never believed that these could have saved it. The enemy was spread out in the jungles.

"American air intervention in case of Communist employment of MIGs in the Delta, on the other hand, would certainly have been effective. This would have necessitated striking Chinese airfields and would have risked going to general war with the wrong nation— China, not Russia. As it was, I feel confident that our capability to do so had a decisively deterrent effect on the Chinese....

"Still another reason for withholding active United States unilateral participation, which I have stated in considerable detail, was a matter of fundamental policy. Members of Congress (who would have had to authorize a state of hositilities) and I were in complete agreement on this. United States defense policy is based upon membership in a system of alliances....The reason for our dependence on alliances is clear: with all its resources, the United States does not have the manpower to police every area of the world. We can provide aid and advice, but with a mere one hundred eighty million people we cannot supply the ground troops to contain forces that could be brought to bear around the entire periphery of the Soviet Union. The nations abutting Russia, those most directly affected, must provide the bulk of the ground forces. Unless our allies were willing to participate along with us—which they were not—action by the United States alone would have been a violation of our firm and wise defense policy.

"But the strongest reason of all for the United States refusal to respond by itself to French pleas is the fact that among all the powerful nations of the world the United States is the only one with a

tradition of anti-colonialism. . . . The standing of the United States as
the most powerful of the anti-colonial powers is an asset of incalculable value to the Free World. It means that our counsel is trusted where
that of others may not be. It is essential to our position of leadership in
a world wherein the majority of the nations have at some time or
another felt the yoke of colonialism.

"Thus it is that the moral position of the United States was
more to be guarded than the Tonkin Delta, indeed than all of
Indochina."

When read against the horrors to come, those Eisenhower
words of 1963 say it all.

And the last two sections, on alliance and anticolonialism,
reflect why Ike made his outburst to Millikin: the United States
cannot and should not fight alone. It must join with others, and join
with them in a just cause. This conviction—like Eisenhower's constitutionalism and his reliance on organization—forms a centerpiece of
his presidency. It explains his knife-edge balancing between war and
surrender during the 1954 and 1958 crises over Quemoy and Matsu;
his opposition to the British-French-Israeli invasion of Egypt in 1956;
his readiness first to go to the rescue of a beleaguered government in
Lebanon in 1958, and then to turn to the United Nations for the final
resolution of the conflict; and it explains his refusal, despite an agony
like that of 1954, to go to war in Laos in the winter of 1960–61.

Eisenhower kept us out of Vietnam primarily because he was,
in peace and in war, an ally. By preventing our disintegration—moral,
financial, political, and military— in the jungles of Indochina, he gave
us what Senator J. William Fulbright—the Democratic chairman of
the Senate Foreign Relations Committee, in his farewell words as he
left the Senate in 1975—called this country's "finest hour" in thirty
years.

VIII

MAY 17, 1954

THE GROUND CHOSEN

M ost presidencies entail a succession of conflicts, warm or cool, between the President and a variety of antagonists, foreign and domestic. To this day, people who have forgotten most of the other controversies of the Eisenhower era can remember one man above all as his principal challenger—Joe McCarthy. To this day, few things irritate Eisenhower's critics more than his apparent refusal, month after month, to "do something"—anything—to stop McCarthy's depredations.

Everybody loves a brawl. But few things reveal more about a president than his selection of battlegrounds; his choice of time, place, and cause for avoiding or accepting or pursuing engagement with an antagonist. For nothing matters more, as Eisenhower's and Lyndon Johnson's contrasting performances in Vietnam demonstrate, than where one fights, whom one fights against, whom one fights alongside, what one fights for, and when.

In good gray words on May 17, 1954, in a letter to Secretary of Defense Charlie Wilson, Eisenhower laid out such a battleground—a battleground of constitutional principle with an immediate consequence: "Because it is essential to efficient and effective administration that employees of the Executive Branch be in a position to be completely candid in advising with each other on official matters, and because it is not in the public interest that any of their conversations or communications, or any documents or reproductions concerning such advice be disclosed, you will instruct employees of your Department that in all of their appearances before the Subcommittee of the Senate Committee on Government Operations regarding the inquiry now before it they are not to testify to any such conversations or communications or to produce any such documents or reproductions."

Without mentioning his antagonist's name, Eisenhower, asserting an abstraction, was aiming his gun at Senator McCarthy, specifically at his demand that members of the White House Staff be subpoenaed to testify before the subcommittee investigating the dispute between McCarthy and the Army. The noisy hearings had reached a climax.

A year and a half earlier candidate Eisenhower had in private in Peoria told a shaken McCarthy exactly what he thought of him and his methods. But the reproof had done nothing to stop the Wisconsin junior senator's hell-raising. Through the intervening months he and his freewheeling Permanent Investigations Subcommittee, purporting to extirpate holdover Communists and Communist sympathizers from the federal government, had been pursuing alleged traitors in the State Department; had been dispatching young Roy Cohn and G. David Schine—derided as "junketeering gumshoes" —on a fast swing through Europe to unearth Communist books in United States overseas libraries; had been chasing an alleged Communist in the Government Printing Office; and, finally, had been looking for Communists and spies in the United States Army.

For an instant in public Eisenhower's rage at these antics boiled over. "Don't join the book burners," he told his audience at the Dartmouth commencement June 14, 1953. "Don't think you are going to conceal faults by concealing evidence that they ever existed. Don't be afraid to go in your library and read every book, as long as that document does not offend our own ideas of decency. That should be the only censorship.

"How will we defeat Communism unless we know what it is, and what it teaches...?" It was a genuinely spontaneous talk, off the cuff. But even in these vigorous words Eisenhower confined himself to a high ground of principle, naming no name.

Dissatisfied friends, advisers, and critics continued to plead for a different strategy, of direct attack. Then on November 24, 1953, in a nationwide TV broadcast, McCarthy, shifted his denunciations from Truman's administration to Eisenhower's—specifically to the

State Department for keeping an alleged security-risk holdover, John Paton Davies, on the payroll; and for giving aid to Britain while Britain traded with Red China. And the heat on Eisenhower reached white intensity.

To Jim Hagerty, McCarthy's performance was "sheer fascism." And to C. D. Jackson of Time, Inc., Eisenhower's outspoken assistant for cold-war planning, McCarthy had declared war on Eisenhower, and Jackson said as much to Scotty Reston of *The New York Times*.

"Reston's piece," Jackson wrote in his diary November 27, "included reference to one [unnamed] White House official who felt that this was a declaration of war on President.... [Conservative Congressional liaison chief Jerry] Persons very upset by all this because declaration of war [by Eisenhower] 'would make it more difficult to get McCarthy and his allies to vote for Presidential program.' ... Can't understand his line of argument, consider it disastrous appeasement which began September 1952, when the campaign train crossed Wisconsin border and the boys persuaded Eisenhower to take out reference to General Marshall in his Milwaukee speech...."

"This has been Milestone Week for more than one reason.

"All the vague feelings of unhappiness I have had regarding 'lack of leadership' over the past many months, which I have always put down, really bounced up this week, and I am very frightened."

On Sunday, November 29, Jackson had a talk with Foster Dulles and found him "profoundly perturbed about McCarthy business, because it messes up his affairs. He is worried about Presidential leadership. He intended to talk to the President first thing Monday morning about what the line should be on McCarthy because of the attack on the State Dept. He also told me two terrifying facts—(1) as of Thanksgiving Day the President had not read the McCarthy speech or been briefed on it. Dulles quote— 'The President asked me if I thought he should read it.' Fact #2—as of Sunday afternoon Herbert Brownell had not read the McCarthy speech. This place is really falling apart.

"*November 30, 1953 (Black Monday)*.... Staff meeting of White House staff called by Hagerty. Unfortunately neither Persons nor Adams present. Hagerty opened up by mentioning the recent Reston, Folliard and Harsch pieces each one of which contained anonymous attribution to White House personnel. He cautioned against talking, saying that it inevitably was embarrasssing to the President, etc., etc. Incidentally, Hagerty was very low pitch and temperate about the whole thing.

"After moment of dead silence, I said that I had told Reston on the telephone the item he had in quotes, namely, that McCarthy had declared war on the President—and that this gave me an opportunity to say some more on the subject....

"Warned them that this Three Little Monkeys act was not working and would not work, and that appeasing McCarthy in order to save his 7 votes for this year's legislative program was poor tactics, poor strategy ... and poor arithmetic, and that unless the President stepped up to bat on this one soon, the Republicans would have neither a program, nor 1954, nor 1956.

"Immediately Jerry Morgan, Homer Gruenther, and to a lesser degree Jack Martin [all of congressional liaison] jumped in on the opposite side. Only two to speak up on my side were [Adams' assistant Charles F.] Willis and [chief speechwriter Bryce] Harlow.... Was appalled to discover that it had been planned to cancel the [Wednesday] press conference and have the President go to Bermuda having said nothing. Big rhubarb. Finally agreed to have press conference. The men have really separated out from the boys.

"*December 1, 1953 (Tues.)*.... Bryce Harlow—on President's press conference, and to discuss Hagerty draft of statement (re McCarthy). Hagerty draft had certain big holes, and other efforts by Jerry Morgan & Co. very very weak....

"Discovered brush-off group about to descend on President, so rushed over with my draft to walk in just as though I belonged there. President left office before they could assemble.

"Big session with [Special Counsel] Shanley, Harlow, Morgan, [Staff Secretary Paul T.] Carroll, Martin, [Assistant Press Secretary Murray] Snyder. Persons still sick although had been pulling strings. Showed them my draft, which though not acceptable did start some spine stiffening. Harlow's inexorable logic also great help. Broke up to convene at staff meeting in the morning.

"*December 2, 1953 (Wednesday)*.... 8 o'clock telephone—no staff meeting. Conclusion: They are trying to freeze me out. Rushed over and found them all assembled unofficially in Snyder's office, and we went at it again.

"Morgan had moved up considerably. Shanley tried to see

President alone with Snyder, but we all trooped in with [Appointments Secretary] Tom Stephens' assistance, and the fight was on.

"Prexy read their current draft with visible irritation, and made some mumbling comments. Jack Martin then pitched in with great courage and said that a vacuum existed in this country, and it was a political vacuum, and unless the President filled it somebody else would fill it. The President twisted and squirmed, but Martin stuck to his point. I pitched in as strongly as I could by telling him that so long as Taft was alive he might have been able to get out of the responsibility of leading the Party, but now he could no longer get out of it, and that the people were waiting for a sign, and a simple sign—and now was the time.

"Big hassle over text started. President read my text with great irritation, slammed it back at me and said he would not refer to McCarthy personally—'I will not get in the gutter with that guy.'

"But gradually an interesting thing developed. The needling and the goosing began to take effect, and the President himself began very ably to firm up the text as he re-read it again, this time very carefully.

"Everyone's mood began to change from divided snarling into united helping him along, and when Prexy dictated the last paragraph exactly as it finally appeared, which contained the real Republican leadership gimmick, the group almost cheered.*

"So what started as a ghastly mess turned out fine. Problem now is, having zippered the toga of Republican political leadership on the President's shoulders, how to keep that zipper shut."

But though the zipper now closed to Jackson's satisfaction, when Eisenhower read his agreed-on text to the assembled reporters, he was still sticking to enunciation of principle: "This most powerful of free nations," he declared, responding to McCarthy's attack on Britain's China trade, "must not permit itself to grow weary of the processes of negotiation. . . . If it should turn impatiently to coercion of other free nations, our brand of coercion . . . would be a mark of the

---

*In his equally candid diary, Shanley, acting staff head in Adams' absence, gives his own straightforward account of his own fair-minded motives: "I was anxious that . . . every one of the staff members have his day in court and get a chance to take a crack at the statement. This was one of the smartest things I have ever done and it left the staff much happier. When the press conference was over, C. D. Jackson was the most enthusiastic of all, which, of course, couldn't have pleased me more."

imperialist rather than of the leader." Given the effectiveness of the administration's security program, he continued, "fear of Communists actively undermining our Government will not be an issue in the 1954 elections.... In any event," he concluded, "unless the Republican Party can develop and enact... a [progressive legislative] program for the American people, it does not deserve to remain in power."

The conflict, like a hurricane, roared on. Asserting he had uncovered evidence of Communists in the Army, McCarthy now focused his attention on an allegedly pink dentist—one Major Irving Peress, drafted into the Army for a year, who refused to answer the Army's questions on his Communist associations and afterward, through bureaucratic bungling, received an honorable discharge. McCarthy haled Brigadier General Ralph Zwicker, commanding general at Camp Kilmer (where Peress had been pulling teeth), up before his subcommittee and demanded the names of the ignoble perpetrators of such disaster. When Zwicker refused to reveal them, McCarthy became insulting, denouncing this gallant soldier of World War II as a man "not fit to wear that uniform," without the "brains of a five-year-old child."

The Secretary of the Army—a nice guy named Robert T. Stevens, who, mixing it up with McCarthy, would inevitably finish last—told Zwicker not to testify any further before McCarthy's committee, and confirmed the Army would release no names. But then he accepted an invitation to eat a fried chicken lunch (in deepest secrecy, unbeknownst even to the President himself) up on the Hill with McCarthy and some Senate "peacemakers," and there he agreed that if McCarthy would behave himself, he could have the names plus Zwicker as a witness again. When the "secret" lunch broke up, and the senators—to Stevens' amazement—gave reporters waiting outside a handout, it omitted McCarthy's promise of reform and portrayed Stevens in a one-sided surrender.

"McCarthy-Stevens row broke wide open today," Jim Hagerty wrote in his diary February 24, 1954. "Agree after meeting with McCarthy, Dirksen, Potter, Mundt and Stevens on 'memo of agreement' giving Joe everything he wants, names, etc.—shouldn't have agreed. Stevens called me late at night (10 P.M.) to say he wanted to release his statement and then resign—told him to cool off overnight—but we were sure dumb—someone let Stevens walk right into a bear trap, and now I'll have to work like hell to get him out of it. What a job!"

126

The next day Hagerty wrote: *"February 25....* Staff meeting broke early so Adams, self, Persons, Martin, Morgan could have meeting with Nixon and [Deputy Attorney General] Bill Rogers—later moved meeting to East Wing where Sen. Dirksen joined us—piecing together yesterday's news seems that the Senators really jobbed up on Stevens, or else he didn't realize what he was doing....

"Pres. very mad and getting fed up—it's his Army and he doesn't like McCarthy's tactics at all. Stevens and [Deputy Defense Secretary Roger] Kyes joined Nixon and all of us at 4 P.M. Worked 'til 5:30 on [Stevens' press conference] statement—cleared it with Pres. who made it stronger and then released it in press conference in my office.

"Quote—Ike on subject: 'This guy McCarthy is going to get into trouble over this, I'm not going to take this one lying down'— 'my friends tell me it won't be long in this Army stuff before McCarthy starts using my name instead of Stevens. He's ambitious. He wants to be President. He's the last guy in the world who'll ever get there, if I have anything to say.'"

Hagerty continued several days later: *"March 2* .... In at 8:15 A.M. Most of day spent working on Pres. statement for press conference on Stevens-McCarthy row. ... Pres. in angry mood [at Joe] all day.... ready to fire back. Repeatedly said during day: 'What's the use of trying to work with guys that aren't for you, and are never going to be for you[?]' Other quotes from Pres. during day: 'You know, what we ought to do is get a word to put ahead of Republican—something like "new" or "modern" or something. We just can't work with fellows like McCarthy, Bricker, Jenner and that bunch.'

"March 3.... At press conference Pres.... read statement [admitting Army wrong in the Peress case; praising General Zwicker; and insisting on courtesy for witnesses before congressional committees]. Went well with some reporters. New Dealers and fuzzy boys disappointed—wanted Pres. to call McCarthy names, crack him over the head, etc.—typical of reaction from these quarters was Reston in N. Y. Times— 'turning the other cheek'—and Doris Fleeson— 'McCarthy can say Pres. didn't lay a glove on him'—Nuts. All these people want is to have Pres. get down in gutter with Joe—personally think Pres. statement strong and dignified.

"Particularly in light of Joe's intemperate rejoinder where he said in effect he'll go right on bullying, etc. Now it's up to our Leaders in Congress—if they take the ball and run with it—if they force changes in rules, then they can come out ahead....They have a chance now to make it good—my bet is they'll kick it over.

"*March 4* ... Stories [in *Washington Post* and *The New York Times*] deliberately needled up by Folliard and Reston....To hell with slanted reporters....

"*March 6*....To White House Correspondents dinner in evening.... Sat next to Bob Stevens at head table—is he jittery(!)—and is he talking—talks about 'Jim's the only one who stuck with me' and stuff like that in front of anyone and everyone—very ... and excited—says 'he's all alone in the fight.' ... [When introduced] he got standing ovation—made him almost drunk with delight—kept muttering to himself 'they're for me. They're my friends' ... someone better ride herd on him but good."

Five days later the Army counterattacked, and the climactic Army-McCarthy hearings began.

Time and again, as Hagerty saw, Ike had nearly exploded in outrage over McCarthy. Then why did he continue to rein in that temper, continue to refuse to close with the enemy?

Not out of fear of controversy. In fact, during the early months of 1954, at the very moment of the Army-McCarthy imbroglio, Eisenhower had overridden wavering Republicans in the Senate and House and gone to the mat on two key issues.

One was the Bricker Amendment, a constitutional amendment introduced by conservative Republican Senator John Bricker of Ohio to limit the power of the President to make treaties. One clause—the hotly debated "Which Clause"—would, in some instances, have required action by Senate, House, and forty-eight state legislatures to put a treaty into effect.

After futile attempts to compromise, to get Bricker to abandon the "Which Clause," at the January 11, 1954, Legislative Leaders meeting Ike announced he had made up his mind to fight to the bitter end. If the "Which Clause" stays in, he declared, "I'll go into every state to fight it."

"Bridges, Millikin, and Saltonstall," Ike wrote in his diary January 18, "are not natural leaders. ... They do not seem to realize when there arrives that moment at which soft speaking should be abandoned and a fight undertaken.... "

"Mad and ready to go," in Hagerty's words, Eisenhower did fight—homing in on legalistic details, phoning, exhorting—to block this "stupid, blind violation of the Constitution by stupid blind isolationists." By February 2 he had become so sick of Bricker ("to hell with him") and his amendment (offered to "gain himself some faint immortality") that he was striding around his office and telling Hagerty: "If it's true that when you die the things that bothered you most are engraved on your skull, I am sure I'll have there the mud and dirt of France during [the] invasion and the name of Senator Bricker." But in the end Ike won: on February 17, the Senate killed the "Which Clause."

From early 1954 into 1955 Eisenhower led a second campaign: for the expansion of international trade. On March 29, 1954, foreign trade adviser Clarence Randall, chairman of Inland Steel, laid before the Republican Legislative Leaders a set of recommendations to this end, including a three-year extension of the Trade Agreements Act, Presidential authority to negotiate tariff cuts of five percent a year or less for three years, and an increase in peaceful commerce with Eastern Europe.

"Can't encourage aid to Russia," conservative Dan Reed of New York broke in.

"We're going to have to fight Russia either in a trade war or in a hot war," Ike shot back. "We've got to win a lot of people to our side. [Our] Allies say, 'All right, you want to limit trade with us; you won't let us trade with Russia. What do you want us to do—starve?'" "[I've] got a doll in my office," Reed replied, "all dressed up [with] hair and clothes. It's from Japan. The price is three cents."

"Never mind the dolls!" Ike cut in. "Let's put our minds to the Pacific testing grounds. Russia can carry those bombs and deliver them—the world is rapidly approaching the crossroads."

Millikin interrupted to say the world reminded him of the fellow who when told of all the terrible things that were going to happen said, "Well, I guess we might just as well paint our assess white and run with the antelopes." "That's quite a story," Ike responded tartly. "Unless we act, we better start running now.... God knows I don't want to start a fight [over free trade] for the hell of it, but I don't see how we can avoid it." (After the meeting Ike said of Millikin: "He's the most fearful man I've ever met—he fears everything.")

No exchanges better than those with Millikin illustrate the virtuoso combination of forthright advocacy and irresistible charm that Ike could bring to a campaign. At the Leaders meeting of March 22, 1955, after the "fearful" Colorado senator had predicted the near impossibility of getting Eisenhower's free trade bill through the Congress, Ike suddenly turned to him and asked: "Gene, did you ever go prospecting?"

"No, Mr. President."

"I'll tell you what we'll do. Let's get a Geiger counter and go up on the Colorado Plateau and prospect for uranium. You prospect and I'll cook. We'll have a fine time and get away from Washington."

Three months later Eisenhower signed into law major legislation incorporating most of his and Randall's recommendations. To Eisenhower the freeing of trade was a principle in which he ardently believed—believed in to surprising lengths, far beyond conservative orthodoxy.

"It is an absolute fallacy," he told the Cabinet August 6, 1954, "to say that no free nation can trade with any Red nation. . . . If China, for example, finds that it can buy cheap straw hats, cheap cotton shirts, sneakers, bicycles, and all the rest of that sort of stuff from Japan, it would seem to me that that would set up the need within China for dependence upon Japan." And after a long talk with Bernard Baruch on March 30, 1956, Eisenhower dictated into his secret diary: "I was quite astonished to find that he now really favors a general plan of removing all restrictions on all trade with the Reds. This conforms to my view, except that we know that there are a few of our types of machinery that the Soviets want as patterns and models. These I would keep on the prohibited list. *Otherwise, however, I believe that the effort to dam up permanently the natural currents of trade, particularly between such areas as Japan and the neighboring Asian mainland, will be defeated* [italics added]." Nearly absolute freedom of trade, even with Red China—an idea whose time had not yet come—remained one of Eisenhower's consistent longings.

The upholding of the treaty-making powers of the presidency, the expansion of trade—these were purposes that gave Eisenhower ground on which he could and would and did do battle. For these he fought tooth and nail. In early 1954 he drew the line against the Bricker Amendment and against protectionism. Why not against McCarthy?

Because, to use a State Department word, he thought such tactics counterproductive. Eisenhower saw McCarthy as a creature and creation of publicity; take away his headlines, and he dies (like the giant wrestler Antaeus of antiquity, who only became stronger when thrown to the ground, into touch with his mother Earth). And it infuriated Ike that others refused to see this fact:

"As for McCarthy," Ike wrote his brother, Milton, on October 9, 1953, "only a shortsighted or completely inexperienced individual would urge the use of the office of the Presidency to give an opponent the publicity he so avidly desires. Time and again, without apology or evasion, I—and the many members of this Administration—have stood for the right of the individual, for free expression of convictions, even though those convictions might be unpopular, and for uncensored use of our libraries, except as dictated by common decency.... Frankly, in a day when we see journalism far more concerned in so-called human interest, dramatic incidents, and bitter quarrels than it is in promoting constructive understanding of the day's problems, I have no intention whatsoever of helping promote the publicity value of anyone who disagrees with me—demagogue or not!"

Five months later, Eisenhower was coming down even harder on the culpability of the press: "No one has been more insistent and vociferous in urging me to challenge McCarthy than the people who built him up, namely writers, editors and publishers," he wrote Bill Robinson March 12. And three days earlier he had written a California friend, Paul Helms: "He [McCarthy] makes a few extraordinary and outlandish charges in the papers, and the whole United States abandons all consideration of the many grave problems it faces in order to speculate on whether McCarthy has it within his power to 'destroy our system of government.' When the proposition is stated as baldly as this, then it becomes instantly ridiculous, without added proof.

"A statement of a code of procedures, law and ethics that should govern the relations among the several departments of government is dismissed to the sixth page of our daily papers in order to dwell upon McCarthy's choice of words in broadcasting his completely unwarranted and despicable insinuations...."

Even as late as 1963, six years after McCarthy's death, Eisenhower resisted giving him—despite editors' pleadings—too much space in the memoirs. He struck out page after page of detail on

McCarthy and Cohn and Schine and told John and me in a letter from Palm Desert: "After having used for the two years of 1953 and 1954 *silence as my strongest weapon to defeat him* [italics added]," he resented going "into a long, dreary story and [giving] his memory far more prominence than I ever did give him in my own mind."

To Eisenhower, throwing McCarthy to earth was not only bad tactics, it was also bad leadership.

"For the past 13 years," Ike wrote Helms in his March 9 letter, "I have occupied posts around which there focussed sufficient public interest that they were considered news sources of greater or lesser importance.... Out of all those experiences, I developed a practice which, so far as I know, I have never violated. That practice is to avoid public mention of any name unless *it can be done with favorable intent and connotation;* reserve all criticism for the private conference; speak only good in public.

"This is not namby-pamby. It certainly is not Pollyannaish. It is just sheer common sense. A leader's job is to get others to go along with him in the promotion of something. To do this he needs their good will. To destroy good will, it is only necessary to criticize publicly. This creates in the criticized one a subconscious desire to 'get even.' Such effects can last for a very long period....

"I am quite sure that the people who want me to stand up and publicly label McCarthy with derogatory titles are the most mistaken people that are dealing with this whole problem...."

With even more adrenaline, he had said the same thing to Milton Eisenhower in his letter of October 9, flaying the "false but prevalent notion that bullying and leadership are synonymous; that desk-pounding is more effective than is persistent adherence to a purpose.... I have not changed. I stand for exactly the same things that I have stood for for many years.... anyone... can go back over my public statements to the very first time that anyone showed enough interest in me to listen to a public statement of mine, and he will find that I have never indulged in bitter personal indictment or attack. To my mind, that practice smacks ... more of the coward and the fool than of the leader."

For these reasons Eisenhower publicly remained aloof. Privately, he and his assistants followed every maneuver on the Hill.

Back in November 1953, one of McCarthy's "gumshoes," G. David Schine, had been drafted. The other "gumshoe," Roy Cohn, had outdone himself—for example, with alleged threats to "wreck the

Army" and efforts to get Schine special privileges: e.g., no duties overseas or on Sunday. At Governor Adams' suggestion, in January 1954, the Army had started compiling a list of these interventions. "Adams tells me," Hagerty wrote in his diary for March 9, "[Republican Senator Charles] Potter [of Michigan] is going to ask Defense for the Schine record tomorrow—that ought to kick up fuss and start ball rolling to get rid of Roy Cohn. . . .

"*March 10*. . . . Good [press] conference. Pres. tough on Joe. . . . is fighting mad, has had it as far as Joe is concerned—'if he wants to get recognized any more,' Pres. told Persons, 'only way he can do it is to stand up and publicly say, "I was wrong in browbeating witnesses, wrong in saying the Army is coddling Communists, and wrong in my attack on Stevens. I apologize"—that's only way I ever welcome him back into fold.'

"C. E. Wilson threw monkeywrench in carefully prepared plans by sending his car to Senate today and picking up Joe for luncheon at Pentagon. Wilson didn't tell anyone in W.H. about luncheon—just let it happen—When I told Pres. he leaned back in chair, muttered a few 'goddamns' and then said, 'You know, Jim, I believe Cabot Lodge is dead right when he says we need acute politicians in those positions. They are the only ones who know enough to stay out of traps—the only ones who can play the same kind of game as those guys on the Hill.' Pres. . . . called me back several times to see if any announcement had been made from luncheon— 'if they are cooking up another statement, then, by God, someone is going to hear from me—but good.'

"*March 11*. . . . Finally caught up with [Assistant Secretary of Defense for Legislative and Public Affairs Fred] Seaton on Wilson luncheon—seems McCarthy called Wilson after Wilson's press conference where he said 'damn tommyrot' Army coddling Reds. Joe wanted to tell Wilson he wasn't against Army—Wilson asked him to lunch but didn't tell anyone over here—went on his own—bawled Seaton out mildly—he said 'listen, if you think you have troubles, come over to the Pentagon'—and I guess he's right—doing good job. . . .

"Army report on Schine-Cohn-McCarthy going up on Hill today—it's a pip—shows constant pressure by Cohn to get Schine soft Army job, with Joe in and out of threats. . . . Should bust this thing wide open. . . ."

It did. The subcommittee voted to investigate the Army's

charges, and the unforgettable Army-McCarthy hearings began: thirty-six ugly and ludicrous sessions of Klieg-lighted nationally televised microscopic examination of the comings and goings of Cohn; phone calls monitored by a clerk in Stevens' office; meetings held and discussions pursued over restaurant butterscotch sundaes; a photograph of Stevens and Schine, cropped. All of this punctuated by endless bogus "points of order" (on a point of order anybody could grab the floor from anyone else), a near fist fight between Cohn and the counsel for the Democratic members, and the near-tears climactic condemnation of McCarthy by Army Counsel Joseph N. Welch of Boston for McCarthy's "cruel and reckless" attack on a young member of Welch's firm for a long-since-abandoned membership in the National Lawyers' Guild.

From the start, Eisenhower watched every move, getting on the phone to talk over ground rules with Majority Leader Bill Knowland (both agreed, to no avail, that McCarthy should have no right to cross-examine witnesses); letting go at the subcommittee's temporary chairman, Republican Senator Karl Mundt of South Dakota ("you can't trust Mundt"); knocking down—to Hagerty's delight—White House staffers Jerry Persons and Jerry Morgan for defending McCarthy's right to sit on the committee as it investigated him ("He can't sit as a judge").

"In at 8 and boiling mad," Hagerty wrote March 25. "Army kicked over their own case by giving story to Wash. Post that they had promoted Schine to Army Criminal Investigators School at Camp Gordon—waived 2 out of 3 requirements—(1) 2 year service in Army (2) physical disability—how dumb can they get—McCarthy can now blow Army report claiming Cohn and Joe had sought preferential treatment for Schine out of the water by say[ing] Army did it themselves. Called Seaton, he's checking and didn't know about it. 'It's deliberate sabotage, and if I can find out Pentagon source of story, he won't be with us any longer.'

"Went to lunch at [Senate Secretary] Mark Trice's office in the Senate with Persons, Martin and Morgan—they said they didn't know who was going to be there—when I walked in there was Joe McCarthy, Welker, Mundt, Malone, Hickenlooper, Butler (Md.), Griswold and Purtell.... McCarthy, Mundt and Malone left right after social luncheon—Then Welker and Hickenlooper started in— proposed both Cohn and [Army Counsel John] Adams resign and case be dropped. I kept quiet and just listened, as did other 3 from W[hite]

H[ouse]—feel being jobbed by McCarthy boys. Hickenlooper criticized 'those who advised Pres. to get into row'—said 'he should have kept out'—arrived at 12:45, left at 2:20—on return to [White] House heard that rumor floating around Capitol of 'compromise luncheon'—called in Persons and Morgan and told them I was going to tell our wire men entire story—they agreed and told wires what happened—no W[hite] H[ouse] approval of luncheon—only 'social'—still think it was a put up job and don't know whether our boys in on it.

"Seaton called ... while at luncheon to tell me Army was flatly denying Schine story—turned down Schine's original application—though still have one pending. Good job by Fred—lot of guts...."

A week later (*April 2*): "Went in evening to Charlie Willis party at Sulgrave Club—just after dinner received urgent call from Seaton—could I come immediately to [Assistant Secretary of Defense H.] Struve Hensel's home—emergency—Marge and I went—Marge visited with Mrs. Hensel upstairs while I talked to Hensel, Seaton and Joe Welch, the Army's new counsel in Stevens' case. Welch accompanied by 2 young assistants—one of them Fred Fisher—earlier in evening while going over each other's background, Fisher admitted that he had been a member of the [National] Lawyers' Guild (on Attorney General's subversive list) and had helped organize Suffolk County Chapter in Mass. with assistance from ... a Communist organizer. I first thought we should not give in on Fisher's membership, but [Communist organizer] association was a different story—it was decided Fisher to drop out and go back to Boston—too dangerous to give McCarthy opportunity to brand Fisher as Red and smear up Army defense...tough decision, but necessary."

Through all of this, the White House publicly kept its distance: it was the Army—nobody else—that was contending against McCarthy. But then suddenly McCarthy crossed onto Constitutional ground. And Eisenhower struck back with a new force.

On May 12 on the witness stand, Army Counsel John Adams revealed that back on January 21 he had conferred in the Attorney General's office with Brownell, Rogers, Sherman Adams, Cabot Lodge, and Jerry Morgan; and that Governor Adams had told him to prepare the memorandum chronicling McCarthy's badgering the Army to help Schine. Naturally the investigators wanted John Adams to tell them more about that meeting—a meeting which for the first time opened an avenue of inquiry right into the White House itself.

"Believe this to be opening of White House action in case," Hagerty wrote, "and probably have to face questions soon as to whether we will stand for subpoena ... of White House personnel. President is opposed and will probably not permit it."

On May 14 at Cabinet, Eisenhower laid down the law: executive branch officials should refuse to testify before congressional committees on (1) security information; (2) *personal* advice exchanged between superior and subordinate, where the consideration of eventual publication could destroy the value of the advice. He went no further. Deputy Defense Secretary Robert Anderson relayed this ruling to John Adams, who thereupon clammed up. "Daily Mirror carried story," Hagerty noted in his diary, "quoting McCarthy that he was going to subpoena White House Personnel....President feels very strongly and said 'This is one we will fight out right up and down the line.'"

"*May 14*....We...discussed the Army-McCarthy hearings and...threat to subpoena White House staff members....The President said that he would not stand for this for one minute. He... looked upon his staff members as confidential advisors...the Congress had absolutely no right to ask them to testify in any way, shape or form about the advice that they were giving to him at any time on any subject—'If they want to make a test of this principle, I'll fight them tooth and nail and up and down the country. It is a matter of principle with me and I will never permit it.'

"*May 15*....Spent most of the morning in conference in Governor Adams' office with the Governor, Herb Brownell, [Assistant Attorney General] Lee Rankin, Persons, Morgan, Martin, Shanley on draft of letter President to send Monday to Secretary of Defense ordering him to refuse to permit employees in the Defense Department to testify concerning confidential and personal matters relating to advice within the Executive departments."

On Monday, May 17, the President met with the Legislative Leaders. "Turning to his letter," Hagerty reported, "the President announced that they all knew that he had been trying to stay out of the 'damn business on the Hill,' that many people have been begging him to get into the struggle, to attack McCarthy personally but that he had refused to do so. However, he said, a situation had come up in the threatened subpoena of his confidential advisers that made it necessary for him to act. He said that he had written a letter to the Secretary of Defense ordering him to refuse to permit their people to discuss confidential matters with the Committee.... 'Any man who testifies as to the advice he gave me won't be working for me that night. ... I will not allow people around me to be subpoenaed and you might just as well know it now." The letter to Wilson not only laid out a sweeping assertion of the President's right to withhold executive branch employees' confidential advice on official matters; it also buttressed this assertion with a long legal memorandum from Attorney General Brownell citing historical precedents back to George Washington.

For months Eisenhower had fought McCarthy by indirection: praising George Marshall, condemning book burning, upholding the need for give-and-take with our Allies, ruling out Communists-in-government as a 1954 campaign issue, insisting on courtesy toward congressional witnesses. Now once again he set forth an abstraction—that of executive privilege—but an abstraction that this time entailed direct action, action against McCarthy himself.

On this new ground the battle now raged. At last the battering rams had struck the presidential fortress. On May 28 Hagerty wrote: "drafted statement designed for President to issue regarding McCarthy's appeal at hearing yesterday to Federal employees to disregard Presidential orders and laws and report to him on 'graft, corruption, Communism and treason.' ... I gave out the statement at 11:00. A few minutes later the President called me in to his office.... He was really mad at what he termed 'the complete arrogance of McCarthy'—Walking up and down behind his desk and speaking in rapid fire order he said....:

" 'This amounts to nothing but a wholesale subversion of public service. McCarthy is making exactly the same plea of loyalty to him that Hitler made to the German people. Both tried to set up personal loyalty within the Government while both were using the pretense of fighting Communism. McCarthy is trying deliberately to subvert the people we have in Government, people who are sworn to obey the law, the Constitution and their superior officers. I think this is the most disloyal act we have ever had by anyone in the Government of the United States.'

"The President then sat down at his desk and said that he supposed he will be asked this question at his press conference.... 'I'll tell you now what I'm going to say—I am going to tell the newsmen that in my opinion this is the most arrogant invitation to subversion and disloyalty that I have ever heard of. I am going to also say that if such an invitation is accepted by any employee of the Government and we find out who that employee is, he will be fired on the spot if a civilian and court martialed on the spot if a military man. I won't stand for it for one minute.'" To arouse public backing, Hagerty called several key journalists, including Edward R. Murrow, strictly following the President's instruction: don't "let anyone even in the White House know what [you're] doing."

"*May 29* . . . Ed Murrow and other commentators have picked up . . . statement of yesterday and characterized it quite properly as a fundamental Constitutional fight between the Administration and McCarthy. . . . The basic question we are making a fight on is simply this: Has a United States Senator, or anyone, a right to publicly urge the formation of a personal Gestapo within the Administrative Branch of the Government, including the military?

"*May 30*. . . . At home in the morning President called me several times regarding his speech at the Columbia Bi-Centennial Dinner. . . . During our telephone conversation the President indicated that he was going to make this a finished fight with McCarthy—He believed the question was a fundamental Constitutional one and was going to the people with it."

In his Columbia address the next day—inspired by the university's bicentennial theme, "Man's right to knowledge and the free use thereof"—Eisenhower delivered his sharpest and most definitive condemnation of his detested antagonist, still unnamed:

"Whenever, and for whatever alleged reason, people attempt to crush ideas, to mask their convictions, to view every neighbor as a possible enemy, to seek some kind of divining rod by which to test for conformity, a free society is in danger. . . . Here in America we are descended in blood and spirit from revolutionaries and rebels. . . . As their heirs, may we never confuse honest dissent with disloyal subversion.

"Without exhaustive debate . . . free government would weaken and wither. But if we allow ourselves to be persuaded that every individual, or party, that takes issue with our own convictions is necessarily wicked or treasonous—then indeed we are approaching the end of freedom's road. . . . Through knowledge and understanding, *we will drive from the temple of freedom all who seek to establish over us thought control—whether they be agents of a foreign state or demagogues thirsty for personal power and public notice.* [italics added]."

To Eisenhower, as to all Jeffersonian believers in freedom of the mind, red fascism and black fascism are one. Communism and Nazism are alike in their totalitarianism and alike in their enemy—republican democratic limited government.

Eisenhower's May 17 invocation of executive privilege made anti-McCarthyists cheer. They cheered for years. The doctrine squared totally with their belief in a strong "activist" president, one who would brook no congressional curtailment of his power or independence. Then came the change. After the "strong" "activist" presidencies of John Kennedy, Lyndon Johnson, and Richard Nixon—with the Vietnam War Exhibit A, followed by Watergate—the liberals had second thoughts. Arthur M. Schlesinger, Jr., for example, who above all had theorized on the need for a president who would seize all the power he could, and who thus helped father the monstrosities of the sixties, now, in his *The Imperial Presidency* (1974), jumped on Eisenhower for the imperiousness of his letter to Wilson; and for Eisenhower's subsequent extension of the claim of privilege from the President himself to everyone in the executive branch—an extension that led Eisenhower officials to refuse information to the Congress forty-four times.

Moreover, Schlesinger pointed out that Brownell's legal memorandum which accompanied the May 17 letter to Wilson, drawing verbatim on an article written in 1949 by Herman Wolkinson, a Justice Department employee under Truman, repeated that article's assertion that the "courts have uniformly held that the President and heads of departments have an uncontrolled discretion to withhold... information and papers in the public interest...." And that assertion, Schlesinger said, was baseless.

Brownell did make a mistake by taking these Wolkinson words out of their qualifying context. But Brownell told me that while he had erred in thus flatly claiming the courts had upheld executive privilege, he had later issued revised documents on the subject—a fact Arthur Schlesinger did not acknowledge and evidently did not know. Moreover, the key evidence in the legal memorandum was not this remark about the courts but the list of instances in which previous presidents, beginning with George Washington, had asserted a right to keep information confidential.

Finally, by the time (October 1974) Brownell told me all this, the Supreme Court of the United States *had* gone far toward upholding executive privilege, in its unanimous 1974 opinion on the Nixon tapes. "The first ground [in support of the claim of absolute privilege] is the *valid need for protection of communications between high government officials and those who advise and assist them* [italics added] in the performance of their manifold duties; the importance of this confidentiality is too plain to require further discussion. Human experience teaches that those who expect public dissemination of their remarks may well temper candor with a concern for appearances and for their own interests to the detriment of the decisionmaking process."

"Eisenhower would have accepted that opinion 100 percent," Brownell told me, as did his successor William Rogers. And he would, both men continued, have accepted the Court's further conclusion: that Richard Nixon had no right to withhold evidence necessary to the investigation of a crime.

For neither Eisenhower nor Brownell nor Rogers believed the claim of privilege absolute. The May 17 letter specifies, as Senator Sam Ervin repeatedly specified in the Watergate hearings, that privilege covers only "official matters." "On crime, on suspicion of wrongdoing," Brownell said, "Eisenhower's view was 'give them everything.'" Indeed, wherever possible, he wanted to be cooperative. If an investigating committee asks for information, he told the Cabinet November 3, 1954, "let's make sure they get it, and let's get it to them within five minutes." In an early draft of the McCarthy chapter in *Mandate for Change*—a draft dated February 14, 1963, a decade before Watergate—Eisenhower wrote these revealing words, hitherto un-published, about the Army's response to the McCarthy subcommit-tee's demand for the names of all Army people connected with the Peress case: "It appeared that Secretary Stevens had already tenta-tively agreed to provide the information, but General Ridgway, Army Chief of Staff, had violently objected on the ground that to give it would establish the practice of subjecting officers to cross-examination and virtual persecution by Congressional committees. I thought that General Ridgway's views were extreme....*As a matter of general principle, I felt that the Army would be well-advised to provide every possible bit of information where security and efficient administration would permit. They should not, I felt, be appearing to cover up* [italics added]."

At last, on June 17, the raucous hearings ended. Some of the figures on the silver tube began to fade away—Bob Stevens, for example, and the various staff cops, photograph croppers, phone-call monitors, and hangers-on. Some would go on to greater glory or notoriety: Roy Cohn, who became a New York financial wheeler-dealer; Schine, who years later became "producer" of *The French Connection;* the witty and urbane Joe Welch, who starred in a movie with Lee Remick; and the Democratic counsel who almost punched Cohn in the nose—Robert Kennedy.

To McCarthy himself, two things happened that sealed his downfall: (a) the American people, especially the daytime-viewing TV audience, had had a bellyful; (b) the Senate, on the recommendation of a select committee chaired by conservative Republican Arthur Watkins of Utah, voted in December 1954 to condemn McCarthy's conduct, finding it "contrary to Senatorial traditions."

As far as I know, Eisenhower pulled no strings behind the Watkins Committee. William Knowland, as majority leader, selected the Republican members (Watkins, Frank Carlson of Kansas, Francis Case of South Dakota) to join the Democrats (Ed Johnson of Colorado, John Stennis of Mississippi, and Sam Ervin, Jr., of North Carolina), and Knowland himself in the end voted against the censure. But staff members made no secret of White House sentiment. (Bern Shanley, for one, met regularly with Ed Thye and other friendly Republicans to this end.) And when the motion carried, Eisenhower on his own initiative invited Watkins to the Oval Office and praised him, in words Hagerty gladly relayed to the reporters, for a "very splendid job."

McCarthyism had ended. No single force had brought it down. And no one knows whether a different presidential strategy might have brought it down sooner—or at all. What one does know is that McCarthyism was over, and that Eisenhower's strategy, at the center of the conflict, must have helped extinquish it.

Of course the McCarthy hearings will always fascinate because they touch fundamental questions. They illustrate how a man can pretend to be protecting freedom at the very time his tactics are destroying it. They show how difficult it is to defend against slander and false accusation. They demonstrate that free speech in the powerful, especially those with congressional immunity, must be separated from persecution of the weak individual. They touch on executive privilege and its limitations. They ask what are the proper methods for handling the demagogue. They cry out for truth and fair play.

In 1952 Walter Lippmann favored the election of Eisenhower

as the best remedy for anti-Communist divisiveness, and I believe Eisenhower's strategy was decisive in ending the McCarthyism obscenity. For what Eisenhower (and Eisenhower above all) did throughout those cacophonous and disgraceful months was, quite simply, what he told his brother Milton he was doing: he upheld constantly a standard of abstract right to which decent men could repair; he engaged the enemy on the ground of principle, and principle alone.

That strategy exemplifies a pattern. Eisenhower succeeded against McCarthy, I believe, because of a strategic sensitivity in selecting his ground—a sensitivity evident also in the Indochina conflict, where he refused to commit the United States without allies; in the Quemoy-Matsu crises, where he walked the gray area between capitulation and the interventionism of those who urged the drawing of a simplistic line against the loss of "one square inch of free territory"; in his reliance on persuasion and persistence to win over Republican recalcitrants ("Gene, you prospect, and I'll cook")—this in spite of temptations to write them off or read them out of the party ("When the President saw the story [of Knowland's vote against the McCarthy censure]," Hagerty wrote in his diary, "he literally hit the roof. . . . 'What's the guy trying to do? Here, he personally picked the Committee to draw up the censure charges. . . and then he turns around and votes against them, using this phony reason. . . .'"); and in the 1958 crisis in Lebanon, where—as in the Bricker Amendment, free trade, and other legislative battles, and as in the fight with McCarthy—he drew an uncrossable line with speed and effect.

The pattern once again exemplifies a man who faced controversy not as a single individual free to follow his instincts, which were more than usually combative; but as a president, subject to the discipline, imposed and self-imposed, of his role and responsibility. Like Lincoln, he would have held the obnoxious McClellan's horse for a victory. Like Lincoln, he could seek to destroy his enemies by making them his friends ("he was," Lucius Clay said, "the least vengeful man I ever knew"). A soldier, he saw and did battle ("When you appeal to force, there's just one thing you must never do—lose"). He knew it great to have a giant's strength, and at Normandy he had wielded more force than any man before him in history. But like the heroine of *Measure for Measure*, he knew it tyrannous to use it as a giant.

THE GROUND CHOSEN

Victory turns on the choice of the ground. McCarthy in the end failed because his conduct did not befit a senator. Eisenhower in the end succeeded because his conduct did befit a president.

IX

SEPTEMBER 23, 1954

DIVIDED PARTISAN

As the presidential plane, the *Columbine*, sped through the September sky toward Los Angeles, where Eisenhower would address a massive political rally in the Hollywood Bowl, Jerry Morgan, Jack Martin, and Bryce Harlow realized the time had come to bell the cat.

The three—with Jerry Persons, General Marshall's Congressional liaison right arm during the War—made up a powerful political team, wise in the ways of the Hill, productive of results, a team indispensable to a President who habitually rose above politics. Lawyer Morgan, an authority on labor legislation, had for ten years been Assistant Legislative Counsel in the House. Lawyer Martin had long been the late Senator Taft's principal assistant. And speechwriter Harlow had done his first day's work under the Capitol dome as a very young man in 1938.

The speech draft which lay before them, though a rouser, had a hole in it: it did not explicitly call for the reelection of a Republican-led Congress in the forthcoming November 1954 election. So they devised a sentence to that end, and shrewd whimsical Jack Martin headed nervously toward the open door into the President's compartment.

The journey to that sentence had been long and tortuous. By the fall of 1954 Eisenhower had had an abundance of headaches with the Republicans in Congress, not only with irreconcilables like Jenner and McCarthy; but with timorous teammates like Millikin and

Saltonstall; unreliables like Mundt; with the assorted "isolationists, high tariff people, union busters, and anti-Social Security" die-hards he had reeled off in a private letter to a friend; and with critics of his foreign policy like the Republican majority leader himself, Senator William Knowland ("I used to think he was a good candidate for President, and now I know he isn't," Ike had sounded off to Hagerty the preceding March 10; and on July 6, after Knowland threatened to resign as majority leader to lead the fight for U.S. withdrawal from the UN if Red China were admitted, Ike let go again: "He thinks he's Horatius at the bridge. All he wants is attention, and he acts like a little boy at times"). In April 1953 Eisenhower had even toyed briefly with the idea of cutting loose the impossible Republicans and setting up a new party.

These and other obstacles had cluttered the road toward any clarion call for a Republican majority in the next Congress. And no one had done more to hasten the President along that road than Morgan and Martin's friend and sidekick on the *Columbine* that September 23, 1954—Eisenhower's chief writer of speeches, Bryce Harlow, a five-foot-four-inch Oklahoma veteran of congressional infighting, who through eight years of the presidency and eight more of the ex-presidency would serve Dwight Eisenhower, as son serves father, with more energy, devotion, tirelessness, street-wise counsel, and selflessness than almost anyone else.

I first met Bryce at four o'clock on Monday, April 5, 1954. As I walked through the iron gate outside the East Wing, I had a first impression, in that blazing spring sun, of a building of blinding whiteness. I climbed the flight of stairs in the two-story building—the only elevator was a cumbersome old freight hauler with doors that close from top and bottom when you pull down on a heavy tape—and into Harlow's tiny office overlooking the roof of the passageway from East Wing to mansion, with a glimpse of trees and lawns to the south.

"Gabe Hauge tells me you'd like to work in this vale of tears," Harlow said, walking around the desk to shake hands. His shortness struck me (I'd never have dreamed he had captained the varsity tennis team at the University of Oklahoma), and his warm and engaging southern-western manner. He spoke of the hazards of working on speeches: "After everybody has mouthed and penciled up anything you write," he said, "if there's a single word in there that you wrote to start out with, it's only an accident."

Harlow was Eisenhower's taproot into the Republican party—

the articulate, facile, bare-knuckled partisan typing at his typewriter or editing his copy "with a dirty pen," coloring the Democrats all black, the Republicans all white; the loyalist standing foursquare always with the team, whether Nelson Rockefeller or Ev Dirksen or Barry Goldwater, fueled by partisan hate and humor.

"That little guy writes with *more venom!*" his friend Gabe Hauge marveled admiringly one day during the Nixon campaign of 1960, as the three of us toured the country by train and plane with the doomed Vice-President. Harlow's brand of partisanship produced results for Eisenhower—results produced by no one else. At times Eisenhower openly welcomed it, even reveled in it. But only for a short span. For at bottom such political partisanship—indeed all partisanship—ignited his impatience.

"I want to be positive!" he exploded at one of our editorial sessions on the memoirs, striking out a "prosecuting attorney" excoriation of some Democratic folly. "I don't believe that things negative promote the happiness of people," he once told a press conference. "I believe that you must go forward in the spiritual and intellectual, cultural, economic development of this country if we are going to make it a place where 161 million people can live in happiness." He had little use for most party platforms, with their assemblage of facts and figures to show the mendacity or stupidity of the other side. The things that would turn him on—the proposals and the people he genuinely warmed to—were things that would foster friendship in the world, enlarge trade among nations, inspire the young. He would have agreed with Eric Hoffer's incandescent reinterpretation of the old saw "whom the gods love die young"—a reinterpretation that discards the old sentimentalism (the darlings of the gods, too tender and good to live in this harsh world, die before thirty, like Shelley and Keats) and substitutes a new insight: the beloved of the gods remain forever young in heart, filled with love and wonder as they view the world, *herrlich wie am ersten Tag*. Ike was young in heart, even when I saw him during his last illness, reading Arthur Krock's memoirs, agreeing totally with the crotchety old conservative newsman's gloomy Jeremiad on the follies and nightmares of the late 1960s, and then turning with shock to ask: "But how can he conclude America has no future? I just can't understand it."

Of his associates, one man above all mirrored this Eisenhower brightness: Kevin McCann—tall, gaunt, gray, tense, nervous, Irish, Jesuit-educated, fiftyish, with steel-trap memory and bright pig eyes;

newspaperman turned Eisenhower speechwriter (Pentagon, Columbia, SHAPE) and then turned small-college (Defiance, Ohio) president.

"Before the starry threshold of Jove's court/My mansion is." Kevin McCann dwelled in the empyrean—in the brave and hopeful and pealing spaces of Ike's great speech to the English-speaking Union in July 1951, calling for Europe to unite; of the homecoming speech at Abilene in June 1952, which assured cynics of his belief in "home, mother, and heaven"; of the Columbia bicentennial address, with its ringing affirmation of mankind's right to knowledge and its free use.

I first met Kevin McCann on the afternoon of May 13, 1954, during a long peripatetic interview that began in the East Wing office he used whenever he came to town. He affirmed the necessity of generalities in speeches: details shift from day to day, even minute to minute; a writer must rise to assertions that the passage of time will not invalidate. (Eisenhower, I learned later, repeatedly and consciously resorted to generality in speeches and press conferences to preclude entrapment in detail.) He took me down the stairs, through the ground floor of the Mansion, out into the colonnade running alongside the presidential swimming pool next to the Rose Garden, and up a slightly inclined plane—replacing steps, for FDR's wheelchair—to the West Wing, and into the office of the President's personal secretaries, Ann Whitman and Helen Weaver. There he discoursed on the subject of presidential messages—short messages to widely disparate groups from churches to conventions coast to coast—and on whether I could write them.

"I don't know a better way to test a man," he declared, "than to embarrass him before women." Presidential messages, he went on, should have three characteristics: "brevity, warmth, and sympathy—above all, brevity." Our floating conversation removed to the Conference Room (ex-Fish Room, now Roosevelt Room), and he motioned to a portrait of Lincoln on the wall. "In the sweep of history, of course, Lincoln will be remembered as the most human of our Presidents. But President Eisenhower will also be remembered for the same thing. At Columbia he spent an entire afternoon composing a letter to a Brooklyn boy who wrote to him complaining that Columbia wouldn't admit him just because he had an Italian name."

The morning of his inauguration Eisenhower had written a short prayer calling for divine guidance to help all to "work for the good of our beloved country and Thy glory." And having entered the

White House, he had found himself embroiled with the tired, the old, and the negative—obstructionists like Mollie Malone, who wanted to keep out foreign goods; Pat McCarran, who wanted to keep out foreign people; John Bricker, who wanted to keep out foreign government; and McCarthy.

Bryce Harlow came from the Hill, the home of such men, with its cigars and one-to-an-office spittoons and Senate bean soup. He was all meat and potatoes—solid legislative proposals, tough argumentation, facts and figures and political statistics (what one partisan called "Republican statistics" to nail [sic] the Democratic hogwash). Singlehandedly as Ike's main speechwriter after Emmet Hughes's departure in October 1953, Harlow had written up in final form the Eisenhower 1954 legislative program, first in the State of the Union address, then in a *mitrailleuse* clatter of special messages on agriculture, labor relations, social security, health, housing. This bone-crushing months-long process—draft after draft, quibble after quibble over each word—produced the most massive set of specific proposals Ike would ever send to the Hill: the St. Lawrence Seaway; new curbs on subversives; a higher federal debt limit; major tax reduction and reform; new flexible—instead of old rigid—price supports for farmers; higher postal rates; changes in the Taft-Hartley labor relations act; more social security and more unemployment insurance to more people; a new federal health program; housing; voting rights for Washington, D.C. and for eighteen-year-olds; more vocational rehabilitation for the disabled; statehood for Hawaii.

For Eisenhower, congressional action on these pieces of legislation would become the focus of his attention during the dark days of the McCarthy-Army hearings—a ray of positive hope. For Harlow, the 1954 record of congressional accomplishment—the greatest in Ike's presidency—would become a club to beat the Democrats with, Exhibit A in a call for the reelection in November of a Congress Republican-led. He could hardly wait.

At 8:30 A.M. on July 26, 1954, I entered the White House to become his assistant.

Coming from Harvard, particularly from English and the humanities, to Washington, particularly during a Republican administration, and particularly during the days of McCarthy, meant crossing quite a divide. Not long before, the Duke University faculty voted 61 to 42 against awarding an honorary degree to one of its law school graduates, Richard Nixon, the Vice-President of the United

States, and he was canceling his planned commencement address there. By contrast, Adlai Stevenson that spring had given the Godkin lectures at Harvard; his admirers had stood in line six hours to get seats in Sanders Theater; and Stevenson would go on to receive that year honorary degrees from both Princeton and Columbia.

After chatting for a minute or two with Harlow, I was taken around to be fingerprinted, sworn in, and otherwise "processed" by Steve Benedict, an assistant White House Staff secretary. As we walked through the corridors of the West Wing and across the street to the Executive Office Building, he said that he had heard I played piano music and wanted to know what. I murmured something about the "standard classical repertoire," fearing exposure as an egghead, believing that anyone in the White House who played or listened to music would like only "Home on the Range," not knowing that Steve himself was a pupil of Karl Ulrich Schnabel, so carefully hidden were cultural accomplishments in the Eisenhower administration.

Thinking to find myself a member of a huge staff stuck far from the East Wing in some remote labyrinth, I was naturally thrilled when Bryce's secretary, Mary Nichols, ushered me into my new office—a small room right next to his with an even better view out across the south lawn, where, Nicky said, you can engage in "President-watching, when he's out there hitting golf balls in the afternoon."

Within minutes, I'd begun to work. First job: to do a rough draft of a speech for the International Conference of the World Council of Churches on August 19, just three weeks away. Bryce already had in hand a draft sent in by a writer for a national magazine which he didn't like and which I also found atrocious. It began with a paragraph about the world, followed by a paragraph about the merits of councils, followed by some praise of churches. So I started in to see whether I could do better.

A couple of mornings later I attended my first staff meeting, presided over by laconic Governor Adams. When it ended, Bryce introduced me. The conversation went like this:

Adams: "You say you studied English?"

"Yes, sir."

"Always get A's?"

"Yes, sir."

"Now's your big chance." He turned on his heel and walked out.

Within an hour I thought I had muffed it. I had brought back my draft to Harlow, and he suggested I stand in the far corner of his little fourteen-by-fourteen office and read it out loud. I did. It was, I thought, a thoughtful essay focusing on the virtues of freedom of the mind and the infinite worth of the individual—something all churches believed in.

But it rang no bells, went nowhere, bent no ears back. Harlow paced the office. "Have you ever been to Jerusalem?" he asked. Taken aback, I answered that I hadn't.

"Well, several years ago, I went there with a group of congressmen. And we visited the Church of the Holy Sepulchre." More pacing. "I think this speech ought to start out like this: Eight hundred years ago a throng of Europeans, moved by their religious faith, left Europe, endured enormous hardships, and went into the Middle East." He had, of course, gone back to the Crusade theme, something in which he could get interested. We talked about it awhile, and I said I'd take a crack at a new draft.

I had met the process of Harlowizing—writing "as though you're arguing with somebody," and driving, polishing, toughening, livening all the way. At its extreme, as Harlow-admirer Fred Seaton once remarked, it could result in "blood flowing in the gutters, virgins raped on every street corner, rockets fired off, purple in every sentence." But from Harlow, this gifted and fertile writer, I began to learn.

By August 6 the speech had Harlow's enthusiastic blessing and extensive editing; it was coming along, we thought, well. But then it began to run into roadblocks. The President let his son, John, read it, and John had some major changes. Following Harlow's conscientious determination to staff everything with care, we sent it to every semiprofessional religious member of the administration—Ezra Benson, of the Mormons' Council of Twelve; Gabriel Hauge, eminent Lutheran; Arthur Flemming, leading Methodist; and assorted Presbyterians, Episcopalians, and Catholics—to ask what they thought; they had flyspeck changes only. But then the national magazine man wrote in asking what was happening to his draft; when he found out, he flew down to Washington in a huff to assert its superiority over the current one. Finally Kevin McCann, Congregationalist, was flown in briefly from Defiance, Ohio, to put a new text together. The final speech ended up containing a little bit of everything: the magazine man's beginning, the crusades, a section on foreign aid that I had devised, and a long section on the need for peace which the President extemporized from notes written up by McCann.

But we had no time for regrets or postmortems. Politics pressed, and one central question: What Republican candidates, if any, would Eisenhower endorse? On July 28 he had said he would not go out stumping for anybody but would travel around the country talking about his program. On August 11 the President implied that he would support candidates as individuals, not party members; he thus would not automatically favor any Republican over any Democrat—a pronouncement that held wavering Republicans' feet to the fire as votes on the Ike legislation came up.

Now to the White House came a showdown in corpulent corporal form: Joe Meek of Illinois, seeking to unseat gray-haired academic Democratic Senator Paul Douglas. Meek had denounced "foreign giveaway programs," favored the Bricker Amendment, praised McCarthy. In contrast, Douglas had backed the President on foreign policy (especially Indochina), the Bricker Amendment, housing, Social Security, and health. But now Meek told the President, for immediate release, "You can count on my loyalties and my support as the junior senator from Illinois." Ike gave Meek his blessing. And liberals—even Republican—winced.

By August 19 at the Illinois State Fair, to more than 20,000 swelterers, Ike was denouncing economic "prophets of gloom and doom" (read: Douglas) and stopping just short of naming Meek by name: "It might be a good thing," he said, "to increase the size of the delegation that you send from Lincoln's party to Washington." Meek, perspiring freely, beamed that that was good enough for him: "Couldn't have said more without being undignified."

Eisenhower had, of course, no secret sympathy with the congressional Democrats, including Douglas. "I'm getting sick and tired of hearing men whom I have about as much political affinity for as a bull in a pen saying they are for us," Eisenhower told the Leaders March 15. "Hell, they're against us and always will be."

But on helping or not helping Republican candidates, Eisenhower could not remain forever ambiguous. Out in the Rose Garden in late August he read from idiot cards before cameras these wind-up words for a rousing campaign film: "All of us who believe in the aims of this [Eisenhower] program should join together to elect Republican Senators and Congressmen who will work effectively with leaders of the Executive Branch toward fulfillment of that program."

In some of the drafts for this message, a comma followed "Congress-men"; in some drafts it didn't. "The whole message turns on that comma," I observed to Bob Kieve, Harlow's other assistant. "If the clause is restrictive, Eisenhower is declaring himself only for Senators and Congressmen who will work with him; if it's nonrestrictive, he's saying that Republican Senators and Congressmen—all of them—will work effectively with him." Bob scoffed. But he stopped when he saw that comma the subject of debate on page 1 of the August 30 *New York Times*. Grammarians were wrestling with its implications. A reporter got to Jim Hagerty and asked him what the wording meant. Jim rode roughshod over him: "It means exactly what it says." Finally a couple of days later Richard Nixon made it clear that the White House of course favored the election of Republicans one and all without qualification.

But in that urging, how far would Eisenhower go? Did he really agree he needed a Republican 84th Congress? And if so, would he go to the mat? Those questions bothered all of us as we looked toward the September 23 monster rally in the Hollywood Bowl.

Our friend the magazine writer weighed in with what he considered a dynamite draft for this political crowd. It featured some great conservative themes—reducing government spending by reduc-ing its purchases of paper clips (*sic*); getting the government out of competition with private business. One sequence wound up with this punch line, which Harlow read aloud, with heavy emphasis, one noon in the White House mess: 'We've even sold, you'll be glad to hear, the Bluebeard Castle Hotel in, comma, of all places, comma, the *Virgin Islands*!" That, and the rest of the draft, didn't fly. (Everyone inside the White House, of course, had an exquisite sensitivity to what was and was not fitting for presidential utterance. I recall another Harlow reading of a suggested draft that had come out of the foreign aid agency about the passage of the foreign aid bill. Instead of remarking on its significance to the free world's defense and economic advance-ment, the whimsical writer had decided to cast the whole thing into the imagery of the Old American West. "A couple of hundred years ago," he began, "our forefathers pushed westward on the frontier, with their guns, their wagons, and their supplies of buffalo meat." This document, which immediately had them rolling in the aisles of the White House Mess, soon became known as the "buffalo meat" draft.)

The Hollywood Bowl audience, Harlow understood, would

include not only Republicans but also friendly Democrats and Independents. "Try to write your way down the middle of that one," he said, as we started into a first draft. Because of the ecumenical character of the audience, he suggested I take a look at a speech Eisenhower had made a year earlier to Republican zealots assembled in Boston—a piece of high-minded oratory drafted by Emmet Hughes, miles away from the kind of gut-cutting Republicanism Harlow secretly liked, a document of the sort that only Hughes could produce. I looked at those lofty words and started a new lofty draft of my own, harking back to Pericles, Thucydides, and the Founding Fathers.

Because Harlow by now had taken up residence near the vacationing President at the Lowry Air Force Base in Denver, and I was working in Washington, I put the whole inspirational thing onto the teletype terminal in the White House West Wing. Instead of commenting on it, Harlow tactfully—and tactically—suggested I show it to one Jim Bassett, who had just flown in to Washington from California to accompany Vice-President Nixon on his forthcoming swing around the country to drum up support for Republican candidates.

Bassett was staying at the old Lee House, behind the Mayflower Hotel. Draft in hand, I knocked on his door and entered a room generously filled by cigar smoke. My heart sank. Here, I thought, is a *real* politician. My spirits picked up somewhat when he told me he had gone to Bowdoin. He flipped through the draft. "That's a very beautiful piece of writing." But, he went on, it unfortunately lacked a down-to-earth political message. He reached for his briefcase and pulled out a sample of what he had in mind: the speech—the standard speech, to be delivered from memory at dozens of airport rallies and rubber chicken dinners with only minor variations—of the Vice-President. It belted Harry Truman for the "mess in Washington 'that's what we called it: a mess'" and the "blueprint for socializing America" that the new Republican administration had allegedly discoverd "in the files" when it took office. Bassett suggested that perhaps my idea and some of this political content could be worked together to make a successful speech. "But don't forget," he added, "Eisenhower is not an intellectual. He's a real down-to-earth guy."

Still optimistic in my newness, I phoned to Harlow Bassett's reaction, suggesting I might take a whack at putting the two approaches together. Meanwhile, however, I feel certain Harlow had heard directly from Bassett himself that I had missed the mark a mile and that the speech should come out as a roistering political attack, a reaction that of course squared totally with Harlow's own inclination from the beginning. So Harlow took over the concoction of the next draft himself.

(One sidelight: After journeying with the Vice-President around the country that year, Bassett served as a confidant to Nixon and an outstanding member of the staff of the Republican National Committee. I last saw him during the Nixon campaign in 1960. Years later, after Nixon became President, Bassett flew in from California to spend a week in Washington. He sent word to the White House that he'd like to drop by for a minute to say hello to the President. In those latter days of H. R. Haldeman and John Ehrlichman and their minions, he never got a phone call back.)

And Harlow knew where he was going. Harry Truman on September 17 would declare: "It seems to me that President Eisenhower should be secretly wishing for a Democratic Congress... and hope that we can save him from the misdeeds of his own party." Even Cabot Lodge was arguing that Eisenhower would do better with a Democratic majority. Harlow now set out to defeat that kind of wrongheaded thinking.

He turned out a ringing pro-Republican slasheroo—a speech that went crashing forward, extolling all the miracles the Republican 83rd Congress had performed for the people, predicting how much more of the same the party stalwarts could accomplish in the next two years, and stomping all over the Democrats. And Ike concurred. By the time his plane took off for Hollywood, he had agreed to everything but one. And now, Jack Martin purposefully approached.

"Mr. President," Martin haltingly began, "I'll leave the door open so that you can throw me out."

Eisenhower misunderstood: "That's okay, Jack, shut the door if you want."

"What I mean, Mr. President," Martin went on, "is that we think the speech ought to include an outright call for the election of a Republican Congress."

Eisenhower harrumphed, looked at the penciled-in wording: "These are the reasons—the compelling reasons—why the completion of your great program requires the election of a Republican-led Congress."

"Well," he snorted, "if you want it in there, here's where it should go, not where you have suggested it." So in it went. And after dozens of other cheer lines that night, it brought down the house.

Eisenhower's inhibitions vanished. By October 15 the President was heading to Indianapolis to deliver another blockbuster, this time on the great works wrought by the Republican Congress for the farmer. Work on the speech had included many hours of long meetings, with White House staffers and agricultural authorities sitting around the conference table, each with a draft before him. Earl Butz, then an Assistant Secretary of Agriculture, would occasionally get off a raunchy joke; but otherwise seriousness, indeed solemnity, prevailed. An early draft complimented our farmers on the hard hours they put in: "When the cows are calving, you don't get much sleep." I can still hear Gabe Hauge intoning those words in the voice, Bob Kieve recalled, "of a Lutheran minister." The experts nodded their assent. Not until Harlow's secretary, Mary Nichols, who had grown up on a farm, pointed out that cows have calves without bothering the farmer at all, did the agricultural wizards shamefacedly admit that yes, come to think of it, farmers do sleep through the process.

Five days later, in the ballroom of the Sheraton Astor Hotel in New York, Eisenhower addressed a totally different audience, at the American Jewish Tercentenary Dinner. Given, as always, Arab-Israeli disquiet in the Middle East, the speech focused on foreign policy. It started out with a draft written by Robert Bowie, head of the State Department's Policy Planning Staff. It then had the attentions of all the White House wordsmiths—Harlow, Cutler, Morgan, Martin, Kieve, and me—plus Solicitor General Simon Sobeloff as guest artist, to turn it from essay into speech.

It had one key point: that the United States wanted the friendship of both sides, Israel and Arabs. So we put all the Jewish writers—Sobeloff, Martin, and Kieve—into the Cabinet Room, put all the non-Jews—Harlow, Morgan, Cutler, and me—into the Fish Room; and thus produced a Jewish module and an Arab module. In those days the White House Mess served only luncheon. So at about eight o'clock that evening, after we'd all been working for hours, the door to the Fish Room opened, and in walked Jack Martin: "When are you Arabs going to feed us Jews?"

With that bit of comedy, we all walked down the street to the Occidental for dinner before returning to the White House to work, literally, the rest of the night. Recognizing Harlow as the key architect, at about 1:00 A.M. the rest of us suggested he take a nap while we worked on. So he stretched out on an old beat-up leather couch in his office. At about 4:00 Jerry Morgan came in, shook him awake, and handed him our latest draft, just typed by an all-night typing pool in the basement of the Executive Office Building.

(None of us, I know, will ever forget night walks from the East Wing down through the moonlit corridor which joined it to the mansion, across through the basement of the presidential dwelling place, past late-hour guards, into the West Wing, and then, if necessary, across West Executive Avenue into the basement of the Executive Office Building, where the round-the-clock typists waited. The thrill of it all kept one wide awake, though I remember reading at the time a squib about a man in England who claimed that he hadn't gone to sleep in ten years: "The White House," I thought to myself, "should snap him up.")

I still recall Harlow's words as we watched the sun eventually lighten Washington, though he was so bleary-eyed that I question whether he could actually have read the draft: "This is a splendid document."

At eight o'clock in the morning he carried it into the Oval Office to go over it with the President. Revisions continued there for another two days.

Eisenhower on October 8 had warned that a Democratic victory would precipitate "a cold war of partisan politics between the Congress and the Executive Branch." Now on October 28, as the campaign climaxed, he expatiated on this admonition to a Washington rally: "Legislative Leaders can stop essential bills in the Legislative Committees, in the Rules Committee, or kill them in the Senate or House of Representatives. . . . For political reasons, they can bottle up program after program to keep the President from doing something no matter how much the people may want it. . . .

"We won't get anywhere with red lights at all the governmental crossroads. Add to this, two drivers at every governmental steering wheel, each trying to go in a different direction, and we shall certainly end up in a hopeless traffic jam."

Harlow was barreling down the turnpike. But inwardly Eisenhower was not. He didn't like partisanship, he didn't like negativism, and despite his willingness to do this political job for his party's advantage and the good of legislation he wanted passed, it rankled.

At one moment in midcampaign he had called on Kevin McCann, still intermittently resident in Defiance, for a draft of a eulogy to Al Smith, for the Smith Memorial Dinner in New York.

The result, after Ike's always extensive editing, was a sand-wich: McCann music on the outside, Harlow meat in the middle. "He [Al Smith] accepted his defeats calmly," McCann began, "for he knew that if he were right, time would vindicate him and truth would prevail.... In every task he was impelled by a fiery faith in the decency and dignity of men and in the purposes of America. So impelled, he labored well.... Monuments of timber and stone and metal have recorded human accomplishment through the years.... To only a few, however, in all the years of the Republic has there been paid the highest of all awards: a public resolve that the causes which they espoused shall not be permitted to die with them....

"Since the beginning of time men have deluded themselves—or have been deluded by other men—with fantasies of life free from labor or pain or sacrifice, of limitless reward that requires no risk, of pleasure untainted by suffering. From such dreams, the awakening has always been rude and the penalty a nightmare of disillusion-ment....

"Among the fruits enjoyed by those who live under the fundamental concepts and principles that define our system are an abundance in all that makes a good life, unparalleled in the entire history of tribes and nations and empires...."

From these ringing generalities, past participles, and triplets ("timber and stone and metal," and "tribes and nations and empires") the speech plunged into some Harlow specifics: on health, and what the Republican-led 83rd Congress had been doing to improve it.

"Newly passed by Congress is a three-year 180 million dollar program to build diagnostic and treatment centers, hospitals for the chronically ill and impaired, nursing homes and rehabilitation facili-ties....

"Newly passed legislation provides more generous tax treat-ment of some 8½ million individuals and families with heavy medical, dental, or hospital bills...."

Though this section, Harlow invidiously remarked later, may not have had the most eloquence, it produced all the headlines. But Ike didn't want gutsiness; he wanted *Aufschwung*.

On the day before Halloween Eisenhower took on one final chore. In a chain phone drive around the country to get out the vote, he called ten staunch Republicans, asking each of them to call ten more—a gimmick intended to flood the polls. The first ten staunch Republicans Eisenhower called had, of course, been screened far more carefully than one would screen a prospective wife—all but one man. When Eisenhower placed the call to him, it turned out the phone company had yanked his phone because he hadn't paid his bill. Then the miraculous White House switchboard called one of his neighbors to say the President wanted to talk to Mr. X. He was, the neighbor reported, on a bus going downtown. State troopers were alerted, and the bus was chased and flagged to the curb. The troopers mounted the steps, called out the man's name, and informed him that the President of the United States was on the phone, waiting. The driver and all the passengers thought the troopers were crazy. But the man finally agreed to go into a nearby drugstore and talk to the White House.

The campaign had reached its finish. Eisenhower had traveled thousands of miles to help Republican candidates. And when Republican Chairman Leonard Hall finally revealed to him his carefully guarded secret—that no other President in history had ever gone to such lengths for his party—Eisenhower roared with laughter.

But he was tired. Between August 12 and November 1, he had made nearly 40 speeches. And by the time he finished his election eve broadcast, urging one and all to vote, fatigue and partisanship turned into anger: "By golly," he burst out audibly as he left the mike, "sometimes you sure get tired of all this clackety-clack."

Harlow, as architect of nearly every one of those forty speeches, felt the full fury and full ingratitude of the blast: "I don't see how you write a goddamned thing," the President exploded at him at last, "with so many people telling you what to do." Thrashing about, he descended on the conscientious staffing of drafts. "I used to write speeches for MacArthur out in the Philippines. And one thing I know: if you put ten people to work on a speech, they'll kill anything in it that has any character. Now the next time you write something that has any character, you bring it right in here. Don't you show it to anybody."

DIVIDED PARTISAN

Those testy words—contrasting so sharply with the common view of Eisenhower's reliance on a bland and structured staff (and with his own high esteem for Bryce)—came and went in Eisenhower's mind. But they stung Harlow to the quick. And for the next two years, until the political exigencies of 1956, McCann, who now moved from Defiance into the East Wing full-time, would produce, with focused dictation and incisive fountain pen, soaring flights of idealism.

It didn't matter that in the 1954 election the Republicans lost control of Senate and House by such narrow margins that the Vice-President could call the result a "dead heat." Ike was weary—weary with talk, weary with partisanship, weary for the moment with the devoted, brilliant, and selfless man who more than anyone, in his 5'4" frame, embodied the vital political process. In that particular season, between Dwight Eisenhower and Bryce Harlow, as between Socrates and Alcibiades, there never could be total peace.

X

OCTOBER 29, 1954

DEVOTED INTELLECTUALS

T he white-haired craggy-visaged guest stared into empty space and asked a question, to no one in particular: "What is the saddest word in the world?"

It was noon on Friday, October 29, 1954. Suddenly in midmorning a dozen younger staff members had had a request from Governor Adams to join him and Robert Frost in the Conference Room for lunch. We finished the tomato juice. The white-coated Filipino mess stewards came around with lobster. Everybody had some. Immediately the stewards came around again, this time with the other Friday option, roast beef. Once again, the entire table, ill at ease, had a helping of that, too.

The conversation turned to staff work. "Why," Frost asked, "should anyone have his writing done for him?" Someone volunteered a bit nervously that the world had become so large that no one man could do all his writing for himself. "When the world becomes that large," Frost mused, in a magnificent galactic allusion, "perhaps it's time to break up into smaller worlds."

It was then that he began to speculate on the saddest of all words. Several people volunteered candidates. Naval Aide Ned Beach: submarine skipper and author, suggested "forlorn." "But then," Ned added, "someone else could top that with 'forlorner.'"

Frost chuckled, then said in a slow and quiet voice, "The saddest word *I* know is 'betrayal.'" I caught my breath.

This arresting incident forms a tiny *tessera* in a pattern: a pattern of varied intellectual forces at work, often, like Frost's visit, out of view—*feux d'artifice*, restless tendencies toward lift, difference, éclat, color, innovation, esprit, within the Eisenhower administration; forces prompted by subordinates to the President who merit the loose label "intellectual" by virtue of scholarly training and knowledge; or a refined and unquenchable love of the beautiful in the arts; or a demonstrated and sustained literary or artistic capability; or an urge toward the constant exploration of abstract questions as a guide to action and innovation in government. In these characteristics they stood somewhat apart from Eisenhower himself; but they loyally devoted themselves to his service. And in a strange and unique fashion no one typifies these men with more poignancy than the one who, almost surreptitiously, brought Frost into the White House that late October day, his old New Hampshire friend Sherman Adams.

Four years later, in the autumn of 1958 Adams, Eisenhower's Chief of Staff, left Washington in disgrace; returned to beautiful impoverished Lincoln, New Hampshire, to write a book and eventually run a ski resort at nearby Loon Mountain; and disappeared from the Washington stage, where he had starred for six years as one of the most powerful men on earth.

I did not see him again for fourteen years, until March 26, 1972, when I drove through the snow to his mountain, with my wife and skiing son, to interview him. Indeed, few of our White House friends had seen him. He avoided reporters. He appeared only occasionally on a college campus. He remained an object of pity and a memory of granite brusqueness.

Dour, slight of build, curt, a frugal Yankee woodsman who drove his own green convertible to work at the White House and wore unaltered a sports jacket purchased as a Dartmouth undergraduate thirty-five years before, Adams came across in his Washington days as a Great Flint Face, ice water in every vein.

"Incorruptible, all square corners," Kevin McCann described him. With Adams, probity and efficiency became indistinguishable from artfully ingenious rudeness. Adams' good friend Republican National Chairman Meade Alcorn, for example, once came to chat with him about a red-hot new idea. He finished. Adams: "Anything else, Meade?"

"No."

"Then why don't you get out?"

Another time Senator John Sherman Cooper of Kentucky

went to ask Adams to let him name a new federal appointee—naturally a Kentuckian.

"We'll make that appointment," Adams cut him off, wheeling in his chair, turning his back on the loyal Republican lawmaker.

Midway in a conversation with Secretary of the Navy Charles Thomas, Adams hung up; unlike many others before him, Thomas got into his car, crossed the Potomac to the White House, entered Adams' office, and took up where the talk had broken off. "You know," Ike told one Gettysburg visitor with a chuckle, "he hung up on me once."

Few questioned Adams' abilities—presidential, some thought, in quality. But through his rudeness he was accumulating enemies, enemies who, when he later got into trouble, would let him sink.

I had always thought of Sherman Adams as one of the splendors of the Eisenhower years. I had come to know him as a man who never offended a younger member of the White House Staff; I saw that he, behind the rough exterior, harbored within a quiet sense of humor and a secret passionate love of the music of Chopin and Mozart.

And never had I felt such nostalgia and such outrage as on that splendid Sunday morning in 1972 when (as his lovely wife, Rachel, with gray hair, ankle-length racoon coat, and sparkling eyes, made maple-sugar-on-snow for the skiers) the governor and I talked in his ski-resort office, with his Ford pickup truck parked outside, the brightly clad boys and girls flashing by on skis outside the window, the fluffy snow gusting through the late winter sunshine. "That's what the New Hampshire farmers call sugar snow," the governor said, in his red lumberjack sport shirt, puffing on his pipe. "This is a beautiful day, a beautiful late winter day."

In the years since that Sunday the nostalgia and outrage have, if anything, intensified—nostalgia for the Eisenhower era; outrage over the intervening Kennedy-Johnson-Nixon years, with their crimes and deceptions that made Sherman Adams' offense—the imprudent acceptance of a rug and a coat as gifts—seem like double parking. The national interest demanded that Adams leave, but the going-out was also a tragedy.

And that Sunday morning, something else struck me as never before: Sherman Adams' generous convictions and restless liberal drive; his thoughtful, informed appraisals of men and issues and events in the seventies, including the unwisdom of revenue sharing, the massive Washington power of the oil industry, and the likability and political maneuvering of Nelson Rockefeller; his dissatisfactions with his old associates in Washington. He was a man still reading, still learning, still searching in his mind for an elusive end—for an understanding of the art of government. He spoke no boiler plate, even about Eisenhower ("What's the most important qualification for a president? That in making a decision he understand his own prejudices," he told me). And as he talked he brought to my mind the perceptive observation of one of his conservative White House colleagues: "The governor was a hell of a liberal inhibition on the President."

To be sure, Adams worked rigidly within the confines of his responsibility, always, as a selfless alter ego of the President. And the opening of his inner mind could at times surprise even close colleagues. After a particularly candid session on Dulles, Wilson, Bedell Smith, and others, C. D. Jackson noted that Adams revealed "far greater perception and knowledge than [his] consistent stone face would lead [one] to believe."

Within his confines during his years in Washington, and now with outspoken candor, Adams did tug. He tugged first against the administration's men of wrongheaded ideas. The Commerce Department, he told Bern Shanley, was "living in the dark ages" on reform of the Taft-Hartley labor law. And Agriculture, he said to me, was headed by an "archregressive iconoclast," Secretary Ezra Taft Benson, a man absolutely uncompromising on farm policy, particularly on the need to reduce the high, rigid price supports of the Truman days. With a touch of wry irony, Adams defended Benson against the charge, made by a knowledgeable White House staffer, that the Mormon Secretary was an operator who could sit in a meeting at the White House, discuss policy, hear the President's decision, and then go back to his department and stimulate lobbying against it. "Benson wasn't underhanded," Adams maintained. "He was just imposing his superior judgment on the decisions of the administration. After all, he had divine guidance. If God had told Benson it was better for the human race to struggle than to enjoy, was it underhanded of him to act on that belief?" (As we had worked on *Mandate for Change*, Eisenhower too had rejected the interpretation of Benson as a schemer, with some testiness: "People may think he was a goddamn fool, but he was a man of integrity.")

Adams tugged also against the administration's men of exhausted ideas, notably, in his view, John Foster Dulles, that "self-centered autocrat" whose conduct of foreign policy was a constant engagement in the suppression of brush fires, not silviculture; who lacked the innovative capacity of a Henry Kissinger opening up China; who could think of nothing but stockpiling nuclear weapons and living in stalemate. "But," Adams reflected at last, "when would you have replaced Dulles and with whom? I don't know the answer."

Finally Adams tugged against a man of no ideas like Douglas McKay, Secretary of the Interior—a department that McKay's successor, Fred Seaton, always believed Adams wanted for himself; a department in which McKay, a former governor of Oregon, seemed always to find himself just one step ahead of the natural resources posse, which was after him for awarding mining claims to the wrong people or letting the oil companies drill on wildlife lands, or "selling" out to the private power companies. "McKay," one of his assistants told me, "was scared to death of Sherman Adams."

When he took over in 1956, Seaton restaffed Interior at the top; gave respectability to federal-nonfederal "partnership" to provide electric power; pacified the conservationists; set aside huge new reserves for birds and animals; got the oil rigs away from the moose; pushed Mission 66—a ten-year program to refurbish the National Parks; forwarded experimentation on making seawater drinkable; and won the praise of ex-President Harry Truman's speechwriter, Bill Hillman, as "the best damned Secretary of the Interior in twenty years."

Yet even Seaton, Adams' admirer and always loyal friend, fell short of Adams' expectations. "The Department of the Interior, while we were down there, got into detailish questions which it failed to counterbalance with foresight." Seaton, Adams felt, should have had his underlings keep the chaff out of the hay in order to free himself to tend the cattle. Republicans, to Adams, were okay on defense or economics but just no good at departments demanding imagination, like Interior or HEW. In these departments, "you can't just stand still and manage what you have."

In another example of tugging liberalism, Adams in 1955 unilaterally took the wraps off some of the secret history of Ike's first term. At his direction Assistant Staff Secretary Arthur Minnich opened his files (principally minutes of Cabinet and Legislative Leaders meetings) to a skilled New York *Herald Tribune* reporter, Bob Donovan, who therewith wrote his *Eisenhower: The Inside Story*.

The book did lift the rock on many activities within the administration and, in fact, presented Cabinet officers and White House Staff members, who too frequently had appeared cardboard figures in their guarded speech and self-righteousness, as human beings. The book did much to confirm the warmth of feeling and trust that the man on the street felt for his President. For it had the ring of an honest reporting job—Donovan was no puffster—about an honest administration that, as its first term ended, had much to be proud of.

Eisenhower, however, knew nothing of Donovan or the keys to the cupboard that Minnich had given him. And when he found out, in March 1956, he hit the roof. In a long memorandum sent to Bill Robinson he threw out one sharp question after another. Did Donovan get advantages denied to other reporters? Did he violate security? Did he reveal confidential advice and counsel? Only a man of Adams' asbestos toughness could have stood the blue flame of Ike's anger. And only a man of Adams' liberal restlessness could have made, and defended, the decision that ignited it.

Finally, Adams' restlessness of mind showed in his love of the beautiful in the arts. I have talked with him about performances of the Mozart *Requiem* and the Bach B Minor Mass, which, even in recollection, moved him so much that he could hardly speak about them coherently. He never told this love. It was not surprising that at his invitation Robert Frost should visit the White House and muse on the saddest of words. And it was not surprising that years later such a man could look back on the administration he so selflessly served and believe it fell short of a dream.

Within the administration, Adams was by no means alone. The presidential staff included others of various intellectual drives and lights. Emmet Hughes, Princeton *summa*, Columbia graduate student in history turned philosophical journalist turned Rutgers professor of politics, has eloquently chronicled his own tuggings—and suggested Adams'—against his colleagues in government. Staff Secretary Andrew Goodpaster, a Princeton Ph.D. in international relations (whose assistant, Arthur Minnich, had a history doctorate from Cornell), would go on to become Supreme Allied Commander in Europe and eventually superintendent of West Point. Professor Malcolm Moos of Johns Hopkins, Eisenhower's last assistant on speeches, would become president of the University of Minnesota. James R. Killian, MIT president, and Dr. George Kistiakowsky, Harvard professor of chemistry, served as Eisenhower's science advisers (another man of

Harvard, its former president, James Bryant Conant, was—over McCarthy's objection—Eisenhower's first ambassador to Germany).

Before joining Eisenhower's White House Staff, Arthur Larson had been a professor of law at Cornell and dean of the University of Pittsburgh Law School; Philip Young, dean of Columbia's Business School; W. Allen Wallis, professor of statistics and economics and dean of the Business School at the University of Chicago; Karl Harr, a Rhodes scholar with a law degree from Yale and a D.Phil. from Oxford. And after leaving Eisenhower's staff, two brilliant younger members, Stephen Hess and Phillip Areeda, would go on to notable careers, Hess as a prolific author on politics and history, Areeda as professor of law at Harvard and a supreme antitrust authority. Robert Montgomery, one of America's most luminous names in film, theater, and broadcasting, served as television adviser.

Foreign trade adviser Clarence Randall, who, unaided by ghosts, wrote a stream of books and articles that amazed his fellow steel executives and delighted readers with their flair and articulateness, had, before World War I, sat in a Harvard English A class that received only two A's from Dean Briggs—one to Randall, one to Frederick Lewis Allen of *Harper's*. And on April 24, 1955, the *Washington Star* carried an article on still more White House staff authors: Commander Edward L. Beach, who had just produced a best-selling novel about submarine warfare called *Run Silent, Run Deep*, later made into a film starring Clark Gable and Burt Lancaster; Kevin McCann, author of the Eisenhower biography *Man from Abilene*; Bostonian Robert Cutler, author of two just-out-of-Harvard youthful novels, *Louisburg Square* and *The Speckled Bird*; Dillon Anderson, who succeeded Cutler as the President's special assistant for National Security Affairs, and who in his spare time wrote short stories for the *Atlantic*; Murray Snyder, a former political journalist. The article also cited two books of mine—one on Jonathan Swift, one on eighteenth-century English journalism.

Then of course there were the economists: Gabriel Hauge, Eisenhower's economics special assistant, a Harvard Ph.D. who had taught at Harvard and Princeton, followed in 1958 by Dr. Don Paarlberg, professor of Agricultural Economics at Purdue; and the successive Chairmen of Eisenhower's Council of Economic Advisers, Professor Arthur Burns of Columbia, and Professor Raymond J. Saulnier of Columbia's Barnard. Like Burns, Hauge had the affection and the ear of the President as an initial advocate of rectitude, wisdom, and force for modern Republicanism—a no-nonsense economic policy of compassion and lift. "The American people," Hauge wrote Ike in 1953, "will not sit content with sound money and a balanced budget; they are a doing people, a building people." And Burns' years as chairman—"a magician," Sherman Adams called him— saw the post-Korean prosperity of 1955–56.

After the recession of 1953–54, unemployment fell. Except for a few years in the twenties and immediately after World War II, it reached the lowest peacetime percentage since 1907. Production soared. The GNP, running at a $359 billion annual rate in the third quarter of 1954, took off, climbing successively through the next quarters until in the fourth quarter of 1956 it topped $420 billion. Between 1952 and 1956 real personal income went up 20 percent. People were investing more than ever. The middle class was growing. We produced so much food we couldn't eat it all. Even Americans on a modest budget could travel the world around and find people everywhere eager to trade: the dollar was as good as gold.

We were a can-do country. By 1956 Congress had enacted what Teddy White in 1961 saw as perhaps Ike's most lasting achievement in office, the giant Interstate Highway System linking all our major cities. Gas was cheap, so were cars, and we became a nation on wheels. New inventions were changing the way we thought and lived—the jet plane, peaceful nuclear power, the Salk vaccine, the electronic computer. Environmental problems and scarcity of resources were problems of the future, and it was thought that future technology would be around to cope with anything. Marilyn Monroe and Doris Day smiled from the silver screen. Eisenhower's favorite drama was Gary Cooper in *High Noon* (his favorite comedy, somewhat later, was *Operation Petticoat*.) Maria Callas sang at the Metropolitan, and Elvis Presley rocked everywhere. The government was dull and sober, and the citizens had all the fun.

Of course, economist John Kenneth Galbraith didn't like affluence. He thought private abundance was bad for people, keeping them from nobler things: money should be transferred to the public sector, where the bureaucrats could have a whack at it. But he typified a minority (as Bismarck reportedly remarked, if you want to punish a nation, let it be ruled by "philosophers").

By October 14, 1955, at the Commonwealth Club in San

Francisco, Hauge could laud Eisenhower's economic conservatism and reveal its formula for success: preserving free markets, private initiative, and incentives; discarding controls, price-fixing, rationing; preserving the integrity of the dollar; cutting the human costs of economic freedom through unemployment insurance, Social Security, public housing, collective bargaining. By campaign time of 1956, Republican orators were quoting George Meany himself: "American labor has never had it so good"; and declaring happily that "everything is booming but the guns."

To be sure, things were not perfect. Black Americans still suffered—a continuing national disgrace. And even as the country prospered, Arthur Burns—and Ike—urged measures to attack the hardships of the 1½ million farm families with annual incomes under $1,000, and of the people in areas, like the Pennsylvania coal fields and New England mill towns, with chronic unemployment. Burns and Eisenhower also focused with care on the threat of inflation. Between January 1955 and November 1956 the consumer price index rose from 114.3 to 117.8—nothing like the Truman years' roaring climb from 76.9 in 1945 to 113.5 in 1952, not to mention the Nixon-Ford-Carter double-digit nightmare, but something to watch, nonetheless.

But despite blemishes on the record, we were indeed moving toward Galbraith—moving away from the old fear of economic failure, born of 1929; moving toward the affluent society—toward the years of our lives in which, as Theodore White says, "the American people were never happier, or, at the least, never more convinced of the opportunity to be happy."

Looking back on the economic brightness of those years, Arthur Burns, in an encompassing metaphor, would always recall the first time he ever saw Eisenhower: as Columbia's new president passed nearby in his 1948 inaugural procession, a flood of sunlight suddenly burst through the clouds— "Eisenhower weather."

All these Eisenhower men, so varied in their intellectual thrust and color, served their President, a demanding boss, with devotion and enthusiasm. The success of his staff was a product chiefly of three principles:

1. He chose highly trained men to work for him.

2. Though they were of varied backgrounds, he got them to work together as a team.

3. He inspired their loyalty, to him and to his decisions. Eisenhower in mufti retained his commanding aura.

Running a modern state requires many types of intellectual accomplishment: the man on the street obviously cannot manage a nuclear reactor. But making the command decisions—setting the goals and policies of the state—primarily requires common sense. No matter what the technological advance, when the problem is one of simple addition, if a hundred ordinary men in a room reach one sum and even Einstein reaches a different one, it is probable that the hundred men are right. This is the wise foundation of democratic thought, a foundation to which, incidentally, Einstein, with the humility of most really intelligent men, himself firmly adhered. And this democratic reasoning was natural to Ike, who thought of himself as a mere generalist.

Eisenhower, one must conclude, belongs in a somewhat different category from that of the men of mind about him. He did, to be sure, share many of their qualities. He was, without question, a man of keen intelligence—an intelligence I've always thought most apparent in the quickness of the movements of his eyes. A famous photograph taken at the funeral of Speaker Sam Rayburn shows three Presidents seated side by side: Kennedy and Truman bowing their heads in prayer, eyes closed; Eisenhower—as the photographer rustled—jaw tensed, eyes suddenly alert.

Eisenhower could write with unabashed enthusiasm to friends in 1959 about his discovery of Eric Hoffer's *The True Believer*, a book of genuine intellectual brilliance written by that magnificent San Francisco longshoreman self-educated in the public libraries of California. He could surprise his Antioch-educated personal secretary, Ann Whitman, with his citations from Clausewitz and military history, and his special counsel, Bernard Shanley, with his recitation of the stanzas from Gray's "Elegy," which end: "the paths of glory lead but to the grave." He could impress his ever-present staff secretary, Dr. Andrew Goodpaster, with the contrast between his public and private personalities: "In private, he was all business, intent, digesting complex issues with great speed." And Goodpaster never forgot the remark of George Kennan, head of the 1953 Solarium foreign policy study by a team of outstanding experts: "In summarizing the group's conclusions, President Eisenhower showed his intellectual ascendancy over every man in the room."

I always found surprising the out-of-the-way words that would surface effortlessly in Eisenhower conversations: "congeries" for example, and "congenital," as in "congenital liar." And when in a draft on the recession of 1954 I wrote that the Republicans, in conquering that recession, had "exorcised" the specter of 1929, some of the Doubleday editors and John Eisenhower balked at the word, less current in 1962 than now, whereas Dwight Eisenhower knew exactly what it meant and left it in. Robert Burns's phrase "in durance vile" Eisenhower introduced into the book himself. And when one editor, describing a windbag politician, suggested a metaphor of a balloon blowing off steam, Eisenhower testily inscribed in the margin, in his small, incredibly accurate, and swift hand: "Steam has no place in a balloon." (Unfortunately, the same editor—after Ike had signed off on *Mandate for Change*—inserted in the galleys the grammatical gaffe "between my staff and I," right in the middle of the sensitive McCarthy chapter, thus inadvertently offering critics another chance to sneer superciliously at Eisenhower's "West Point English." Eisenhower was dumbfounded to learn of this mistake, one he would never have made himself. His style was sometimes stilted, but his grammar was nearly impeccable.)

But *intelligent* and *intellectual* are two different words: one fits Eisenhower, and one for many reasons doesn't. Gabriel Hauge had a Picasso hanging on his office wall, "but the President," Hauge knew, resignedly, "wouldn't like it." Hauge admired Special Assistant Meyer Kestnbaum's familiarity with Rousseau and urged me to try to leaven Eisenhower's speeches and messages with literary allusions, but to no effect.

Milton Eisenhower, amateur pianist, could play Chopin's E-flat Waltz. And as we worked on the memoirs, he would insist on including the names of outstanding singers and cellists and pianists who had performed at his brother's White House. But the President himself would carry such display only a limited distance; he would never, for the sake of effect, have led a phony cultural revival in the East Room. He himself enjoyed the process of painting; but he didn't have a passion for the fine arts. He enjoyed writing, and he wrote with flair; but he didn't particularly like literature. He loved to sing, in an enthusiastic tenor voice; but he didn't sit still long for classical music. "The folks' tastes," his son, John, once remarked, "are strictly cornball."

Moreover, Eisenhower didn't feel very much at home in professional intellectuals' company. He did have friends from Columbia days whom he invited down to Washington to stag dinners from time to time—notably economist Eli Ginzberg, a leading authority on manpower policy, and physicist Isidor Rabi, Nobel laureate. But Eisenhower would probably have preferred, to Dr. Johnson's famous prescription "let me smile with the wise and feed with the rich," this variant: "let me talk with the rich and dine with the rich." Eisenhower saw a man's financial success as an indicator of his intrinsic interests. He felt comfortable primarily with such tycoons as "Slats Slater," Pete and Charley Jones, and Cliff Roberts—often partners in bridge games. Kevin McCann has noted the physical energy that Eisenhower could put into slapping a card down on the table; and having read through all the White House correspondence in Gettysburg, I can testify to the intellectual effort he also put into the game—letter after letter to Al Gruenther, Bill Robinson, and others outlining bridge problems and his proposed solutions. But the moneymakers formed a largely nonintellectual group. Perhaps Eisenhower's chief reason for liking them came through in some remarks he made at an elegant private party in his honor at the 21 Club in New York. Some time earlier, Pete Jones had died in a plane crash on a flight from New York to California, where he planned to meet the ex-President for a fishing trip to Mexico; he was carrying—no one knows why—$56,000 in cash. At 21, when friends presented him with a leather saddle Pete Jones had owned, Eisenhower commented impromptu: "Some people try to do nice things but just don't have the means. Others have the means but never have the impulse to generosity. But Pete Jones had both." Eisenhower's wealthy friends frequently gave him gifts. He enjoyed these; saw nothing wrong in accepting them; never let this largesse tilt a presidential decision; and genuinely enjoyed relaxation with such men—high achievers like Eisenhower himself.

The restless administration intellectuals did have a brief moment in the sun during the heady summer of 1956. The Republicans, their campaign underway, courted men of thought and art whom, in 1952, and sadly again in 1960, they largely considered off limits. On August 7, 1956, a new Committee from the Arts and Sciences for Eisenhower—CASE for short—announced its intention to corral the "egghead" vote. Helen Hayes, James Phinney Baxter, president of Williams College, Isidor Rabi, sculptor Felix de Weldon, Dr. Detlev Bronk, all signed on. There followed a "nonpolitical" launching of a new international People-to-People Program, which brought the distinguished to Washington in droves to head an array of citizen committees—George Meany for labor, Eugene Ormandy for music, Eugene Carson Blake for religion, William Faulkner for literature, Al Capp for cartoons. Only one saw through the momentary Republican facade, Robert Frost. Invited to head, in Frost's words, "a committee of intellectuals," he declined. "Intellectuals!" he snorted to a friend. "Do they think I've spent my life writing my one book just to throw it into one of their campaigns? . . . an invitation to head a committee, but never an invitation to dinner. . . . Do you know why they don't invite me? They are too honest. They're too decent honest to pretend they are interested in what I am interested in."

He was right. In July 1954, with the Indochina war and the Army-McCarthy hearings still hovering over Washington, Eisenhower exchanged a succession of letters with an opinionated old Army friend, Brigadier General B. G. Chynoweth, Ret'd., with whom, years earlier in Panama, Ike had had some "fine and heated arguments." The exchange flashed like summer lightning—they never corresponded before or afterward—unmatched in good humor and unbuttoned candor.

Nothing illustrates better than this exchange the validity of Frost's magnificent insight into the Eisenhower honesty. And nothing better illustrates both Eisenhower's consanguinity with the intellectuals and his distance from them.

Throughout the letters Chynoweth emerges as a true troglodyte of the far right—a man who favors cutting the executive branch in half, stopping our "good uncle" act toward the United Nations and India, *raising* the voting age, passing the Bricker Amendment, and launching a crusade against the "Marxist" income tax.

Facing this mind-set, Eisenhower in a letter of July 13 argues for the middle way—"the path that marks the way of logic between conflicting arguments advanced by extremists"—contending that, outside "the field of moral values, anything that affects or is proposed for masses of humans is wrong if the position it seeks is at either end of possible argument"—a contention that reveals Eisenhower's strength as a man of day-to-day decision; a man who, listening to right, left, and center, constantly works a gray middle area, trying to bring the greatest number to agreement. "It seems to me," Eisenhower writes, staking out his specific middle ground, "that no great intelligence is required in order to discern the practical necessity of establishing some kind of security for individuals in a specialized and highly industrialized age. . . . We have had experiences of millions of people—

devoted, fine Americans—who have walked the streets unable to find work or any kind of sustenance for themselves and their families.

"On the other hand, for us to push further and further into the socialistic experiment is to deny the validity of all those convictions we have held as to the cumulative power of free citizens, exercising their own initiative, inventiveness and desires to provide better living for themselves and their children. . . ."

A week later, Eisenhower sends Chynoweth a far more discursive letter, bridling at Chynoweth's undefined term "radical Republican": "You call Lincoln a radical, but every bit of reading I have done on his life convinces me that in many ways he was the greatest compromiser and the most astute master of expediency that we have known. Now, of course, this agrees with my definition of 'radical' but from what I can gather from reading your letter, not with yours. I believe that the true radical is the fellow who is standing in the middle and battling both extremes.

"You decry the teachings of Rousseau, and I must say that I share your dislike for the man's writings, although obviously I have not read him as deeply or thoroughly as you have. I waded through his initial essay, called, I think, 'Origin of Inequalities Among Men,' and read also through the six books on 'The Social Contract.'

"To me it is useless to read about Rousseau unless first you read something of his life. He seems to me to be a bundle of contradictions—a sort of frustrated man who was constantly changing professions and localities through fear or similar motive; but who discovered that he had a considerable facility in dealing with abstractions.

"He read a number of ancient philosophers and historians and from this reading began to picture 'the world as it ought to be.'

"While I never thought about it before, it is entirely possible that his writings have had a far greater influence with our so-called 'intelligensia' [sic] than would seem reasonable. By the way, did you ever hear that definition of a member of the intelligensia that runs, 'One who uses more words than necessary to tell more than he knows'[?]. . .

"I find myself in enthusiastic agreement with your rebellion against the reduction of every value, every incentive to the materialistic. If man is only an educated mule, we should eliminate him and turn the earth back to the birds and the fishes and the monkeys.

"But the very fact that a man is a spiritual thing makes it

impossible for any durable governmental system to ignore hordes of people who through no fault of their own suddenly find themselves poverty-stricken, and far from being able to maintain their families at decent levels, cannot even provide sustenance. Mass production has wrought great things in the world, but it has created social problems that cannot be possibly met under ideas that were probably logical and sufficient in 1800.

"What I mean by the 'Middle of the Road' is that course that preserves the greatest possible initiative, freedom and independence of soul and body to the individual, but that does not hesitate to use government to combat cataclysmic economic disasters which can, in some instances, be even more terrible than convulsions of nature."

Few documents in Eisenhower's official writings—and, indeed, few in his private correspondence—reveal as much as this one: his rough-and-ready approach to philosophy, intelligent but untutored; his digression into a wisecrack about the "intelligensia," misspelled twice—by his typist?—and used ungrammatically once (Eisenhower seldom misspelled words, and he was ordinarily a purist on grammar; but he did at times harbor suspicions of people with an advanced education, particularly if coupled with political antipathy to him); his minting of the phrase "educated mule"; his imaginative and specific speculation on turning the earth back to the "birds and the fishes and the monkeys"; and his human sympathy for people caught in cataclysms "even more terrible than convulsions of nature."

Good humor on both sides; crisp, decisive disagreement; evidences of Eisenhower's sympathy with particular conservative tenets; and proof of his capacity to win people even in this extreme group because of their trust in him and the frankness with which he could talk back to them—all run through these warm letters. Eisenhower could charm anyone. And so, in his final letter, after four pages of single-spaced self-typing and table-pounding, Chynoweth concludes: "Now please take the sky off my shoulders! Back to the bush league for me. But even a bush leaguer can pray for you to hit the ball a *mile*, Ike."

One old soldier had written to another. Eisenhower's intelligent, decisive, concerned letters in this exchange do not reveal an intellectual's systematic training, cultivated sensitivity, or innovating contemplative restlessness of mind. But they do reveal why intellectuals—and countless others, of widely varying persuasions—would gladly and obediently follow him as their acknowledged leader. Common sense is uncommon, and in practical affairs it outranks brilliance. One or two men in history, of course, have had both, but Dwight Eisenhower was not one of them, nor for that matter was George Washington.

XI

FEBRUARY 9, 1956

ARCHITECT OF SUCCESSION

O n February 9, 1956, Republican National Chairman Len Hall came, at his own request, to see the President. Eisenhower, still recuperating from his heart attack of five months earlier, had not yet decided to run for reelection. But he was already looking ahead to possible running mates. And that morning, when Ike switched on the tape recorder in Ann Whitman's office, it picked up the most arresting political possibility of his entire presidency: crossing the line, running not with his first-term Vice-President or any other Republican but with a Democrat—specifically, Governor Frank Lausche of Ohio.

Lincoln, Hall pointed out, had run with a Democrat: Andrew Johnson. Putting Lausche on the ticket would, Hall believed, mark a "turning point in history." And at that turning point, Hall and Eisenhower recognized, almost as an afterthought, the hopes of Richard Nixon for a second term as Vice-President would have to come to an end.

In 1952, when Ike's inner circle of advisers, led by Herbert Brownell and Lucius Clay, had selected Nixon as Eisenhower's running mate from a small list (now lost) of men acceptable to the General—including Cabot Lodge and Governor Dan Thornton of Colorado—no one was looking four or eight years ahead, foreseeing the young California senator as the necessary heir apparent to the presidency, any more than such predecessors as Alben Barkley,

Henry Wallace, Cactus Jack Garner, or Charles Curtis. But once in office, Eisenhower kept Nixon better informed (through regular weekly Cabinet and NSC meetings, for example) than any previous Vice-President (compare FDR, who never told Truman about the atomic bomb). Eisenhower gave Nixon assignments of substance (eliminating racial discrimination among federal contractors, journeying in late 1953 on a goodwill mission that included Australia, Pakistan, and India). And he looked to Nixon for tough and distasteful political infighting (answering Stevenson and McCarthy on nationwide TV in the spring of 1954, campaigning coast to coast that fall).

Nixon took on all these jobs and did them to Eisenhower's utter satisfaction. Without question he was both loyal and intelligent, with a mind, one observer noted later, like a computer. In public Eisenhower repeatedly praised him. And in private Ike never wrote a list of possible running mates or successors without including Nixon's name. (In fact, I never heard Eisenhower say a single word against Nixon even in the years 1961–65 as we worked on *Mandate for Change* and *Waging Peace*, years when one and all believed Nixon had forever gone down for the count.)

But Nixon was never at the top. In a secret diary entry of May 14, 1953, Ike lists Nixon ninth among sixteen "somewhat younger" people in his administration without singling him out, as he had Cabot Lodge and Herbert Brownell, for example, for comment on his exceptional qualifications. A distance did divide the two men, President and Vice-President—a distance more significant than the generation gap, twenty-two years, in their ages; a distance perhaps like the one that separated so many Americans from their Vice-President. Again and again one heard the old refrain: I don't know why, but I just don't like him. Sometimes people would try to specify a reason. One White House Staff member, for example, who sat through Cabinet meetings for eight years remarked that in all that time, the characteristic of Nixon that struck him most was Nixon's constant attention to the outside of issues: how would they strike the press, the voters? In this man's view, the Vice-President seldom looked beyond surfaces to substances.

What bothered me most about Nixon was his imagery. Beneath the unctuous evenhandedness and studiedly casual gestures of his nationwide TV answer to Adlai Stevenson's attack on the Republican administration in March 1954, for example, one glimpsed a dark pit of mind as Nixon spoke about traitors in government:

"As a matter of fact I've heard people say, 'After all, they're a bunch of rats. What we ought to do is to go out and shoot 'em.' Well, I'll agree they're a bunch of rats, but just remember this: When you go out to shoot rats, you have to shoot straight, because when you shoot wildly it not only means that the rat will get away more easily, you make it easier on the rat...." From the metaphor of 1954 to the obscene tapes to the saccharine and egocentric farewell of 1974, the trajectory is, in retrospect, unfortunately and in Nixon's phrase, "perfectly clear."

This image of rats illuminated for an instant a black id. Another, from the 1954 fall campaign, illuminated the glib huckster: his image of the Eisenhower administration's having "found in the files a blueprint for socializing America," a "dangerous, well-oiled scheme [that] contained plans for adding 40 billion dollars to the national debt." The words had the ring of specificity: a green metal file cabinet with a drawer containing the wicked blue drawing of some villainous political architect; a $40 billion debt increase; a scheme "well-oiled." Indeed, they recalled Edmund Wilson's comment about Swift's evocation of the chink and feel of gold coins in the fingers. Yet when one looked at the words, the substance vanished. What building? What office? What file? What plan? What architect? The Vice-President of the United States had told us nothing. Like the concoctions of the snake-oil salesman, these words were distortions and betrayals, not clarifications of the truth. In contrast, Eisenhower's platitudes lacked graphic sharpness; but they had the ring of reality, of a mind faithful to fact.

As Nixon hit the congressional campaign trail in 1954 and again in 1958, worried Republicans would come running to Eisenhower to report on the Vice-President's alleged atrocities, and Eisenhower would invariably stand by him. So when we came to writing up the 1954 campaign in *Mandate for Change*, an early draft had Eisenhower once again backing Nixon's oratory all the way. But when that draft went to Milton, it elicited this comment: "I have always felt that Nixon's 1954 campaign speeches were of the Truman type; it took him a long time to have the public regard him as a statesman rather than as a low-type politician. Your praise of him here endorses his 1954 tactics. I hope I am wrong, but I think knowledgeable folks will raise their eyebrows at this." Responding, Dwight Eisenhower scrawled a note to his son, John: "There may be some validity in Milton's comment. The fact is that I've never had the opportunity to read the texts of Nixon's talks. It is possible that their content is something of which I would not approve. Please have Ewald look up. It would be no real loss to the text to eliminate the whole of this story." And on that cue, we did take it out.

In late 1954, fed up with partisan "clackety-clack," Eisenhower was balking at the incipient effort to make him run again. On November 18 Lucius Clay came to see him, and afterwards, Ike vented his rage in a secret memorandum to himself: "A drive to force from me a commitment that I will be a candidate for the Presidency in 1956 has suddenly developed into a full blown camapaign." Clay had come at the question, Ike noted, "circumspectly and even in roundabout fashion, but when he once got on to the real purpose of his visit, he pursued his usual tactics, aimed at overpowering all opposition and settling the matter without further question...."

"I am ready to work for you at whatever sacrifice to myself because I believe in you," Clay told Eisenhower bluntly. "I am not ready to work for anybody else that you can name."

Clay "insisted that he and his friends needed now the assurance that I would not 'pull the rug out from under them.' This is exactly the phrase they used on me in 1951, and I well know how such a foot in the door can be expanded until someone has taken possession of your whole house."

Three weeks later Eisenhower was reiterating to Swede Hazlett his decision, "long ago communicated to you... that the *only* thing that could possibly make me change my mind would be an unforeseen national emergency that might possibly convince me that it was my duty to stay on." By June 4, 1955, Eisenhower was writing Hazlett that he believed his "special duty" had already been "largely fulfilled." And by late summer, when Len Hall came to talk reelection politics at the President's vacation office in Denver's Brown Palace Hotel, he found Ike in no mood to be persuaded.

The phone rang. It rang a second time. "Damn it," Ike exploded, "I suppose I'll have to answer my own phones." The irascibility spilled over onto the subject of a 1956 campaign.

"Damn it, Len, I've given my adult life to my country. I've done enough. I'm not going to run again." Hall left, "shell-shocked."

Then came the September heart attack, followed by months of convalescence and of speculation on such possible successors as Earl Warren (front-runner in a November poll reported in *The New York Times*), Nixon, Dulles, Knowland, Dewey, and Harold Stassen.

Len Hall remarked to Sherman Adams that if Eisenhower didn't run, the contest would boil down to Nixon and Knowland; got Adams' instant reply: "Neither of 'em!"; and glimpsed for the briefest instant, he thought, the governor's hope that lightning might just possibly strike Sherman Adams.

In a series of conversations in December, Eisenhower with characteristic candor explored the outer reaches of possibility with Jim Hagerty:

"*Saturday, December 10....*The President brought up the question of 1956 himself....He said that he was appalled by the lack of qualified candidates on the Democratic side and particularly pointed to Stevenson, Harriman, and Kefauver as men who did not have the competency to run the office of President.

"*Sunday, December 11....*While we [Hagerty and Sherman Adams] were still with the President, he said that he wanted particularly to talk with Governor Dewey about the political situation. Then he grinned and said, 'You know, boys, Tom Dewey has matured over the last few years and he might not be a bad Presidential candidate. He certainly has the ability and if I'm not going to be in the picture, he also represents my way of thinking.'

"Neither Governor Adams nor myself said anything at that time....

"*Monday, December 12....*During the Republican legislative meeting Harriman's name came into the conversation....The President declared that as far as he was concerned, Harriman was.... 'nothing but a Park Avenue Truman.'

"*Tuesday, December 13....*Following the bipartisan meeting Tuesday morning, the President decided to fly to Gettysburg, and I went with him and Jim Rowley [of the Secret Service] in the Aero Commander. As we left the White House and were driving to the airport, the President himself brought up the question of '56.... 'I don't want to run again, but I am not so sure I will not do it. We have developed no one on our side within our political ranks who can be elected or run this country. I am talking about the strictly political men like Knowland. He would be impossible....'

"Once in the air he came back to '56. 'What do you think about my suggestion on Tom Dewey? You're a friend of his. Do you think it would work?'

"I told him that I did not think that it would. I said that

rightly or wrongly Dewey was looked upon by the Midwest Republicans as an easterner who represented all the views of easterners. I said that I thought it would split the party badly and give encouragement to the midwest, determined to defeat Dewey, to rally around someone like Knowland whom they wouldn't really be for....

"The President then said, 'What do you think about Nixon's chances?' I told him that I thought Nixon was a very excellent vice-presidential candidate on the ticket of Eisenhower and Nixon, but that I did not believe that Dick on his own could get the nomination even though the President himself would actively support his candidacy....

"By this time we were nearing Gettysburg....On the ride from the airport... the President pointed out an English rifle cannon that the Confederates used that could shoot four miles with a great deal of accuracy....

" 'Unfortunately for the South,' the President said, 'they... could get only a very few through the Union blockade. If they had been completely equipped with those British guns, the Civil War might have been a different story.'...

"*Wednesday, December 14.*...I arrived at the farmhouse shortly after 9, and the President was alone on the front porch.... 'Now, getting back to 1956,' he said.... 'I've been trying to think of a ticket that could gain widespread support and could be elected. Let me try out this one on you—George Humphrey for President and my brother for Vice-President. Let me tell you why. George is one of the ablest men I know. He is a fine administrator and could rally the conservatives, particularly in the midwest to his support. Now George really isn't a conservative because every time we have an argument along these lines and the facts are presented to him, George usually ends up going along with the liberal point of view or my point of view, which I think is fairly liberal. Now, my brother would lend the Eisenhower name to the ticket and I of course could give my support completely.' I asked the President if he thought George Humphrey could get the nomination. He grinned and said, 'Well, that's the trouble. I don't know. But if he could, I think he could be elected.'...

" 'We have four people that I think are mentally qualified for the Presidency....One is George Humphrey, one is Herb Brownell and the third is Sherman Adams, but I don't think either Herb or

Sherm can get the nomination, but I do think there is a chance for George. I would also like to see Bob Anderson in there, but I don't think he can be built up for the Presidency, maybe Vice President.'"

For weeks Eisenhower's introspection continued. On January 23, 1956, he got off a long letter to Hazlett:

"... ever since the hectic days of the North African campaign, I find that when I have weighty matters on my mind I wake up extremely early, apparently because a rested mind is anxious to begin grappling with knotty questions. Incidentally, I never worry about what I did the day before. Likewise, I spend no time fretting about what enemies or critics have said about me. I have never indulged in useless regrets....

"I am to avoid all situations that tend to bring about such reactions as irritation, frustration, anxiety, fear and, above all, anger. When doctors give me such instructions, I say to them, 'Just what do you think the Presidency is?' Finally, the instruction that I simply have not learned to keep is 'eat slowly.' For some reason I have never been able just to sit leisurely at a table and take my time enjoying food. I am always hungry as a bear when I sit down and I show it. For forty years I have been a trial to Mamie. She has done her best, but she still has made little impression.

"As I have tried to tell so many people, I do not think it is of any great importance just what this job might do to me as an individual. I recognize that men are mortal. Moreover, during the war there were sometimes situations involving decisions compelling temporary and occasionally fairly acute personal danger. I had to become sufficiently objective to realize that great causes, movements and programs not only outlive, but are far more important than the individuals who may be their respective leaders."

Then a theme that repeatedly haunted him: "We well know that when advancing years and diminishing energy begin to take their toll, the last one that ever appreciates such a situation is the victim himself. Consequently, he can slow up operations, impede the work of all his subordinates, and by so doing, actually damage the cause for which he may even think he is giving some years of his life. (And loyal subordinates will not break his heart by telling him of his growing unfitness—they just *try* to make up for it.)"

Finally on the evening of February 28 Eisenhower phoned Lucius Clay in New York: can you come down?

Clay and Mrs. Clay joined the President and Mrs. Eisenhower on the second floor of the mansion. And then, after dinner and before they went in to see a movie, Eisenhower took Clay aside, as he had years before in London. "I've made up my mind. Tomorrow I'm going to announce I'm going to run again."

As the news broke the next morning, no one captured the elation better than Joan Blondell, who sent Eisenhower a one-word wire: "WHEEEEEEEEEEEEEEE!"

Why had he changed his mind? Eisenhower in the memoirs gave a number of reasons. But nothing better describes the tortuous process he had gone through—better reflects his own inner longings, his detachment, his ability to let others help make up his mind—than a letter, hitherto unpublished, he wrote to Hazlett on March 2: "I suppose there are no two people in the world who have more than Mamie and I earnestly wanted, for a number of years, to retire to their home, a home which we did not even have until a year or so ago.

"When I first rallied from my attack of September 24th, I recall that almost my first conscious thought was 'Well, at least this settles one problem for me for good and all.'. . . As I look back, I truly believe that could I have anticipated in early October what later public reaction was going to be, I would have probably issued a short statement to the effect that I would determine as soon as possible whether it was physically possible for me *to finish out this term, but that I would thereafter retire from public life.*

"Having missed the opportunity to do this (and again I say I cannot be so certain that I would have done it), it seemed to me that I had no recourse but patiently to wait the outcome of all the tests the doctors wanted to make on me and gradually come to a decision myself as to whether or not I could stand the pace.

"I wish I could tell you just exactly what finally made me decide as I did, but there was such a vast combination of circumstances and factors that seemed to me to have a bearing on the problem—and at times the positive and negative were delicately balanced—that I cannot say for certain which particular one was decisive.

"*One, and this has been mentioned to no one else, had to do with a guilty feeling on my own part that I had failed to bring forward and establish a logical successor for myself. This failure was of course not intentional. To the contrary, I struggled hard to acquaint the public with the qualities of a very able group of young men; I will not bore you with the repetition of the story I told you many months ago. But the evidence became clear that I had not been able to get any individual to be recognized as a natural or logical candidate for the Presidency* [italics added]...."

Then a poignant passage which, intended for Hazlett's eyes only, shows the genuineness also of Eisenhower's stern sense of duty: "When I consider how many times I have been driven away from personal plans, I sometimes think that I must be a very weak character. I think that one mistake I made was assuming, in 1948, that I had forever destroyed the possibility of a political career for myself. When I finally, in January of '52, acknowledged publicly that I was a Republican, I realized that I had gone a long way from the personal objectives that Mamie and I had laid down for ourselves. Having gotten into the struggle, however, I naturally was not going to take any chances of defeat that I could avoid. I worked hard.

"The next time that I had a defeat of a similar kind was when I allowed myself to be talked out of my purposes of announcing, in my Inaugural Address, that I was a one-term President only. However, all of the people who persuaded me to do so agreed that, at my age, one term was all that should be expected of me, or that I should attempt. My recent decision represents another of the same kind of defeat...."

Personal defeat perhaps, but Ike had decided. Before and after his decision, however, the question of his vice-presidential running mate remained open—a question rich in possibilities, with the future of Richard Nixon only an incidental feature. So on February 9, Ike and Len Hall had found themselves speculating on running Ike with Lausche, Democrat and Catholic, of Ohio.

Ike liked Lausche: he had considered naming him to a high administration post in the summer and fall of 1953. Moreover, the idea of running with Lausche had at least fleetingly crossed Ike's mind before. On January 28, 1955, the Ohio governor came in to see the President and, as Hagerty observed in his diary, "When he told the President that the people of the country, particularly the people of the State of Ohio, supported him, the President was visibly affected.... the President...said to him that he had been reading some stories in the papers to the effect that Lausche might be the Democratic candidate for President. Lausche said that he had heard those rumors too but as far as he was concerned, the President was the best qualified man in America to lead this country through the present difficult situation. The President then said, 'You know, they tried to get me to run as early as 1946. Twice in that year in this very room Truman personally asked me to run on the Democratic ticket for President with himself as the candidate for Vice President. I told him no both times. . . .' Then he laughed and asked Lausche how his golf was. Lausche said he plays a little in Ohio even during cold weather and the President slapped him on the back and said, 'I'll tell you what we'll do, Governor. When I go down to Augusta in April would you come down and play golf with me a few days if I asked you[?]' Lausche said he would be delighted. The President laughed and said, 'Let's do it. We'll confound all the political experts. They'll think we're trying to make up a combination ticket. O.K.?'"

During his recuperation from his heart attack Eisenhower speculated to Hagerty on Lausche's attractiveness as a possible Democratic presidential nominee.

"Look, Jim, Lausche would be a natural. In 1952 many Democrats voted for me because they didn't like Stevenson and the Truman Fair Deal-New Deal boys. Furthermore, despite all we have done in four years, I'm the only Republican that the young folks will support. With me out of the picture, they will support a Democrat. Lausche would appeal to the youth, and hundreds of thousands of Democrats who left their party to vote for me would go back to their party, I am convinced, to vote for Lausche."

So when Hall expatiated on an Ike-Lausche ticket, Eisenhower was intrigued. Eisenhower reminded Hall that labor hated Lausche.

"Labor leaders don't like *you*," Hall countered, "but the laboring people vote for him and vote for you. . . . [Moreover], the Republicans seldom do something different; here you would break that bugaboo of a Catholic." Even Ohio Republicans, Hall said, told him that Lausche was an able man. If they could work out something of this sort, he remarked, Nixon would become a sort of hero and drop out of the race; a new alignment of parties would result.

"It would just knock the props out of the [opposition]," Ike replied.

A "shocker," Hall agreed.

"I'd love to run with a Catholic," Ike said, "if only to test it out." If the Republicans didn't run a Catholic this time, Hall rejoined, the Democrats would next time. And he specifically mentioned young John Kennedy, an "attractive guy."

It would be the "easiest thing," Hall believed, "to get Nixon out of the picture willingly. The question is whether to build him up some way in doing it. . . . Mr. President, I have known Dick a long time. I think I should go have a talk with him about all this."

"I want you to," Eisenhower replied. In talking with Nixon, the President went on, Hall should ask him what he wanted to do. If the President did not run, he said, Hall should tell him that he would have a wide-open field and the friendship of the President, the knowledge that the President believes in him. But he should look first at what is the best thing for him to do—for himself, and thus for the party.

"I think that at this moment, if I could have my favorite fellow," Eisenhower continued, "my first choice would be Bob Anderson, if this job he has taken [in private industry] hasn't [seemingly] ruined him. Lausche for my money. . . , you could not improve on him. . . he is a great patriot. Here would be a point—could you take a poll of the County Chairmen [and ask them this:] 'A number of people have been suggested for Vice-President. One of [them freqeuently mentioned] is Governor Lausche. Would you like to see [him] nominated for Vice President on the Democratic ticket?"

So here, in a remarkable conversation, was Eisenhower looking backward toward the hope that he had expressed in a memo to himself in April 1953—that he could get all the good people, the enormous majority who agreed with him, into a single political party. This was the Eisenhower who had flown in the face of all his political advisers and made up his mind to campaign in the South in 1952, going after the votes of the conservative majority down there, people who had always admired him and whom he in turn admired, whether they were southern Democrats in the Senate—like Walter George, whom he included on his list of greats at least once—or Democrats-turned-Republican, like Bob Anderson and Jerry Persons. And here were Len Hall and the President together not only predicting the 1960 Democratic nominee—months before he came to national prominence in the Democratic convention of 1956—but actually antedating the famous memorandum of Ted Sorensen and Connecticut State Chairman John Bailey, which outlined how that Catholic nominee would win a national election.

"All right," the President concluded, "you see [Nixon] and talk to him. But be very, very gentle."

Hall did take a poll. Because of its sensitivity, he avoided the well-known opinion samplers and instead went to a detective agency, getting results written out in longhand. And what the poll proved, Hall recalled years later, was that only one name on the ballot counted—Eisenhower's—but that Lausche would run as well as anybody else in the number two spot.

Moreover, Hall—and his second in command, Bob Humphreys—did carry the word to Nixon (Humphreys because, in Hall's words, at that time he was the closest man he knew to Nixon: "they had both been Commie chasers years before"). And what was Nixon's reaction?

"I never saw a scowl come so fast over a man's face. But beyond that, we got no response at all. He was so uptight when he heard the suggestion, he just stared at the ceiling." (As another memorable example of Nixon's oblivious uptightness, Hall recalled a luncheon at the Pavillon in New York. Renowned restaurateur Henri Soulé approached Nixon's table: "You should meet the lady at the next table, Miss Garbo." Nixon to Soulé: "Oh, you're from Chicago.")

In exploring this Nixon-Lausche episode I have had curious reactions from the few people who ever knew about it. Hall tended to play it down. And when we were working on the memoirs, Eisenhower seemed genuinely incredulous. I have no doubt that he had put this extraordinary maneuver out of his mind, though he did mention, on reflection, that he had a high opinion of a number of Catholics who would have made excellent vice-presidential nominees. (He mentioned specifically Connecticut's Judge John A. Danaher, whom he had appointed to the U. S. Court of Appeals; Secretary of Labor Jim Mitchell; and NATO Commander Al Gruenther. He recalled also that he had looked over a list of Catholic Republicans in 1956—I had seen such a list, put together by Fred Seaton, though I doubt Seaton knew why Eisenhower wanted it—and acknowledged he even considered a Democrat.) But like Hall, he seemed to see little significance in the episode.

Not so Bob Humphreys. "Someday," he said mysteriously during one of our conversations as I was working on the book, "I'm going to write up one of the strange things that happened in that 1956 campaign."

I couldn't resist: "You mean the idea of crossing the line?"

Bob blinked: "That's right, crossing the line and getting a *Catholic.* I was the guy who took that suggestion to Nixon."

Humphreys never did write it up. And he never told me anything more about that meeting. But as he thought back on that bit of history, he could see its fire and drama.

Needless to say, Ike didn't cross the line. He didn't put Lausche on the ticket. Indeed, in an irony of politics, he ended up that fall crusading *against* Lausche in Ohio and crusading *for* Lausche's bumptious Republican opponent for the Senate, 100 percent loyal Congressman George Bender, who had led the Taft singing forces at the 1952 convention, who long after Joe McCarthy's downfall could still mindlessly conduct a tipsy Christmas crowd of Republican reactionaries in a bellowing chorus of "McCarthy is my leader, I shall not be moved," and who after his inevitable defeat by Lausche could be seen in his office (a shelter concocted for him in the Department of the Interior), a bottle of bourbon on the desk, discussing with a reporter his planned autobiography entitled *Onward Christian Soldiers.*

The Lausche stratagem came and went. Eisenhower liked the Ohio governor. The possibility of running with a Catholic Democrat momentarily piqued his interest as a political maneuver. But it did not reflect his greatest longing—to select as a vice-president a man who had his wholehearted enthusiasm as a successor to the presidency: a man who could bring stars to Eisenhower's eyes as he himself had brought stars to the eyes of the young in 1952.

Eisenhower was not a man to display such feeling. Back in the summer of 1951 he had written to his close friend Bill Robinson a long letter—the "kind of letter I have never written to any other person"—outlining an Eisenhower regimen for the restoration of Robinson's once "glowing health" (yogurt and black coffee for breakfast, only one pack of cigarettes a day, no drinking except just before dinner, and then only two weak highballs), concluding almost apologetically:

"Anglo-Saxon men usually find it difficult to exchange direct expressions of sentiment and affection. I am as subject to this inhibition as is any other person, but I am not exaggerating when I tell you this letter is dictated only by sheer affection and esteem."

As we worked on the memoirs, I often heard the President mention this reserve. He had seen it in the man he probably admired more than any other in his lifetime, General Marshall. "Marshall," Eisenhower said, "never to my recollection called me 'Ike' except once. And after he realized what he'd done, he caught himself up short and in the next breath called me, almost as if in correction, 'Eisenhower' at least three or four times." I don't believe I ever heard

Eisenhower praise any subordinate directly face to face (except, of course, in a political campaign as part of the ritual). In his writing of *Mandate for Change*, one could detect the warmth and enthusiasm of his words for, say, Al Gruenther or Jim Hagerty. But when he wrote about others, one could feel the tightening, particularly in his mention of Governor Sherman Adams, Interior Secretary Fred Seaton, and other members of his Cabinet and White House Staff. Even his inscriptions on photographs tended to come out terse. To Douglas M. Black, for example, chairman of Doubleday & Company, who with Robinson had worked up the handshake deal to publish *Crusade in Europe* in 1948, a deal that was to make Eisenhower's personal fortune, Eisenhower once inscribed a photo, "whom I proudly label, real friend!" Eisenhower's was not the terseness of a cold heart; he just didn't like fat effusions of sentiment.

To my knowledge, only three men alive in 1956 broke through such reticence and kindled Eisenhower's unqualified affection and enthusiasm as possible presidential successors. The first was his brother Milton: family liberal, career civil servant (from State and Agriculture in the days of Coolidge to Office of War Information with his friend the eminent liberal journalist Elmer Davis), admirer of FDR, president successively of Kansas State, Penn State, and Johns Hopkins, a man kept out of Ike's Cabinet only by his being Ike's brother.

Dwight Eisenhower never wavered in his personal devotion to Milton or in his conviction that he would make a superb President of the United States. (Indeed, in May 1953 he had confided in his secret diary that he believed Milton "the most highly qualified man in the United States to be President. This most emphatically makes no exception of me.") He called on him again and again and again for informal counsel: as personal envoy and adviser on Latin America; as member (with Nelson Rockefeller and Arthur Flemming) of his tiny Advisory Committee on Government Organization; as political consultant, speech doctor, and reader of the memoirs (the only outside person who read the entire text before publication); and as beloved friend. "In all our discussions," Milton recalls, "we disagreed on only two major things—the St. Lawrence Seaway and the wisdom of putting complete faith in Richard Nixon."

During his heart attack convalescence Dwight Eisenhower adverted briefly to the idea of a Milton Eisenhower candidacy for the presidency ("I think," Ike told Jim Hagerty, "my brother ... would run for President, if I wanted him to"; "long before I became President," Ike told Milton himself, "you were my favorite candidate"), as well as for the vice-presidency (on that improbable ticket headed by George Humphrey). But idea died: "I could never have seen myself elected President just because I was Dwight Eisenhower's brother," Milton reflected years later. "I guess we're just different from the Kennedys."

The second man was General Alfred M. Gruenther, Eisenhower's brilliant chief of staff at SHAPE. Al Gruenther, uniquely, had a place in three of Eisenhower's hermetically sealed groups of associates. He belonged among the esteemed public servants—in Ike's own characteristically enthusiastic words in the memoirs, "one of the ablest all-around officers, civilian or military, I have encountered in fifty years." (Contrast his description of Matthew Ridway, whom Truman chose over Gruenther to succeed Ike at SHAPE: "an unusually competent combat commander.") Gruenther had also been one of Eisenhower's personal Army friends, a group so close to Ike that before he was buried in an $80 military coffin, his honorary pallbearers outside the family included only old and close military associates, of whom Gruenther was one. Finally Gruenther was an intimate of "the red-blooded boys from New York"—the tycoons or near-tycoons like Bill Robinson and Slats Slater and Pete and Charley Jones, who knew nothing of military affairs and little of politics and who had in common principally money and a devotion to bridge, of which Gruenther was an internationally esteemed master.

Both as an intellectual companion and as a wit—indeed, clown—Gruenther had a further uniqueness among all Ike's acquaintances. On December 31, 1956, Gruenther retired as Supreme Allied Commander at NATO and came to Washington as president of the American Red Cross. From its ornate white headquarters just a few hundred yards from Ike's Oval Office, he would frequently drop over for cocktails. Many of these visits he would instigate himself by a Gruenthergram—a long piece of cardboard like an IBM card on which he might pen this kind of irreverent note: "The President of the American Red Cross, a splendid organization, invites the President of the United States to join him for cocktails at the White House at four-thirty this afternoon."

Beneath the bantering and horseplay rested uncommon devotion. And it never came through with more poignancy than in the dark days of late 1957, when Eisenhower had suffered a sudden stroke as he prepared to go to Paris for the long-scheduled meeting of the NATO heads of government—a trip that would decide whether he did or did not have the physical capability to remain in the presidency. On December 10 Gruenther wrote Eisenhower a letter "enclosing a few French phrases which I should like to ask—as a very special favor—that you learn before you take off on Friday. Oh yes, I know the objections. You will say: (a) 'I already know them.' (b) 'What business is it of yours?' and (c) 'What will be accomplished?'

"In answer to the first question, I respectfully submit that your French never was that good, not even in your cadet days, and certainly not during the 1951-52 period. Secondly, it is *very much* my business. I have a vital interest in NATO, in France, and I want to see you succeed there because that will help everybody. Thirdly, what will be accomplished? You are working industriously and most commendably, I am glad to say, to pull some tear jerkers from your bag of tricks. I can promise you that you will make a tremendous hit if you can sound off a cheerful '*bon jour*' as you appear for the first time before other members of the press at Orly. ...

"I shall be prepared to give you individual instructions starting tomorrow afternoon at 4:00 o'clock at appropriate moments. I would, however, be grateful to you, if you would study the lesson sheet prior to that time. I would also prefer to have no cracks about my accent...."

Gruenther signed it "your devoted French teacher." Ike, uncharacteristically, sent back an equally bantering reply: "*Cher General*.... I will have ready for you one or two passages of elementary English that I have rendered into French, to see with what facility you can re-translate them into the original text."

Through the jesting on both sides, one feels the anxiety, the veneration, the affection. But Gruenther, like Milton, never took seriously the thought of a presidential or (1960) vice-presidential candidacy, though Ike urged Gruenther, more than once, to consider it. In his modest wisecracking way Gruenther replied: "I just told him it was a lot of baloney."

Eisenhower turned to a third man, of integrity, breadth, studiousness, and intelligence like the first two: Robert B. Anderson of Texas, member of the Texas Legislature, professor of law at the University of Texas Law School, general manager of the W. T. Waggoner Estate (all before thirty), steely-eyed, soft-spoken, mild-mannered, walking with a slight limp, unshakable in purpose. Anderson had entered the Eisenhower administration at age forty-two as Secretary of the Navy.

The association between the two men had begun in January 1951. On the limousine ride from the airport to the White House after Eisenhower's arrival from his tour of the NATO capitals, President Truman began talking about how the Federal Reserve Board was balking at doing what he wanted it to do—constantly purchase enough Treasury bonds to keep their interest rates down. Eisenhower, totally ignorant of all this, continued to wonder about it, and later in his hotel suite, he brought up the subject with his old friend Chief Justice Fred Vinson, formerly Secretary of the Treasury. "If you want to know about that, why don't you ask Bob Anderson, who's here in town?" So Ike's aide Al Gruenther picked up the phone and put in a call. Anderson arrived. And there in the presence of Vinson, Anderson's fifteen-year-old son Dick, and, curiously, the only two men who ever rivaled Anderson in Ike's esteem, Gruenther and Milton, Anderson and Eisenhower talked about bonds and the Fed. And as the Andersons left, the Supreme Commander gave young Dick a crisp salute.

Thus began a financial tutelage that would extend to the end of Eisenhower's White House days. And thus began the association between Eisenhower and the man of whom, a dozen years later in Gettysburg, I heard Eisenhower say, with dead seriousness: "I'd rather have turned the presidency over to him than to anyone else I know."

At the Pentagon, Anderson shone first as Navy Secretary (where he deftly desegregated the Charleston and other southern Navy yards), then as Deputy Secretary of Defense, particularly by contrast with his boss, stocky, white-haired, round-faced Charlie Wilson, who at times could drive Ike wild. The Secretary of Defense ("preposterously opinionated" in Adams' phrase) had views on everything and no hesitation in expressing them (give him a draft of a State of the Union message, for example, and you'd get his comments not on defense but on civil rights or agriculture). He loved to take digressionary "short trips around the world," causing Eisenhower to sit there grinding his teeth. "Damn it, how in hell did a man as shallow as Charlie Wilson ever get to be head of General Motors?" Ike once exploded. Worst of all, Wilson would lateral to his five-star boss Pentagon problems that Ike expected Wilson to solve: "Why does he have to talk to me about things he should be deciding or himself?"

To be sure, Eisenhower admired Wilson's head-knocking and organizational talents; his skill in recruiting future administration stars (including Anderson, Fred Seaton, and eventual Labor Secretary Jim Mitchell); his quips ("I wouldn't give the Ethiopians anything but spears"); and above all his bluff courage: reflecting on confrontations with the Russians at the brink of war, Ike once snorted: "I never thought the Russians were doing anything but bluffing, and neither did Charlie Wilson." Eisenhower valued his Secretary of Defense, but Wilson had blemishes.

Anderson did not. By December 8, 1954, he had taken a commanding lead in the presidential succession sweepstakes: "Bob Anderson of Texas is just about the ablest man I know anywhere," Ike wrote Swede Hazlett. "He would make a splendid President of the United States.... Another fine man is Herbert Hoover, Jr. In addition there are Dick Nixon, Cabot Lodge, Herb Brownell and Charlie Halleck...."

Eight months later, after going to Europe as one of the advocates of Nelson Rockefeller's Open Skies plan at the Geneva Summit, Anderson left the Pentagon to go back into business (an organization called Ventures, Ltd.) to make some money. And from there Eisenhower and Dulles called upon him to undertake one of the most sensitive and secret of all presidential missions—to try to persuade Egypt and Israel into peace in the Middle East. By twenty years he was foreshadowing Kissinger's shuttle diplomacy and the Camp David accords.

Through 1955 the danger signals from the eastern Mediterranean had become ominously insistent. In February the Israelis had mounted a devastating raid on the Egyptian-held Gaza Strip. Egyptian terrorists attacked an Israeli wedding party. Incursions, reprisals, border clashes escalated. In April Nasser journeyed to the Bandung Conference of Asian and African leaders and discovered himself a symbol on the world—and cold war—stage, alongside such giants as Nehru and Chou En-lai. And in September he announced his agreement to barter Egyptian cotton for heavy arms from the Soviet bloc.

On the afternoon of January 11, 1956, Dulles and Anderson came to the White House to plan with Eisenhower Anderson's down-to-earth talks with Nasser and Israel's Prime Minister David Ben-Gurion, talks to avert an arms race, with the U.S. and U.S.S.R. as competitive suppliers. And when Anderson left, though they had not talked politics, the President wrote in his secret diary: "My confidence in him is such that at the moment I feel that nothing could give me greater satisfaction than to believe that next January 20, I could turn over this office to his hands. His capacity is unlimited and his dedication to this country is complete."

The mission, put together in deepest secrecy by Foster Dulles and CIA chief Allen Dulles themselves, was of necessity a cloak-and-dagger enterprise all the way. The preliminaries were conducted through guarded phone calls between the brothers (for example, on "northerners" [Israelis] and "southerners" [Egyptians] and how much they should tell the British and "Hank" [Byroade, the U.S. Ambassador to Cairo]), and through meetings at Foster's home. Traveling was done in disguised ("black") flights by a small plane that shuttled from Cairo to Jerusalem by way of Rome or Athens, and which at least once got caught in a violent storm which, the cabin being unpressurized, drove all occupants to their oxygen masks. Anderson's dictated cables reporting on the progress of the meetings were sent to Foster Dulles through a special channel of the CIA, not the State Department, with no copies; even the code clerks couldn't read them. And the entire mission was anchored by two of the Agency's most capable officers: in Cairo, Kermit Roosevelt, who had masterminded the overthrow of Mossadegh in Iran in 1953; and in Jerusalem, the skilled and controversial James Angleton, both reporting directly to the "case officer," Allen Dulles himself.

Anderson carried in his pocket a letter from a man both Nasser and Ben-Gurion admired, General Dwight Eisenhower, naming him Eisenhower's personal representative, with full authority to speak for the government of the United States. And Anderson had a clear and simple purpose: to persuade Nasser and Ben-Gurion to compose their differences, and to commit to them whatever they wanted in aid from the United States to seal that agreement, as the bedrock of peace throughout the entire Middle East. "Eisenhower," Anderson told me, "just about gave me carte blanche."

Armed with such authority, Anderson left on his initial flight to Cairo, via Athens, of a hopeful mind. The plane touched down. He and his CIA associates drove to a Cairo suburb for a clandestine midnight rendezvous with Nasser and his close confidant Interior Minister Zakaria Mohieddin. (On the periphery of the mission's meetings was Nasser loyalist Hassan el-Tohamy, a living link between the Anderson discussions and those at Camp David two decades later).

Anderson outlined his proposals. Nasser seemed to nod his agreement. Anderson returned to the American Embassy and began dictating a long and buoyant cable reporting success. And then he ran into a stone wall.

Nasser had asked his old friend Kim Roosevelt to remain behind a moment after the others left. "What," the Egyptian President wanted to know, "was Mr. Anderson talking about?" He hadn't understood the Texas accent. He hadn't understood the Texas idiom. He was genuinely puzzled.

"Well, Gamal," Roosevelt replied, not without some self-satisfaction, he having had from the outset little optimism about either this mission—indeed any such mission—or about this particular missionary, "I think he believes he was getting your firm pledge to meet with Ben-Gurion and resolve all your differences."

Nasser was stunned. "I could never do that. I'd be assassinated! Go stop him. Don't let him send that cable!" And on that rock, largely, through the next two months the negotiations foundered.

Anderson had made his entry into the steamy world of Middle East and CIA intrigue—a world of venomous backbiters, ingenious conspirators, and suspicious bureaucrats, where the first job of American intelligence at times seemed to be to find out what the State Department was up to ("penetration begins at home") and prevent it if necessary (by, for example, getting some Egyptian to deny a visa to a high-ranking State functionary who might fly into Cairo and mess things up); where a skilled American agent, Miles Copeland, could get into Egyptian cabinet meetings and even to the regular Thursday night movies at Nasser's house; where Egyptians played endless cute tricks on Americans and Americans on Egyptians ("we'd catch them; they'd catch us"). Anderson knew little of Middle East politics. He had no personal acquaintance with its principal antagonists ("I didn't know these people"). He was starting from scratch, suffering by comparison with more experienced regional negotiators, like Eric Johnston, whom some of the career men professed to prefer.

But whatever his initial limitations in that jungle, he came in—more than one shrewd observer remarked—like a breath of fresh air. Tough and able, as he'd been when running the Navy; scrupulously evenhanded between Arab and Jew; modest in manner; patient in listening to his knowledgeable advisers and in using Roosevelt and Copeland as "interpreters" to help get through to Nasser; gradually winning the respect of both sides; focusing always on the overriding human questions—the food, clothing, and shelter of peace, the tragic toll of war; always searching for a way, never taking no for an answer, Anderson incisive throughout—one observer said at the end—was "Lincolnesque."

He tried everything. To join Egypt and Jordan without forcing Israel to sacrifice its non-negotiable port at Elath, at the southern tip of the Israeli-held Negev, Anderson proposed an east-west Arab corridor across the Negev, with an overpass over the north-south Israeli highway to Elath. The plan met with gleeful derision from Zakaria Mohieddin ("Ha! I can see the Israelis now, down below our elevated highway, shooting up at us!") and even from Nasser himself ("If an Arab on the upper level had to relieve himself and accidentally hit an Israeli, it would mean war! Besides, if you want to construct an east-west Arab corridor, don't put it way down south in the Negev. Put it here." And with a flourish he drew a line farther north, right across the heart of Israel).

To join Egypt and Jordan or Saudi Arabia, Anderson proposed a bridge from the Sinai Penninsula across the Gulf of Aqaba. "We may have to finance a bridge high enough for ships to go under," he told Eisenhower. This plan, too, met with Nasser's rejection—his insistence on Israeli territorial concessions which would permit Egypt to have its own territory in the Negev join that of its Arab neighbors.

To solve the overwhelming problem of the Palestinian refugees, Anderson proposed grants of American money to help them resettle outside the Middle East. The plan not only raised the question of who would accept them, it met with the fanatical opposition of the refugee leaders themselves, who ignored the distended bellies of the children and warned the parents: "We're going to return to our homeland. The first one who accepts resettlement will be shot."

To get Ben-Gurion and Nasser to agreement, Anderson tried two things. First, he offered to serve as intermediary, shuttling back and forth carrying offers and counter-offers, steadily narrowing the differences. The plan met with Nasser's assent ("you serve as mediator, we'll come to terms"). But not Ben-Gurion's: he insisted on sitting across the table from Nasser himself. So Anderson offered to set up a face-to-face meeting between the two in deepest secrecy—on board a U.S. aircraft carrier far out in the Mediterranean. This time Ben-Gurion agreed. Nasser did not. Even there, he feared the fatal news leak that could bring him down.

On this last conflict, above all, the mission failed—failed to avert the war that both sides knew would come. On March 12 Anderson came to the White House with Acting Secretary of State Herbert Hoover, Jr., to report the result to the President. In his secret diary Eisenhower later recorded their conversation. In Israel, he wrote, Anderson had found officials anxious to talk to the Egyptians. But no concessions, they insisted: "Not one inch of ground." Clamoring for arms for their own protection, they knew that they could get them more cheaply from almost any country in Europe. But they wanted them from the U.S., to make us a virtual ally.

On the other side "Nasser proved to be a complete stumbling block," with his dream of becoming political leader of the entire Arab world. He had many fears. He feared the military junta that put him in power, a group extreme in its opposition to Israel. He feared to antagonize the Egyptian people in any way, constantly remembering the fate of deposed King Farouk. He feared public opinion in other Arab countries. The upshot: Nasser believed that he could take not one step toward peace; he could only continue to make speeches—all breathing defiance of Israel.

Eisenhower accepted the failure and its tough implications. More and more he reflected in his diary, Europe was becoming dependent on Arab oil; if that were cut off, European economies would collapse, and the United States would find itself in deepest difficulty. On the other side, Israel—a tiny nation surrounded by enemies—had the recognition of the United States, plus a strong pull on the emotions of the Western World as a result of its people's tragic suffering through 2500 years.

"It is," the President concluded sadly, "a very sorry situation."

The collapse of Anderson's mission did not diminish his stature one millimeter. Indeed, Anderson's performance as a secret international mediator wrestling with this most intractable of diplomatic problems stirred Eisenhower to new heights of enthusiasm and to an unprecedented action. Late one afternoon, as Richard Nixon, urged by Ike to chart his own course, agonized over his future, Eisenhower invited Anderson to the Oval Office with a single-minded purpose: "I want," he said "to talk with you about *your* future." And there, in the course of a memorable conversation, the President definitely and specifically offered Anderson the second spot on the 1956 ticket. "I've observed what you've done. We work well together. As President I have to spend all my time on international affairs; I'd like you, as Vice-President, to spend most of yours with the leaders of the party."

To Anderson the offer did not come as a total surprise. Sometime earlier Sherman Adams had forewarned him of the President's speculation on him as a possible running mate. And with the offer now before him, Anderson understood Eisenhower's purpose at once: "You want me to run in order eventually to succeed you in the presidency." And Ike did not disclaim this intention.

Anderson demurred. He could never, he said, get the nomination. "I'm a political realist," he told Eisenhower. "*You* could win without a long Republican record behind you. But I'm a nominal Democrat. You say you know a lot of people who would back me. But can you tell me that a life-long Republican in Kansas would? He'd ask: How long has this guy been a Republican? He's just walking in and asking for the nomination." Matching political considerations were personal ones: Anderson did not have and never would have a great ambition to become President; and he recognized that without that kind of drive, no one would enter—and ever hope to win—a bruising political battle to the top.

Throughout, Eisenhower said not one word against Nixon. And to Anderson's knowledge, Nixon never knew, during Eisenhower's presidency, of Eisenhower's offer. But with this conversation began an Eisenhower campaign to build up Anderson as a political figure, a campaign that would extend even into Eisenhower's postpresidential years.

As Eisenhower's first term ended, he and Foster Dulles offered Anderson the post of Undersecretary of State—replacing Herbert Hoover, Jr., who was returning to private life—with the understanding that he would eventually succeed Dulles as secretary, and that Dulles might move up to a new super-Cabinet post. Again Anderson declined. "I sometimes regret not accepting the position," Anderson years later recalled. "And I say to myself, 'You can't blame foreign policy makers for things they do wrong; you had a chance to do something about them, and you refused.'" Some months later Eisenhower offered Anderson another Cabinet post, the departing Charlie Wilson's Defense. Anderson turned this down also. Finally Eisenhower made a third offer—Treasury. And this time Anderson accepted. Why? "Ever since I went on the Dallas Fed Board," he told me, "I'd always been interested in our monetary and financial system. If you'd walk down Park Avenue and ask all the heads of the big banks, 'How does a dollar bill come into being? How does it go out of existence?' you'd get the worst jumble of answers. If they can't answer that simple question, how can they understand international financial problems?"

Through the second term Eisenhower drew on Anderson's financial knowledge, in hours-long economic tutorials. He used the Texan relentlessly as an intermediary to Anderson's fellow Texans (and longtime friends) Johnson and Rayburn ("Don't tell me anything you don't want the President to know," Anderson warned them at the outset, "because I'll tell him.") And Ike continued his build-up campaign, touting Anderson to friends, touting him to the media, throwing attractive speaking invitations his way, trying to project the younger man as a close confidant. As the 1960 election approached, Ike not only urged Oveta Hobby to help send Anderson to the Republican convention as a Texas favorite son; he also urged Anderson himself to go after the nomination: "I'll quit what I'm doing, Bob, I'll raise money, I'll make speeches. I'll do *anything* to help. Just tell me I'm at liberty." And after the Kennedy victory, Ike pleaded with Anderson repeatedly to build himself up for 1964.

Thus three times Eisenhower begged Anderson to run: in 1956, 1960, and 1964. And three times Anderson refused. The affection and admiration of the older man for the younger never diminished. In the 1964 campaign Anderson, who just could not stomach the candidacy of Barry Goldwater, became a charter member of a business committee for Johnson and Humphrey. Some of Eisenhower's former subordinates, jealous of Anderson's place in Eisenhower's esteem (to this day he has detractors), now began to gloat. I recall that some of them even asked me—then deep in the Eisenhower papers—to look into the alleged mysterious circumstances surrounding Anderson's original appointment as Secretary of the Navy: Who had recommended him?

At this moment in 1964 Eisenhower himself, of course, was biting the bullet and loyally going down the line for nominee Goldwater, despite his considerable qualms. And in the midst of all this politicking I had to telephone Anderson to check some of our memoirs narrative. Not knowing the President's reaction to his political defection, Anderson inquired cautiously how the President was feeling and then asked me to send him his "very affectionate regards." Not knowing the President's reaction either, I relayed the message; and I shall never forget the instantaneous bright look that came into the President's eyes—even at this moment of political divergence—as he heard this friendly message from the man who, of all men, he always thought most worthy to succeed.

Eisenhower always vigorously maintained that he had urged Richard Nixon in 1956 to take on the management of a major government department—Defense, say—to strengthen himself as a candidate in 1960. He resented Nixon's assertion (in *Six Crises*) that he considered this suggestion an affront ("Hell, I offered him anything in government he wanted"). But seen against the record of Eisenhower's enormous enthusiasm for Anderson, and specifically against Eisenhower's flat offer to make Anderson Vice-President in order to succeed to the presidency, Eisenhower's protestations appear disingenuous.

The carpenter, however, must work with the material at hand. When on March 14, 1956, Eisenhower spiritedly told reporters, "Anyone who attempts to drive a wedge of any kind between Dick Nixon and me has just as much chance as if he tried to drive it between my brother and me," he was, as he said, speaking "the plain unvarnished truth." And when on April 26 Nixon, after weeks of writhing, came to the White House to let Ike know he would be honored to run again, Eisenhower could with honesty tell Jim Hagerty to inform the reporters he was "delighted." Richard Nixon, always acceptable to Eisenhower, was once again accepted, *faute de mieux*.

Years later I told General Lucius Clay that I didn't believe Eisenhower would have been heartbroken if events had replaced Nixon with another. "I don't either," Clay replied. "But he wanted somebody else to do it. And he had no other candidate."

XII

NOVEMBER 7, 1956

"OKAY,
LET'S LOOK
AT THE RECORD"

In early November 1956 Great Britain and France, faced with outraged American condemnation, agreed to a cease-fire after their invasion (concerted with the Israelis) of Gamal Abdel Nasser's Egypt. And on the morning of November 7 British Prime Minister Anthony Eden phoned President Eisenhower to patch up their differences, suggesting that Eden and French Premier Guy Mollet fly to Washington that very day for a friendly talk. Ike, Eden's longtime friend, readily agreed. But Foster Dulles demurred. And Eisenhower had to pick up the phone again, call Eden, and cancel the plan for an immediate conference.

The incident illuminates a recurrent pattern in Eisenhower's presidencey: resistance to the will and thought of the Chief Executive by a lieutenant strong on his assigned turf—resistance foreign or domestic, forward-looking or retrogressive, which at times prevailed, for worse or for better.

If Dwight Eisenhower had, for example, followed his own inclinations instead of Interior Secretary Fred Seaton's, Alaska would never have become a state while Eisenhower occupied the White House. Since 1947, when he had visited Alaska and nearly frozen to death, Ikc had thought statehood for such a territory ridiculous. To him, Alaska was an outpost, a military reservation, with only one city worthy of the name. When Senator Eugene Millikin declared, "I can come around to [statehood for] Hawaii after a lot of mental retching and vomiting but not Alaska," Ike for once agreed with him. "Gene, you reflect my sentiments exactly. This linking of Alaska to Hawaii is just the old Democrat game of promising for years ... a compulsory FEPC. What did they do[?] nothing, not a damn thing."

Eisenhower had gone along with Alaskan statehood reluctantly in the 1952 Republican platform; had threatened to veto it in 1954; had continued to qualify his assent—he didn't want statehood to interfere with national defense—in the campaign of 1956. But in that year Seaton replaced Douglas McKay at Interior. And back in 1952, serving out an unexpired term as senator from Nebraska, Seaton had made Alaska statehood the subject of his maiden speech. So when Eisenhower submitted his 1957 Budget Message, it included for the first time an outright call for admission of the Territory to the Union, along with the usual Republican call for the admission of Hawaii.

The legislative drive began, including—to remove a key Eisenhower objection—a provision for federal defense establishments in north and northwest Alaska, edging the U.S.S.R. But inwardly Ike remained reluctant. As the statehood bill picked up momentum in the summer of 1958, he demanded from Interior some facts and figures. Seaton sent him on June 24 a crisp rundown showing that Alaska general revenue per capita in 1957 exceeded that in thirty-nine of the existing states. And in the margin of the memorandum Eisenhower scribbled in pen impatiently: "I don't believe it—unless we take into consideration Federal expenditures."

Alaska became a state within a month, and Ike signed the bill with fanfare. But as late as 1963, as we worked on *Waging Peace*, he would still cuss about it: "They were nuts to want to start paying their own way."

In one draft on the episode that he dictated himself, he almost said as much. And when we mailed that draft out to Seaton in Nebraska for comment, Fred nearly had a heart attack, got on the phone at once to ask me what had happened to my sense of historical perspective, and inundated me with additional information to turn the chapter around ("don't make the President a reluctant dragon; give him full credit. I didn't disregard his counsel and insist on statehood for Alaska before Hawaii: we wanted to set a trap—get Alaska in, and thus make Hawaiian statehood inevitable—and the President agreed.

Tell how LBJ predicated death for Ike's foreign aid bill in 1957 if I kept pushing Alaska statehood"). As I started working on a corrective revision, Seaton flew East to confer with the President. By the time they met in Gettysburg, he no longer had to use his arguments. Eisenhower had swallowed his opposition and accepted the new draft.

In the history of Alaskan statehood, Fred Seaton, of course, deserves all acclaim for his resistance to the President and for the result. So does his assistant and legislative counsel, now United States senator from Alaska and majority whip, Ted Stevens, who worked night and day on the Hill, at one time provoking Republican Minority Leader Joe Martin, an old foe of statehood, to go straight to the White House to protest Interior's "blitz." On this cause, Fred was a zealot, Ted a fanatic. Without them, Alaskan—and Hawaiian—statehood would not have happened.

But in the end, as in our final draft of *Waging Peace*, the greatest glory must go to Eisenhower. He chose his lieutenants, gave them freedom to think and to innovate, backed them to the hilt despite his qualms, and thus produced an outcome that in retrospect remains a triumph of his administration. They worked in his name; and history will, and should, honor him for what they did.

Another Cabinet officer, Attorney General Herbert Brownell, also had a difference of opinion with the Boss from time to time. And Eisenhower would regularly allow Brownell full freedom to express and pursue his independent judgment.

In the 1952 campaign, for example, Eisenhower had gone to Texas and committed himself to granting outright ownership of the oil-rich offshore submerged lands ("Tidelands") to the states. But in March 1953 Brownell, testifying for the submerged lands bill, urged—with Eisenhower's permission—that it give the states not ownership but only the right to remove the submerged lands' minerals. Moreover, Brownell urged the Congress to amend, and thus possibly jeopardize, the 1952 legislation—which Truman had vetoed and which the oil-state Senators knew Ike would sign—by drawing on a map the states' offshore boundary lines. Eisenhower thus allowed his lieutenant to modify even a campaign promise.

In 1956–57 the differences between Brownell and Eisenhower on civil rights became demonstrably—at times devastatingly—clear. On April 9, 1956, the Attorney General sent the administration's first major civil rights legislative proposals to the Hill. Two headed the list: a new Civil Rights Commission to look into civil rights violations and a new Assistant Attorney General for civil rights in the Justice Department. For each, Brownell sent along draft legislation.

With these two requests came two suggestions (with no draft legislation) for the consideration either of the new commission or of the Congress: a strengthening of legislation to protect the right to vote, and a new authority for the Attorney General to initiate civil actions to protect all civil rights.

Testifying before the House Judiciary Committee, Brownell walked a narrow line. The administration, he said, favored immediate action on the commission and the new assistant attorney general. (These two, and nothing more, would soon appear on Eisenhower's legislative "must list.") Suggestions three and four, Brownell made clear, he was merely serving up for "the consideration of the Congress and of the bipartisan commission." But he did volunteer that he "personally" favored immediate action on them too, and when Republican Ken Keating—who of course knew all about them and about the tug of war between civil rights activists and standpatters within the administration—asked him to have the department draft them up in legislative form, Brownell gladly agreed. And when another congressman, picking on the word "personally," asked Brownell whether he spoke for the administration, Brownell hedged, saying he did, and then taking refuge in his original letter, which urged "consideration" only.

J. W. Anderson, in *Eisenhower, Brownell, and the Congress* (1963), charged Brownell with flagrant insubordination. So did some White House Staff members, muttering once again about the "Department of Just Us." Eisenhower himself did not.

As far as I know, Brownell enjoyed the confidence of the President without interruption from their first meeting in 1952, through two conventions (when he received Eisenhower's list of possible vice-presidential nominees, and appeared himself on one of them), and through Eisenhower's postpresidential years. In fact, in 1963 when Anderson's book appeared, Ike picked up the phone and called Brownell from Gettysburg:

"Say, Herb, I've just read that you and I had a big fight over the 1956 civil rights bill. Can you tell me what that's all about?" Brownell just chuckled, and the two remained trusting friends.

Despite Brownell's urging, the Congress passed no civil rights legislation in 1956. At the height of the election campaign later that year, Eisenhower at last endorsed all four of Brownell's proposals, and they became part of the administration's legislative program as the 1957 congressional session began.

As we wrote up that year's civil rights battle in *Waging Peace*, I never felt Eisenhower's enthusiasm for the four proposals kindle; at heart they were Brownell's, not his. In our sessions on the book, Eisenhower outlined the kind of plan for school integration that personally appealed to him: start with the graduate schools, then work down one grade each year, accelerating to two grades each year in the primary schools, all the while improving the quality of the schools that remained temporarily segregated.

He was no instant reformer. And he was not a cynical grandstander. "I want something meaningful or nothing on civil rights," he once told his White House civil rights specialist, Max Rabb. "Everybody knows that Roosevelt and Truman had a formula: Every election year they would come up with a bill for an FEPC, an end to the poll tax, or an outlawing of lynching. The liberals could vote for it, the southerners could filibuster, and everybody got what he wanted. It was nothing but a hollow gesture."

So in 1957 the President found himself in the awkward middle: between the aggressive Brownell and the obstructionist Democrats who, with a two-vote majority in the Senate and a 33-vote majority in the House, controlled Congress and the fate of all legislation.

Ike resisted both. He resisted the many roadblocks thrown up that year by the Democrats, northern and southern, which included a gutting amendment to assure a jury trial for those accused of civil rights violations; and a move by Georgia's Senator Richard Russell to send the House-passed bill to the Senate Judiciary Committee (and certain death under the chairmanship of Eastland of Mississippi) instead of directly to the Senate floor.

But Eisenhower also resisted Brownell. On July 2 Senator Russell declared Eisenhower's bill "cunningly designed to vest in the Attorney General unprecedented power to bring to bear the whole might of the Federal Government, including the armed forces if necessary, to force a commingling of white and Negro children" in Southern schools. Russell was adverting to Title III of the bill, which gave the Attorney General the power to go into federal court to get an injunction against anyone trying to deprive a citizen of his civil rights. Eisenhower respected Russell; and Russell's claim, in Brownell's words years later, "stunned" him. The next day at his press conference

Ike hedged: the civil rights bill, he declared, contained "certain phrases I didn't completely understand"; he would confer with the Attorney General about them. He reasserted what he said was his principal purpose: to prevent any illegal interference with the right to vote. Give people the vote, Eisenhower reiterated in our conferences on the memoirs, and their economic improvement would follow.

At the White House meeting of the Legislative Leaders on July 9, everyone agreed that Eisenhower did not seek authority to use the armed forces to enforce school integration or any other civil right. And on July 16 in a brief press release, Eisenhower set out the four things he believed a civil rights bill should do: protect the right to vote; "provide a reasonable program of assistance in efforts to protect other constitutional rights of our citizens" (a refusal to abandon Title III); establish the new commission and the new assistant attorney general.

The next day, July 17, reporters probed the administration's ambiguities: Should the attorney general have power to bring suits on his own motion to enforce school integration? Eisenhower muddled: "A. Well, no. . . . without any request from local authorities. . . ."

Q. "That is what the bill would do, part three."

A. "Well, in that, we will see what they agree on. . . . my own purposes are reflected again in the little memorandum I published last evening. . . ." In conclusion he warned that in this kind of legislation, you can't go too far too fast. It was not a crisp performance.

From the start, Brownell had not hidden what Title III might permit. In his February 1957 testimony before a Senate Judiciary subcommittee, he stressed that he wanted the Title III authority primarily to protect the right to vote; but he also mentioned other civil rights, and specifically the right to attend a non-segregated school. He cited a case in Hoxie, Arkansas, in which a school board had decided to integrate the town's schools; had been intimidated by a crew of segregationists; had defied the intimidators; and had gone into a federal district court and got an injunction against them. In other instances, Brownell reasoned, a local school board might cave in; and in those instances, given Title III, the Department of Justice could sue for an injunction.

Now, howerver, the President himself was balking. And Justice began playing down school desegregation. By July 18, when Senator Jacob Javits released a list, handed to him by the department, of twenty-four civil rights that the Attorney General wished to protect under parts 3 and 4 of the civil rights bill, the list omitted school integration.

On July 22, in a long and hitherto unpublished letter to Swede Hazlett, Eisenhower spoke candidly about his uncertainties:

"The plan of the Supreme Court to accomplish [school] integration gradually and sensibly seems to me to provide the only possible answer if we are to consider on the one hand the customs and fears of a great section of our population, and on the other the binding effect that Supreme Court decisions must have on all of us if our form of government is to survive and prosper. Consequently the plan that I have advanced for Congressional consideration on this touchy matter was conceived in the thought that only moderation in legal compulsions, accompanied by a stepped-up program of education, could bring about the result that every loyal American should seek.

"*I think that some of the language used in the attempt to translate my basic purposes into legislative provisions has probably been too broad. Certainly it has been subject to varying interpretations. This I think can be corrected in the Congress. . . .*" [italics added]

Given Eisenhower's ambivalence, plus the opposition of the Senate Democrats, Title III was defeated. But in the end a compromise bill was produced, containing the Civil Rights Commission; the assistant attorney general; power for the attorney general to seek an injunction against voting rights infringements; and a jury trial provision with a few teeth. It was the first civil rights act since Reconstruction.

Brownell had tugged, with effect. Without his spearheading, the year 1957 would never have seen passage of a civil rights bill of adequate—or possibly any—force. Eisenhower had wavered on Title III, but only on Title III. With that exception he backed his attorney general, and in face of enormous temptations not to. Eisenhower that year needed the help of the powerful southern Democrats to get through any legislation, foreign or domestic, especially for foreign aid money; and he could have bought that help—as they told him in words of one syllable—by caving in on civil rights. In the squeaker Hayes-Tilden election of 1876, Brownell recalled years later, Hayes won out by making a deal with southern senators emasculating the civil rights acts of Reconstruction. "Eisenhower could have done the same thing. But he didn't."

In the Little Rock crisis several weeks after the civil rights bill passed, Brownell didn't have to tug. Eisenhower, faced now not with legislative strategy but with a constitutional imperative, saw his duty and did it—did it, history will record, perfectly. When Governor Orval Faubus defied a federal court order integrating the Little Rock public schools, and angry mobs assembled around the city's Central High School to prevent the entry of black students, Ike, after futile attempts at conciliation, moved with dispatch: he phoned Chief of Staff Max Taylor and sent in a thousand Army paratroopers.

"When you appeal to force, there's just one thing you must never do—lose."

The next day, under this protection, nine black boys and girls entered Central High. He used enough power to accomplish the law's intent. No one was injured. The crisis would end.

Eisenhower allowed episodic resistance—a Seaton's or a Brownell's—to help shape domestic policy. But resistance of even greater significance helped shape international policy. And this resistance resulted not—as with Alaska statehood and civil rights—from Eisenhower's habit of delegation, but from outright disagreement between two men who regularly worked on every detail together and who shared together a broad sweep of agreement both on their convictions and on their strategy—Eisenhower and his Secretary of State, John Foster Dulles.

One cannot overdraw the intimacy of their day-to-day, hour-to-hour working relationship. I once got out a metal tape and measured the exact length of the Eisenhower-Dulles correspondence (1953–59) housed at the ex-President's Gettysburg office, on that sunny glassed-in back porch that held all Ike's personal green file cabinets. The papers stretched more than five feet, and they didn't even include the detailed minutes of National Security Council meetings, Cabinet meetings, and smaller conferences that both men attended. (At least once, in the midst of a major crisis, they went together to a World Series game. Dulles didn't much like ball games, but no one turns down an invitation from the President of the United States. There's a wonderful photograph in John Eisenhower's office that shows Dulles, dressed in diplomatic starched shirt, dark tie, and black hat, looking like a Presbyterian elder, with a skeptical lawyer's expression on his face, sitting in a box with Ike, hands on the railing, yelling out advice to the players.)

The area of national security, obviously, was where Eisenhower spent most of his time: on those tiny turns at the wheel of history that make or mar the Grand Design.

Who today, for example, remembers Trieste—the bitter quarrel between non-Communist Italy and Tito's Communist Yugoslavia over a boundary for that border territory at the head of the Adriatic, a quarrel that had festered since World War II and that might have sparked World War III? Through 1953–54 Eisenhower and Dulles (and Dulles' alter ego, Bedell Smith) spent hours on this, hatching tactics, hearing reports, dispatching emissaries, writing memos back and forth.

For example, June 3, 1954, Dulles to Eisenhower: Yugoslavia has agreed on a line that gives the Trieste-City part of Trieste Province to Italy; the U.S. is granting Yugoslavia $20 million more in foreign aid in the current fiscal year; the U.S. proposes to grant similar aid to Italy.

July 10, Eisenhower's "Notes to Discuss with Foster Dulles": Bases in Italy are not vital to the U.S. If Italy knew we were losing interest, they would become more cooperative.

September 6, Bedell Smith to Eisenhower: Could he have Eisenhower's okay on sending veteran diplomat Robert Murphy to Rome and Belgrade, authorized to warn both sides of a "future less sympathetic U.S. attitude" toward both economic and military aid if the disputants should refuse the "concessions we seek?"

September 6, Eisenhower to Smith: He approves Murphy's mission and these verbal messages: to Tito, "a warning"; to Scelba, words "mild, even...encouraging."

And so on, to an ultimate composition of the crisis and its disappearance from front pages and, what is more significant, from memory.

Men whom Eisenhower liked best were "students"—a favorite word. Bob Anderson was a student. So were Milton and Al Gruenther. And so, supremely, was Foster Dulles. And one cannot exaggerate the closeness of their collaboration as for six and a half years, hour by hour, they focused on those tiny details that eventually decide war or peace. In Dulles' own words, in a phone conversation with Eisenhower only a few weeks before his death in 1959, "I don't think we are going to reach a settlement [on Berlin], but what we can do is patch things up and prevent them from becoming acute, and keep things out of war. We must convince the world we are only striving for liberty....We must get the initiative."

One cannot exaggerate, either, the closeness of Eisenhower's and Dulles' convictions as revealed in the unpublished minutes of the meetings of the National Security Council. In September 1954, when the Chinese Communists began to shell Quemoy Island (which lay between the Chinese mainland and Formosa and which was held by Chiang Kai-shek's Nationalist forces), and a majority of the Joint Chiefs of Staff believed the United States should go to the defense of Quemoy and the other offshore islands, it was the always unflappable Dulles who formulated the problem as both men saw it: The Council, Dulles said, faced at that moment "a horrible dilemma." The Chinese Communists were probing: failure to stop them could produce disaster in Korea, Japan, Formosa, and the Philippines. But a flat resolve to defend the offshore islands would put us at war with Communist China—all alone. And it was Foster Dulles who came up with the answer that Eisenhower wholeheartedly approved: to take the offshore islands question to the United Nations in order to get an injunction to preserve the status quo. And thereby save the islands and avert war.

Thus the crucial knife-edge decision was taken. And from it flowed the brilliant strategy of ambiguity that Eisenhower and Dulles followed for eight ensuing agonizing watchful months, never committing, never retreating, leaving the enemy guessing, restraining Chiang, saying only that the United States would move to defend the islands if at the time of a Communist attack we judged it a prelude to an assault on Formosa.

It was not an easy strategy to hold to. "They [the Chinese Communists] are certainly doing everything they can to try our patience," Ike told Hagerty February 3, 1955. "Sometimes I think that it would be best all around to go after them right now....I have a feeling that [they] are acting on their own on this and that it is considerably disturbing to the Russians." But the moment passed. The ambiguity remained. And the next month when Admiral Carney made a bellicose "off-the-record" prediction to reporters that the Chinese Reds would invade Matsu by April 15 and Quemoy a month later, Eisenhower exploded. "By God, this has got to stop," he told Hagerty as he angrily paced the floor March 28. "I think you should tell the reporters ... we are trying to keep the peace. We are not looking for war and I think the stories like the ones they get from Carney, when published, are a great disservice to the United States. They're going to look awful silly when April 15th comes along and there is no incident, because honestly our information is that there is no build-up off those islands as yet to sustain any attack, and believe me, they're not going to take those islands just by wishing for them...."

The frustrations passed. The strategy stood. The crisis ended. And the episode rests as one of the signal triumphs of the Eisenhower-Dulles years—a triumph produced by two men who thought as one.

Nearly always, Eisenhower and Dulles thus agreed *in toto*. But not invariably. And when they differed, Dulles would at times have his way, as in the Suez crisis of October-November 1956.

The United States had refused—largely on economic grounds—to help Egypt's Nasser build a monumental Aswan Dam across the Upper Nile. In fury, Nasser announced he was nationalizing the Suez Canal. In response, Britain, France, and Israel secretly conspired to attack Egypt. Simultaneously Hungarian patriots, following the example of Polish patriots only short weeks before, broke into bloody revolt against the Soviet Union, rampaging through the streets, tearing down Soviet flags, hurling Molotov cocktails. Soviet tanks and troops rolled into Budapest to gun down the uprising. And Israel, Britain, and France, by infantry knifing across the Sinai Desert, and by paratroopers taking off from later-arriving warships in the Mediterranean, executed a clumsy aggressive invasion of Egyptian soil.

On Hungary, Eisenhower and Dulles were once again as one. Not once, in any meeting of the National Security Council in late October and early November did either consider U.S. entry to help the freedom fighters. As we worked on *Waging Peace*, Eisenhower commented on the geography of the problem, the fact that U.S. forces couldn't have got to Hungary except by crossing neutral or Communist territory—Yugoslavia, Czechoslovakia, or Austria. But this consideration does not appear in the minutes of any single conference written at the time. The option never came up. And the reason was clear. "With the deterioration of the Soviet hold over the satellites," Eisenhower speculated to the NSC, October 26, "might not the Soviet Union be tempted to resort to extreme measures, even global war? We must watch this possibility with the greatest care. After all, Hitler knew in February of '45 that he was licked. But he kept on, pulling down Europe with him in defeat."

On the British-French-Israeli aggression against Egypt, however, one can detect between President and Secretary of State the slightest divergence, with Eisenhower harking back toward his old wartime sympathy for our Allies, Dulles harking back to the Wilsonian anticolonialism of *War, Peace and Change* ("in the colonial areas the sovereignty system is operated by the colonizing...power to the end that its nationals may have a preferential right of exploitation").

The tension, small though it was, surfaces in the minutes of the meeting of the National Security Council on Thursday morning, November 1. Foster Dulles reviews the weeks of perfidy: The French did the planning, the British acquiesced, and the French covertly shipped the Israelis military equipment without telling the United States, in violation of the 1950 tripartite agreement. And Dulles proposes unequivocal action in the United Nations: The United States must reassert its leadership against this use of force in the Middle East. If it does not, the Soviet Union will seize that leadership; newly independent countries will turn to the Soviet Union. He advocates a suspension of all military and some economic assistance in the Middle East. He throws off attempts to water down the severity of censure. When Harold Stassen suggests the United States introduce a U.N. resolution calling for a cease-fire only, Dulles warmly disagrees. The President suggests a mild resolution in an effort to block a "really mean" one. Dulles diplomatically goes along, but pointedly adds that Cabot Lodge has just phoned saying that if the United States tries to walk a tightrope, the Soviet Union will introduce an extreme resolution. Eisenhower suggests a suspension of military aid to the entire Middle East and deferral of a decision on economic aid. Dulles does not concur: we've already argued in the U.N. for economic aid suspension; we can't change now, though we don't necessarily have to make our decision public.

Dulles thus affirmed—with Eisenhower's complete concurrence—United States condemnation of "colonialism." But underneath, Ike's instinct for North Atlantic friendship remained, through this grievous moment, intact. As he wrote Swede Hazlett on November 2 in the eye of the hurricane: "No one could question the legal right of Egypt to nationalize the Canal *Company*....The real point is that Britain, France and Israel had come to believe, probably correctly, that Nasser was their worst enemy in the Mid East and that until he was removed or deflated, they would have no peace. I do not quarrel with the idea that there is justification for such fears, but I have insisted long and earnestly that you cannot resort to force in international relationships because of your fear of what might happen in the future. In short, I think that the British and French seized upon a very poor vehicle to use in bringing Nasser to terms....

"I think that France and Britain have made a terrible mistake. Because they had such a poor case, they have isolated themselves from the good opinion of the world and it will take them many years to recover. France was perfectly cold-blooded about the matter. She has a war on her hands in Algeria, and she was anxious to get someone else fighting the Arabs on her Eastern flank[;] so she was ready to do anything to get England and Israel in that affair. But I think the other two countries have hurt themselves immeasurably and this is something of a sad blow because, quite naturally, Britain not only has been, but must be, our best friend in the world...."

When the fighting stops in Egypt, the divergence between Eisenhower and Dulles breaks into the open. At 8:43 in the morning of November 7—the day after Ike's landslide election to a second term—Eden phones him.

The President says he would be delighted to have Eden and Mollet come to the United States. Eden suggests they fly over that evening.

"After all," the President tells his old friend, "it is like a family spat."

Dulles, confined at Walter Reed after a sudden operation, does not so see it. With George Humphrey and Herbert Hoover, Jr., he votes no on the meeting. So at 10:27 A.M. Eisenhower phones Eden: the Cabinet, he says, thinks "our timing is very, very bad." The English and French will have to put off the visit.

It has been postponed, not canceled. Driving out to Walter Reed to see his ailing Secretary of State later that morning, Eisenhower emphasizes that when Eden does come over, they'll want to talk about "what the Bear will do and what we would do in the face of the Bear's acts"; he sees no point in recrimination; he stresses the need for a military study on what the United States should do if the Russians move into the Middle East, and calls for coordination with the British on intelligence estimates. Already—in the heat of battle— Ike has laid the groundwork for reconciliation. But at this crucial moment, while the barbed arrows of angry words are still flying, it is Foster Dulles who has called the shot.

He did so again on another major Eisenhower initiative in 1958. In January of that year, in the anxious season after *Sputnik*,

Eisenhower got from Kevin McCann, now back at Defiance College, an idea the President found incandescent: a proposal for the United States to bring ten thousand students from the Soviet Union to study in American universities.

The idea ignited the irrepressible enthusiasm that Eisenhower had for great schemes that could leap across the tired nitty-gritty of diplomacy: the Atoms-for-Peace plan of 1953; the Geneva Open Skies proposal of 1955; the People-to-People initiative that Eisenhower had unveiled in 1956; and even the Kennedy Peace Corps ("Those kids," he once remarked, "are wonderful"). Far more than overtaking the Russians in satellite launchings or in ICBMs or leaving them in the dust in an economic race, the idea of massive student exchanges—not by scores, but by thousands—was the kind that turned Eisenhower on; he felt about international politics the way he felt about concilia-tion and moderation in the United States; he disliked strident summons to international competition as much as he disliked the hard-hitting negativism of the Republican National Committee.

Asked to study the suggestion, the Department of State, needless to say, stalled. Weeks passed. By March 14 Eisenhower, taking the bit in his teeth, phoned his brother Milton, who shared his international enthusiasms: "I'm tired of dealing with mature men already set in their prejudices." He had in hand a draft of a letter to Soviet Premier Nikolai Bulganin that would set the plan in motion. But on March 20 back the idea came from Foster Dulles covered with cold water and accompanied by a departmental memorandum listing all the reasons it couldn't be done: The Russians would never agree (read: assume defeat before you start). The plan would produce a snarl of red tape in the Justice Department. American universities had too many students already. The whole thing would cost too much. It would make more third world students accept grants to study in Russia. And on and on. Eisenhower must have wanted to fire the whole bureaucratic building. As Kevin McCann once remarked, in all seriousness, "We ought to get rid of every career State Department functionary and fill the whole place with cabdrivers."

Responding to Dulles, Eisenhower wrote with a cold reserve through which one senses a searing blue flame: "Only this morning you were pointing out the great disadvantages that we incur by reason of the fact that people in the Far East do not understand America and what is going on here. Even though a supposedly 'free press' reaches those nations, the misunderstanding is not only very noticeable but its consequences are serious to us. The proposal that I am considering would be aimed at clearing up such misunderstanding.

"Now, with respect to some of the problems mentioned.

"(a). I checked the security matter with Edgar Hoover and he said that the volume of the security problem would be slightly increased, but in reality it would be little more difficult. Personally, he was in favor of the idea, saying, in effect, 'It is high time that we were doing something positive; we cannot always be merely negative.'

"(b). If the information provided to me is reasonably accurate, there is a period for the next two or three years during which our undergraduate bodies will *not* be filled; I am told that numbers of undergraduate institutions are anxiously striving to fill up their student bodies.

"(c). Of course the program would not be cheap. I had been calculating a total of three thousand dollars per student for one year, and I was thinking of something on the order of five thousand students. This would cost us $15,000,000 per year."

Speechwriter Arthur Larson had already made the student exchange plan the centerpiece of a speech Eisenhower planned to deliver to the American Society of Newspaper Editors on April 17. Eisenhower sent a draft to Dulles: "we need some vehicle to ride in order to suggest to the world, even if ever so briefly, that we are not stuck in the mud...."

Once again, back came a two-page single-spaced memorandum: The speech, the Secretary wrote, "seems to me to be unnecessarily somber. After all, quite a lot of your [April, 1953] 'Chance for Peace' aspirations have been realized.

"There is the Korean armistice. There is an IndoChina Armistice. There is an Austrian State Treaty. There is an International Atomic Energy Agency. There is great progress in the development of a 'European Community, conducive to the free movement of persons, trade, and of ideas'....

"The 'Chance for Peace' has been greatly increased by the apparent abandonment by the Soviet leaders of methods of violence such as were used in the prewar and postwar period up to 1953.... The principal aspect of your April 1953 speech which has not been realized is the limitation of armaments and any permanent reduction of the costs of armament. I do not think, however, that it is necessary to be despairing even as to this...."

So there the two stood: Dulles, ironically, extolling the

betterments in the world, even the monolithic world of Atheistic Communism; Eisenhower somber, restless, realizing that peace still lay a long way off, yearning to get on with the job, wanting—in Sherman Adams' phrase—to throw a rock through the window to get the world off dead center.

But Ike didn't throw the rock. He deferred to Dulles. In frustration and disgust he canceled the foreign policy speech. And the student exchange plan died.

The story does not end there, in a portrait of a weak President overawed and overruled by a strong Secretary of the Interior or Attorney General or Secretary of State. Facing intolerable freewheeling, Dwight Eisenhower was completely capable of punitive action without loss of sleep. When in the 1957 disarmament talks chief negotiator Harold Stassen failed to coordinate with the British and went straight to the Russians with new proposals of his own, leaving Ike (as he wrote Ambassador Jock Whitney) furious, Eisenhower with finality brought his powerful and headstrong negotiator to heel.

The story does not end, either, in a portrait of a President like Warren Gamaliel Harding, wishy-washy of conviction. Eisenhower had not only stood up to Winston Churchill in hours-long arguments on strategy during the War. He had defended his unpopular Secretary of Agriculture, Ezra Taft Benson, against all comers; against all powerful persuaders—including even Milton—he had held firm to his chosen course against Joe McCarthy; against liberal pleaders in his party, he had refused to declare himself on the Supreme Court's school desegregation decision.

In the words of Al Smith's most famous quotation, the story must end with a look at the record, a record produced, under presidential leadership, by strong organization. That record encompasses failures (the 1952 deletion of the Marshall paragraph), shortcomings (the collapse of the student exchange plan), and imponderables (the disinvitation of Eden and Mollet). But that record also encompasses overriding successes: Alaska statehood, the writing of the first civil rights act in this century, and the Eisenhower-Dulles chronicle in international conduct.

Adlai Stevenson, Emmet Hughes, Nelson Rockefeller, and John F. Kennedy all voiced frustration with the Eisenhower-Dulles performance. So also did Eisenhower's powerful Chief of Staff, Sherman Adams, saddened by Stassen's fall ("Stassen was like an IRA activist throwing a bomb into a Belfast hotel: he wanted to do something—anything—to produce new approaches to the Russians"); frustrated by the intransigence of Foster Dulles ("an autocrat, a self-centered autocrat. A President makes an error to lock himself in for eight years with Cabinet officers who may become devoid of ideas. Maybe Stassen and C. D. Jackson and Nelson Rockefeller didn't have the greatest ideas in the world, but at least they were trying to come up with something new. And just building up a bigger and bigger nuclear capability and deploying it around the world accomplishes ultimately nothing").

Yet not one of these critics proposed an alternative of substance, a road rejected that looks right in retrospect. Adlai Stevenson's panting after "new ideas," which resulted only in feckless urgings, in caricature, to ban the bomb and end the draft, did not even survive to the end of the 1956 campaign. Emmet Hughes's foreign policy prescriptions in *The Ordeal of Power*—more foreign aid, more "diplomatic engagement" with the Russians, less affection for Franco—remain similarly frothy. When I asked Nelson Rockefeller what he would have done differently in the foreign policy of the 1950s, he replied vaguely that, like Henry Kissinger, he would have constructed a comprehensive global strategic design, got the free world better organized to counter its foes, and given the Eastern Europeans better help in rebellion. And Sherman Adams in the end candidly admitted his inability to have improved on the record, despite his visceral unhappiness with it: "When would you have replaced Dulles and with whom? I don't know the answer."

And no one does with certainty. Perhaps in 1953 we might have forestalled all future troubles in Iran by helping Mohammed Mossadegh override the Constitutional monarch and become a popularly acclaimed dictator, instead of backing the Shah, and seeing Mossadegh as an erratic neurotic, the unwitting entering wedge for Communist control of the Persian Gulf. Perhaps in 1956 we might have advanced the cause of human liberty by intervening to aid the Hungarian freedom fighters, instead of holding back for fear of igniting World War III. Perhaps in early 1957, after opposing the invasion of Egypt, we might have made a firm friend of Nasser and his admirers throughout the Middle East—and thus further alienated the British—instead of trying above all to restore the North Atlantic alliance and establish an Eisenhower Doctrine aimed against Middle East intervention by the Soviets, with Nasser their perceived surrogate. Perhaps later in 1957 we might have pursued an agreement with the Russians on Harold Stassen's disarmament plan and thus arrested the worldwide proliferation of nuclear weapons, instead of, once again, deferring to the objections of the bypassed British. And perhaps in 1960, after Dulles' death, Eisenhower might have taken a small chance to preserve the momentum toward peace in the forth-coming Paris summit conference, instead of ordering the continuation of intelligence-gathering through one more flight of a U-2. Maybe one or all of these actions might have improved things. But who knows for sure?

Of all the critics, only John Kennedy had an opportunity to institute his own alternatives, and the result Eisenhower himself summed up in a Boston speech in what *Time* magazine called "the most succinct and devastating paragraph" of the 1962 congressional campaign. As Ike pointed out, "In those eight years we lost no inch of ground to tyranny. We witnessed no abdication of international responsibility.... No walls were built. No threatening foreign bases were established. One war was ended, and incipient wars were blocked.... [In] the past twenty-one months there has [not] been anything constructive in the conduct of our foreign relations to equal any part of that eight-year record."

That is the end of the story: the record—the record in domestic policy, and above all the Eisenhower-Dulles record in foreign policy—a record marked mainly not by brilliant new schemes (Atoms for Peace, Open Skies, Alliance for Progress), but by tiny turns, many of which kept possible disasters from happening, and thus preserved the peace: eight years of peace with no ground and no men lost. That is the Eisenhower-Dulles record.

The end result, to paraphrase Aristotle, is everywhere the chief consideration. And in Eisenhower's building of this result, foreign and domestic, the organization—strong leader, strong lieuten-ants—was central. "No one can be completely objective," Governor Adams once remarked when asked what he considered the most crucial of all presidential attributes. "But I believe a president should above all understand his own prejudices."

Dwight Eisenhower had powerful instincts: on Alaska, on civil rights, on foreign policy. But in his use of his organization one can read a drive toward objectivity, toward getting outside one's own confirmed prison to find the answer. In none of his exchanges—with Seaton, with Brownell, with Dulles—did Eisenhower, or his adver-saries, attach primary significance to the genesis of ideas, to the fact they were his or theirs. He showed no resentment over their crossing him, and no vindictiveness afterward. He and they argued each question on the facts in hand, and if in the end he accepted subordinates' judgments, he did so in the belief that they, not he himself, were probably right.

The greatest attribute of a president, to Adams, was an understanding of his own prejudices. The greatest attribute of a commander, to George Marshall and Dwight Eisenhower, was self-lessness. In the end the two desiderata are one. Selflessness is the possession of the objectivist; the man who sees that the truth is greater than himself.

But with Eisenhower its pursuit was not a bloodless, nerveless process. "I have the best people I can find giving me advice," he once remarked to Andy Goodpaster in a contentious moment, "and I take their advice. But," he added, his eyes flashing with irritation, "I don't have to like it!"

Book Three

DAYS OF
SHADOW

XIII

APRIL 29, 1957

WOUNDINGS

O n the floor of the 1952 Republican convention, the leader of the Eisenhower forces, Governor Sherman Adams of New Hampshire, was seated across an aisle from the Oregon delegation and maverick Senator Wayne Morse.

"Morse wanted the vice-presidential nomination," the governor mused some twenty years later, as he puffed his pipe and we talked in his Loon Mountain ski resort office. "He argued that he could hold labor and liberal votes for the Eisenhower ticket. Nixon's selection infuriated him, and eventually he came out for Stevenson and bolted the Republican party.

"I've often thought I should have crossed that aisle. If I had, the future might have been different." What might Adams have done: made some deal, some gesture of conciliation? He didn't say. But he continued to speculate on such turning points in history. Such turning points often involve divisions between men.

"There comes a time when you have to deal with a potential enemy—when, as Senator [Ralph] Flanders of Vermont used to say, a man has to lay conscience aside and do what he has to do. That time came with Wayne Morse.

"And that time came with Emmet Hughes."

It came during a dramatic confrontation between Hughes and John Foster Dulles in the Secretary of State's office on a winter Monday afternoon in early 1957 and with a decision sealed by

223

Eisenhower himself in a letter to Hughes dated April 29 of that year. And that decision set in motion powerful currents of effect, personal and political.

For of all who felt frustration with Dulles—and eventually with Eisenhower himself—no one voiced it with more bitterness or eloquence than former speechwriter Hughes in two books, *America the Vincible* (1959) and *The Ordeal of Power* (1963). Those books did three things: They discolored Eisenhower's account of his relationship with Hughes as we worked on the memoirs, just as Harry Truman's personal attacks of 1952 discolored Ike's account of their association in 1945–51. They left a residue of bitterness (in those closest to Eisenhower) over Hughes's betrayal ("You came down hard on Emmet Hughes in your book," I observed to Milton Eisenhower after his *The President Is Calling* appeared in 1974. "Yes, and I could have said a lot more. He was an arrogant sonofabitch"). And Hughes's books and subsequent career left a trenchant impact on the future course of American politics.

Emmet Hughes—brilliant young Time-Life reporter, Princeton *summa*, devout Catholic, and former aide to Ambassador Carlton J. H. Hayes in wartime Spain—was brought into the Eisenhower 1952 campaign by Clare Boothe Luce to write the Milwaukee speech condemning Communism. In the weeks thereafter and in the first nine months of the Eisenhower presidency, he turned in a blazing performance. In the Eisenhower texts he fused vibrant rhetoric and a generous nonpartisan view of foreign policy: "these new lands... should be the ones—from Israel to India, from Syria to Indonesia— whom we should be quickest to help. For they should be the quickest to share our faith in freedom's future—in the brotherhood of man under the fatherhood of God."

And he had brought the campaign to a screaming climax in just five words: "I shall go to Korea."

C. D. Jackson of Time-Life and Harold Stassen had brought those words by hand from New York to the campaign train in Buffalo; but it was Emmet Hughes, writing back in Manhattan, who would quickly receive press credit for having thought them up, and for years no one seriously questioned his authorship. By the time we were writing up this episode in the memoirs in 1963, however, Hughes had attacked Eisenhower, and Ike had soured on Hughes. So, as we worked on the galleys of *Mandate for Change*, the General was delighted when I discovered a fact that seemed to torpedo Hughes's claim to prior invention: that back in mid-August of 1952, more than two months before the thunderclap, Harry Kern, foreign affairs editor of *Newsweek*, had phoned Bob Humphreys at National Committee headquarters with an interesting suggestion: Eisenhower should announce his intention to make a personal trip to Korea. Not long thereafter Humphreys got the same suggestion from a leading Pennsylvania Republican, Frank Hilton. Like a million other ideas that pop up in any campaign, this one's time had not yet come. No one rejected it. No one pushed it. And there it lay. But Kern and Hilton had indubitably made the suggestion. That fact undercut Hughes. And Eisenhower swiftly added it to the book. Moreover, in his narrative he insisted on looking over Hughes's head to C. D. Jackson as the staff man who had brought him the text.

No one can trace the trajectory of the idea from the time when Harry Kern brought it in. It was in the air. Ed Clark also proposed it in early September. And as Hughes himself admits, even the Stevenson people had hit upon this same possibility, only to reject it because of the ludicrousness of the thought of Adlai on that rugged wartime front; and they hoped against hope that the Eisenhower camp wouldn't think of the same thing. Whether the notion sprang unprompted into Hughes's mind, or whether he got the germ of the idea from one of these other sources, and had it flare into consciousness when he had to think up a rousing ending for a talk on the Korean War, no one knows. Given the evidence, one can hardly credit him with having unilaterally brought the design into the world. But he did the crucial thing—put it into the speech.

And though Ike almost mangled it with the Germanic phraseology of his editing, it hit like a blockbuster.

So did Eisenhower's Inaugural Address, again largely written by Hughes, who was again in the memoirs demoted to second place behind C. D. Jackson. But the address rings with Hughes's alliteration, balanced antithesis, and dramatic tension: "Since this century's beginning, a time of tempest has seemed to come upon the continents of the earth....The enemies of this faith know no god but force, no devotion but its use. They tutor men in treason....Whatever defies them, they torture, especially the truth....The peace we seek, then, is nothing less than the practice and fulfillment of our whole faith among ourselves and in our dealings with others. This signifies more than the stilling of guns, easing the sorrow of war. More than escape from death, it is a way of life. More than a haven for the weary, it is a hope for the brave."

Revisionist liberal Peter Lyon in his 1974 biography of Eisenhower hears the whole speech as a "clarion...unmistakable" that "called to war." Unreconstructed liberal Elmer Davis, an observer far more literate and intelligent, heard just the opposite, a call to peace: "He reassured the few here and the many abroad who complain that we are not willing to talk to the Russians, by saying that we are willing to join with any and all others in joint efforts to remove the causes of fear and distrust among nations—if those efforts provide methods by which every participating nation will prove its good faith in carrying out its pledge. In other words, we won't just take their word for it....The foreign policy outlined today deserves the support of all of us; for the President has erected a standard to which the wise and honest may repair."

Ninety days later, on April 16, Eisenhower—with Hughes's massive help—raised another standard, one of the most pivotal of his presidency.

Stalin had died March 5. By April 8 Allen Dulles was reporting to the NSC on the "shattering departures" of his successor, Georgi Malenkov: a Communist peace offensive had started; the U.S.S.R. was trying to avoid a global war. In the President's view the Soviet leaders perhaps had decided to produce civilian goods and thus lift the living standard of the Soviet people. He hoped so. "Let us study," he said, "to see whether, at long last, a *modus vivendi* might become possible."

This hope informed Eisenhower's April 16 address to the American Society of Newspaper Editors. After an early inadequate draft from C. D. Jackson, in the Oval Office, as Hughes himself excitedly recounts, Eisenhower came alive with the central blazing idea—his weariness, and the world's weariness, with the drain of armaments, the threat of war; his demand for concrete proposals toward peace. Hughes returned on the run to the East Wing, closeted himself, and began to type. His secretary, Mary Nichols, has never forgotten her own excitement as she first saw the words unfold from smudged pages produced through a long night of drafting. The speech retained the Eisenhower realism about the Soviet menace. But then it broke into a heartfelt yearning for peace, for a good life for the whole family of man. "Every gun that is made, every warship launched, every rocket fired signifies, in the final sense, a theft from those who hunger and are not fed, those who are cold and are not clothed.

"This world in arms is not spending money alone.

"It is spending the sweat of its laborers, the genius of its scientists, the hopes of its children.

"The cost of one modern heavy bomber is this: a modern brick school in more than thirty cities.

"It is two electric power plants, each serving a town of sixty thousand population. . . .

"We pay for a single fighter plane with a half million bushels of wheat.

"We pay for a single destroyer with new homes that could have housed more than eight thousand people."

And then, in a striking metaphor from his Catholic amanuensis—a metaphor too religious, too literary, too emotional for Eisenhower's own invention, but irresistible—he summed the Good Friday tragedy of mankind: "This is not a way of life at all, in any true sense. Under the cloud of threatening war, it is humanity hanging from a cross of iron."

The words light up the future of the Eisenhower presidency: his Open Skies at the Geneva summit; his impatience with an international contest in *Sputniks* and missiles; his alarms, repeatedly in private and finally in public, against the military-industrial complex. All lie like seeds in this address—an address that reflects Eisenhower the soldier's weariness with the negativism of the Pentagon, a weariness that parallels Eisenhower the President's weariness with the negativism of Republican politicians.

What did Eisenhower the President initiate? Above all, this: a *Sehnsucht* toward a "sunny upland of peace" for the world—a longing that one senses with poignancy throughout his eight presidential years, a longing that rode over every lesser consideration again and again. That's what Eisenhower left us.*

---

*Eisenhower's love of peace was recognized even in Russia, and one of the most unfortunate consequences of the U-2 spy plane disaster was the cancellation of his visit there, where he was a hero, known as the good friend of General Zhukov. Premier Khrushchev was no Satanic Stalin, and real rapprochement may have been possible. But after the Russians had proof that their boundaries had been violated, the hard-liners made Khrushchev's position untenable. He withdrew his invitation; at the Paris Summit he banged on the table with his fist; at the United Nations he banged on the table with his shoe. Eisenhower, however, understood his problem: The last comment I heard him make on the subject was, "Khrushchev was an interesting man."

And he left it to us all by himself. He had no precedents. When Harry Truman stopped the Russians in 1946 in Azerbaijan, when he moved into Greece and Turkey, when he deployed the Marshall Plan, when he ordered U.S. forces into Korea, he had a precedent that he had read, marked, learned, and inwardly digested— the precedent of Munich: Don't feed the ravenousness of a dictator. Stop him cold. And stop him early. Or in the end he'll have you, back to the wall, fighting for your life.

Truman read that lesson, and practiced it well. Eisenhower, too, had that lesson of 1938 as precedent—plus the precedents added by Truman—and he, too, practiced it well: in Guatemala in 1954, in Quemoy and Matsu in 1955, in Lebanon in 1958, in Berlin in 1959. But in his search for peace—in his attempt to turn the world away from war, hot or cold—he had no precedent, in that dismal year of his taking office. He was a soldier longing with head and heart for arms control, for an end to the world's "mad race" in weaponry. And never did he voice this longing with more poignancy than on April 16, 1953, with the superb and soaring words of Emmet Hughes.

But underneath, all was not well. Less than three months later, on July 17, Hughes went to see his friend C. D. Jackson to tell him about his plans for leaving Washington, and his reason: despite the success of the Inaugural and ASNE addresses, he had had it—had it with the shortcomings of a foreign policy largely administered by a man whom the ASNE address had largely bypassed, Secretary of State John Foster Dulles.

Jackson shared the same frustrations. In his diary he had groaned (6/1/53) over Dulles' converting a gold mine of information into a dreary audience-numbing NSC presentation; predicted (7/8/53) when McCarthy "exposed" Red authors in State Department overseas libraries, that neither press nor public would now allow Dulles "to continue doing a Pontius Pilate"; writhed (also 7/8/53) over State's "business-as-usual attitude" in the face of widespread popular unrest in East Germany, telling Allen Dulles (who "didn't even know what his inventory was") that his CIA "should be prepared [to] supply clandestine arms in Berlin," and prompting Bobby Cutler to call a meeting "quickly in order [to] get Foster Dulles to *understand* what it was all about." And (8/18/53) Jackson had sympathized with Undersecretary of State Bedell Smith when Smith revealed to Jackson he had "finally cracked under JFD's penchant for two-timing maladministration."

Jackson himself came close to cracking in the ensuing months as he battled not only Persons, Morgan, and others he considered "appeasers" of McCarthy, but also the stick-in-the-muds in State and Defense whom Jackson had to drag along kicking and screaming on the project code-named "Wheaties"—Ike's triumphant announcement, at the United Nations on December 8, of United States willingness to contribute from its nuclear stockpile to a U.N. agency to serve the "peaceful purposes of mankind." Jackson's diary recalls the agonies:

"*November 17, 1953 (Tues.)*. . . . Meeting in Foster Dulles' office with [Atomic Energy Commission Chairman] Lewis Strauss. Unfortunately [State Department Policy Planning Chief] Bob Bowie invited in. Subject—Wheaties, and UN appearance on December 8. Dulles went into reverse, ably needled by Bowie—he didn't like UN idea; he didn't like Strauss' proposal; he didn't like anything. Bowie kept repeating that this was not the way to do things—quiet, unpublicized negotiations were the only thing that would get anywhere with Ruskies. . . ."

"*November 25, 1953 (Wednesday)*. . . . Big meeting in Foster Dulles' office. Foster, Allen, Lewis, Roger [Kyes, Deputy Defense Secretary], Radford, Bowie—on Wheaties. Red lights started blinking all over the place. Joint Chiefs and Defense have laid their ears back. Kyes sarcastic and offensive, talking for effect and not recognizing substance of problem. . . ."

"*November 27, 1953 (Friday)*. . . . Real problem is very deep and goes beyond any disagreement on wording or technical details. Real problem is basic philosophy—are we or are we not prepared to embark on a course which may in fact lead to atomic disarmament? Soldier boys and their civilian governesses say no. Foster Dulles doesn't say yes or no, but says any atomic offer which does not recognize ultimate possibility is a phony and should not be made. Strauss and I say we won't be out of the trenches by Christmas, or next Christmas or the next one, but let's try to make a start and see what happens. Foster considers this mentally dishonest (he should talk!). . . ."

"*November 30, 1953*. . . . Prexy meeting on Wheaties. Present— the Dulles brothers, Wilson, Kyes, Radford, Strauss. Two agonizingly awful hours. Kyes read a 6-page memo as a substitute for the speech which was in effect his plan to budget defense on a three-year instead of a one-year basis. This was going to restore confidence at home and abroad and solve all problems.

"Wilson proposed doing nothing, since the Soviets were now

beginning to educate their youth, and an educated youth would overthrow the Soviets.

"Foster Dulles at his most judicial, and therefore straddling fence.... Kyes overstepped himself by making a reference to somebody handing the President an umbrella if he offered in a speech to turn any fissionable material over to a United Nations pool.

"Finally passed note to Allen Dulles saying I couldn't fight this alone, at which he got into the act with startling vehemence...."

"December 3, 1953. ... President on Wheaties. Foster Dulles, Kyes, Wilson. Went over latest draft. Wilson still mumbling around in his cave, but Kyes completely reversed, and desperately trying to recoup his shocking performance of Nov. 30.... Did some editing and another draft (#7) prepared."

Five days later Eisenhower appeared before the U.N. General Assembly, and Wheaties became Atoms-for-Peace.

The volatile Jackson soon softened his complaints. By December 18 he was rejoicing that the "UN speech has triggered the new Eisenhower" and hoping that this, plus the McCarthy statement of December 2, plus "State of Union, plus Budget, plus solid accomplishments in Defense, HEW, FOA, State, etc., will not only reverse 'where is leadership' trend but create an atmosphere by spring or summertime that will absolutely snow the electorate and the Congress." And by February 25, 1954, on the eve of his amicable departure from the White House, he was writing to Henry Luce that "the Eisenhower-Dulles foreign policy is not just a tougher 'me too' to Truman-Acheson foreign policy, but something distinctive, something on its own, and something with its own hallmark—and the name for it is virile diplomacy at work with long term objectives....

"What did come out of [the Berlin Foreign Ministers Conference] was that the display of virile diplomacy under the field generalship of Foster Dulles produced (a) voluntary if not enthusiastic Western unity such as has not been seen for one hell of a long time, (b) smoking out Soviet foreign policy intentions which had been pretty well smothered in question marks prior to Berlin in spite of the experts, (c) facing Molotov and Co. with the kind of attitude and the kind of words that he has never heard before...."

Hughes had by now left the White House and returned to Time, Inc. Not for a decade would the world know of *his* inward disaffection with the administration "team"; know of the minutes he made on Cabinet meetings he sat in on; know of his scorn for Charlie

Wilson, whom he protrayed as a benighted protectionist refusing to award contracts on Army Engineers dams to British firms (here again in *Mandate for Change* we straightened the record by adding what Hughes had left out: that though the Army did award an American firm, as low bidder, one $4.2 million contract, it awarded the British a $1.7 million contract the same day, and a $3.6 million contract some months later, despite the fact that the department might under the law have thrown all the business to the Americans).

Hughes kept his disaffection hidden, particularly from Eisenhower. He returned to the White House for eight weeks at the height of the 1956 campaign and once again shone like a star, with an initial foreign policy speech that contained, not callow crowing over past triumphs, but somber concern over future difficulties; with smart-aleck talks taunting Stevenson ("they fled from the scene... in headlong silence"); and with noble "rule of law" rhetoric at the campaign's end, as the Suez-Hungary crisis forced the curtailment of Eisenhower's appearance at partisan rallies. So great was Eisenhower's confidence in Hughes that Hughes could begin the drafting of a talk scheduled, say, for Seattle as Ike's plane went wheels up, Seattle-bound, from Washington's National Airport; or finish drafting a speech for seven o'clock on nationwide TV at 6:50 P.M., pushing the pages across the desk to the relaxed and waiting speaker.

In the flush of November's victory Hughes emerged a hero. And then came the moment Sherman Adams saw.

In January 1957 Hughes drafted Eisenhower's second Inaugural Address, warning a complacent West of the "winds of change" sweeping the earth. And now, in Adams' phrase, Hughes became a "serviceable citizen," proud of his powers, eager to take on new challenges on the international stage, and presenting "a rather tall order" for a new administration assignment. Over the succeeding weeks, one event led to another, and in a long letter from Hughes himself dated April 8, Eisenhower heard the whole tale:

"Several different positions came into discussions between Governor Adams and myself," Hughes wrote, "and this is what happened to each:"

First, Hughes said, Adams suggested that Hughes might go to London as a minister under Ambassador Jock Whitney—an idea that though it appealed greatly, Hughes could not accept because of the need to remain in the United States near his parents, then in precarious health. Adams next suggested the post of Assistant Secretary of State for Public Affairs—a position that Hughes quickly vetoed because of his aversion to mixing journalism and government, and because of his interest not in press agentry, but in the direct conduct of foreign policy. So Adams came up with a third suggestion: what about Assistant Secretary of State for European Affairs? And this one ignited Hughes's enthusiasm. In fact, he said, he became so stirred that he had the "presumption" to confide that there was, of course, one diplomatic post that, if offered, he would accept even though it might mean the renunciation of his journalistic life forever— the post of U.S. Ambassador to the United Nations. To this "gratuitous" overture the governor made no response; he kept his "superbly laconic poise," muttering simply that he had no idea when anything would open up there. But by this time Hughes had made up his mind: if the State Department did want him as Assistant Secretary for Europe, he would, despite personal difficulties, accept.

Then came the culmination: a half-hour interview with Foster Dulles—a half hour that brought to engagement four years in the life of the two men, going back to Hughes's drafting of the April 16 foreign policy speech of 1953; his constant end-running of the State Department to get into presidential speeches and messages his own more capacious sentiments on international conduct; his opportunity, after his departure from the administration in 1953, to observe it and its foreign policy and its chief foreign policy architect from a European distance with mounting impatience and mounting frustration; his drafting of the climactic speech on Suez in 1956, a drafting that began with the wastebasketing of a text composed by Dulles himself.

All that sat on one side of the table. And on the other sat the aging, authoritarian, autocratic, self-centered, rigid, inflexible Presbyterian who viewed all such foreign policy amateurs with consummate distrust for daring to invent and present ideas that he himself had not invented or presented; all that shrewdness, all that learning, all that ambition, which had come to a lifetime climax when Dulles assumed the post that both his grandfather and his uncle had held, and for which he had prepared himself since 1907; all that superb intelligence, in which Eisenhower reposed absolute confidence—a sentiment that contrasted with the affectionate warmth that Eisenhower felt for his young and brilliant and imaginative Catholic speech drafter who sat opposite.

The talk, Hughes reported with his accustomed alliteration, was "cordial and clear and conclusive." The Europe Assistant Secretary post, Dulles explained gently but precisely, was already being filled. In any event, he felt it was not the slot for Hughes, for it required perhaps more experience than Hughes had to offer. So Dulles had a suggestion: why not instead join the Policy Planning Staff and concentrate there on long-range thinking?

With a twist of irony, Hughes remarked that happily he could reply with equal candor: Dulles had framed his proposal in exactly the form Hughes could not accept: as an opportunity for him to get a sort of high-level on-the-job-training. Leaving Time, Inc., he told Dulles, would end eleven years there; he could not justify canceling his current career simply to become an apprentice somewhere else. Civilly, Dulles replied that he did not find Hughes's reaction surprising. Hughes continued: the kind of change they were talking about would make sense only if he were to fill a specific post that needed filling and that he could, given his capabilities, fill well. He acknowledged that the State Department had a great many posts for which he had few qualifications. He acknowledged Dulles' point that speech drafting did not necessarily prove mastery of foreign policy issues, though he added, again with irony, that it might occasionally have *some* relevance. He was centering his argument for a serious responsibility not on this, he said, but on ten years of direct knowledge of Europe, a speaking knowledge of foreign languages, and four years in the wartime embassy in Madrid.

So there the conversation ended. Hughes reported to Adams and returned to New York.

If Hughes intended this April 8 letter to Eisenhower as a last-chance appeal over Dulles' head, it didn't work. For nearly three weeks Eisenhower didn't answer. But when he did—in a letter that bears traces of the draftsmanship of Ann Whitman, who admired Hughes but who in any showdown always came down loyally on the side of the President—he not only refused to rise to any bait but spoke with a suavity worthy of Dulles himself: "This is in no sense an acknowledgment of your letter of the eighth (I would not dare in view of your dire threats). But I do at least want to tell you that I am glad to have your explanation of why the Administration is to be deprived of your contribution—and to tell you, too, that I understand thoroughly the decision you reached.

"Don't ever feel badly that you are, for the present at least, not to be working on a day-to-day basis for the government and for our country. You have already given so freely of your talents that I would not dare to ask you to make further sacrifices to continue to do so; and I have never promised, have I, to refrain from calling upon you for a particularly sensitive and demanding job?" He concluded chattily with a comment on the weather and the coming battle with Congress on appropriations.

Eisenhower would, indeed, call upon Hughes again, just once, within the coming weeks, to do an emergency message on mutual security for a nationwide TV broadcast. But he never called on Hughes thereafter.

Hughes was left to bitter reflection. By January 1959 he was again writing an inaugural address, but this time for a new kind of Republican, the incoming buoyant and liberal governor of New York State, Nelson Rockefeller. Before 1959 ended, Hughes, now a close associate of the governor's, published his eloquent *America the Vincible*, lauded by John Kennedy among others—a book that savaged Dulles and all his works; and that caused Eisenhower to send Hughes only a curt reminder that he, not Dulles, bore principal responsibility for America's foreign policy. By 1960 Hughes would be writing declarations for Nelson Rockefeller on the inadequacies of Eisenhower's defense budget. And by 1963 he would write *The Ordeal of Power*, a book this time striking at Eisenhower himself.

More than anything else, I have always believed, it was Rockefeller's association with Hughes that soured Eisenhower on Rockefeller. Indeed, I believe the course, from the beginning, of the relationship between the two men—the President and future governor—offers a supreme illustration not only of the influence of a subordinate but also of a central feature of Eisenhower's personality, an exquisite sensitivity to personal attack.

Rockefeller had signed on for the campaign in 1952 with stars in his eyes, and joined the team in Washington in 1953 first as an able adviser—with Milton Eisenhower and Arthur Flemming—on reorganization of the government, including the Pentagon (as he nervously waited outside the Oval Office with Charlie Wilson to tell the five-star Commander in Chief, successfully, how to organize Defense, he had found the "absurdity overwhelming"); then as loyal and admiring Undersecretary to Oveta Culp Hobby in the new Department of

Health, Education, and Welfare; and finally as C. D. Jackson's successor as Eisenhower's adviser on cold-war planning.

An activist like Jackson and Hughes, Rockefeller had from the start run into trouble with Foster Dulles and George Humphrey. Learning in early 1953 that Dulles was leaning negative on a $300 million loan to Brazil, pledged by Truman and Acheson, Rockefeller went to see Eisenhower, who at once phoned the Secretary of State ("Nelson is here, and he tells me. . . ."), heard Dulles' confirmation of the tentative turndown ("George Humphrey thinks the loan is inflationary"), and directed Dulles to reverse the decision—a conclusion, Rockefeller reflected ruefully years later, that "was good for Eisenhower, good for the U.S., good for Brazil, but that finished me with Foster Dulles." Discovering in 1955 that the Tata Iron and Steel Company of India wanted a one-half percent reduction in the Export-Import Bank interest rate in order to buy a steel mill from the United States (even so, at more than the price of a German plant) and that George Humphrey was refusing, thus alienating America's best free-enterprise friends in India, Rockefeller once again sought a reversal, this time in vain (though Kaiser did eventually get the contract). Hearing from Egypt's Foreign Minister Mahmoud Fawzi a face-to-face plea for an increase in U.S. economic aid—aid that would encourage Egypt to concentrate on its internal progress and move toward recognition of Israel—Rockefeller ran once again into a Dulles stone wall. Finally, seeing that Eisenhower was planning to go to the 1955 Geneva summit conference with only a sterile Dulles recommendation that the heads of government there should merely identify problems, leaving their solution to the foreign ministers, Rockefeller—assisted by Henry Kissinger, Walt Rostow, William Kintner, and other thinkers assembled at Quantico, Virginia—devised the Open Skies aerial inspection scheme, entailing overflights by the United States and the Soviet Union of each other's territory; encountered first Ike's delight with the innovation, then Dulles' cold water (nothing new; an old idea, long since discarded), then Ike's fury with Rockefeller's persistence ("Goddammit, Nelson, I've told you we're not going to do that! I don't want to hear any more about it"), and at last the thunderclap of success as—at Ike's own gracious invitation—Rockefeller came to Geneva to hear the President, finally persuaded, announce the electrifying challenge to the startled Russians and the world.

Restless under restraints (George Humphrey saw him as a "left-wing spendthrift"), Rockefeller left Washington, returned to New York, ran for the governorship in 1958, and won in a landslide. And as he was readying himself for the race, on October 4, 1957, the Russians put *Sputnik* in orbit. Public alarm immediately erupted over the sufficiency of our national defenses, and a distinguished Rockefeller Brothers Fund panel called for additional defense spending of $3 billion a year for the next several years—a direct slap at the Eisenhower Administration.

Nelson Rockefeller always believed that report fatally flawed his friendship with Eisenhower: "He never forgave me for that." Doubtless the criticism—which came only indirectly from Nelson himself—did hurt. But the Eisenhower presidential papers' evidence—some of which Rockefeller overlooked, some of which he never knew—confirms a different analysis.

Not only did Eisenhower volunteer to come to New York late in 1958 to campaign for Rockefeller (an offer Nelson declined, to keep the focus on Democratic Governor Averell Harriman's record, not on international relations); not only did Ike praise his decisive victory against the Democratic tide that that year drowned Republican candidates coast to coast; even after the advent of Emmet Hughes and the publication of *America the Vincible* in 1959, Eisenhower, despite his brusque note to Hughes himself, remained receptive to the possibility of a future Rockefeller presidency.

For the President continued to distinguish between the governor and his adviser. Even after Rockefeller's criticism of his defense budget in 1960, Eisenhower had a friendly frank phone talk with him on June 11, pointedly urging him to write his own speeches. And Ike wrote Henry Luce the same day that Nelson is "being too much influenced by a man who has no capacity for giving sensible advice." A few months earlier, on April 14, Eisenhower had received from Johns Hopkins political scientist Malcolm Moos, now his chief writer of speeches, a memorandum citing a historical precedent for a possible agreement by Nixon, candidate for President, that if elected he would serve only one term, then turn the candidacy for the succeeding term over to his loyal Vice-President, Nelson Rockefeller. In two single-spaced pages, Moos instanced Rutherford Hayes's public letter accepting the Republican nomination in 1876, where Hayes announced his "inflexible purpose, if elected, not to be a candidate for election to a second term." The declaration, Moos said, had won Hayes widespread praise; and if Nixon were to follow Hayes's example, by advance agreement with Rockefeller, Nixon might cite these reasons for his decision:

"1. He jumped out of his naval uniform directly into politics in 1946.

"2. By 1964 he will have been in Congress and high public office 18 years.

"3. He intends to do the things he believes are in the transcendent public good without regard to personal self-interest in re-election.

"4. After service either in the Armed Forces or political office for a quarter of a century, he believes that he should step aside in favor of new leadership in the Republican party.

"He also has a sincere interest in returning to private life to see more of his family and do some of the things that heavy demands of public office have precluded."

Moos also held out some bait for Rockefeller: If he accepted the vice-presidential nomination, he'd build up a great goodwill in the party. Moreover, he'd risk nothing. Even if the ticket lost in November, he would still be governor of New York and a leading prospect for the presidency in 1964.

Eisenhower did not rush to Nixon with Moos's arguments. But on July 19, after Gabe Hauge wrote Eisenhower that only a Nixon-Rockefeller ticket could hope to match Kennedy and Johnson, and "the only man who could persuade Nelson is you, sir," Eisenhower immediately got on the phone to Hauge, and the long conversation that ensued—a conversation recorded by Ann Whitman in two single-spaced pages—shows how seriously Eisenhower still regarded the Moos formula.

"I have talked to this man two or three times," Eisenhower told Hauge. "His attitude has been just as adamant as what you have read in the papers. He said this morning, or yesterday, 'I will not run . . . even if the President asks me.' I don't see very well how I can get down on my knees to him. He is apparently possessed with a popular appeal that people feel—but he is no philosophical genius. It is pretty hard to get him in and tell him something of his duty. He has a personal ambition that is overwhelming. . . . There is only one formula by which Nelson would take the second spot," Eisenhower continued. "If Nixon would, very confidentially, tell Nelson that he would serve only for four years if victorious, I believe Nelson would agree to run for vice president. I don't think Dick would agree with this, but if Dick does ask my opinion, I'd say that 4 years in the presidency [would be] enough...."

Nothing, obviously, came of this conversation. Indeed, within less than a week Rockefeller and Eisenhower once again came into confrontation—with Nixon in the middle—this time over Rockefeller's insistence, to which Nixon agreed in a late-night secret meeting at Rockefeller's New York apartment on July 22–23, that the Republican platform include these words critical of Ike's defense policy: "The U.S. can afford and must provide the increased expenditures to implement fully this necessary program for strengthening our defense posture. There must be no price ceiling on America's security."

When Ike got these sentences—soon made public—from his representative at the platform committee, Bob Merrian, over the phone, he sent word through Jim Hagerty that he would not accept them. By 12:30 that afternoon, Saturday, July 23, Nixon was phoning Eisenhower, then in Newport, Rhode Island. As Ann Whitman recorded the conversation: "The Vice President apparently told him of the meeting with Nelson Rockefeller, the getting together of suggestions for Party platform. What he did not tell him was that it was being interpreted by the convention as Nixon undercutting the President." The next day the two had a longer and franker talk; in Ann's words: "The President called the Vice President and said there had been reported to him some unhappiness because of the Nixon-Rockefeller agreement, apparently, on the platform. Some of the things were completely at variance with what the platform committee wanted. Its members felt there was implied an indirect criticism of the Administration.... Eisenhower threatened indirectly no enthusiasm for the campaign if the platform criticized the administration (this I must say was very veiled but it was there)." Nixon pledged that he would see to it that the platform gave a ringing endorsement of everything the administration had done.

In the end, Eisenhower amended the objectionable wording on defense. The platform committee adopted his changes to the letter.

And Nelson Rockefeller dropped off the Eisenhower list of vice-presidential possibilities.

Through the postpresidential years Eisenhower's resentments intensified. In early 1962, though he sent one draft chapter of *Mandate for Change*—on the Geneva conference—to Rockefeller for comment, he sent not one page to Hughes. And later that year, when Eisenhower's publishers, Doubleday & Company, relayed to him Hughes's request for permission to quote Eisenhower letters verbatim in Hughes's forthcoming *The Ordeal of Power*—also under Doubleday contract—Eisenhower exploded.

As Doubleday Chairman Douglas M. Black, editors Ken McCormick and Sam Vaughan, and John Eisenhower and I were working downstairs in Ike's Gettysburg office one morning, the General suddenly entered. Without a preface he began scoring his old friend Black and "you Doubleday people" for publishing an author "who writes books against me." And he went on to ask pointedly how Nelson Rockefeller (who was then, before his divorce, the prospective front-runner against John Kennedy for the presidency in 1964) could expect Eisenhower's backing with a man like Hughes in his employ. The discussion ended inconclusively, with Ike agreeing Doubleday should not summarily "kick out" Hughes's book. In the event, however, it was published not by Doubleday but by Atheneum; and Hughes left the Rockefeller family to write for *Newsweek*.

In 1965 one late draft of *Waging Peace* included a sentence, suggested by an assistant, that said what many—indeed most— political analysts believed about the 1960 election: that Nelson Rockefeller could have won it. Eisenhower left the observation in for several retypings, then one day suddenly struck it out, with a testy comment on Rockefeller's "divisiveness" as a party leader. And in 1968, when Hughes returned to serve as Rockefeller's principal assistant in his doomed run for the Republican nomination, Eisenhower wrote Ann Whitman deploring the re-association; it would mean, Ike said, that Nelson would never be nominated. And abandoning his years-long earlier neutrality, the mortally ill former President called a news conference, got up from his hospital bed, and announced for Richard Nixon.

Many forces led to this result, including Rockefeller's own restiveness under Eisenhower's leadership and Dulles' foreign policy; Rockefeller's divorce; the approaching marriage of Julie Nixon and David Eisenhower; and Ike's own increasing conservatism. But the key force was Emmet John Hughes.

When I suggested this analysis to Rockefeller years later, he did not leap to agree; the Brothers Fund report, he maintained, marked the crossroads. But as he reflected—on Hughes's role in the negotiations over the 1960 platform; on his gubernatorial secretary

Ann Whitman's bitterness over Hughes's betrayal of the President, he admitted: "You may be right." And he added a memorable piece of perception: "After Emmet's love for Eisenhower turned to hate, he used his intellect to serve his emotions"; a memorable aside ("I'm not sure Emmet did *me* a great deal of good"); and a memorable piece of irony: "I haven't read either of Hughes's books on Eisenhower." Nelson Rockefeller suffered from dyslexia. But of a certainty he—like Dwight Eisenhower—knew the embarrassments those books, particularly the second, contained. And like Dwight Eisenhower—who also "never read" them—he was putting them beneath his sight.

No one knows whether an Eisenhower endorsement of Rockefeller could, in the end, have stopped Nixon's advance to the White House. But I must believe, with Sherman Adams, that the outcome might have been otherwise.

If Eisenhower did have a tragic flaw, it was sensitivity to personal attack. Hughes was not alone: Harry Truman of the 1952 campaign; Adlai Stevenson of the taunts and smears of 1952 and 1956; and Jack Kennedy of 1960—mention of these people's names would forever bring a tightening of the jaw and a reddening of the face. A man who always declared his thick-skinned good-natured indifference to any and all attacks, a man who claimed he did what Tom Jenkins, his old West Point wrestling coach, always told him to do—come back off the canvas with a grin on your face—Eisenhower's insouciance was an exercise in iron self-discipline. Underneath, the venom worked; and it shaped the course of history.

"There comes a time when a man has to deal with a potential enemy." What if Sherman Adams had crossed the narrow aisle that divided him from Wayne Morse? What if Dwight Eisenhower had seen what Adams later saw: that the time had come to deal differently with Emmet Hughes; to keep close the glory of wording and fertility of passionate imagining brought to his White House by—and only by (for no one ever replaced him)—this gifted young aide; that the time had come *not* to create out of alienation and hatred and hurt an inevitable, implacable foe?

No one knows. But history does have turning points of choice, some of them personal. Hughes was to influence the link between Eisenhower and Rockefeller. Of course, there were philosophical differences between the President and the governor, but their relationship was colored primarily by events, both large and small. "There comes a time. . . . "

XIV

JULY 14, 1958

COMMANDER
IN CHIEF

At 2:30 on the afternoon of July 14, 1958, Eisenhower summoned twenty-two congressional leaders, Republicans and Democrats, to the White House to tell them he was planning to send U.S. forces into Lebanon. Facing what he and his advisers perceived as a Communist threat, through internal rebellion, to that lovely land of mountains and beaches, Maronite Christians and antipathetic Moslems; acting in accordance with the U.N. Charter and the 1957 Eisenhower Doctrine; responding to a plea from conservative Maronite President Camille Chamoun, who had triggered the crisis by reportedly approving a drive toward a constitutional amendment to permit him an unprecedented second term; spurred by the news of a military revolt in nearby Iraq and the assasination of its King Faisal II, Crown Prince Abdul Illah, and Premier Nuri as-Said, Eisenhower that afternoon was poised for the decision that would send the Sixth Fleet into action; airlift Army battle groups eastward from Germany; and send Marines splashing ashore amid startled swimmers south of Beirut. The action would restore calm and avert a take-over. Within a little over three months the Lebanese would peacefully elect a new President; and Eisenhower would order the last of the troops out again.

For the first and only time during his presidency, Eisenhower was sending American forces into possible overseas combat. And he was providing an arresting demonstration of his recurrent maxim, "When you appeal to force, there's just one thing you must never do—lose," and its corollary, repeated again and again to his staff: "Remember this: there's no such thing as a little force. You have to use it overwhelmingly."

Ten months earlier he had overwhelmed the crisis in Little Rock with the dispatching of a thousand paratroopers of the 101st Airborne Division to the streets around Central High School. And now he was overwhelming the crisis in Lebanon, again without bloodshed or loss of life, with an unparalleled peacetime eruption of power—ultimately a force of fourteen thousand on Lebanese soil, backed by seventy warships and more than eleven hundred SAC aircraft on heightened alert, "bombed and crews ready."

Nothing exemplifies better than the Lebanon intervention, I believe, the American people's reason for wanting Eisenhower as Commander in Chief. He had twice won election by massive margins because, above all, the electorate trusted him to hold the security of the nation in his hand; trusted his capability to bring us through roiling international waters without fear, without defeat, without Armageddon. Here lay Eisenhower's supreme personal expertise; here, more than anywhere else, he spent his waking hours. Hydroelectric power, Social Security, conservation, housing—these he could extensively delegate. But on national security he was the master.

To hour after hour of nuts-and-bolts conferences on this subject, he brought a soldier's vision of the world at midcentury. To him it was a world characterized by protracted conflict, a world in which the spasmodic stop-and-start defense planning of his predecessor had become an anachronism. No longer could we let our defenses deteriorate, as the Truman administration did after V-J Day, a deterioration that, Ike told the Legislative Leaders May 12, 1953, forced us to pull out of the Korean peninsula and thus invite attack.

No longer could we make the opposite mistake the Truman administration made, once the Korean War started—ordering defense spending without adequately counting the cost. Truman had left Eisenhower, for fiscal year 1954 (beginning July 1, 1953), a budget $9.9 billion in the red; an overestimate of tax revenues of $1.2 billion; and $81 billion in additional spending authorizations—C.O.D. deliveries that somehow would have to be paid for in the next few years.

And no longer could we theorize, as the Truman administration had, about a single desperate D-Day of maximum danger toward which to direct all planning. All of these errors Eisenhower rejected; our defense "must...be one which we can bear for a long and indefinite period of time. It cannot consist of sudden, blind responses to a series of fire-alarm emergencies...."

To Eisenhower the world at midcentury was, secondly, a world transformed by a revolution in weaponry.

In graphic words on January 3, 1955, the old soldier lectured the Cabinet and the Legislative Leaders on its realities: "In the kind of war we are faced with, how long do you think it would take us to ship ten divisions to Europe or six to Japan? Enemy submarines would be swarming the seas, and troops at either the port of embarkation or debarkation would be sitting ducks for atomic aerial attack. What we have got to do in our new thinking is to realize that there will be a period when all we can do is to [a]vert disaster. If we have time to do that job and hit back hard, then we can do the rest in time. But unless we do this, gentlemen, take my word for it we are going to be shot to pieces."

And a month later, when Senator Styles Bridges mentioned that Army Chief of Staff Matthew Ridgway was complaining that cuts in Army personnel would jeopardize U.S. security, Ike continued the lecture to the Leaders, pounding the table: "Gentlemen, Ridgway is Chief of Staff of the Army. When he is called up on the Hill and asked for personal convictions, he has got to give them....But...as Commander in Chief, I have to make the final decisions. I have to look at this whole question of the military establishment as one which must be kept in balance....

"Actually, the only thing we fear is an atomic attack delivered by air on our cities. Suppose that attack were to occur tomorrow on fifteen of our cities. Goddamn it, [it] would be perfect rot to talk about shipping troops abroad when fifteen of our cities were in ruins. You would have disorder and almost complete chaos in the cities and in the roads around them....Do you think the police and fire departments of those cities could restore order? Nuts! That order is going to have to be restored by our military forces and by our Reserves. That's what our military is going to be doing in the first days of an all-out atomic attack....Anyone who thinks we are going to immediately ship out of this country division after division is just talking through his hat. It couldn't be done and if I tried to do it, you would want to impeach me. That's the trouble with Ridgway. He's talking theory—I'm trying to talk sound sense....We have to have a sound base here at home. We have got to restore order and our productivity before we do anything else.... What do you people think would happen if this city were hit today by an H-bomb? Do you think you would vote or ask me to send the troops at Fort Meade overseas—or would you be knocking on my door to get me to bring them in to try to pick up the pieces here in Washington?"

"As the President was talking," Hagerty observed in his diary, "you could hear a pin drop in the room."

In such a midcentury world—a world of protracted conflict and of ultimate weapons—a decisive deterrent became an imperative. This entailed not only today's delivery system, a strong retaliatory air force; but also tomorrow's ballistic missiles.

As Truman left office, the United States was spending on such missiles just $3 million a year. In Eisenhower's first fiscal year, 1954, the figure jumped to $14 million, and in the next year to $161 million. But something else happened: in 1953 the administration set up, to advise the Air Force, a Strategic Missiles Evaluation Committee of civilian scientists under the chairmanship of the brilliant mathematician John von Neumann. On February 10, 1954, Von Neumann reported the possibility of a major breakthrough in reducing the size of a nuclear warhead carried by an intercontinental (range: 5,000 miles plus) ballistic missile (ICBM). In May the CASTLE tests in the Pacific confirmed this finding.

In February 1955 another committee of scientists urged a speedup of work on an intermediate-range (1,500-mile) missile (IRBM). By late summer Eisenhower accorded the Air Force's pursuit of an ICBM top priority. By December the same top priority went to two ICBMs (Atlas and Titan) and two IRBMs (Jupiter and Thor). All three services were into long-range missile research—a fact that gave Eisenhower some qualms: as he wrote Charlie Wilson December 21, 1955, he had had an uneasy feeling that the August to November delay in issuing the Defense directives on this research had stemmed from interservice squabbling. But Wilson assured the President that all such differences would be eliminated and that separate programs would produce beneficial competition. And Ike went along, repeating to Wilson what he had earlier told the NSC: that "the political and psychological impact upon the world in the development of an effective [IRBM]...would be so great that early development of such a missile would be of critical importance to the national security interests of the United States."

"Because scientific progress exerts a constantly increasing influence upon the character and conduct of war," Eisenhower had written Wilson a year earlier, "and because America's most precious possession is the lives of her citizens, we should base our security upon military formations which make maximum use of science and technology in order to minimize numbers in men." When an interceptor can't go as high as a bomber, he told the Legislative Leaders, ground forces can't help.

Along with powerful systems for retaliation and for early warning against attack, other subsidiary requisites would of course remain, including ships to clear the ocean lanes, U.S. NATO forces which could become swiftly engaged, improved Reserves to help preserve order after a nuclear attack, and "mobile forces to help indigenous troops deter local aggression, direct and indirect."

But the figures reflect the hierarchy: U.S. Army strength of 1.5 million men in December 1953 went by June 1955 to 1 million; Navy strength of 1 million, to 870,000; Air Force strength of 950,000, to 970,000—the only increase. Between FY54 and FY55 Army and Navy budgets declined; that of the Air Force went up. "We are certainly not going to fight a ground war in Europe," Eisenhower told reporters March 11, 1959, at the height of the crisis over Khrushchev's threats against Western rights in Berlin. And short weeks after those words, both threats and crisis came to an end.

In the world at midcentury efficiency became another Eisenhower imperative. "I have advised the Secretary of Defense," Eisenhower wrote Budget Director Joe Dodge December 1, 1953, "that to achieve real savings at an early date in the Defense Department, he will be required, as I see it, to establish personnel ceilings in each service.... I believe that the divisions, combat units, and air squadrons in Korea should be kept up at full strength.... Likewise, the Strategic Air Force (at least that part of it that would be expected to carry out instantly any retaliatory operation), together with certain interceptor squadrons, should be kept at full strength. But I believe, on the other hand, that practically all supporting units, schools, detachments of all kinds of civilian duty, can safely be reduced by a definite percentage....We are no longer fighting in Korea, and the Defense establishment should show its appreciation of this fact and help us achieve some substantial savings—and without wailing about the missions they have to accomplish...."

Ike wrote dozens of memos like this.

To heighten the Pentagon's efficiency and responsiveness, Eisenhower reorganized it twice: once in 1953, when he sought limited changes, with Nelson Rockefeller's help, through a reorganization plan which the Congress permitted to take effect; and once in 1958, when he sought major changes, through the enactment of legislation, to vest more power in the Secretary of Defense and pull into line the conflicting and competing Army, Navy, and Air Force.

On January 25, 1958, accompanied by Harlow and Goodpaster, Ike drove to the Pentagon for a full-scale shootout on the problem. There they were (as seen by a canny observer): Defense Secretary Neil McElroy, who had recently succeeded Wilson; Chairman of the Joint Chiefs Nathan Twining, "a good soldier, trained in the tradition that whatever the Commander in Chief wants, he will fight for," a man "not too effective but loyal"; General Thomas White, Air Force Chief of Staff, "inclined to say one thing and [then] go around the corner to tell the *Air Force Journal* to print [the opposite]"; Chief of Naval Operations Arleigh Burke, also a "good soldier," who had kept the "Navy under control, [with] no big explosions"; General Max Taylor, an old Army man "but a little bit of an aesthete"; General Randolph Pate, who "would fight to the last breath for the Marines"; the three service secretaries, all "captives of [their] various services"; and perhaps the most brilliant man in the upper reaches of the Pentagon, Deputy Secretary Donald Quarles—the "true scientist," a man "who goes to the heart of the matter," an ardent believer in the need for reorganization. "It won't do simply to justify everything now being done," Eisenhower told them. For example, the services then had some one hundred thirty liaison officers assigned to the Hill; each service had more public relations flacks than the Secretary of Defense.

The present Joint Chiefs of Staff system, Ike continued, was too complicated ever to work in wartime, too full of frictions, differences, complications of effort; he wanted to clear command channels and to set up under the Joint Chiefs a really effective, integrated staff, with the whole organization directly under the Secretary of Defense.

By April 3 Eisenhower was sending to the Hill the details of his recommendations for reform: organization of the actual fighting forces into truly unified commands, under full control of a single officer of whatever service; orders directly to that unified command (thus to "the man with the gun") from the President and the Secretary of Defense, not by a meandering route through various service secretaries; a strengthened military staff to advise the Secretary of Defense; a new Director of Defense Research and Engineering under the Secretary, to supervise all Pentagon research and development; and more legal authority for the Secretary of Defense over his department, including its $40 billion annual budget.

Eisenhower's key adviser on the reorganization, Bryce Harlow, as staff director of the House Armed Services Committee in the years after World War II, had worked hand in glove with its chairman, the venerable Carl Vinson of Georgia, and he regarded Uncle Carl with an almost filial affection and esteem. Now Harlow found himself in the middle, engineering the President's reorganization bill through the legislative tunnel.

As soon as Eisenhower's proposed legislation appeared, Vinson attacked it. The President, he said, was seeking to merge the Armed Services; to produce a Prussian-style general staff; and, in his proposal to appropriate all funds directly to the Secretary of Defense, to undermine the "constitutional responsibilities" of the Congress.

Eisenhower took the offensive. In a speech to the American Society of Newspaper Editors, he fired back a salvo of Harlowisms: the administration bill would mean no Prussian general staff, no undermining of congressional authority, no czar, no $40 billion blank check. And then, in what Harlow called a "tour de force" effort, the President went to the people, launching a personal letter-writing and lobbying campaign in which "for the first time Dwight Eisenhower used all his powers as President; it was sheer muscle all the way." Ike wrote to some four hundred business friends; he "dropped in," in business suit, on a black-tie meeting of the U.S. Chamber of Commerce to thank its members for their help. And the heat began to reach the Hill. Harlow's phone rang. Uncle Carl was calling: "Bryce, the ox is in the ditch. Can you help the old man get the ox out of the ditch?" Harlow agreed to help. He, Vinson, John R. Blandford (Committee Counsel), and Representative Paul Kilday of Texas sat around a table and redrafted a bill; it contained nearly everything Eisenhower had wanted from the start. On its passage, Ike sent Harlow two bottles of Chivas Regal. They had engineered a signal victory.

Finally, in the world at midcentury, a world of protracted conflict, of ultimate weapons, balance became an imperative:

—Balance to prevent the flow of overwhelming power (as Eisenhower said, in words well remembered, in his Farewell Address) to the "military-industrial complex"; or (as he said in the same address, in words less well remembered) to a "scientific-technological elite."

—Balance to prevent interservice contention and to replace loyalty to service with loyalty to country. On the morning of August 5,1957, Ike picked up the phone hopping mad and called General White, Air Force Chief of Staff. In a public speech White had "made comparisons," Ike wrote in his diary, "between the Air Force and its sister services in the matter of their readiness to appreciate modern conditions and adapt their methods and equipment to those conditions.

"I told him that I had no objection to his praising his own service as much as he pleased, but I did object to any representative of one of the services comparing himself or his own service with the others to their disadvantage and his own advantage. This in my opinion is destructive in terms of the whole general service morale.

"It is the old question of whether servicemen are working first of all for their own service or for the good of the United States."

A year earlier, Eisenhower had written Swede Hazlett about this "most frustrating domestic problem.... Time and again I have had the high Defense officials in conference—with all the senior military and their civilian bosses present—and have achieved what has seemed to me general agreement.... Yet when each Service puts down its minimum requirements for its own military budget for the following year and I add up the total, I find that they mount at a fantastic rate. There is seemingly no end to all of this. Yet merely 'getting tough' on my part is not an answer. *I simply must find men who have the breadth of understanding and devotion to their country rather than to a single Service that will bring about better solutions than I get now* [italics added].

"Strangely enough, the one man who sees this clearly is a Navy man who at one time was an uncompromising exponent of Naval power and its superiority over any other kind of strength. That is Radford....

"Some day there is going to be a man sitting in my present chair who has not been raised in the military services and who will have little understanding of where slashes in their estimates can be made with little or no damage. If that should happen while we still have the state of tension that now exists in the world, I shudder to think of what could happen in this country...."

Perhaps it was such a shudder, four and a half years later, with a young Massachusetts Democrat about to enter 1600 Pennsylvania Avenue, that prompted Ike's farewell warning against the power of the military-industrial complex, a power that could make a man green to the ways of the military a victim to their constant drive for more, more, more.

—Balance to prevent (as Eisenhower said in a nationwide telecast his first year in office) the country's transformation into a "garrison state" through the self-defeating pursuit of absolute safety. "There is no such thing as maximum military security short of total mobilization of all our national resources," Eisenhower declared in that telecast, a form of security that "would compel us to imitate the methods of the dictator." "American strength," Eisenhower said in his letter to Hazlett, "is a combination of economic, moral and military force. If we demand too much in taxes in order to build planes and ships, we will tend to dry up the accumulations of capital that are necessary to provide jobs for the million or more new workers that we must absorb each year. Behind each worker there is an average of about $15,000 in invested capital. His job depends upon this investment at a yearly rate of not less than 15 to 20 billions. If taxes become so burdensome that investment loses its attractiveness for capital, there will finally be nobody but government to build the facilities. This is one form of Socialism.

"Let us not forget that the Armed Services are to defend a 'way of life' not merely land, property or lives. So what I try to make the Chiefs realize is that they are men of sufficient stature, training and intelligence to think of this balance—the balance between minimum requirements in the costly implements of war and the health of our economy."

—Balance to prevent panic. On November 4, just one month after *Sputnik*, Mr. H. Rowan Gaither, Robert Lovett, Frank Stanton, William Foster, and other distinguished citizens came to see Eisenhower to report the results of a study they had made, at government request, of America's national security. It was gloom, gloom, gloom. As the notetaker for the meeting scribbled on his yellow legal pad: "The group appraised the threat very thoroughly. They found that our active defenses are not adequate. They had concluded that our passive defenses are almost insignificant. They felt that our Strategic Air Force could be knocked out on the ground today, and that by 1959 SAC will be highly vulnerable to the ICBM and our population critically vulnerable. . . . In the event of hostilities, they concluded, the U.S. could expect to lose half its population as casualties."

Gaither and associates then made a host of recommendations: pool economic, technological, and political resources with our allies; lessen the vulnerability of the Strategic Air Command to Soviet attack; increase SAC's offensive power; increase our forces for limited warfare; eliminate weaknesses in our active defenses; increase our antisubmarine effort; establish a nationwide fallout shelter program.

Eisenhower and Dulles eyed all these alarms and solutions and began to sort them out one by one. By January 6, when the NSC met to go over these recommendations, they found that the executive agencies completely concurred with putting more SAC bombers on alert; fractionally concurred with other suggestions—for example, increasing the number of ICBMs planned for July 1, 1963; and discarded only one suggestion outright—blast shelters, at astronomical cost, for SAC runways. Eisenhower himself took great interest in the panel's recommendations on the alert and dispersal of SAC.

Ten days later the NSC once again peered over the rim of Hell and considered the recommendation for fallout shelters—$22 billion worth—to save 50 million lives. Rejecting it, Eisenhower came to a cold conclusion: "To talk about a hundred million dead," he said, "is to talk about the complete paralysis of the United States.

"It would be silly to talk of recuperation if everything were destroyed. We could destroy Russia. The result would be two wounded giants doing nothing. Civilization could not be rebuilt in two centuries."

Given such numbers, no nation could "win," and it would be folly to plan for such a "victory." As Eisenhower had told top military officers assembled at Quantico more than three years earlier, on June 19, 1954:

"No matter how well prepared for war we may be, no matter how certain we are that within 24 hours we could destroy Kuibyshev and Moscow and Leningrad and Bakhu and all the other places that would allow the Soviets to carry on war, I want you to carry this question home with you: Gain such a victory, and what do you do with it? Here would be a great area from the Elbe to Vladivostok and down through Southeast Asia torn up and destroyed, without government, without its communications, just an area of starvation and disaster. I ask you what would the civilized world do about it? I repeat there is no victory in any war except through our imaginations, through our dedication, and through our work to avoid it."

In the upshot on the Gaither report, while deciding to give some further study to shelters, Eisenhower and his advisers agreed to keep nuclear retaliatory power as our principal reliance. Though modifying specific features of U.S. defense, they refused to make a slam-bang switch in frenzy. And time has proved them right, and vindicated the balance of the man at the center of the fire storm.

The word "balance," which reverberates like a pedal point through Eisenhower's conduct of his country's defense, recalls once again that moment of tension in the White House July 14, 1958. For on that summer afternoon, with its bursting evocation of firepower—of ships, troops, planes roaring eastward toward Lebanon—one single, tiny, silent detail shines out, like a point of brilliant light in a Vermeer. As Ike told the congressional leaders the Marines were going in, one lone observer, keen of eye and sensibility, heard the senators and congressmen draw in their breath with apprehension. And then he happened to look at the President, and what he saw was this: one big hand (Eisenhower had outsized hands, with knuckles broken in football, made for wielding an ax or kneading the dough for a pie crust), dangling over the arm of his chair—a hand relaxed, with no sweating palm, no agitation, no nervousness—a single arresting symbol of the man: of a capacity to make agonizing decisions which could entail death and sorrow; of objectivity and command; of detachment, of his ability to remove himself, to delegate details, to do his duty as he saw it; of that magnificent nervous system, the silent center on which a whole earthshaking event turned.

A symbol, in a word, of courage—courage which is itself a balance: balance between cowardice and rashness, between blind surrender and blind assault.

Eisenhower saw life steadily, saw it whole, and saw it un-afraid. In the midst of the furor over the 1944 Battle of the Bulge, William Robinson found Ike at SHAEF "the only unworried, un-harassed man I had met in four days." In the midst of the 1956 Suez crisis, facing a dictatorship "furious and scared" on the brink of World War III, Emmet Hughes watched Ike bang golf balls across the White House lawn, doubtless cussing the insanity of it all, and the particular perfidy of the British and French. In the midst of the 1962 Cuban missile crisis, I remember Eisenhower's returning to our Gettysburg editing sessions from a briefing call from the White House, exclaiming: "Boy, *that* was good news!" and reflecting: "You know, most of the worst things you expect to happen never do happen." And in the midst of his final illness, several months before the end, as the nationwide TV news reported the Walter Reed physicians' fear that Ike would probably not live through the night, I can still hear John Eisenhower's words over the phone as he confirmed the stark prognosis: "The only person who's not gloomy around here is Dad. He's kidding with the nurses and having a great time. But all the doctors looking at all those dials just can't say anything hopeful."

Eisenhower saw the terrors in each of these moments of impending death; and he saw another terror, a terror that particularly haunted him, the terror of death-in-life itself—the loss of faculties, unperceived. This prospect haunted him as he watched his old friend Winston Churchill slip into incompetence, unaware, and as he himself struggled with his decision over running again. It haunted him on repeated visits to Walter Reed as he watched the scientist he admired most in the world, Dr. John von Neumann, dying slowly of cancer, that mind of incandescent genius not even recognizing the President, imperceptibly becoming a nothing. It haunted him in 1959 as he again traveled to Walter Reed to visit both Foster Dulles and George Marshall, silently slipping away into oblivion. It haunted him in 1968, as he himself recuperated at Walter Reed after multiple electric shocks for heart fibrillation, asking General Gruenther, worry in his voice, "Have I turned into a vegetable yet?" And surely the specter must have crossed his mind as, working on the book, he would recall an event, only to discover his recollection radically wrong, confuted by documents written at the time of the event itself.

Courage is not the absence of fear, but the mastery of fear. In 1964 Eisenhower's superb personal Air Force pilot, Colonel William Draper, came to Gettysburg to confer with his old boss about his imminent and forced career change after a heart attack, from professional pilot to airline executive. The prospect terrified Bill Draper, and he asked Ike what he should do. And he got this magnificent answer: "Go ahead, *be* scared, and do it anyway."

At the heart of our national security for eight critical years were the experience, the wisdom, and above all the courage of a single man.

XV

AUGUST 26, 1960

AT ARM'S LENGTH

O n August 26, 1960, CIA Director Allen Dulles dictated and
dispatched an urgent cable to the agency's station chief in the
Republic of the Congo, a new nation just eight weeks independent of
Belgium and racked with tribal violence, a rampaging pillaging revolt
of its armed forces, the secession of its mineral-rich Katanga Province,
and the threat of continuing chaos or a Communist take-over. In
circumlocutious wording ("targets of opportunity may present themselves to you. . . . You can act on your own authority" if the ambassador
does not wish to be consulted and if time does not permit checking
back with Washington), the cable gave the station chief his unmistak-
able order: effect the removal of the Congo's Prime Minister—in U.S.
eyes a frenzied Soviet tool—Patrice Lumumba, if necessary by
assassination.

There followed many weeks of bizarre—and ineffectual
(Lumumba was eventually murdered, but not by the CIA)—maneuvering to this end, monitored personally by Dulles and his deputy,
Richard Bissell, and capped by the arrival in Leopoldville, exactly one
month after the urgent cable, of a scientist spook from CIA headquarters carrying in his luggage rubber gloves, syringe, mask, and "lethal
biological material" (which apparently soon lost its potency) to be
squirted into Lumumba's food or toothpaste.

Surveying all these events fifteen years later, after Watergate,
the Senate Select Committee to Study Governmental Operations with

Respect to Intelligence Activities—Frank Church (Democrat, Idaho) chairman, John Tower (Republican, Texas) vice-chairman—issued a portentous pronouncement: the evidence it had seen would "permit a reasonable inference that the plot to assassinate Lumumba was authorized by President Eisenhower."

He, in the committee's eyes, knew. And, the committee's "reasonable inference" went, to protect the presidency—or himself— he kept the deed and its perpetrators at arm's length.

Did he?

An organization man, a man who habitually saw himself in a constitutional role, Eisenhower without question used his organization again and again to preserve detachment—to avoid bespattering himself or the office he held or both. In campaign speeches he never asked anyone to vote for him. He never attacked an opponent by name. He never himself accepted a vanquished enemy's sword. On V-E Day in 1945, it was Bedell Smith, not Eisenhower, who accepted Jodl's surrender at Rheims. (The event measures the distance between Eisenhower and MacArthur, who accepted the Japanese surrender on V-J Day himself.) On election night in 1956 it was his political lieutenants whom Eisenhower ordered to accept, metaphorically, the surrender sword of Adlai Stevenson. He let others at times take flak directed at his decisions ("If I give the reporters that answer," Jim Hagerty once protested, "they'll give me hell." "Better you than me, boy," Ike chuckled. "Now go out there and tell them"). Thus preserving his detachment, Hagerty admiringly commented years later, Eisenhower in confrontation always left an escape route open, "for himself and for the other guy." He was not only Hamlet or Lear, the protagonist in the midst of events; he was also the symbol of moral order at their end—the Fortinbras or Albany, uncorrupted.

From the start Eisenhower had, detached, pursued the 1952 Republican nomination through trusted lieutenants, Lucius Clay and above all Herbert Brownell, who worked always in his name and occasionally without his knowledge. Tom Dewey's man, a Wall Street lawyer, short, mild-mannered, gently paunchy, deferential, quick of smile, unflappable, nasal-voiced from his Nebraska boyhood, likable, suspicious of fine print, politically tough and sharp, Brownell had run both of Dewey's presidential campaigns and served (1944–46) as chairman of the Republican National Committee.

In late March 1952, after the New Hampshire primary victory, Brownell, at Clay's dispatch, came to see Ike at SHAPE. He hadn't wanted to leave his lucrative law practice and get back into the nitty-gritty search for convention votes, but at that meeting the Eisenhower personality worked its magic, and Brownell left with his "marching orders"—an understanding of what he had to do in the months ahead, yet without any explicit declaration from Eisenhower that he would make the race at all. All he had, Brownell later recalled, was "the distinct feeling that if Eisenhower had decided in his own mind not to be a candidate, I would have known it before I left that day." Indeed, in public Eisenhower still professed indifference to the nomination. Brownell found himself soliciting people who knew that if they announced for Ike and he left them holding the bag, they would face their own political extermination. So for anxious weeks, Brownell kept his fingers crossed, swallowed his uncertainties, and stuck his neck out. "I told them flatly he would run," Brownell recalled. But like Cabot Lodge, Brownell recognized gray areas of indefiniteness where Eisenhower would not lay out explicit ground rules. "There were things I never said to him," Brownell recalled later, "and things he never said to me," on subjects of crucial significance on which Brownell nevertheless had to act.

Far from the view of their war-hero candidate, political officers and foot soldiers took on various dirty necessary jobs. Brownell himself, for example, became nervous about the impending publication of Kay Summersby's first autobiographical book, *Eisenhower Was My Boss*; asked the publisher to let him see an advance copy; found it innocuous except for a lurid blurb on the jacket; and persuaded the publisher to tone that down.

Others of far lower rank pulled off the usual variety of rough tricks, as in most campaigns. In the dead of night they removed the clapper from a huge Taft bell. One key Eisenhower agent, with a bankroll of $365,000, projected a huge image of Eisenhower onto the Tribune Tower of Taft die-hard Colonel Robert R. McCormick. He floated a dirigible over Michigan Avenue above the colonel's office with a voice booming: "You *read* the Chicago *Tribune?* Ho! Ho! Ho!" He hired a helicopter to descend at the precise moment of General MacArthur's airport arrival and blow to the four winds the pages of the General's address. He discovered (some ex-CIA operatives on his payroll having penetrated the Taft organization's inner recesses) how big booming Ohio Congressman George Bender, heading Taft's singing forces, was planning to use "I'm Looking over a Four-leaf Clover" as Taft's theme song; and he promptly organized counterperformances using the same melody with the words "Taft Is a Loser, a Four-time Loser." He got three busloads of Gary steelworkers to form a flying wedge to crash onto the convention hall floor, breaking three front teeth and the arm of a Taftite doorman. He found out that the Taft people had paid the organist $500 to play seven minutes longer than the official demonstration time, and shelled out $1,000 to make him play *fourteen* minutes overtime for Ike.

Of all this, Eisenhower knew nothing. Indeed, I recall the day he learned of it from the man himself, who came out to Gettysburg in 1961 and regaled the General for a couple of hours with these war stories. Intrigued, Ike remarked, "We ought to put some of those into the book." Such tactics were his organization's, however, not his.

The 1952 nomination and election won, Brownell and his chief cohort Tom Stephens continued arm's length lieutenancies in a variety of forms. Early in 1955, for example, Stephens, then White House appointments secretary, peeled off from the staff, ostensibly to return to New York to practice law, but actually to scout out Republican leaders coast to coast and make the 1956 convention an Eisenhower convention. Specifically, his top secret mission—known to Eisenhower, Clay, Adams, and few others—entailed manipulating state political conventions, uncovering problems that could cause trouble there, and informing Adams regularly on what the administration should do to "decapitate" (Adams' word) any obstacles. His mission also entailed a surreptitious sampling of Republican opinion of Richard Nixon.

Brownell himself, as Attorney General for nearly five years, bore for Eisenhower the delegated responsibility of knowing and controlling the work of the FBI. Perhaps the knowledge and control were imperfect: the Church Committee alleges that no Attorney General, from 1946 to 1963, was informed of the bureau's "black bag jobs" (surreptitious entries of foreign embassies to get hold of their codes). But in the large, Brownell believes, he knew the "mechanics" of the FBI's activities. The more controversial of these (particularly the Counterintelligence Program, or COINTELPRO, used in the sixties to harass Martin Luther King and domestic dissidents) were, under Brownell—as under his successor, William Rogers,—directed against Communist agents. Only spies were investigated through wiretaps. "Nothing we did," as revealed by the Church Committee, Brownell asserts, "has given me any pause. They found no evidence of wrongdoing."

Of all this, Eisenhower knew only what he had to know. "Do you have to tell me?" he once interrupted his Attorney General sharply as Brownell began to recount how—with the FBI's "help"—a suspected Communist accomplice had twice mysteriously "lost" his briefcase. To know such detail was the charge of the Attorney General, not the President. Similarly, Eisenhower, while opposing legislation to ban the dissemination of Communist propaganda from abroad, could wink at the fact that within the Post Office a lot of the stuff would mysteriously disappear.

The "dirtiest" (Eisenhower's own word) arm's-length job of all Eisenhower gave to Republican National Chairman Meade Alcorn: to ask for and get the resignation of Sherman Adams in 1958. On June 10 of that year John Bell Williams, acting chairman of the Legislative Oversight Subcommittee of the House Interstate and Foreign Commerce Committee, announced he had in his hand evidence that Adams had occupied hotel rooms in Boston paid for by one Bernard Goldfine, a New England textile manufacturer, plus evidence of Adams' intervention with both the FTC and the SEC to help Goldfine's companies. The high priest of sanitary government, one wag said, had been caught defiling the altar.

With Eisenhower eschewing executive privilege, Adams went to the Hill June 17 and under oath made his defense: he admitted having accepted Goldfine's generosity (payment of hotel bills in Boston, Plymouth, and New York City; the temporary loan of an oriental rug, the gift of some wool fabric and a vicuna coat, the vicuna of which cost Goldfine $69); conceded his mistake ("If I had these decisions before me now, I believe I would have acted a little more prudently"); and stood his ground ("Did Bernard Goldfine benefit in any way in his relations with ... the federal government because he was a friend of Sherman Adams? Did Sherman Adams seek to secure any favors or benefits for Bernard Goldfine because of this friendship? My answer to both questions is: 'no'").

Eisenhower resolutely defended Adams. But as successive revelations came in (particularly the shocker on July 1, previously known neither to Adams nor the administration, that Goldfine had taken deductions for his gifts to Adams on his federal tax return), Eisenhower recognized he had a problem. At arm's length he began to work. On July 15 he invited Richard Nixon to breakfast. Subject: Should Adams resign? Eisenhower never asked the Vice-President outright to talk to Adams. But when the breakfast ended, Nixon—like

Brownell—knew, subliminally, that was what Eisenhower wanted. As Eisenhower had sent Len Hall to Nixon in early 1956, Eisenhower now sent Nixon to Adams, to be, once again, "very, very gentle."

That same afternoon, Nixon talked with Adams and then came back and dictated to Ann Whitman a long series of notes on the meeting, notes intended for the President's eyes only.

At the outset he had made it very clear to Adams, Nixon reported, that Eisenhower had neither dispatched him nor indicated which course of action he believed Adams should follow. Nixon, well organized, then weighed to Adams the pros and cons of resignation (Goldfine had made a bad appearance before the committee, which reflected on Adams and through Adams on the administration; the overwhelming majority of Republicans in the House and Senate believed Adams should resign; Eisenhower would obviously get embarrassing press conference questions about his standard of ethics—one standard for Adams, one for everybody else. Obviously, no man had worked as hard, as efficiently and decisively as Adams had; filling his shoes would present Eisenhower a great problem. But if in the coming congressional elections the Republicans should suffer substantial losses, Adams would inevitably get the blame).

In 1952 during the Fund furor and in 1956 before the writing of the national Republican ticket, Eisenhower, detached, had told Nixon to chart his own course; now in 1958, through Nixon, he was giving Adams the same message. The results would mirror not Eisenhower's method, but his lieutenants' characters: Nixon had charted his course to help Nixon; Adams would chart his course to help Eisenhower and the country they both served, and thus do himself formidable hurt. Years later, as the Watergate crisis unfolded, and as Nixon once again looked at the pros and cons of a resignation—charting his course by his own star—I wondered what bitterness Adams might have felt reflecting in 1974 on the irony of using Richard Nixon as emissary back in 1958 on a moral and political question, a question rooted in no evidence of crime or coverup or wrongdoing but only in the acceptance, temporarily, of an oriental rug and of a $69 vicuna overcoat, a gift from a friend whom Adams mistakenly trusted.

Nixon spoke. Adams did not budge: the decision, he insisted—as Nixon himself had insisted in his own crises of 1952 and 1956—rested with Eisenhower.

The uproar around Goldfine intensified. By August 25 Eisenhower was once again talking to Nixon, this time phoning him in

White Sulphur Springs to discuss—in the guarded words of Ann Whitman, listening in—a plan for "a certain individual." Eisenhower, Ann detected, had seemingly made up his mind: Adams should resign. And once again he implied, though not in so many words, that Nixon should go to Adams and have another talk.

Nixon returned to Washington at once. This time when he spoke to Adams, Nixon was, he reported to Ann, "as blunt as it was possible to be": The Republicans were going to lose seats in the Congress; rightly or wrongly, they would blame Adams; he would find it more difficult to operate in the future than in the past. Still Adams remained the Great Stone Face. He just didn't know, he reiterated, whom the President could get to replace him. This response triggered a partisan outburst from Ann, forever loyal to only a single man, Eisenhower; this was, she said in her diary, "the most alarming part of the whole business to me. It reflects Governor Adams' apparent belief that he is indispensable," a belief reinforcing the myth "that he...is running the Government, not the President." Adams' response may also reflect Nixon's failure to communicate, or Adams' failure to hear the message. For to this day, Adams told me, he believes that Nixon never did urge him to resign; indeed, he felt that Nixon praised his performance—particularly as a butt of McCarthyism and as a loyal caretaker during Eisenhower's heart attack; that Nixon noted how much in recent speeches he'd stung the Democrats, who now sought vengeance; and that Nixon tried to get him to see that the Goldfine mess did not mean the end of the world.

The force that Nixon and rational analysis lacked, money and politics now supplied. On September 4 from Newport, Rhode Island, Eisenhower wrote a long reply to a letter from his good friend, investment banker Cliff Roberts in New York: "The thing that disturbs me most about your report is that a spirit of 'hopelessness' seems to you to be a Republican attitude discernible throughout the country. This defeats me.... One man [Adams] admittedly made a mistake, but no one has ever accused him of crookedness. Yet this circumstance, almost alone, seems to account for the alleged 'hopelessness.'...

"No one can feel worse than I about the entire Adams affair. Indeed, in view of the fact that I know better than anyone else the extraordinary dedication the man has exhibited through six years, the constant pressure under which he has worked, the round-the-clock days that he has devoted to the service of the government and the country, all now seemingly forgotten by the public with a consequent readiness to make him a greater villain than almost anyone in current history, you can understand that I get not only puzzled but sometimes resentful as well.

"But that is the way it goes, and I am forced to agree that the situation is not greatly different from your portrayal of it."

Before long Eisenhower was picking up the telephone to call National Chairman Meade Alcorn. He mentioned some disturbing messages he had just received in the past two days, which, he said, "put the most extraordinary weight on the Adams affair." One was Roberts' letter (Eisenhower didn't tell Alcorn Roberts' name). Another was a conversation the President had had that very morning with his good friend and former ambassador to England, Winthrop Aldrich.

"This man has got to go," Aldrich had said, "or we (the Republican party) are done."

"My mind is pretty well cleared up as to what would be the better thing to do," Eisenhower concluded to Alcorn. "The difficulty is to find a good way to do it." He asked Alcorn to take no action until after the Maine election four days later.

On September 8 Maine's Governor Edmund Muskie defeated Republican Senator Frederick G. Payne by sixty thousand votes and became the first popularly elected Democratic senator in the state's history. The morning of September 10 Eisenhower again phoned Alcorn from Newport, "Meade, we can't wait any longer. This is the toughest, dirtiest assignment I could ever give to a National Chairman. I want Sherm's resignation. I don't have the heart to ask for it myself, but I want you to get it." He suggested that both Alcorn and Nixon see Adams together.

Adams at that moment was in Canada fishing. Alcorn phoned Adams' secretary at the White House. She called the governor and he agreed to pack up and come home. Nixon and Alcorn were to meet with Adams at the White House at 2:00 P.M. on September 15. When the morning of that day arrived, however, Nixon suddenly told Alcorn: "Meade, you'd better go see him alone. My office is swarming with reporters; they're following my every move."

"They're following mine too," Alcorn replied, miffed at Nixon's withdrawal. "But if you won't go, okay."

"I'll be right here in my office. If any problem comes up, just call. And in any event, give me a call afterward."

Alcorn met with Adams. As frankly and gently as he could, Alcorn told Adams of the damage he thought Adams' continued presence in the White House was doing, and now, for the first time, he added the missing clue: "The President will not ask for your resignation. But I know he would prefer that you leave."

"The President tell you that?"

"Yes."

There was nothing more to discuss except the process. Alcorn suggested getting network time and on the spot outlined what Adams should say. Two days later Adams approved the idea, asked Alcorn to write up a text, looked it over when Alcorn brought it back to the White House and suggested, without any thanks, that Alcorn get Nixon's clearance. (Adams in his broadcast used Alcorn's draft nearly verbatim, with some additions.) Special Counsel Jerry Morgan flew to Newport, at Adams' request, to verify Eisenhower's word to Alcorn. Ike confirmed it.

Adams' friendship with Alcorn had gone back to 1952, when Alcorn headed the Connecticut Republicans for Eisenhower and delivered the whole delegation at the convention. During the Goldfine crisis Alcorn had fended off Adams' attackers again and again. But now forever afterward Adams would treat Alcorn, in Alcorn's own bitter words, "as though I didn't exist. He thought I was the architect of the the whole thing. After he made his decision, I wrote him a warm personal note. He stuffed it into his pocket. I've never had even an acknowledgement.

"This was the one time in my three years in Washington when I wished I'd never heard of the Republican National Committee. This was the one time when I thought the President might have done it himself." Alcorn felt himself used.

The next day, after Eisenhower had talked with Adams' emissary Morgan alone, Ann Whitman observed that the President felt extremely bad but appeared relieved that the conclusion had been reached; he commented on how dreadful it was that cheap politicians could pillory such an honorable man. That afternoon the President telephoned Cliff Roberts to make sure that Sidney Weinberg repeated to Adams his offer to get him a better paying job in industry. At 10:28 the next morning, a rainy September 17, Adams telephoned the President. Eisenhower motioned for Ann Whitman to remain in the room. Adams said he would resign, asked for some time to think over his statement, and indicated he would stay around for about a month to get the personnel straightened out.

"If anything is done," the President said, "and we make any critical decision, as I have always said, you will have to take the initiative yourself." Later the President called Governor Adams back to try to pin down some dates for the announcement. (In the first conversation, Ann observed, he had the feeling that the thing would be delayed too long.) He of course understood Adams' wish to have time to decide what he wanted to say, and emphasized again that he wanted to protect him from anything that looked cold and indifferent.

Ike put down the phone and began dictating: "Governor Adams has been one of the finest public servants I have ever known. . . . It is idle to pretend that his going is not an official loss, but of course I understand the circumstances, and I must accept his decision." The die was cast, the throw was speedy and final, and Ike had protected his administration rather than Adams.

Toward Eisenhower, Adams never looked back in rancor as a result of this episode. Ironically the man who did was Richard Nixon. With his White House Staff at bay and the Watergate hounds closing in, the embattled Nixon on March 22, 1973, assured his cronies on one of the tapes that by God he wouldn't throw his faithful followers to the dogs as Ike had. He wouldn't do to Haldeman and Ehrlichman what Eisenhower did to Adams. "I want you all to stonewall it. . . . [Eisenhower] only cared about—Christ, 'Be sure he was clean.' But I don't look at it that way. . . . We're going to protect our people, if we can."

Nixon was speaking with bitterness and with a memory that went back more than twenty years: to 1952, when Eisenhower had cut him loose to prove his innocence of the Fund charges; to 1955, when Eisenhower had accepted the resignation of his Air Force Secretary, Harold Talbott, for a peccadillo—the inadvertent use of Air Force stationery for a private business purpose; to 1956, when to the jeers of calloused Republicans, Eisenhower had vetoed a natural gas deregulation bill he personally favored because he found the bribery and goon-squad tactics of its proponents reprehensible ("they make crooks out of themselves," he wrote in his diary, and as we worked on the book his eyes flashed as he recalled the cocktail party aside of one gas lobbyist, speaking of one senator: "I've got him in my pocket"); to 1958, when Nixon himself helped ease out Sherman Adams.

Nixon, however, was showing himself purblind to the central fact Ike saw: that the presidency is not the President; that men come and go, but the office rests; that nothing—nothing at all—must discolor or obscure or undermine or betray the trust that must run between the American people and the occupant, any momentary occupant, of that office, which a President holds at their sufferance. Lies, coverups, an atavistic affirmation of the primacy of loyalty to tribe or gang could only exacerbate a problem, as Nixon's own fate proved.

Was the American presidency, to use Nixon's word, "clean"? That's what Eisenhower *did* care about.

To preserve the integrity of the office, called into public question, his most valuable aide had to go. And given Adams' innocence of any substantive misconduct, it was far better, for him and for the presidency, that he go on his own volition, not through a harsh, even unjust, act of presidential retribution. That, I believe, was the end Eisenhower was trying to accomplish. And his arm's-length maneuverings were his means to achieve it.

To this day the fate of Adams throws long shadows. Nothing is more difficult for staff members to face. But for the President, it was also a necessity. One thinks of the Roman general, Manlius Torquatus, who had ordered that any man who attacked before he gave the command would be executed; when he was told that his son had broken the line, he ordered him killed: after that, the line held and the battle was won. Eisenhower, like Torquatus, had to face the consequence, not just of what would happen if he carried out his mandate, but also of what would happen if he did not. With Adams, Eisenhower's standards had been broken, the fact had become public knowledge, and he reasoned that if a member of his own White House family were allowed to escape the effects, the end result would be a loss of public trust. Reluctantly, he enforced discipline, although he never doubted Adams' honesty, as Torquatus never doubted his son's zeal against the enemy. Both men had deputies carry out the punishment, not because they were cowardly, but because that made it easier on their own feelings and on the feelings of those they loved.

In his televised interview with David Frost in May 1977, Richard Nixon volunteered a crisp account of the getting of Adams' resignation: "You know who did it? *I* did it." The next day, while Alcorn was still smarting with disbelief—given Nixon's flight from the moment of truth with Adams—the phone rang. Rose Woods, Nixon's secretary, was calling: the Boss, she said, wanted Alcorn to know how sorry he was about how that broadcast had turned out. He couldn't edit the tape, and he'd been misquoted. But Alcorn shouldn't worry; the Nixon memoirs, forthcoming, would have the whole story right.

And sure enough, a few months later a copy did arrive, carrying an account much closer to the truth, and a flowery inscription to Alcorn praising his services to Nixon and the party.

Nixon's effusiveness, Alcorn told me, contrasted ironically with another earlier episode. In the 1968 presidential campaign Alcorn, with several other former National Chairmen, came out for Nelson Rockefeller. In 1969 Nixon entered the White House, and the next year, as Alcorn's small hometown of Suffield, Connecticut, where his family had lived in prominence for generations, readied itself for its three-hundredth anniversary, Alcorn phoned the White House to request the President's presence at the celebration. Nixon agreed. The program was reshuffled, security arrangements were made, special tickets and programs were printed—all to fit the presidential requirements. A crowd of thousands assembled. Overhead the presidential plane was seen descending, to touch down at nearby Bradley Field. And that was it: the President and his aides ducked into waiting limousines and headed straight for a meeting in Bridgeport, not even slowing down as they zipped away from Suffield. "You know why he did that?" Alcorn asked years later, still furious at the recollection. "Because I announced for Nelson in 1968. Nixon just wanted to show me you don't do that to him. God, he could be petty."

Eisenhower's use of arm's-length strategies, on missions great and small, trivial and grave—from a little political job to a nasty announcement to the press, to control over the FBI, to the dismissal of the second most powerful man in the government—forms a persistent pattern in his presidency, a pattern that confirms Murray Kempton's perception of the cunning beneath the presidential shell, and Richard Nixon's assertion of an Eisenhower far more devious than most people recognized. The pattern also reveals, on occasion, the flickerings of an instinct toward self-protection—an Eisenhower who, in Bedell Smith's words, needed the shielding of a "prat boy." Nelson Rockefeller, for example, never forgot Eisenhower's irritated response to a

Rockefeller survey (during his stint as a presidential assistant) that showed the United States approaching a period of mortal peril from the Soviet Union, and Rockefeller's recommendation that the President so inform the nation: "Why," Eisenhower bristled, "do I always have to be the one who breaks the bad news to the American people?"

Throughout all these instances of arm's-length maneuvering Eisenhower did not insist on, indeed sometimes didn't want, absolute knowledge. But he did insist on control, through trusted lieutenants—a Brownell, an Alcorn, a Nixon. And in the end (as when he confirmed Alcorn's words to Morgan) he did not seek to disguise—all self-protection discarded—his ultimate responsibility.

Such unqualified trust as Eisenhower reposed in his leading lieutenants, he did not repose in Allen Dulles. Throughout the Eisenhower presidency runs a steady effort to tighten control over the CIA Chief and his agency—an effort culminating in 1960, after the U-2 disaster.

When Eisenhower entered the White House, the Director of Central Intelligence had the power to launch all covert actions on his own authority, with only the advice—not the approval—of an interagency group, including representatives of State and Defense. From 1953 until March 1955 the director, now Allen Dulles, coordinated his covert projects with the Psychological Strategy Board (under C. D. Jackson) or with its successor organization, the Operations Coordination Board (under Jackson's successor, Nelson Rockefeller), though he himself still had final approval authority. On March 12, 1955, under NSC 5412/1, this approval authority shifted to the OCB's Planning and Coordination Group, directed by the President to "know in advance" of all major CIA undertakings. And nine months later, on December 28, 1955, through NSC 5412/2, the authority shifted to what eventually became known as the "Special Group" (later the "Forty Committee"), including representatives of the Secretary of State, the Secretary of Defense, and the President. And there it rested throughout Eisenhower's presidency and far beyond. Six weeks later, by Executive Order, Eisenhower established the President's Board of Consultants on Foreign Intelligence Activities—a group of distinguished citizens, including Dr. James R. Killian, Jr., of MIT, Benjamin Fairless of U.S. Steel, and General James H. Doolittle—

empowered to look specifically at Allen Dulles' recurrent shortcomings in management of the agency and coordination of the government's entire "intelligence community."

The reforms appeared far better on paper than in practice. Again and again the board made recommendations for strengthening the CIA's internal management, and again and again these broke on the personality and practices of the agency's director. "To put in all the administrative improvements they propose," Ike once remarked, "I'd have to fire Allen Dulles. And with all his limitations, I'd rather have him as chief of intelligence than anyone else I can think of. In that business you need a strange kind of genius."

Meanwhile the Special Group seldom met. Allen Dulles himself balked at attending (for one thing, he couldn't stand the Pentagon representative, a man Dulles suspected as "not secure.") He sent instead such scattered agency substitutes as Frank Wisner (chief for covert operations) or Deputy Director Charles Cabell. No advance agendas were written out. No formal minutes were kept. Little staff work was done ahead of time. During this period monitoring of major CIA projects evidently fell to adventitious mechanisms outside the Special Group. It fell, for example, to frequent meetings and phone calls betwen the DCI and his brother, the Secretary of State ("I saw Foster Dulles far more often than did State Department officers of my rank," one CIA operative recalled. "He liked to talk to us. You know most of us flunked the Foreign Service exam. But we were—the word that comes to mind is: sly. And the agency could also outdo the State Department socially: Des FitzGerald, Kim Roosevelt, and Frank Wisner were much more impressive to the two Dulleses than most State Department people. The two brothers," he concluded, "formed a lead wall between Eisenhower and their organizations"). It fell to White House Staff members who would alert the President to conspicuous problems with particular CIA actions (for example, the Indonesian operation of 1958, when the pertinent question was "which side are we on?" inasmuch as we were simultaneously helping both President Sukarno and the rebels who were trying to oust him). And the monitoring fell to ad hoc White House meetings on major enterprises (like the Berlin tunnel, which enabled the CIA to tap into East German telephone conversations. "After the secrecy of the tunnel was blown in late 1957," Gordon Gray recalls, "the President insisted the Special Group know in advance of every CIA action that impinged on another nation's sovereignty").

"Pretty damn informal," Gray labeled the process he found when he became special assistant to the President for National Security Affairs in July 1958. Early in 1959 Eisenhower ordered the whole mechanism tightened up. Meetings began to be held once a week, in the office of the deputy Undersecretary of State for Political Affairs, the group's informal chairman. The criteria for projects to be examined were widened. Thomas A. Parrott, Allen Dulles' assistant, was directed to keep formal minutes (one copy only, in CIA custody, at Eisenhower's explicit direction).

The attendees came regularly: Allen Dulles, frequently accompanied by Wisner's successor, Richard Bissell, Deputy Director for Plans (read: "dirty tricks"); the informal chairman—the State representative—first Robert Murphy, then Livingston Merchant; the Defense representative, Deputy Secretary Donald Quarles and later Deputy Secretaries Thomas Gates and James Douglas or Assistant Secretary John Irwin; Gray of the White House; and notetaker Tom Parrott. Allen Dulles brought forward his major projects for inspection—projects that before they got to the Special Group had ordinarily been intensively discussed between CIA and State, at the Assistant Secretary level.

After the group deliberated, Gray would report—usually alone—to Eisenhower. In so doing, Gray, like Brownell, exercised selectivity: he brought up only subjects of significance—disputes for appeal and actions for which the President's personal approval was advisable. Like Brownell (and like Rockefeller, when he had the CIA oversight responsibility), Gray told the President only what he *had* to know to understand a proposed CIA action, omitting details Eisenhower didn't need or want (Eisenhower, for example, wanted to know about U.S. monitoring of Soviet missile tests, but not about the location of specific surveillance devices on Turkish soil, though, as Staff Secretary Andrew Goodpaster remarked, Eisenhower would want to know that such details were known to "his people," principally Goodpaster or Gray).

Emerging from his presidential conference, Gray would brief Goodpaster on the President's decisions and at times write up a memorandum of conversation, like this one on his meeting with the President August 17, 1960: "suggestion in connection with the more vigorous aspects of the cold war" was discussed, which the President said to talk over with the Secretary of Defense (the mysterious subject Gray described in a handwritten note attached to the memo in a sealed envelope). Finally, Gray would, if necessary, advise the Special Group members themselves, who did not consider a project approved until after Gray had got back to them—by phone or by word of mouth at the next meeting—with an okay from the President. As a result of this oral procedure, the Special Group minutes might or might not reflect presidential knowledge and decision.

All this elaborate detail, conducted in deepest secrecy in Eisenhower's final years, was designed to assure control over Allen Dulles and the CIA by a committee, by Eisenhower's lieutenant Gordon Gray, and ultimately by Eisenhower himself. It was not designed to provide insulation.

The most sensational covert actions of all, indeed, Eisenhower followed closely—or even directed himself in detail—out of the Oval Office.

In August 1953 he received regular reports on the CIA action to help the Shah of Iran—the constitutional monarch, denounced by the erratic tearful semi-invalid Prime Minister Mohammed Mossadegh—accomplish what the constitution permitted him to do: replace Mossadegh (who was swiftly becoming the Dr. Benes of Iran, believing he could ally himself with the Communists and then outwit them) with a Prime Minister of the Shah's choice, Fazlollah Zahedi, thus arresting Iran's slide toward a Communist take-over and restarting its desperately needed flow of oil income from the West, shut off after Mossadegh in 1951 had put Iran's entire oil industry under national ownership, ending British control.

These reports included NSC intelligence briefings from Allen Dulles on the probability of financial assistance to Iran from the Soviet Union and the certainty of political backing for Mossadegh from the Communist Tudeh party.

They included State Department cables from U.S. Ambassador Burton Berry in Baghdad recounting his conversations with the Shah after the Shah's Beechcraft flight from Iran in the belief that his attempt to appoint Zahedi had been thwarted by a bizarre combination of bad weather, vacillating accomplices, an Iranian holiday, and Mossadegh.

They included a crucial August 18 memo from Bedell Smith to the President on the apparent failure of the "counter-coup" against "the old boy" and the probable need now "to snuggle up to Mossadegh if we're going to save anything there."

And finally the reports included a rousing cloak-and-dagger

White House briefing (like a "dime novel," Ike said) on the whole harrowing episode—after victory had been snatched from the jaws of defeat—by the CIA's man on the scene, Kermit Roosevelt, who had spearheaded the covert triumph: the ouster of Mossadegh, the installation of Zahedi, the return of the Shah.

The success had not resulted from an American deployment of strength. The Shah selected Zahedi and gave the order. The Iranians supplied the two key activists and all of the pro-Shah mobs in the streets. No American arms or armed forces played any significant part. Roosevelt had only the tiniest handful of non-Iranian accomplices in Tehran. Little money changed hands—less than $100,000.

So what, I asked Kermit Roosevelt in the fall of 1979, was the American value added? And his answer was simple: He personally assured the Shah—and the military officers loyal to him—that if he named a new Prime Minister, the United States and the British would not—as the Shah had feared in the Truman days—back Mossadegh. That was what the CIA did in Iran in 1953. And through his lieutenants in State and the CIA, Eisenhower followed every step of the action. (The retention of the Emperor of Japan helped stability because of a later growth of democracy; the retention of the Shah could have had the same effect, had subsequent policies been different.)

In June 1954 he personally refereed a dispute between Allen Dulles and Assistant Secretary of State Henry Holland, a dispute about the wisdom of escalating the United States' secret effort in Guatemala to overthrow the crypto-Communist Arbenz government. Eisenhower himself approved the use of a handful of obsolete small planes to fly over the country dropping a few bombs—and empty Coke bottles, which make a comparable bang—to frighten Arbenz into flight (he ultimately turned up in Czechoslovakia) and confer victory on the 200-man ragtag liberation army of Castillo Armas.

From Goodpaster Eisenhower received regular reports on the Defense Department's ill-fated surveillance balloons, free-flying from east to west across Siberia (against Eisenhower's explicit order, the Pentagon attached a time-clock shutdown device, and one balloon went down in the Ukraine); this episode doubtless colored Goodpaster's laconic phone message to Air Force Chief of Staff General Nathan Twining on March 13, 1956: the President is not interested in any more balloon projects.

Throughout 1960 Eisenhower himself conducted in the White

House a series of meetings by an ad hoc interagency task force on Cuba which had been organized by Gordon Gray. Prompted by the initial presentation of Allen Dulles and two or three aides, which featured a diagram of a sugar refinery, with a description of how it could be sabotaged, Ike commented: "Instead of this one-shot action, Allen, why don't you come back with a complete program?" The program eventually entailed training anti-Castro Cuban troops for a return to their homeland, a return that Ike's successors planned and executed so ineptly via the Bay of Pigs.

Through Goodpaster Eisenhower got briefings on the later 1960 photographs of Soviet territory by American reconnaissance satellites. And with meticulous secrecy—for a while not even Gordon Gray knew—Eisenhower, assisted by Goodpaster, monitored the far more sensitive flights (because they violated Soviet airspace) of the satellites' predecessor, the U-2. Personally Eisenhower approved the November 1954 recommendation of a committee headed by Edwin Land that the United States build the high-flying spy plane. Personally he followed its progress (under contractors Lockheed; Pratt and Whitney, who made the engines; and Hycon and Perkin-Elmer, who made the cameras) through its first test flight, through the recruiting of pilots from SAC, through its first flight over Eastern Europe, and through its first flight over the Soviet Union (including Moscow and Leningrad) in the summer of 1956, and through a succession of missions—as necessary—over not only Soviet soil but also Indonesia, Tibet, the Middle East, and China. And personally Eisenhower approved every flight in advance; he entertained each request for permission to overfly, always holding it to a specific time period; he received in the Oval Office a small committee (ordinarly Allen and Foster Dulles, Cabell, Richard Bissell, the Secretary of Defense, the Chairman of the Joint Chiefs, and Goodpaster) before each venture; he examined their large map detailing specific photographic targets; at times he made his own modifications of routes; he always ended by thanking the group, with the understanding that if he approved their request—with a clean cutoff time—he would have Goodpaster phone the project director, Bissell, within a day or two.

If this whole voluminous record of Eisenhower's various mechanisms for overseeing the CIA establishes anything at all, it establishes this: that Dwight Eisenhower did not direct CIA actions via private one-on-one conversations with Allen Dulles. This fact the

White House appointment records abundantly confirm: In 1953 the two met in the Oval Office (apart from NSC and Cabinet meetings) exactly sixteen times, in 1954 sixteen times, in 1955 seven times, in 1956 twenty times, in 1957 sixteen times, in 1958 twenty-seven times, in 1959 twenty-four times, in 1960–61 twenty-four times. These 150 meetings average 19 a year. Of those 19, approximately 80 percent included at least one additional person—White House or Cabinet officer. The meetings of Dulles and the President alone—sometimes for less than ten minutes—therefore average about four a year.

Even this is not the complete story. After the U-2 debacle of May 1960, both Gray and Goodpaster specifically recall the President's telling them in an unambiguous directive that henceforth *in no circumstances did he ever want to meet with the CIA alone:* so upset was he with the U-2 performance that he wanted to preclude any possibility that the agency would *privately* get his approval for anything.

This, then, was the elaborate apparatus Eisenhower established to control the CIA. And despite his efforts, and those of Goodpaster and Gray, it remained—and remains in retrospect to this day, despite all allowances one must make for the cold-war ethos that prevailed under Eisenhower as under Truman and Kennedy—a "very," in Goodpaster's words, "weakly controlled business."

The apparatus did not prevent the agency's excursions into drug experimentation on American citizens who never knew they were serving as guinea pigs; such experiments, not being covert actions overseas, fell outside the Special Group's purview. It did not prevent the agency's engaging in attempts to use newsmen as intelligence agents or to disseminate false information abroad: these, being "accepted" and "routine" practices, would never have got onto the Special Group's agenda for scrutiny of their ethical implications. It did not prevent the CIA—and the NSA—from intercepting and reading letters and cables to and from U.S. citizens ("I doubt Allen Dulles would have told the President about that," Richard Bissell told me, "except possibly by circumlocution. Allen was a lawyer; he knew that that knowledge would put the President in a peculiar constitutional position"). It did not prevent the CIA's unilateral initiation of an assassination plot against Fidel Castro in early 1960—a plot that Allen Dulles reported neither to the Special Group nor to the series of ad hoc meetings on Cuba held in the Oval Office. It did not prevent the U-2 fiasco and the Soviet capture of pilot Francis Gary Powers, a fiasco that eventuated in part because of Eisenhower's understanding—an absolute understanding from Allen Dulles—that no U-2 pilot would ever be taken alive.

The suspicion between White House and agency, John Eisenhower summed up most succinctly when I phoned to ask him about the Church Committee's thunderclap revelation of CIA horrors during his father's administration: "That goddamned CIA! There's no telling *what* they were doing! You know they lied to Dad about the U-2." Indeed, so far removed was the agency from the usual White House purview that even as knowledgeable and sophisticated an observer as Eisenhower's personal secretary Ann Whitman told me that she remembered the CIA as an independent entity, like the Federal Reserve Board.

This was the apparatus—with all its strengths and weaknesses—that was in place on August 26, 1960, when, the Church Committee alleges, Allen Dulles, with Eisenhower's knowledge, cabled Leopoldville to order the assassination of Patrice Lumumba. But there was something else in place also: Eisenhower's repeatedly expressed unconditional aversion to assassination as an instrument of American policy.

Again and again in candid informal remarks—words not spoken for any record—Eisenhower affirmed this aversion. His naval aide, Vice Admiral E. P. Aurand, for example—a man with no responsibility whatsoever in the NSC area—vividly remembers Eisenhower's telling him, in an off-hand moment, that the United States wanted no part of any such murder; that it could only set in motion a chain of events whose end no one could foresee. Dr. Karl Harr, special assistant to the President for Operations Coordination, believes he recalls hearing Eisenhower say almost the identical thing. Ed McCabe, an administrative assistant with responsibilities largely in the fields of labor and congressional relations, recalls a similarly startling Eisenhower pronouncement in a pre-press conference briefing in July 1960—just a month before the Congo crisis.

Agents of Dominican Republic dictator Trujillo had attempted to assassinate the liberal President of Venezuela, Rómulo Betancourt, by blowing up a car filled with explosives just as Betancourt's own car drove by—an attempt that had killed the riders in the front seat, though not Betancourt. In McCabe's recollection, the atrocity infuriated Eisenhower; he condemned it with a vehemence that, if anything, struck McCabe as extreme.

Others, including General Gruenther, remember, out of long years of the closest association with Eisenhower, no mention whatsoever of assassination. "We'd get together late in the afternoon in the mansion," Milton Eisenhower recalls, "and never once did Ike discuss assassination with me in those conversations. And believe me, we talked about everything under the sun."

One witness who might have shed a particularly revealing light on Eisenhower's opinion of assassination, the Church Committee didn't even call. In fact, on a Sunday afternoon in August 1975, he and I watched Frank Church on *Meet the Press*, and I remarked that the Church Committee had produced no evidence against Eisenhower on assassination.

"Nor will they find any," my friend exploded. "In fact they will find just the opposite: it will blow up in their faces. As you may know, Eisenhower sent me to the Dominican Republic actually to try to keep Trujillo from being killed."

I did know the outlines of the story: In early 1960 Eisenhower and his advisers were trying to find some way to remove the hated Dominican Republic dictator from the scene, before violence removed him and perhaps replaced him with a Castro-type successor. Accordingly, on April 25, 1960, my friend met with the President and Secretary of State Herter to discuss a plan for getting Trujillo to resign, induced by the provision of a generous trust fund for him. The United States wanted Trujillo to leave the Dominican Republic immediately, his departure to be followed by the seizure of power by an American-approved junta, which would guarantee free elections. Though the scheme did not work—Trujillo declined—it once again illustrated Ike's convictions against political murder.

Yet despite the existence of this abundance of evidence—evidence it did get or should have got—the Church Committee clung to its "reasonable inference" that Eisenhower knew about the plot against Lumumba. It came to this conclusion, it said, not because it had discovered a single smoking gun but because it perceived a "chain" of events extending through several weeks late in Eisenhower's presidency—a chain strong enough to link President and plot but a chain nebulous enough to permit "plausible denial" and keep him at arm's length.

That "chain" has three crucial links.

It begins with the meeting of the National Security Council on August 18, 1960—the meeting most likely, the Church Committee concluded, to fit the indefinite recollection of its key witness. Fifteen years after the event that witness, one Robert Johnson (described by the committee as third in command on the NSC staff, after James Lay and Marion Boggs) told the committee that at an NSC meeting in the summer of 1960 (he couldn't remember which one exactly), during an extended and vigorous discussion of the Congo, he definitely recalled hearing Eisenhower order Lumumba's assassination, and even more vividly recalled his own shock at the command.

The second link comes a week later, at the August 25 meeting of the Special Group. The CIA had under way, Parrott's notes show, several anti-Lumumba measures—covert actions through labor organizations as well as an attempt to produce a Congolese Senate vote of no confidence in the Prime Minister. Gray breaks in to remind Allen Dulles that "his associates" (read: the President) "had expressed extremely strong feelings on the necessity for very straightforward action," and questions the adequacy of what the agency intends to do. The group finally agrees "that planning for the Congo would not necessarily rule out 'consideration' of any particular kind of activity which might contribute to getting rid of Lumumba." In interpreting these minutes, the Church Committee leaned heavily on the testimony of a man who wasn't there that day, Richard Bissell, DDP. The words, Bissell insisted, afforded a "prime example" of circumlocution: rule out no means equals assassinate if necessary; Eisenhower "in effect" was giving Dulles a message through Gray. The next day, in the third link Dulles fired off his cable.

That, in brief, is the evidence. Now to look at it, starting with Mr. Robert Johnson and his recalled shock at the NSC August 18.

First, only Mr. Johnson heard the alleged presidential order. Without exception, every other attendee asked by the Church Committee to testify about that meeting—including Undersecretary of State C. Douglas Dillon and Dr. Marion Boggs—flatly denied any similar recollection whatsoever. Without exception all other living attendees of that meeting—men whom the Church Committee for some reason failed or declined to call as witnesses: Defense Secretary Thomas Gates, Treasury Secretary Robert Anderson, Defense Mobilization Director Leo Hoegh, Budget Director Maurice Stans, Acting Chairman of the Joint Chiefs General Lyman Lemnitzer, Special Assistant Karl Harr, Assistant Secretary of State Gerard C. Smith— all have told me in equally unequivocal words exactly the same thing, that no assassination was ordered or even considered.

Indeed, the attendees most knowledgeable and closest to Eisenhower went even further. Gray, Goodpaster, and Goodpaster's assistant, John Eisenhower, all three, told the committee flatly that they had no recollection whatsoever of any consideration by Dwight Eisenhower of any assassination of anybody at any time. Karl Harr told me exactly the same thing: "totally alien" to Eisenhower's way of thinking, he said. And so did Nelson Rockefeller, interviewed on his monitoring of the CIA for Eisenhower in 1955.

So as witnesses to the August 18 meeting, on one side stand Gray, Goodpaster, Dillon, Gates, and seven colleagues—all of them well-known men who were in close relationship with the President, men who had regularly attended NSC meetings for years. And against them—and alone—stands Mr. Johnson, who in his entire lifetime was permitted into two NSC meetings—just two, this being the first—at which Eisenhower presided. And Johnson himself confessed to the Church Committee doubts about his own memory!

One central witness could not testify: Allen Dulles, who was dead. But on the evidence he too failed to hear the Eisenhower assassination command Johnson thinks he heard. Because after the meeting Dulles took no assassination action whatsoever. He appeared before the Special Group a week later, in fact, with an assortment of plans that Gray told him fell short of the "very straightforward action" Eisenhower wanted.

To Bissell, reading these minutes fifteen years later, Gray's words meant murder. To Gray himself, they did not; never in this meeting or any other, he testified, did anyone plan any assassination. To Tom Parrott, who wrote these words down, they had no such meaning either. The other living participants in the August 25 Special Group meeting, Livingston Merchant and John Irwin, similarly recall no discussion of Lumumba's assassination. If Gray and the others had discussed assassination, Parrott told the Church Committee, he would have used the word. He did not write euphemisms (the only exception, he told me, was "Gray's associates" or "higher authority" for the President—a nearly transparent fig leaf employed to afford a scant measure of protection if the notes ever fell into outside hands). To Parrott, his notes were a record, an accurate record, not a bureaucratic CYA device. They belonged, by presidential order, to the agency alone.

The plain fact was, Parrott told me, that *nothing* was ever said in the Special Group about assassination—any assassination. And on this fact (with the single exception of the attempt against Lumumba) even Richard Bissell would agree. Though CIA operatives, he told me, had from time to time discussed the murder of one foreign leader or another, never before the fall of 1960 had anyone requested formal approval for action.

In these circumstances one must choose among four scenarios. Which is right?

The first is simplest: The Church Committee is right. The surmises of Bissell, longtime director of dirty tricks, mirror truth. Gordon Gray is a liar or amnesiac. And so are all the other well-known witnesses except confused Robert Johnson.

The second scenario reflects the antagonism between the White House officials and the CIA that remains to this day: Did the agency arrogantly take off on its own, thumbing its nose at Eisenhower's control apparatus, concealing its actions (as they actually did in the U-2 episode—"they'll never take him alive"—and in their scheme to kill Castro)? Perhaps the agency did. But Tom Parrott recalls vividly Allen Dulles' scrupulousness about getting explicit approvals ("don't ever tell me they had no objection; tell me they asked me to do it"). And, as Gordon Gray asks, wouldn't a DCI who got presidential permission to sabotage a sugar refinery also have got clearance to attempt an assassination?

A third scenario goes like this: In the Congo in 1960 it was almost wartime. A general, Ike knew all about the morality of the battlefield: life is cheap, troublesome prisoners are routinely shot "trying to escape." Why be squeamish? Why not forget all the control mechanisms and—just once—give Allen Dulles a secret unilateral circumlocutious okay to snuff out one major single bad actor?

Through such private understanding, Bissell speculated to the Church Committee, Dulles must surely have got Eisenhower's approval—in a periphrastic subliminal unrecorded conversation—for the attempt against Castro. Goodpaster, who knew Eisenhower's ways of working far better than Bissell, angrily denounced this speculation as "completely unlikely." "Bissell," he told me, "was in on the plot against Castro, and I think he was just trying to spread the blame around in implicating the President."

Thomas Parrott also found incredible the theory that Ike would have mounted a covert action on his own. Allen Dulles, Parrott told me, never had a close relationship with the President, as the appointments records amply confirm. Moreover, if Ike gave Dulles a secret set of marching orders—known to no one else—when could he have done so? Between the August 18 NSC meeting and August 26, though Dulles attended three big group conferences, he had not a single minute with the President alone. (In fact, not until November 25 did he see Eisenhower by himself, for exactly ten minutes.) No human records can be absolutely watertight. But at this period the White House appointments list was kept, minute by minute, with great meticulousness. And of the private instruction theory these records provide not a chemical trace of evidence.

Another thing: The secret meeting theory hinges in great part on Bissell's allegation to the Church Committee that Dulles regularly used circumlocution to inform Eisenhower of sensitive plots afoot. Yet when I asked Bissell in an extended interview to name a specific instance, out of certain knowledge, he could produce not one that would fit. He *speculated* that Dulles *might* have used circumlocution to apprise Eisenhower of mail intercepts. He recalled that Dulles would avoid naming names (and dollar amounts) of European political beneficiaries of agency largesse, though Eisenhower knew about the practice of bankrolling candidates abroad. Bissell *doubted* Dulles would have told Eisenhower explicitly that the United States was backing both sides in the French war against Algeria. But he could cite not one instance—not one—in which Allen Dulles used circumlocution to inform Eisenhower of a major new CIA initiative. Those he did cite—like the alleged circumlocution to inform Eisenhower about the killing of Castro—rested not on firsthand knowledge, but on conjecture.

There's a final scenario: misinterpretation. And this I believe the most likely.

The President did have strong feelings about Lumumba, as the NSC attendees heard August 18. He did want vigorous action against him, as Gordon Gray told the Special Group August 25. And being reminded of the strong feelings and the need to get moving, Allen Dulles (perhaps still smarting from the U-2 fiasco) sprang into action, not only directing Lumumba's removal but citing "highest quarters here"—a breach of caution that surprised Bissell himself— thereby telling his man in Leopoldville that the President had given the order. Perhaps Allen Dulles did this, arrogantly, on purpose, thinking he knew more than the President; but probably he did not. In Francis Bacon's idol of the theater, each man responds in terms of his own philosophy, a tendency that always stands between men and their understanding of each other; and surely the spy mentality becomes such a singular way of viewing the world that it should come as no surprise that individuals who work in intelligence and individuals who do not will on occasion fail to communicate accurately.

If Allen Dulles believed Ike had ordered Lumumba's death, nonetheless, he grievously misread Gray's words. For I believe Gordon Gray when he denies any assassination thought—his or the President's—behind them. Not to believe Gordon Gray on this crucial question is not only to impugn his veracity but also to ignore all the other firsthand witnesses who unanimously confirm his account.

In that world of cold-war conspiracy, words deceived. To Bissell without question, the words "dispose of" or "eliminate" or "get rid of" included among their meanings "kill if necessary." To Allen Dulles, reporting to the NSC in Eisenhower's presence September 21, they included the same meaning; for at that very moment his nefarious technologist was packing his poisons and needles for the flight to Africa. Yet to Eisenhower—and notetaker Boggs and Gray and Goodpaster who were listening—Dulles' affirmation of the urgency of "disposing of" Lumumba did not, on all the evidence, mean murder.

One final underscoring: In March 1957, after the Suez crisis, Eisenhower met in Bermuda with his old wartime friend, British Prime Minister Harold Macmillan.

There, Eisenhower's own dictated memoranda reveal, they talked about Nasser of Egypt—to the British "an evil, unpredictable and untrustworthy man.... ambitious to become a second Mussolini—" and about the urgent need of obtaining promptly a satisfactory arrangement for the use of the [Suez] Canal.... I immediately pointed out to them the inconsistencies in their approach to these two problems. If we were at this moment to begin an attack on Nasser... *and do everything in our power overtly and covertly to get rid of him* [italics added], then the hope of getting an early and satisfactory settlement on the Canal would be completely futile."

Some hurried historians may read the italicized words as shorthand for assassination. Less hysterical historians, I believe, will remember one other fact—that Eisenhower himself quoted them in *Waging Peace*; and they will recognize its corollary—that if these words meant murder to Ike, he would never have dreamed of putting them into print for posterity.

Throughout this whole tragicomic tale, I can't help recalling—for its intriguing insight, not its historicity—the comment of a wily veteran observer who told me: "You know, I've read all through that episode, and I'll bet the whole thing's a joke. I knew those agency types. And a lot of them weren't worth a damn. All they cared about was lateral transfer—switching into the State Department, maybe even becoming an ambassador, so they and their wives wouldn't have to sit below the salt. Then all of a sudden here comes this cable: Assassinate Lumumba. Assassinate Lumumba! Hell, most of them couldn't assassinate anybody. Some of them couldn't even give a good cocktail party. So while this poor guy's sitting there, thinking of how to resign and hoping the order would blow away, here comes Dr. Strangelove with his suitcase full of bottles of poison...Christ, I'm convinced Eisenhower never knew anything about any of it."

I concur that Eisenhower knew nothing about the attempted murder of Lumumba. He worked at arm's length. He relied on trusted lieutenants. He failed to get complete control over the CIA. He took final responsibility on himself. And he ordered no assassinations. *Especially* no assassinations. After all, he had been the target during World War II of too many such attempts on his own life, attempts that help explain the vehemence McCabe noted in his deprecations on the subject. To hell with that; that was one way of solving problems he refused to allow ever to come into his consciousness; in assassination lay chaos.

King Henry II grew to regret the slaying of Thomas à Becket, which eventually caused Becket to be revered as a saint. It is a specious argument to say that a few assassinations are better than war, which kills millions: war represents the breakdown of law and order, whereas covert murder represents their absence, in the long run a still greater calamity for mankind.

When one rereads the record of how the President conducted the nation's security and sees his courage, or how he finished McCarthy and sees his principle and cunning, or how he organized the flow of government business and sees his common sense, or how he heeded his experts and sees his grudging humility, or how he spoke with foreign statesmen and sees his wisdom, the reader is left with a good feeling about Ike, about men, and about human events. But when one reads how he pulled the rug out from under his loyal servant Adams, or how he dealt with foreign nations through the CIA, one is left with a feeling of hesitation, of incompleteness, of questioning. Even when one approves the course taken, one is inevitably also torn. The reason, I believe, is that these episodes illustrate not just the exercise of power, but also the unavoidable dilemmas in the exercise of great power.

A leader, in accomplishing his task, must at times stand aloof and use men for the best interests of his task, not of the men. He must put the nation's interests first, even when he harms, perhaps unfairly, an Adams: in some cases the good doesn't triumph, just the better. These two particular dilemmas of power have been met by all nations in their histories. In the relations of America with foreign countries through the CIA, however, new questions have been raised, or old ones have been so intensified that they can justly be considered new. And one cannot answer these basic questions by saying we were merely responding to Russia's KGB: Russia has to think through these questions also.

What rule of God or man gave the United States the right to consider certain actions permissible overseas which we would not allow at home? Universality is the harbinger of justice; every great religious leader has said to do unto *every* man as you would have him do unto you. This issue remains today among the most acute of those disturbing world order. In the long run men armed with illegal lethal needles and dirty tricks can never be considered any nation's ideal representatives. Their techniques, like a broken sewer, were eventually to sully the White House even as the Kremlin.

Men rule, using the technology of their century; and the quality of the man in power is everything. As Germany suffered under Hitler, America prospered under Eisenhower. To the rest of the world his policy, while of course imperfect, was above all peaceful. He let the earth breathe. History, however, admits no gods. Each leader rules within a framework of ideas, a framework that belongs to and is limited by the period in which he happens to live. And the cold-war ethos of midtwentieth-century America approved clandestine interferences in the affairs of those who lived overseas.

When all the excuses have been made, we must admit that understanding a foreign government is quite different from understanding a foreign culture: without knowledge, money and goodwill are wasted; without skill, intervention does more harm than good. One's ignorance can create a desert and call it peace.

Human power is always exercised with human error, and every nation has to bow its head, finally. It is destiny that shapes our ends, rough-hew them how we will.

Book Four

HOW SWIFT
HOW SECRETLY

XVI

JULY 12, 1956

THE ROAD NOT TAKEN

O n or shortly after July 12, 1956—probably without even a second thought—Dwight Eisenhower made the most fateful decision of his presidency. For on that day Charles G. Ellington, special assistant to Deputy Secretary of Defense Reuben Robertson, forwarded to White House Staff Secretary Andrew Goodpaster a small sheaf of reports responding to a presidential question: Should the U.S. Army get a go-ahead to put an earth satellite into orbit in late 1956 or early 1957, that is, ahead of the Navy's attempt, which had been scheduled for late 1957 or early 1958, in order to come within the International Geophysical Year (IGY)?

Up through the bureaucracy came the reply, from a distinguished Advisory Group on Special Capabilities to the Assistant Secretary of Defense for Research and Development to the Deputy Secretary of Defense to Goodpaster to the President. And the reply was no. The decision was to influence many issues, national and international, and all of the bureaus of government, from State and Defense all the way to the department, new in Eisenhower's first term, of Health, Education, and Welfare. Furthermore, the decision was to determine, as much as any single action, the outcome of the 1960 election.

The experts, military and scientific, had the best of reasons for their conclusion: the Navy's progress was "reasonably satisfactory."

An Army attempt would have at best only a 50 percent chance of success. Tracking equipment was not yet ready. An early launching would not satisfy the U.S. commitment to the IGY and the international scientific community. It would require the diversion of top scientists from the main Jupiter missile effort.

No one mentioned a race with the Russians, also known to be planning an IGY satellite launch. No one mentioned the seismic shock to public opinion of a Soviet first in space. Goodpaster laconically scribbled across the bottom of Ellington's memo, "Secy. Robertson feels no change should be made—per Mr. Ellington. Reported to President." And history took a decisive turn, a turn memorialized by the launching of *Sputnik* October 4, 1957.

Before *Sputnik* the occurrences of the Eisenhower presidency form little pattern. All, or almost all, is light: the shaking off of Harry Truman and Korea and McCarthy, of cronies and distrust and recession in 1953–54; the high plateau of peace and prosperity in 1955, punctuated by the facing down of the Communist threat to Quemoy and Matsu; the euphoria of the campaign of 1956, punctuated by the resolution of the Suez crisis.

After *Sputnik*, in 1958–59, parallel successes appear, with the facing down of the threats to Lebanon, Quemoy and Matsu (again), and West Berlin. But behind these flashes of heat lightning, one sees a single implacable sequence of events arching from the Soviet satellite shot to the final election of 1960—an Aristotelian sequence that throws its shadow over the U.S.-Soviet space and defense and economic race; over our conduct in Africa, Latin America, and faraway Laos; over Ike's trips to India and the Far East; over Kennedy's win and Nixon's loss. It is a sequence driven by negativism and partisanship, ending in bitterness and defeat.

Ike knew *Sputnik* was approaching; he did not foresee its force. In a ho-hum mood on January 24, 1957, he and the National Security Council routinely discussed the Soviet Union's plan to put up an earth satellite—a plan known for nearly two years. They saw, they noted, they moved on to more pressing problems. On May 10 the subject came up again, this time with a slightly sharper edge. The Soviet Union, Allen Dulles reported, could orbit a satellite that very year; if they put one up and the United States didn't even try, they would score an enormous propaganda victory.

Galvanic U.S. action did not result. "You know those scientists," George Humphrey laconically observed. "When they've put up one satellite, first thing you know, they'll want to put up another."

To Eisenhower and his associates other things seemed more urgent—missiles with warheads, for example. When Joe Martin told the Legislative Leaders May 14 that the House would probably cut the Pentagon's appropriation by about $2 billion, mostly in missiles and aircraft, Ike reacted with force: "To cut the Defense Department budget further now is to take a gamble with our national safety," he said. "The U.S. must get the first missile."

On June 22, when the Soviet Union reported to an IGY work group that it planned a satellite launch within the next few months, *The New York Times*, unconcerned as the NSC, printed the news on page 12. On July 31, after Eisenhower's staff, briefing him for his news conference, reminded him that a small Soviet satellite was "going up in August," no reporter even brought the question up. And no great public clamor arose on August 27, when *The New York Times*, this time on page 1, blared out the claim of the Soviet Union that it had successfully tested a multistage ICBM, adding that the only U.S. attempt so far had flopped.

At last, when on October 4 *Sputnik* circled the earth, the scattered warnings came crashing together. And so did the multitude of petty political grievances that the Democratic party had against the lame-duck President. Since January seriatim they had grumbled over Eisenhower's criticism of Israel for failing to vacate the Gaza Strip fast enough after the Suez war; chipped away at his budget; quarreled over civil rights legislation; and harped on Ike's too much or too little intervention at Little Rock. Now at last with *Sputnik* they had a focus and a theme.

At his news conference only the day before the word of the launching broke, Eisenhower had stood before the reporters as a resolute champion of civil rights. He fielded questions with sure-footedness on Faubus and Little Rock, and when he finished, reporters praised his performance as one of his best ever. Twenty-four hours later he became what he would remain throughout his final years in office—a symbol of an America grown complacent, fat, and unconcerned; an America about to be overtaken by a smart, hungry, dangerous rival, not only in science and engineering but in education and economic advance as well. As the attacks grew more venomous, more fearless, and—given his inability to run again—more personal,

Eisenhower took them more and more to heart. With bitterness, he turned defensive. And more and more he turned for these defenses to a solid alliance with his Republican party—Left, center, and Right—in order to vindicate the honor of what he had done and honor of what he himself was.

From that moment until the years 1961–65 when he worked on the memoirs, Republican apologists would scour the history of America's performance in missiles and space, looking for facts to counter the shock of *Sputnik;* they tried to tilt the Republican ship upright again. Joe Martin and Bill Knowland would assert that in January 1948, Harry Truman's Presidential Air Policy Commission, warning that other nations might be outstripping us, had urged that our missile project be given highest priority—advice that Truman rejected. Republican researchers would turn up the intriguing statistic that under Truman we spent less for missiles than we did for peanut price supports. Administration spokesmen, fortified by "Fact Sheets" disseminated by the Pentagon (through the Republican National Committee), would cite Wernher von Braun: "The United States had no ballistic missile program worth mentioning between 1945 and 1951. Those six years, during which the Russians obviously laid the groundwork for their large rocket program, are irretrievably lost." They would trace with pride the multifold increases in spending on missiles under Eisenhower, citing the scientific group under John von Neumann which told the President in 1954 of the possibility of a major technological breakthrough, multiplying explosive power while reducing warhead size—a breakthrough that would at last mean a U.S. intercontinental missile without the need for an enormous thrust.

Along with the charges and countercharges, action started. Ike gave the Army the go-ahead to ready the Jupiter rocket as a backup to Vanguard, an action that ultimately gave the Army our first success in space just four months later. Work began that in 1958 would result in boosts in defense spending, reorganization of the Pentagon, passage of the landmark National Defense Education Act, and establishment of NASA. Drafting commenced, too, on a series of presidential "chin-up" speeches designed to buttress the shattered confidence of the American people.

Behind all this lay two crucial facts that Eisenhower could not divulge. One was that for more than a year the U-2 had been overflying the Russian landmass, recording on film the extent of the

Soviet Union's military capabilities. The other was that, ironically, *Sputnik* had done us a good turn by establishing the principle of the freedom of outer space, specifically, the freedom to orbit reconnaissance satellites. As Eisenhower well knew, the United States could get far more from these than the Russians could. And we did. Though Eisenhower could never claim credit during his lifetime, *Waging Peace* includes, buried in an appendix, a direct quote from *The New York Times* of August 14, 1960, describing the flight and recovery of an American reconnaissance satellite capsule—a citation that went to the brink of revealing the success that American scientists had had with this successor to the U-2 during Eisenhower's years in office.

These things, of course, had to remain secret: they were truly national security issues.

(A question remains to this day, of course, over the proper balance, in a democracy, between what must remain hidden and what ought to be made public. This is—and will always be—a problem over which, in difficult cases, intelligent men will disagree. What seems to be most needed by politicians is a basic understanding of the theory of democracy, especially of its relationship to scientific method. Things work when they touch truth, and truth is established openly. Authoritarianism and secrecy succeed only in the short run; employed routinely, they will eventually make the United States look like Russia. And even in the short run, a wise president is as open as possible, taking into his confidence the public, not just his advisers: *Sputnik*s, like Vietnams, cannot be hidden.)

Out of the spotlight in which he and his associates were fighting tooth and claw to defend themselves, Eisenhower would do something rare indeed: concede to his diary that his attackers had two valid criticisms: the delay preceding the late 1955 Camp David decision on ballistic missiles; and the Pentagon decision to hold up progress on the Army's Jupiter rocket. But he would concede no more.

Bitterness, indeed, infected his responses. With retrospective disapproval, Sherman Adams recalls Eisenhower's sardonic locker-room wisecrack to his NSC associates: "Any of you fellows want to go to the moon? I don't. I'm happier right here." And ironically, Adams himself most lastingly capsulized this political disdain, in his rollicking political speech ghosted by the effervescent Bryce Harlow: "The serving of science, not high score in an outer space basketball game, has been and still is our country's goal."

In the midst of all this nonsense, one voice, in my view at the time, sounded the right note, clear and true of pitch, the voice of the Vice-President of the United States. On October 15 he declared that the Soviet feat should impel the United States to a renewed military effort, even at the expense of budget economies and tax cuts.

"We could make no greater mistake," he warned the country, "than to brush off this event as a scientific stunt of more significance to the man in the moon than to men on earth."

Many Republicans who up to this time had had little use for Dick Nixon began to take notice. He had said what we hoped to hear and what the country would soon hear incessantly from the Democrats: let's get America moving.

To make everything worse, the economy started into a downturn. And with it came a codicil to *Sputnik:* the allegation that the Russians would soon overmaster us not only in satellites and missiles but also in economic power. In vain would administration spokesmen cite CIA statistics to show not only that the Soviet Union had a GNP approximately 40 percent of ours, but also that its claimed rate of economic growth had been declining over the years, from 26 percent in 1948 to 16 percent in 1951 to 10 percent in 1957. *Sputnik* panic was sweeping the land.

At home, as in the recession of 1954, the lines on the economists' charts continued to move downward; one month of anxious waiting followed another. In early 1958 Eisenhower was determined not to let the recession turn into a depression; determined to spend what had to be spent on space and defense; and determined not to emerge from the recession with deficit-producing policies that would make trouble later on. Therefore he drew a line beyond which he would not go—a line that divided him from the Democratic advocates of big federal spending which would lead, by an easy step, to the ultimate cheapening of the dollar. And therefore, on the advice of Professor Raymond J. Saulnier—Arthur Burns's successor as chairman of the Council of Economic Advisers—and Gabriel Hauge, and the even more adamant advice of Treasury Secretary Robert Anderson, Eisenhower, while holding a general tax cut poised as an antirecession tool, held off on asking the Congress for it. And as events turned out, the economy began to rebound in March 1958; Eisenhower never had to make his request. Once again, as in 1954, sunshine returned without drastic remedies; Ike had won.

This outcome fortified Eisenhower's habitual economic conservatism—a streak evident long before *Sputnik*. In January 1957, for example, Eisenhower had, without resentment, countenanced George Humphrey's criticism of the excesses of the administration's FY58 budget and his forecast that, unless federal spending and taxation were cut, we could get a recession "that will curl your hair."

After the badgering of the Democrats during the succeeding months of 1957, when they overslashed his budget, gutted foreign aid, and played civil rights politics, Eisenhower, looking for friends, moved closer than ever toward a recognition of his compatibility with the Republican Right, including Bill Knowland.

"It would appear," Eisenhower wrote Chairman Meade Alcorn August 30, 1957, in a six-page landmark letter, "that some new kind of approach is necessary to convince all Republicans that we are essentially of the same general group in political thinking.... Senator Knowland stands among the first four or five of the Republican Senators in his record of voting for measures which I have proposed. ... He and I [agree] that we are conservatives. While I have recognized the necessity of the Federal government undertaking functions and responsibilities that far exceed those in which it was engaged forty years ago, yet I have consistently fought against the needless and useless expansion of these functions and responsibilities. Senate members of the so-called 'right wing' have acted similarly. Among them are such men as Bridges, Ed Martin, Capehart, Dirksen, and Hickenlooper...."

Now, after *Sputnik*, after the Democratic attacks on his complacency, and after the vindication of his antirecession moves in the spring of 1958, Eisenhower's economic conservatism took on a new militancy. And compounding it were some changes in his inner circle of advisers.

Back in the heady summer of 1956, no one had epitomized administration liberalism-triumphant more than handsome, academic, articulate Arthur Larson, Undersecretary of Labor. A former Rhodes scholar and law school professor, he had written a short, clear, fluent, and descriptive book, *A Republican Looks at His Party*, in which he took the often ponderous and stodgy rhetoric that surrounded the Republican President and his accomplishments and tooled it into readable, ordered, and ingenious argument. The 1956 Republican party of Eisenhower, Larson reasoned, was neither the party of McKinley nor the party of Franklin Roosevelt. It was something new.

It rejected the mossbacks who wanted to go back to 1896 as it rejected the liberals who yearned for the second coming of 1936. And it held the strategic center of the American political battleground—a position of unbeatable strength.

Eisenhower read the book, admired it, called Larson in, and asked him to draft an acceptance speech for the forthcoming nominating convention—an address that, like Larson himself, turned out kindly, friendly, optimistic, generous, imaginative; that appealed not only to Republicans but to independents and "discerning" Democrats to pitch in and help; "There are still enough needless sufferings to be cured, enough injustices to be erased, to provide careers for all the crusaders we can produce and find."

Riding the crest, Larson had become head of USIA; had delivered a too-heady speech in which he asserted that "throughout the New and Fair Deals, this country was in the grip of a somewhat alien philosophy, imported from Europe"; had left USIA after a savaging of the agency's budget by suave, hypocritical appropriations subcommittee chairman Lyndon Johnson ("We look to you as the distinguished author and spokesman for your party to enlighten us"); and had served a stint in the White House as Ike's chief speechwriter, where he often tugged against the inclinations of the speaker ("dammit, Art, put that sentence in there; and if you don't I'll ad lib it in anyway").

Now, in late 1958, Larson was gone from the staff, succeeded by the more responsive Malcolm Moos ("I try to find out what the President wants to say, and help him say it in the best way"). Other White House Staff members were gone, too: Gabe Hauge, chief economic architect of "Modern Republicanism," succeeded by a former assistant to Ezra Benson, the capable Don Paarlberg; Arthur Burns ("fiscal responsibility with human compassion") succeeded by the more conservative Saulnier; and above all, reflective and restless Sherman Adams succeeded by General Wilton B. Persons—delightful, knowledgeable, totally loyal to Eisenhower, wise in the ways of the world, a genius in assessing the aims of Congress, and a man of no individual philosophical bent: Whatever Eisenhower wanted—Left, Right, or center—Persons would deliver.

With a man like Eisenhower, who thought aloud, liked to talk, shaped his ideas out in the open, these changes told. With them his presidency lost something, as it had with the departure of Emmet

Hughes and C. D. Jackson in 1953 and the death of Pete Carroll in 1954.

Another thing steeled Eisenhower's economic conservatism: his growing concern over a recrudescence of inflation.

After three years of negligible change, in April 1956 the consumer price index had started upward again. In 1957 it rose nearly 3½ percent and continued going up through the 1957–58 recession itself. In 1958 wage rates also continued to climb, faster than historical increases in productivity. With production declining (from the recession's peak to its trough real GNP dropped nearly 4 percent), unemployment mounting (to 7.4 percent, against the 1953–54 recession's top of 6 percent), and an election approaching, Eisenhower and his advisers might well have lost interest in price stability. But they didn't. "We face a choice," Anderson told Eisenhower: "preventing a little more unemployment or preserving the value of the dollar. I favor the second course. Because if inflation ever starts snowballing, it will require so much unemployment to stop it that even a Dwight Eisenhower couldn't survive politically." And the President agreed.

Vindicated on this decision (and it was a heroically correct decision), surrounded by a less liberal palace guard, goaded by Democratic attacks on his inaction, Eisenhower proceeded to make economic conservatism his centerpiece in the 1958 congressional election campaign. His old detachment gave way to a new willingness—even eagerness—to roll up his sleeves, to get his hands dirty in the detail of partisan politics, and to act with a new enthusiasm in league with the Republican Right. He would show, in Bryce Harlow's phrase, that "a second-term President was not a eunuch." He was even phoning Nixon about raising money for the fall campaign, a campaign with one key issue: the Democrats' fiscal irresponsibility, leading to deficits and inflation.

For his kickoff speech at an October 20 Republican rally in Los Angeles, Ike, as in 1954, called Harlow in for help. Harlow went away, spent an evening or two at his typewriter, and produced a blockbuster—a copy (pale but still recognizable) of the speeches he'd done earlier for Sherman Adams, speeches that had prompted a new sharpening of knives within the Democratic ranks on the Hill, and that had helped seal Adams' fate. Once again, the Democrats were all black, the Republicans all white. The Republicans were united, the Democrats divided. Half the Democrats looked north, half looked south. Half were deeply conservative, responsible statesmen, half radical free-spending nuts. And so on. Eisenhower saw this draft. And for once its bare-knuckled indictments delighted him.

"Now for the first time," he jubilated, "I know why I'm going out to Los Angeles:"

It was the Hollywood Bowl speech of 1954 all over again, but with this difference—this time it was negative and divisive, and it marked a significant turn in the road from *Sputnik* to November 1960. In the 1952 campaign Ike had run against the Truman record; in 1954 on the record of the Republican 83rd Congress; in 1956 on his own record of peace, progress, and prosperity. But now in 1958 he was running *against* the opposition party, particularly the opposition Congress.

And he failed.

The Republicans lost in a landslide. The vote left Eisenhower with only 34 in the Senate, against 64 Democrats; with only 153 Republicans in the House, against 283 on the other side. The Democrats won their first Senate seat in Indiana in twenty years; Iowa, Nebraska, and Kansas elected Democratic governors. In Utah Frank Moss beat the honored Senator Arthur Watkins; in California Knowland lost the governorship, and Goodwin Knight his Senate race.

"They obviously voted for people that I would class among the spenders," Eisenhower told the reporters November 5. "And I promise this: For the next two years, the Lord sparing me, I am going to fight this as hard as I know how." He would keep this vow to the end, his resolve fortified not only by his abhorrence of inflation but also by his increasing concern over U.S. balance of payments deficits and concomitant threats to the dollar in international money markets.

He had, however, scarcely enough votes to sustain a veto. But in January 1959 he sent the top-heavy Democratic Congress his budget for FY60 (running from July 1959 to July 1960)—a budget with a tiny surplus of $100 million. And he dared them to bust it. On February 5, when Senator Joe Clark of Pennsylvania proposed an amendment expanding a housing bill by $450 million a year for four consecutive years, the Republicans banded together as a man, with just one defection, to reject it, 33–56. In July and September the President vetoed the still excessive housing legislation, and the Senate failed twice to override. Not until September 10 did the Congress manage to overcome a veto—of the public works appropriation bill—one of only two overrides of all 181 Eisenhower vetoes in eight years. A remarkable record.

And in the end Eisenhower got his surplus—$269 million, a figure in stark contrast to the nearly $13 billion deficit of the year before. And when the good news came in, in the summer of 1960, Budget Director Maurice Stans and his staff celebrated with a barbecue in Stans's backyard.

The celebration, however, soured. For between April 1958 and April 1960 the American economy had produced the shortest trough-to-peak expansion of the postwar period. And between April 1960 and February 1961, it headed downward. Unemployment, which had fallen from its 1958 average of 6.8 percent to 1959's 5.5 percent, began once again to climb. It climbed right through the November 1960 election and helped hang Dick Nixon.

Looking back through the Kennedy-Johnson years, economists of various persuasions would throw these specific charges at Saulnier, Anderson, and independent Federal Reserve Chairman William McChesney Martin, who constantly conferred on economic action:

1. In going from a $13 billion deficit to a quarter billion dollar surplus, they turned the budget around too fast, choking off the recovery.

2. The Federal Reserve Board kept the money supply too tight: Between December 1956 and December 1960, the M-1 supply increased at an annual average rate of less than 1 percent. In 1959 the Fed raised the discount rate from 2½ percent to 4 percent, and not until June 1960 did the rate start coming down again, with recession already under way.

3. They should have cut taxes or otherwise stimulated the economy in 1960.

In early March of that year Arthur Burns, looking toward the election, came to see Nixon to warn him of recession's onset and urge him to convince the President to (a) loosen credit and (b) increase national security spending. Nixon did see Eisenhower. But, in Burns's view, Anderson and Saulnier showed themselves "stonewalls of resistance," and Eisenhower, true to his organization in place, followed their advice. (Though Nixon brought the subject up at Cabinet March 25, the minutes do not reveal any vigorous advocacy of policy change by him, or any comment at all by Anderson or Saulnier, also present.) Eisenhower thus, in Burns's view, became the victim of the wrongheaded counsel of the admired Anderson, a man who didn't know enough economics, and of Saulnier, a trained professional who had in his office the National Bureau of Economic Research's indicators of oncoming recession and refused to heed them. The administration failed to intervene. And Nixon lost.

No doubt Eisenhower and his advisers might have done better. But seen against the nearly unbroken deficits of the later sixties and early seventies and the double-digit inflation they helped produce, one fact emerges sharp and clear: the Eisenhower economic conservatism stopped the threat of inflation—stopped it cold.

In fiscal years 1956, 1957, and 1960 Eisenhower gave us three of our five balanced budgets in the thirty years since the Korean War began. Particularly in the 1959–60 steel strike settlement, he resisted wage increases which outstripped growth in productivity. He agreed that the Fed should not "turn loose" an abundance of cheap money. Between April 1958 and February 1960—nearly two years—consumer prices increased only 1.5 percent, the capstone of an eight-year Eisenhower record that saw them rise from 1952's index of 79.5 to 1960's 88.7, just 11.6 percent in eight years, 1.4 percent a year. It was an admirable performance.

But none of this helped Richard Nixon in 1960.

More and more, as Eisenhower fought this economic fight, he became a symbol of conservatism embittered. And more and more he became a contrast to the youthful senator from Massachusetts who seized on the accident of *Sputnik* and became a symbol of liberalism resurgent, aware, concerned with the movement of international forces.

In 1952 John Kennedy, a young Massachusetts congressman, had entered the Senate by defeating Cabot Lodge. Within two years he suffered his near-fatal illness—an event that led Eisenhower, speaking in Boston in November 1954 to ask his audience's prayers for the stricken young senator. Recovered, Kennedy lost the 1956 Democratic vice-presidential nomination to coonskin-capped Estes Kefauver by a whisker, thereby simultaneously saving himself from the Eisenhower landslide and putting himself into the national public eye.

Soon Kennedy would begin to ride the tide of the newly awakened—and newly discovered by politicians—third world: of that world espied above all by Adlai Stevenson and Chester Bowles and Barbara Ward Jackson.

The world's population, which had reached only 1 billion by 1850, had reached 2 billion by 1930 and would reach 4 billion by 1975 and a projected 8 billion in the early years of the twenty-first century. This growth was exploding most wildly in Latin America, Africa, and Asia. And this third world—impoverished, often subjected to colonial control, resentful—was on the march.

Although, as on civil rights, Eisenhower could from time to time voice ambivalence about this thrust ("Why the hell did we ever urge the Dutch to get out of Indonesia?" he burst out in facetious exasperation at an NSC meeting in December 1954), he understood this emergence and tried to frame sensible American action toward it. He appointed his brother Milton as an unofficial emissary to Latin America. And he himself gave it much attention. "I probably have written you more often on the subject of Mexico than any other single matter," Ike wrote Dulles on June 14, 1955. "I have the uneasy feeling that somewhere along the line we are not really appreciative of Mexico's economic and political and social problems. I believe that there is a holdover in our country today of the thought that Mexico is inherently an enemy of ours.... Visits from foreign heads of state are normally a bore, but I am so earnestly of the opinion that the soundness and friendliness of our relationships with Mexico must be a first and continuing concern of ours, that if we could arrange for an early visit of President Ruiz Cortines I would be perfectly willing to go through with it. I think that possibly you and I could profit a lot to hear his personal thoughts about his own country and its needs, especially capital—public and private.... I understand that the Soviets have the largest Embassy in Mexico City and that they are constantly carrying on a real propaganda drive in order to gain advantage in that region...."

On the other side of the world Eisenhower spent many hours intrigued with the personality of the leader of the world's greatest nonaligned power, India. On May 25, 1955, Eisenhower had a long talk, recorded on tape, with *Newsweek's* Malcolm Muir on colonialism and Nehru. Eisenhower told Muir of his failure to convince Churchill that colonialism was dead and that Britain could capitalize on its death by insisting that all its colonies have the chance to decide for themselves whether or not to remain part of the British Empire. Eisenhower had also, he said, begged the French in 1950 to do the same thing; he had succeeded in convincing only one man—General de Lattre de Tassigny. "When de Lattre died," Eisenhower continued, "France suffered a mortal blow from which it may never recover..." It is a "tragedy," Eisenhower went on, "an example of the stupidity of men, that we cannot see it clearly enough to make a virtue out of a necessity."

But however fast Eisenhower moved or wanted to move in action in the third world, he would frequently find a Kennedy or a Stevenson or a Bowles one step ahead of him. By July 2, 1957, for example, Kennedy was calling for the independence of French-owned Algeria.

"The time has come," he declared on the Senate floor, "for the U.S. to face the harsh realities of the situation and to fulfill its responsibilities as leader of the Free World....These countries are moving ahead. They desire cooperation with us....Moderate people become extremists, extremists become revolutionaries, revolutionaries become Communists. I think time is running out."

Meeting with the Legislative Leaders, Eisenhower, for the first of many times, swatted at the gnat. Republicans, he observed, couldn't take the floor to argue with Kennedy; but they should chide him for pretending to have all the answers. He didn't want to say that Algerians should not have some degree of independence. He did, however, feel it was somewhat out of order to get up and make ringing speeches in support of it.

But Kennedy had seized an initiative. And with *Sputnik* three months later, he and the other Democratic critics had a full-throated scheme: the United States was standing still; the Soviet Union was forging ahead on international battlegrounds, chief among them the third world.

The restless dissatisfaction that animated Kennedy and the Democrats extended over to Nixon and many Republicans. As all eyes turned toward 1960, the forward force was moving imperceptibly out of the White House to other sections of the government—to the office of the heir apparent Vice-President, and to the offices of his close colleagues, Secretary of Labor Jim Mitchell and Secretary of the Interior Fred Seaton.

Having gone with Fred Seaton after he left the White House

to become Secretary of the Interior, I shared these concerns. Fred had been repeatedly mentioned for greater things: for Sherman Adams' replacement in 1958 and now in 1959 as a possible vice-presidential candidate; so also Jim Mitchell. Both had lively, capable staffs: Jack Gilhooley, Walter Wallace, and Steve Horn (now president of the California State University at Long Beach) in Labor; Elmer Bennett (first choice of all of us as eventual Secretary of the Interior), George Abbott (later Nevada Republican state chairman), and Ted Stevens (now United States senator from Alaska and majority whip) in Interior. All had high hopes for the future—a future that hinged on their association with the future success of Richard Nixon.

Never had hope seemed brighter or victory surer than in July 1959 when around the world there flashed the photograph of the young Vice-President of the United States, in the model kitchen at the American Exhibition in Moscow, scoring debating points, forefinger into pudgy abdomen, over our national adversary, Nikita Khrushchev. At that moment I myself still had some lingering doubt about Richard Nixon. But this demonstration of force and direction, like his earlier dead serious response to *Sputnik*, I found arresting.

At that precise moment, in August 1959, as bearers of an Eisenhower Exchange Fellowship, my wife, Mary, and I set out on the most intensive learning experience of our lives, not excluding even the experience that went into our Harvard doctorates—an eleven-month tour which took us to the Soviet Union, Africa, the Middle East, India, and Japan. I was studying the substance and impact of the United States government's information and cultural programs over-seas. And we carried in our hearts that magnificent utterance of Thomas Jefferson carved around the inside of the Jefferson Memorial in Washington: "I have sworn upon the altar of God eternal hostility against every form of tyranny over the mind of man."

Starting in the Soviet Union we met with members of the Writers Union who read and spoke English and revealed they had never heard of Milton's *Areopagitica* or Mill's *Essay on Liberty*—the two most monumental tracts in the language on freedom of thought and speech. We met professors of English literature at the University of Moscow who had heard of Milton and condescendingly professed to understand why he opposed licensing the press: in the context of the seventeenth century, they pointed out, it was necessary for him to believe in freedom of speech. "But aren't some concepts, such as freedom of speech," we asked, "separable from any historical context?" "No."

We visited Moscow's Lenin Library, where we saw a highly touted display of American books translated into Soviet languages, not one volume of which contained anything to counter the dogmas of an obscurantist order; and where we at last found Milton and Mill in Russian translations, all dating back to the days of the czars. One copy of *On Liberty* had been read seventeen times in the ten years since 1950, a second copy fourteen times; the name of every reader had been recorded by the vigilant "librarians."

Here, if anywhere, was the heart of the darkness. We had been sending Arthur Schlesinger and Paddy Chayefsky and Lenny Bernstein to the Soviet people. Why not send along also a few old books—say, 50,000 copies of *On Liberty*, or 100,000? Why not forge a new strategy to confront the messianic obscurantist enemy hand to hand, mind to mind, throughout the world?

Could we not, by helping others to understand us, help peace? Why not give the great Russian people, one of the most long-suffering in history, a chance at new concepts? Guns represent power, but the direction in which one fires them is determined by ideas.

XVII

NOVEMBER 8, 1960

ALL THE
DIFFERENCE

O n the night of July 28, 1960, as Richard Nixon delivered his
acceptance speech at the Republican convention, we heard a
strategy of victory announced.

In words full of forward motion and drive, he struck the
theme of international challenge—the theme set forth by *Sputnik*: "We
are in a race tonight, my fellow Americans, a race for survival, in
which our lives, our fortunes, our liberties are at stake." Accordingly,
he went on, one task above all would devolve upon the new president:
to devise "a brand-new strategy which will win the battle for freedom
for all men, and win it without a war."

For a flickering instant as he uttered these words I thought
back to the metaphors of 1954—the blueprint for socialism, the rats in
the barrel. And then those images vanished. For now Richard Nixon,
there on the TV screen, speaking to millions of Americans, calling for
victory in the battle for men's minds, was detailing his formula to
produce that victory. "The complex of agencies which have grown up
through the years for exchange of persons, for technical assistance, for
information, for loans and for grants—all these must be welded
together into one powerful economic and ideological striking force. . . .
We must develop a better training program for the men and women
who will represent our country at home and abroad. We need men
with a broad knowledge of the intricacies and techniques of the
strategies of the Communists, with the keen knowledge of the great

principles for which free people stand, and, above all, men who with a zeal and dedication which the Communists cannot match, will out-think, out-work, and out-last the enemies of freedom wherever they meet them, anywhere in the world."

He was leaguing himself with a drive from thaw to thought in the cold war, with the exchange of ten thousand students, with a free traffic of ideas and documents and words. He was talking to complacent American cocktail party artists and cookie pushers he had seen in his travels around the world. And he was talking to the members of the Composers Union and the Writers Union whom we had met in Moscow, to the professors, and to the officials of the Lenin Library. He was throwing a blazing light on a course ahead, and in it my doubts vanished.

Richard Nixon was shaking himself free at last. From Dwight Eisenhower, sitting in the audience, Nixon felt he needed little or nothing now. He would do it all himself. His campaign, he declared, would begin that very night. And he would visit all fifty states—every one of them. Already he had his own staff in place, with a horde of eager helpers. One early meeting brought together more than fifty people, representing every agency of the federal government, in one room, under the leadership of Professor George Grasmuck of Michigan, master of the campaign's research. Studies were undertaken. Position papers were written. Dozens of experts were tapped for ideas, to be funneled to Jim Shepley, a young tiger on leave from Time-Life who sat at Nixon's elbow. The future seemed bright indeed for Nixon and his men, particularly by comparison with the awkward beginning of young John Kennedy, tapping his fingers nervously in Los Angeles before his acceptance speech in July and mired down in the embarrassments of the concluding weeks of the Senate session in August.

Then two things happened. On August 17 in Greensboro, North Carolina, Nixon accidentally banged his right knee against a car door he was entering. A painful infection resulted, putting him into Walter Reed Hospital until September 9. The hospitalization forced him to cancel some planned trips, including one to Alaska, and thus put his campaign behind schedule until its final frenzied days.

The second thing happened on September 26: disaster—the first of the televised Nixon-Kennedy debates. Not only did Nixon look pale and sickly under the studio lighting in his light gray suit against a light gray background His responses to the attacks of the underdog seemed likewise sickly and pale: "The things that Senator Kennedy has said, many of us can agree with...I subscribe completely to the spirit that Senator Kennedy has expressed tonight, the spirit that the United States should move ahead." Shifting to what would become his major theme through the campaign, Nixon asked a rhetorical question: "Is the United States standing still?" For all the statistics that he then reeled off to answer that question with a negative, and for all the assertions he would make over the coming six weeks to prove America's forward movement under Republican management, he had boxed himself onto no-win ground. And Senator Kennedy, in his final summation in the debate, seized his advantage: "If you feel that everything that is being done now is satisfactory....I think you should vote for Mr. Nixon....I don't want historians ten years from now to say these were the years when the tide ran out for the United States. I want them to say these were the years when the tide came in, these were the years when the United States started to move again."

With these words, the Kennedy campaign itself began to move. It would attack the Republican administration for everything: for letting the Russian economy grow at three times the rate of ours; for letting unemployment in the United States double in the past eight years; for letting American prestige plunge; for—somehow—letting a child in two villages in Brazil have a life-span of less than one year; for letting things drift in Little Rock and then suddenly calling out the troops; for failing to stop Castro's takeover of Cuba; and, always, for standing with "the contented" against "the concerned." The attack—and the hollowness of the implied promise that Kennedy could right everything, if only given the chance—infuriated me. And what infuriated me even more was Kennedy's own vulnerability to attack, the rashness and callowness of so many of his own words.

As September became October, Fred Seaton was now traveling full-time with Nixon around the country, and more and more becoming Chief of Staff. So back in Washington I began drafting up suggestions and, unsolicited, firing them off to him: one on Kennedy's fatuous assertion that we might well have avoided all trouble with Castro if only we had "given the fiery young rebel a warmer welcome in his hour of triumph"; one on Kennedy's dangerous weakness on the defense of Quemoy and Matsu and Berlin. The water wore the stone. On Sunday, October 23, Fred phoned me to come to Washington's Union Station and get on the campaign train.

By now, newsman Seaton had become supreme in the Nixon palace guard. Attorney General Bill Rogers, Nixon's capable longtime friend from their days on Capitol Hill together, was, at this moment, just going along for the ride. So, largely, was Jim Shepley.

The big hitters in the group, under Seaton's direction, were his good friends from the White House Gabe Hauge, on leave briefly from Manufacturers Trust in New York, and Bryce Harlow, who divided his time in those last weeks between helping Nixon and helping Eisenhower. And on that Sunday evening of October 23, there would be these new additions: Karl Harr, a White House special assistant in the national security field; Roemer McPhee, associate special counsel to the President, a man with a background in economics as well as law; and I.

At ten that night the staff gathered together to go to work. The candidate would be making a platform speech every half hour or so the next day, Fred told us, starting in York, Pennsylvania, at 8:00 A.M. Few of these had yet been written, and because we were going through coal country a mile at a time, I got my first assignment: to do ringing declarations on two subjects—coal research and residual fuel oil. These subjects didn't exactly have the glamour of Berlin, Quemoy, and the Kremlin; but there they were, and I set to work. Around midnight, before the train pulled out of Washington, I got off, and from a pay station phoned my friend Royce Hardy, Assistant Secretary of the Interior for mineral resources. He sounded sleepy, having indeed been asleep. I asked him for some figures, and he gave them to me, right to the point. (Only weeks later did I learn from him that the next morning he had asked his wife: "Do you remember that Bill Ewald called me up last night? He asked me for some figures, I think. I wonder what I told him?") With his authoritative facts and figures in hand, I confidently knocked out a draft demonstrating, dollar by dollar, that on minerals and fuels research, the Eisenhower appropriation figures outstripped those of Truman by 30 percent. In fact, the draft revealed, no president in U.S. history ever did more for coal research than Dwight Eisenhower.

We assembled for yet another brief staff meeting, at which Roemer McPhee mentioned that "what we need is another idea like the one Emmet Hughes came up with in 1952: 'I shall go to Korea.'" Nettled, Seaton jumped all over him. "In the first place, Emmet Hughes didn't think that idea up. And in the second place, we've got something up our sleeves three times as big."

302

As we stumped through Pennsylvania, I began working on, of all things, a draft excoriating Kennedy's farm proposals—a rough and tough document Hauge and I concocted, alleging that Kennedy's plan, if enacted, would raise grocery prices 25 percent and throw 2 million Americans out of work.

We released it Tuesday night, and the next morning I had the pleasure of sitting down to breakfast with a couple of reporters I didn't know and hearing them grumble: "That excerpt on Kennedy's farm plan was uncalled for. It was *too* rough."

Actually in his Tuesday evening address, in Cincinnati, Nixon had not even mentioned agricultural policies—Kennedy's or anybody's. He had repeated his canned speech on the nation's need for experience rather than inexperience in times of crisis. And so the counterpoint would sound throughout the campaign: the candidate giving his standard speech from the platform while a variety of handouts, labeled "excerpts," on a variety of subjects sailed off from his train or plane from coast to coast. The counterpoint did not please the reporters: "If he didn't say it, goddammit, I'm not going to write it up."

For me there was one salient exception to all this niggling carping on coal and oil and butter and eggs—the excerpt I began writing Monday night on the captive nations of Eastern Europe, harking back to Nixon's acceptance speech, and his moving account of his triumphant 1959 welcome in the streets of Warsaw.

My draft was a proposal to keep hope for liberty in Eastern Europe alive; and to this end it included the Vice-President's promise, if elected, to visit every one of the Soviet Union's captive nations. Hauge and Seaton read it with instant enthusiasm. But now I began to discover pitfalls. Karl Harr objected to having the Vice-President of the United States announce he would go to Eastern Europe; you have to have, he argued, an invitation. Bill Rogers found the draft too severe on the Russians. ("I guess we'll have to change it a bit to satisfy him," Seaton snorted, as a vista suddenly opened on the tension between two tough and able men. "He's not the least of the crosses I have to bear. If he knows a goddamned thing about politics, I sure don't know where he learned it.") So we cut and softened and accommodated: Richard Nixon wouldn't just go crashing into Eastern Europe uninvited: he'd seek ways to set up a visit. Then we encountered another problem: by total accident and sheer ignorance I had stumbled onto the Great Idea—the surprise three times as big as

"I shall go to Korea"—that Seaton had alluded to a couple of days earlier. It was, I learned, a brainstorm of Jim Shepley's: an Eastern Europe visit by Eisenhower. A hitch therefore came up: Should we announce a Nixon visit now? Happily the answer came back yes; we'd announce the unleashing of the ex-President later.

So on the night of Thursday, October 27, Press Secretary Herb Klein gave the reporters my Eastern Europe excerpt. And that night Nixon did actually speak of Poland and the captive nations and the weeping cheering crowds. And when the staff returned to the train, they told me that they had seldom heard him make so moving an address.

But I had not heard it. For in that empty train that night, assisted by one loyal secretary, I had seized upon the invaluable time—two uninterrupted hours of silence—to dictate the first draft of what I hoped would be an even more significant contribution to the campaign—a document soon titled "Mission Liberty."

Like the captive nations excerpt, it recalled the acceptance speech, attempting to add muscle and detail to some of its outlines. It proposed a strategy that included: *First,* a spreading throughout the world of the books that set forth and argue for democratic government and the freedoms of thought and speech—the *Federalist Papers*; Madison's *Notes on the Constitutional Convention*; a one-volume selection of the writings of Jefferson and Lincoln; Milton's *Areopagitica*; John Stuart Mill's *Liberty*—books to be put into the cheapest possible paperback editions and translated into the major languages of every country.

Second, the organization of trained and intelligent professionals ready and able to speak for the United States to foreign audiences with a mastery of the arguments for freedom the books set forth; these men to be our "barristers of liberty throughout the earth."

Third, the Open Bookshelf proposal to the Soviet Union: an offer to exchange selected translated books on a massive scale. "It is in a sense an indictment of western civilization," the paper concluded, "that today so many people ask of a man, 'Is he a Marxist?' The prevalence of that question must end. The day must come when the Marxists will begin to ask of a man, 'Is he a Jeffersonian? Is he a believer in the ideas of Abraham Lincoln? Is he an adherent of Milton and a follower of Mill...?'"

The next morning I came down to earth with a bump. The train was now rolling through Illinois, and between whistle stops the staff got together for its one and only meeting with the candidate himself, back in his private dining room at the rear of the train. Nixon was all business, looking ahead to the writing we'd be doing. "You have to use colorful language," he instructed us. "You can have all the fine phrases in the world, but if the writing's not colorful, the papers won't print it." Then he looked ahead to future subjects. He'd been trying to terrify his audiences by revealing to them the perils in inexperienced international leadership. Now, he said, we had to frighten them on the domestic side, by showing them the perils of inflation and recession, by asking the blunt question: "Where are you going to get the money?" Prime Minister Macmillan, Nixon said, had told him that the Labour government in England had advocated programs that just couldn't be paid for. We had to scare people by showing them what would happen if the other side won—what would happen with jobs, what would happen with prices. He thought he might cover this domestic threat in a short TV broadcast: Nixon at Nine.

Another such short broadcast, he said, could focus on foreign policy. Then in a third one we could "do all that welfare crap." Laughter—some nervous, some raucous—followed.

"Dr. Flemming," Herb Klein broke in archly, since the HEW Secretary was not present just then, "refers to such things as 'meeting human needs.'"

"I don't care," Nixon said irritably. "It *is* crap. We'll have one broadcast on it—things like education, health, and housing."

The candidate left to go to the rear platform to talk to a small band of Illinois farmers. He was suffering from a heavy cold. As we waited for him to return, the minutes dragged on. "What the hell's he doing out there?" Seaton asked. "He's wasting his voice on ten people." Finally the wait became unbearable. Seaton got up: "Let's go." We all walked out. We never had another such gathering.

The week ended with a little group of us agonizing late into the night over the scare theme. "Monday is Halloween," Nixon had said: "Every campaign needs a Halloween speech." So after many drafts we produced a text that sought to portray Jack Kennedy as the Master Halloweener, trying to frighten the American people by conjuring up hollow hobgoblins—recession, defeat in outer space, unemployment. It never saw the light of day.

After a quick flight back to Washington for what was left of the weekend, we took off again on Monday, October 31 late in the afternoon, this time by plane. As the wheels went up, we had in fact no idea of our immediate destination. This ignorance reflected a constant problem with the campaign: "Dick reacts viscerally, like a cat," one perceptive observer told me. "He keeps responding to Kennedy's moves, day by day. Instead, I think he should belt him a good one in the morning but then every afternoon try to do something more constructive."

But Nixon didn't. He kept hammering away at his negative theme: America has not been standing still. And we kept slashing away at Kennedy's follies. But we weren't in fact counterpunching minute by minute. On the train or the plane one exists in a hermetically sealed tube, hurtling through space at 60 or 400 miles an hour, completely cut off from the world. When the train tube stops, someone plugs a long wire into an outlet, and you can phone Washington; the conversation ends with a slice when the train pulls out of the station. When the plane lands, you can get to a pay phone and renew your touch with reality. You may, if you're lucky, see an occasional newspaper. But its headline will report what the foe said hours ago or yesterday, not what he's saying at the moment. And out in the plains and prairies, the detail of what he said can be maddeningly short. So you're fighting not a flesh and blood opponent but a phantom image in gray outline—an image whose changing day-to-day detail you can't see.

We were now riding a 707—the Nixon family in front, the staff in first class, the press corps in tourist in the back.

We had long known of the reporters' hostility to the candidate. In fact, Nixon even had hard evidence that in the TV debates some of the newsmen were allowing themselves to be used as conduits for questions selected by the Democrats. Ironically, my own recollections of individuals in the accompanying press corps are largely beneficent: of my friend Pat Munroe, trying without success to get an appointment with his old friend Seaton; Teddy White, a typewriter on his lap, chatting amiably with his friend Hauge; Maggie Higgins, bright and beautiful even at seven in the morning, her shoulder-length auburn hair ungroomed and tumbling. Moreover, some of the Nixon staff viewed the abrasiveness of the press with amusement; at 25,000 feet, one staffer observed with a twinkle, if you open a window you create a vacuum that will suck out anybody sitting next to it. So, he went on, perhaps somebody should just walk down the aisle with a six-shooter and shoot out windows next to a few select reporters.

One of these, in the view of all of us, would surely have been Nebraska-born bull-shaped William H. Lawrence of *The New York Times*. Nixon had planned to visit all fifty states. He had not yet visited Wyoming. So he was going to keep his pledge and fly into Casper. Unhappily, on the morning selected, the Casper Airport was enjoying a massive snowstorm. The skilled pilot, consulting with Nixon's aide Air Force Major Don Hughes, made a first attempt at a landing. It didn't work. We felt the huge 707 pull out of its descent and soar upward again. And at that moment the sotto voce mumbling and growling of Lawrence became audible. "What the hell is that maniac trying to do—kill us all? He's risking the lives of all these press people, all of whom have wives and children, just so he can keep his goddamn commitment to go into every state!" At that precise moment, some of the press stories later claimed, a few reporters began singing hymns. I personally heard none, though I did know that the bar back in their section had been open for business since early morning. Finally, after another pass, the pilot brought the plane safely down. And having received word of the hysterics in the rear section, Hughes himself went back to explain to the reporters that he knew what he was doing; that he too had a wife and children; and that at no time would he have endangered the life of anyone. Then he turned on his heel and marched back to the cockpit, muttering under his breath something like: "Those stupid bastards."

The bitterness persisted. From Casper we flew to Spokane. A reporter from the St. Louis *Post-Dispatch* sat in the front row, watched as Nixon, speaking with emphasis, expectorated involuntarily small flakes of saliva, and repeated in a loud stage whisper: "That's right. Spit at 'em, Dick!" Nixon, as the reporter doubtless intended, heard. And as I passed through the candidate's cabin as we got ready to take off from Spokane, I saw him in a rage: "Get me the name of that reporter. We're going to get that guy!"

It was rare to have such a glimpse of the candidate *in camera*. On the 707, in flight, a closed door separated him and Pat from the rest of us. We would sit there in our comfortable first-class seats, just a few feet away, and look at that door. Fred Seaton went through it at times, but no one else. And so, I learned, did "Mission Liberty." Bryce Harlow had done some editing on it. Gabe Hauge's enthusiasm—like Harlow's and Seaton's—remained strong as ever. Fred initialed the draft—the ultimate mark of approval. Don Hughes carried it to Nixon. The rest was silence.

And now time was running out. Nixon was in Los Angeles, poised for his final discharge of his fifty-state commitment: his flight to Alaska. Len Hall had had a frantic last-minute call from Illinois: Illinois was wavering between Nixon and Kennedy; one more big visit from Nixon might push Republicans over the top. So Hall asked H. R. Haldeman. And he got a brusquer brush-off: "We're not going to Illinois. We're going to Alaska." That decision may have cost Nixon the election.

But so may many others. Since 1960 I have talked to dozens of people, all of whom believe that if their single idea—go to Illinois, send a wire to Martin Luther King, give a talk on the rule of law—had been accepted, Nixon would have won the election. I'm sure they're all right. And at times I too like to believe that one thing might have changed the outcome: a return to the forward thrust of the acceptance speech with the promulgation of an idea like Mission Liberty.

For we lost by the closest margin in years. Kennedy and Johnson got 49.71 percent of the total vote, Nixon and Lodge 49.55 percent. A switch of just 11,874 votes in five states, Hawaii, Missouri, New Mexico, Nevada, and Illinois, would have reversed the result.

As the vote rolled in, that long night in Los Angeles, we absorbed the shocks of despair—all but one, which came the next morning. As I entered the coffee shop of the Ambassador Hotel, looking for a few breakfast friends to commiserate with, the waitress approached, and recognizing it as a table of campaigners, beamed. Then she looked straight at me, seated next to the Republican Secretary of the Interior, and said, awestruck:

"I know who *you* are. I saw you on television last night. You're *Ted Sorensen!*"

Of all possible causes of Richard Nixon's defeat in his race for the presidency, two undeniably came from Eisenhower himself: (1) his fatal bequest of negativism; (2) his ambivalence. Nixon had always been an attacker, not a defender. Starting with his first campaign for Congress, in 1946, he had challenged Jerry Voorhis; hounded Alger Hiss; labeled Helen Gahagan Douglas a pinko; socked the Truman record in 1952 with 3 C's and a K—Communism, Controls, Corruption, and Korea; had gone around the country in 1954 waving the "blueprint for socialism" found in the files; and in 1958 had piled onto the Republican excoriation of the Democrats' "radical spending wing" and mounted a counterattack of his own against the Acheson foreign policy which "resulted in war." But now in 1960 Nixon had become a defender, protesting from coast to coast that "America has *not* been standing still." And saddled with negativism, he had become a loser. Though his loss was in part traceable to Eisenhower, it was ultimately traceable to Khrushchev, and specifically to *Sputnik*. The tree, notched on October 4, 1957, had never righted again. It fell on November 8, 1960.

The second Eisenhower contribution to Nixon's defeat—ambivalence—Eisenhower always vehemently denied. Hadn't he stood by Dick from the start—from 1953, when he sent him out on a goodwill mission to Australia; to 1954, when he backed his method of campaign stumping; to 1956, when he let him chart his own course—offered him any job in the government he wanted—and then welcomed him on the ticket; to 1958, when he came out to the airport and praised him at his triumphant return from near death by mob violence in Venezuela; to 1959–60, when he accepted with enthusiasm the certainty that Nixon would be the nominee?

Eisenhower had done every one of these things. He had done more with and for Nixon than any other president had done for any other vice-president in memory. Yet withal the ambivalence—though in dilute measure—remained.

It surely crossed Eisenhower's mind as he sat listening to Nixon's acceptance speech. In drafting an account of the 1960 campaign for the memoirs, I included some high praise for Nixon's proposed strategy of victory. With a snort, Eisenhower struck the words out. "It's a great idea. The only problem is how do you do it?" He was not only objecting to the setting of an impossible dream. He was reading underneath those Nixon words—and I believe reading rightly—a slur on his own shortcoming, his own failure to achieve that victory in eight long years in the Oval Office.

Ambivalence surely came through also in Eisenhower's renowned reply to a press conference question on August 24 from *Time*'s Charles Mohr about Nixon's contributions to administration thought. Actually, at that news conference the question was asked three times in three different ways, and with every answer Ike grew more impatient. First Sarah McClendon of the El Paso *Times*, never a presidential favorite, asked Eisenhower to lay out "some of the big decisions that Mr. Nixon has participated in since you have been in the White House. . . ." Eisenhower bristled: "Well, Mrs. McClendon, no one participates in the decisions. Now let's see, we just—I don't see why people can't understand this: no one can make a decision except me if it is in the national executive area. . . ." A few minutes later the same question came up again, this time from Mohr: Had Nixon then "been primarily an observer and not a participant"? Eisenhower reddened. Once again he stressed his own primacy in executive decision-making. "That has to be in the mind and heart of one man."

But now Mohr, as the strict half hour of the news conference approached its end, pushed one step further: "I just wondered if you could give us an example of a major idea of his that you had adopted in that role, as the decider. . . ."

Eisenhower had had enough: "If you give me a week, I might think of one. I don't remember."

"Thank you, Mr. President," said timekeeper Jack Bell of the AP, and it was all over.

All over—except for the fallout. Eisenhower, embarrassed by the implication that reporters drew from this reply, tried to dismiss it as "facetious." But he wasn't being funny. Whenever Eisenhower used the word "facetious" or "jocular," or whenever he spoke of laughing off an attack, he was often concealing a wound or an irritant. The reporters that morning had struck a nerve: the allegation that Eisenhower didn't run the government. ("One thing this book is going to demonstrate," his son, John, told me as we started in to work on it, "is that Dad knew what was going on.") So Ike bridled at the faintest trace of this implication in the reporters' questions, and Nixon became the victim. The plain fact was that Eisenhower did not so unqualifiedly favor Nixon—especially now that Nixon was moving to replace him at the apex of government—that he would sacrifice his own self-defense (even against so slight an attack as this one) in order to help him.

Indeed, it is probably fair to say that Eisenhower did not so much wish victory for Nixon—the minor, often merely subliminal critic of Eisenhower and his work—as he wished defeat for Kennedy—the major, overt attacker of his presidential performance. The difference emerges subtly but indelibly in a remark Eisenhower made in a phone call to his friend Ben Fairless of U. S. Steel on August 19: "Motorcades kill me, but I'm going to do them to try to arouse enthusiasm. I'll do almost anything to avoid turning the country over to Kennedy." Ike would have rolled up his sleeves to go to work *for* Bob Anderson or Al Gruenther or his brother Milton. But when he finally rolled up his sleeves in late October 1960, he was going to work *against* the young upstart from Massachusetts.

Overriding all objections Richard Nixon agreed to meet Kennedy in televised debates. And on the eve of the first one, on September 25, he rejected Eisenhower's strategic advice: "I am going to play it in a low key—be gentlemanly, let Kennedy be the aggressor. Because of the religious angle, I can't be too tough." Though Eisenhower concurred, he still warned against softness: "Don't be too concerned about Kennedy's looking bad." Ignoring that advice had helped to sink Nixon in the first encounter.

Whether this rejection nettled Eisenhower or not, he was doing all that Nixon asked him to do. Between September 1 and October 27 the President made approximately twenty speeches, most of them "nonpolitical" appearances before key groups, often with political overtones. He phoned and wrote Nixon (and Lodge) a stream of congratulations and suggestions: the campaign needs more zip, don't appear too quick and glib with answers in the debates, pay particular attention to young people. He became increasingly frustrated and irritated under the Democratic attacks and he became increasingly hurt and chagrined that Nixon wasn't asking him to do more.

Finally, by agreement, he swung into real action. At 10:23 on the morning of October 21 he talked with Nixon by phone from San Diego. Ann Whitman recorded that tycoon-friends Pete Jones and Sig Larmon overheard the conversation. The President, she said, apparently spoke "fairly firmly" to Nixon, and agreed to do everything he could to help "what is generally regarded as Dick's lost cause"; but he intended to help "in his own way."

Eisenhower plunged into the campaign with the greatest vigor of his political career. He made barn burning addresses in Philadelphia, New York, Cleveland and Pittsburgh. He lashed at the callow "young genius" on the other side, at "the juggling of promises by the inexperienced, the appeal to... and selfishness, the distortion of fact, the quick change from fantastic charge to covert retreat."

But even in the midst of this blazing finish—decorated with congratulatory Eisenhower-to-Nixon and Nixon-to-Eisenhower phone calls—differences and bitterness persisted.

On October 31 the President invited Nixon to the White House to have lunch with him and with Len Hall, speechwriter Malcolm Moos, Bob Merriam, Jim Hagerty, and several others. "I know you have trouble in some key states," Eisenhower said. "Tell me how I can help." Eisenhower had already agreed to his final-week appearances in the New York City area, Cleveland, and Pittsburgh. And with Len Hall he'd agreed also to an expansion of this schedule to include upstate New York, downstate Illinois, and Michigan. He was fired up, ready to go. But when he asked his question, Nixon never gave him a straight answer. He tightened, and in effect turned Eisenhower's offer down. Why? The reason Nixon gives in his memoirs (1978) was fear for Eisenhower's health, a fear underscored by secret imploring phone calls, only hours before, from Mrs. Eisenhower and Dr. Howard Snyder, Eisenhower's physician. Exasperated, Eisenhower afterwards asked Hall straight out: "Why didn't Dick pay attention to what I was saying?"

"He was uptight, Mr. President," Hall, also stunned, replied. "You could have fired a gun off and he wouldn't have noticed."

"Goddammit, he looks like a loser to me!"

To confidants Eisenhower would advert with some irritation to the advice he had given Nixon in 1956. As Secretary of Defense or Commerce, Ike argued, Nixon could have resigned eight months before the election and given full time to a winning campaign.

On November 5 Ann Whitman set down in her diary that out of desperation the Nixon camp was suggesting that Eisenhower call on all candidates to make public their health records. Jim Hagerty saw this as a "cheap, lousy, stinking policital trick." And Eisenhower himself flatly refused. He would be "no party to anything that has to do with the health of candidates." So the health ploy—an attempt to exploit Kennedy's alleged Addison's disease and other infirmities—never came off.

A second ploy, however, did. Jim Shepley had sent in a draft of a talk in which Nixon would propose that if elected he would invite heads of government of the Communist countries to the United States and in return ask President Eisenhower to visit the Communist bloc countries in 1961. When Ann showed it to Eisenhower, on November 4, he was, in her words, "astonished, did not like the idea of 'auctioning off the presidency' in this manner, spoke of the difficulty of his traveling once he is not president, and felt it was a last-ditch hysterical action." He did, however, make some changes in the wording of the text and asked Hagerty to phone Shepley.

"They will not use this tonight," Jim told Ann after he hung up. "They may come back at us tomorrow." But despite Eisenhower's editorial changes, it was clear he had disapproved of the proposition, and Jim had conveyed this disapproval to Shepley. But two days later, on Sunday, November 6, just before Nixon left for Alaska, Rose Mary Woods phoned Ann from California to ask her to be sure to have the President tune in on Nixon at nine that night. When Ike did, he heard Shepley's proposal, which now had a new feature: not only would President Eisenhower go to Eastern Europe but ex-Presidents Truman and Hoover would also.

The deception made Eisenhower livid. He got on the phone to Hagerty: issue a retraction saying I won't go. Finally, he thought better of it, cooled down, and did what he had to do: he sent Nixon a congratulatory message on the eve of his defeat.

Through months and years after the election, the Nixon zealots resented Ike's reservations about their hero, just as they ignored Nixon's drive to do everything unassisted, rejecting dependence on Ike. Yet in retrospect, one cannot fault the President's ambivalence. Without doubt, as Nixon's longtime friend William Rogers observes, the later defeat in California humiliated and embittered and changed Nixon into a man consumed by vengeance, determined to kick his perceived enemies. Yet long before California, long before Watergate, bits of mosaic form a pattern: the picture of the loner, trusting no one; the labeling of education, housing, and health as "welfare crap"; the flare-up threat to "get" the *Post-Dispatch* reporter; the peremptory order that Jim Bassett received from a key Nixon aide, about a scheduled meeting with some black leaders in Chicago: "Cancel that meeting; the Vice-President isn't going to meet with those niggers"; the scene that remained painted in our memories after Mary and I came away from the Nixon Washington home following a pre-Christmas farewell, the tree twirling on an electric stand as we heard our host's first words of greeting: "We won, but they stole it from us" (words that revealed his obsession with nothing but himself, his own campaign and his own loss): intense personal struggle over so many years does not produce magnanimity.

There were further bits of evidence that seemed to bear out the terse summary of Sam Rayburn, long before Watergate: "Nixon doesn't give a damn about the truth." During the 1960 campaign, for example, Gabe Hauge and I would listen again and again as Nixon spoke of inflation under Truman: the cost of living, he would say, went up 50 percent; the buying power of the dollar was therefore cut in half. Hauge, a Harvard economist, would shake his head: if the cost of living went up 50 percent, the buying power of the dollar went down not by a half but a third. One could see that the problem bothered Gabe: "He's careless about things like that." Finally there was Nixon's diction, a feature the Watergate tapes would underline. One close confidant of the Nixons—a man who had grown up with barracks language all about him—noted as early as 1960 that "Nixon would use shocking words, words never used even in unmixed company, words I'd even forgotten existed." Years later, I, too, would recoil in shock at the former Vice-President's vocabulary when I got a firsthand report of his characterization of Eisenhower in 1964: "that senile old bastard." Had I been more analytical, I should have known the truth before this: Eisenhower was ambivalent toward Nixon; Nixon was deeply resentful of Eisenhower.

If the Nixon cream was soured, some of the bacteria came from the environment. Running for office too often has become, in America, a hunt in which a fox is savaged by the hounds. A candidate can learn to hate his public. Dirty trick behavior is often beneath human dignity, Democrats like Muskie, becoming its victims as well as Republicans. Our political campaigns need revision in both length and tone.

In retrospect, one should doubtless give thanks that a man of Nixon's character never got the opportunity to lead a worldwide moral crusade in 1961. (By 1968 he had apparently dropped the idea.) For if we had read the acceptance speech with care, we might have seen that its root motivation was not international love, but international hate. The Nixon strategy of victory was a strategy of defeat for a detested foe. Intellectuals would become a strike force: even the thought of Thomas Jefferson would become a weapon for strategic deployment. Clearly the difference between Nixon and Ike was more extreme than its surface appearance. Dwight Eisenhower, lifelong soldier, never thought this way, since he sought not a plan of conquest, but simply a union of friends around the world. A strategy for victory was an impossible strategy, as Eisenhower said: rooted in hate, not compassion, it could never have resulted, even if it had succeeded, in a triumph for humankind. What the world needs is cooperation under law.

For all their differences, however, Nixon's defeat was also Eisenhower's. The President viewed the election result, in part rightly, as a "repudiation of everything I've done for eight years." And the bitterness that flowed from it fortified his scorn for Kennedy, his associates, their capabilities, and their work.

This scorn enlivens the most vitriolic single letter in Eisenhower's personal Gettysburg files—the one he wrote to Coca-Cola's Bob Woodruff January 3, 1961, on the incoming Kennedy Cabinet: "Ralph McGill," Eisenhower wrote, "has hailed the assembly of brains with which the President-elect is to be surrounded. I think he is possibly correct in his high opinion of Rusk. Everything I have heard about that individual seems good. But when you have a menagerie in the State Department comprising one individual who is no less than a crackpot, another noted for his indecisiveness, and still another of demonstrated stupidity, and, finally, one famous only for his ability to break the treasury of a great state it is very difficult for me to share Ralph's high opinion... of such a group."

This scorn, plus outrage, filled the ex-President in midsummer 1961; he snarled—the angriest I ever saw him—at the Kennedy's plan to take President Ayub of Pakistan to Mount Vernon for an evening of wining, dining, and dancing: "What a desecration! these goddamn..." And then Ike leaned back and grinned: "The doctors say I shouldn't get my blood pressure up; so I guess I shouldn't say any more."

Such scorn remained even in 1965 as Eisenhower told a crowd of reporters off the record in Gettysburg that if he had had charge, the Berlin wall would have been knocked down; and that "you can always tell a Harvard man, but you can't tell him much."

And I feel certain that total lack of confidence in his successor's competence was the ambience of the advice Eisenhower gave Kennedy in the weeks before the inaugural—advice not only on the balance of payments problem ("I pray that he understands it") but above all on Laos.

As 1960 came to a close, the Communist Pathet Lao, backed by the Soviet Union and North Vietnam, was threatening to seize this small landlocked kingdom bordering China, Vietnam, Burma, Thailand, and Cambodia. Once again, a dilemma. Assuredly, Eisenhower did not want Laos to fall. If it fell, he believed, the one domino could knock down others throughout Southeast Asia. Assuredly also, Eisenhower knew the perils of unilateral U.S. intervention; and he could not persuade the British and French to join us. Accordingly, as in the previous parallel crises in Indochina in 1954 and the Formosa Straits in 1955 and 1958, he said conflicting things. Gordon Gray vividly recalls Eisenhower's vehement insistence that landlocked Laos would be the last place where he'd want to commit U.S. troops. Former Joint Chiefs chairman General Lyman Lemnitzer recalls that though studies were made, no form of decisive action was ever found. Defense Secretary Gates, Deputy Secretary Douglas and Assistant Secretary Irwin concur. Democratic historians have pointed to what Eisenhower told his advisers on December 31, 1960 (and later reportedly told the President-elect), that perhaps the time might come when the United States would have to go into Laos "with our allies or without them"—clear proof, they say, that Eisenhower, like Kennedy and Johnson, might have got us bogged down in Southeast Asia all alone. Perhaps. But three considerations remain:

1. Ike never did.

2. He left office with the agonizing question unresolved, even in his own mind. Indeed, in reading the presidential files on Laos, one senses most the familiar walk down that narrow middle line—the line of ambiguity, between capitulation and intervention—that had long been a central characteristic of the Eisenhower performance.

3. As Eisenhower looked at Laos, he perforce looked also at Kennedy. And he therefore tended to tilt tough, not only in the 1960–61 meetings but also in *Waging Peace;* sensing in the men of the New Frontier, on the evidence of the campaign and their writings, (a) inexperience, (b) a tendency to tilt soft.

To Eisenhower, the cold war he had inherited on January 20, 1953, was still a stark fact. When he turned over the presidency to John Kennedy on that bitterly-cold, snowy, brilliant Washington January noon, he was turning it over at a moment when—it was suggested at a twilight NSC meeting—the Soviet Union might decide to launch a nuclear attack. "I share your concern," Eisenhower told the Council. But, he went on, he'd been unable to get the new administration to understand the danger.

He never did trust their appreciation of the threat we faced, or their capacity to cope with it. After he had left Washington, on the Saturday morning when I first journeyed to Gettysburg to confer with him about the memoirs, John and my wife and I drove the President from his office back to the farm. That afternoon he would helicopter over to Camp David, at Kennedy's request, to discuss the disaster at the Bay of Pigs. As we let him out of the car, he leaned in the window and told us with a chuckle of a piece of advice he had just recieved in a wire from a woman in Iowa: "You go down there and tell that little boy to be careful. In fact, you'd better go and take over yourself."

EPILOGUE

DAYS REMEMBERED

I f the trumpet give an uncertain sound," James Reston quoted First Corinthians during the anxious days after *Sputnik*, "who shall prepare himself for battle?" Each of us listens for a presidential peal to respond to. But the trueness of intonation resides not only in the soloist but also in the surrounding orchestration.

"He spoke in trumpets," a John Kennedy eulogist declared, and a restless nation was roused by his summons to "pay any price, bear any burden, meet any hardship, support any friend, oppose any foe to assure the survival and success of liberty." Yet against the later orchestration of Vietnam—not to mention the gradual public realization of what the necessarily secret reconnaissance photographs had long since made clear, that the alleged "missile gap" never existed—the clarion of open-ended international activism seems less compelling. So does the clarion of open-ended domestic activism when heard against the flawed background music, including inflation in crescendo, of the wartime-launched Great Society.

Those who began by making fun of General Eisenhower, announcing a new generation, heralding an advent, calling on American youth to flex its muscles in limited wars and new domestic frontiers, ended by destroying a whole decade, in a nasty, wasteful, unwinnable conflict, the students in revolt, crazed by drugs and riots, their long hair flying, and singing a lonely, wistful lyric, "Let the Sunshine In."

317

Richard Nixon in 1960 had demanded cold-war victory. Some of us also leaped to his instrument's call, we, too, failing to detect the falseness of its timbre—a falseness glaringly clear against the orchestration of Watergate.

To James Reston, however, and to received opinion for years after the 1960 defeat, the obviously uncertain trumpet was that of befuddled old Eisenhower—a man who could manage only a three-fourths-hearted "muted blat" (the Washington *Post*'s phrase) for post-*Sputnik* action; a derided exhumer of negative and antiquated causes—sound money and a balanced budget; a man constrained by his perception of the limits to U.S. power. But against these cacophonies of his success, the Eisenhower trumpet sounds across the years with a newly understood certainty, a call clear, rich, and simple, like the final "Dona Nobis Pacem" of the B Minor Mass.

Future events will recolor our perception of the Eisenhower sound. Eisenhower himself recognized this fact: "If the South had won the Civil War," he once remarked in a sentence with a surprise ending, "think what would have happened to our opinion of President George Washington." Inevitably we view the past from the present's perspective.

Our opinion of Washington, if the South had won, *would* have changed. And yet, as Eisenhower also knew, it wouldn't. Because in a president, any president, there is a legacy beyond the power of events to modify—the legacy not of what he *did*, but of what he himself *was*. And this is the most notable bequest that Dwight Eisenhower—and indeed George Washington—has left us.

Eisenhower was not a man without faults. And he was not a man without hidden recesses. Jim Hagerty, for example, recalls going to the President's upstairs painting room more than once and finding Ike sitting by himself, staring at his untouched easel, absorbed in reflection. His landscapes are often remarkable in capturing a feeling of loneliness. And Jackie Cochran, who after Eisenhower's presidency invited him to make his winter office at her Cochran-Odlum Ranch in Indio, California, hard by his Palm Desert home, recalls Eisenhower in his small office-cottage of a Sunday, all alone, not reading, not working. "He came here year after year," Miss Cochran mused, "and I frankly never understood him."

Nonetheless some principal features do form a pattern. First, he was a man of extraordinary personal force—force that takes many forms: the flashing eyes, the speed of intellect, the surge of adrenaline in anger, the excoriation of New Frontiersmen, the energy with which he slapped a bridge card onto the table, the tigerlike pacing of the office in his seventy-fourth year ("I've got to get outside or I'll just die"), the electricity of his presence ("you knew he was in the room even before you saw him"), the ebullient enthusiasm for all things worthy and of good report, the unquenchable eagerness to break down the barriers—of trade, of ideas, of old habit—dividing people, the furiousness with tired Old Guard grumblers against modern Republicanism, the quickness of his affection for the young with stars in their eyes who sailed balloons for him in 1952, the decisiveness—whether in Little Rock or Lebanon—that prompted his son John's observation that his father came from the Abilene of Wild Bill Hickok, who shot first and asked questions later; above all, the forceful tenacity with which he held to simple commonsense convictions—convictions that led him to seek peace in 1953 as in 1961, to stress the peril of a distended military complex at the end as at the beginning, and to make plain to his countrymen, whatever their political persuasions, that where he had made mistakes, they were mistakes of the head, not of the heart.

Eisenhower was a man of force. He liked to get up in the morning. He was also a man of discipline, which reined in that force. To George Washington, Eisenhower's supreme hero among American presidents, as to Robert E. Lee, Eisenhower's supreme hero among American military men, discipline was the soul of an army. To Eisenhower, it was also the soul of public service. Specifically, it was the means of constraining and subduing and directing the power of individual personality to the purposes of a hierarchy of organizations and causes greater than oneself, from Army to party to administration to nation to international alliance to the family of man, to each of which he had a loyalty, in an ascending order. Nothing more explicitly describes this process than Gerard Manley Hopkins' magnificent poem "The Windhover," a poem that, for all its religious sublimity, speaks of the glory of the reining in of animal excellence and force to the service of a transcendent purpose:

> *Brute beauty and valor and act, oh, air, pride, plume here*
> *Buckle! And the fire that breaks from thee then, a billion*
> *Times told lovelier, more dangerous, O my chevalier! ...*

Eisenhower was a man of force, discipline, and loyalty. And to think of him in this formula is, I believe, to understand many things about him.

It is to understand, first, his agreement with General Marshall on the cardinal attribute of a successful officer: selflessness; and his most often repeated maxim: take your job seriously, never yourself.

It is to understand Eisenhower's unwavering self-subordination to men he personally disliked, like Harry Truman, whose defense budget he publicly upheld despite his own powerful reservations, on the eve of the Korean War; like Lyndon Johnson, whom Ike trusted about 50 percent but whom he backed to the hilt once American troops entered Vietnam; like Barry Goldwater, whom Ike considered a sporadic personal critic ("dime-store New Deal," "moderation in the pursuit of justice is no virtue") and an intellectual lightweight, but on whom, as the 1964 nominee of his party, he bestowed public praise; and like scorned John Kennedy, to whom, as constitutional Commander in Chief, Eisenhower personally pledged his backing on all national security policies.

To think of this formula is to understand the personal struggle Ike went through—a struggle over conflicting loyalties, to nonpolitical and political forms of service—before he accepted the Republican nomination; and his voicing of this struggle, similar to George Washington's, in gray noble-Roman words reminiscent of Washington's own.

It is to understand Eisenhower's love of our "sturdy old allies," the British, as well as of the Germans under the ramrod integrity of Adenauer, and, albeit with a few more personal reservations, the French.

It is to understand Eisenhower's willingness to abide by the Allies' refusal to go into Vietnam in 1954 and his anguish over their refusal to help save Laos in 1961, as he was leaving office.

It is to understand his rigid adherence to a constitutional role during the McCarthy uproar—his selection of presidential ground for counterattacking the senator; and it is to understand his behavior after the Supreme Court school desegregation decision—his enforcing it to the hilt within the areas under his constitutional responsibility, including Little Rock, without ever affirming or denying agreement with the decision itself.

To think of this formula is to understand the unthinkableness of Eisenhower as a man on horseback, a law unto himself, a loner imposing on others his self-perceived truths.

It is to understand instead his habit of thinking aloud, of working through problems with a group about him, and frequently of accepting organization decisions that went counter to his own—like the deletion of the Marshall paragraph, the veto of his plan to invite Eden and Mollet to Washington after Suez, the cancellation of his project for an exchange of ten thousand students.

And it is to understand Eisenhower's expectation of similar self-denial by his subordinates, including a readiness to undertake, at arm's length, chores that he, as leader, wished to remain detached from.

To think of this formula is to understand Eisenhower's refusal, despite his liking for the company of the rich, ever to trade his loyalty to the United States of America for a mess of pottage—a refusal he evinced in 1956 when, despite his many friends in the oil business, from Sid Richardson to Charley and Pete Jones, he vetoed the gas bill even when he wanted it enacted, purely because of the venal lobbying that had pushed it through the Congress; a refusal he evinced in 1961 when, as he was leaving office, his good friend and White House staff member, Clare Francis, the distinguished chairman of the Studebaker Corporation, suggested that as ex-President, Eisenhower might agree to accept a new Studebaker and give it his endorsement: Eisenhower wrote back a polite letter, with steel in every line.

It is to understand, despite Eisenhower's lifelong loyalty to the Army, his rage at the "goddamn three-star general" who, having no higher loyalty, had rejoiced at the news that the Navy's Vanguard, in an attempt to launch a space satellite after *Sputnik*, had fizzled on the launch pad.

It is to understand his willingness to tolerate "the tyrannies of the weak" as an unavoidable by-product of the pursuit of "the equality of sovereignty" between the great and small nations of the world.

Above all, to think of this formula is to understand Eisenhower's longing for peace and to understand the kind of peace he longed for. He did not revel in cold war. In 1953, in command of the full panoply of American power and prestige, he had begun his presidency with the ending of the wasting war in Korea—an action that recalls the heroic Othello's magnificent calming words at his first entry on stage, in the midst of a bloody street brawl: "Put up your bright swords, or the dew will rust them." In 1957 after *Sputnik* those who gloried in cold war wanted victory. Eisenhower wanted concilia-tion: "What the world needs today even more than a giant leap into outer space is a giant step toward peace." In the age of ICBMs "what will ... be needed is not just engineers and scientists, but a people who will keep their heads and, in every field, leaders who can meet intricate human problems with wisdom and courage ... not only Einsteins and Steinmetzes, but Washingtons and Emersons."

The cold warriors were wrong. He was right. Their "piecemeal peace," in Hopkins' phrase, was "poor peace." It came from an inferior loyalty, to a nation-state; his came from a higher loyalty, to the whole family of man.

All hierarchies order by means of a power structure, but all hierarchies also order by means of rules, and though it is often disregarded in discussion, it is the rules that are the true power; rules represent the ethical component in man's nature, man's nature which is extended into his organizations, organizations which mirror men's qualities. Even the President of the United States—every President—must know himself at all times subservient to the law. It was the bedrock of Eisenhower's greatness that he did.

In a lawless international jungle with cold-war marauders abroad on every continent, he repaired without apology to the law of tooth and claw, clandestine thrust and covert subversion, with concern for his country and for the survival of freedom in the world. But he always hoped for a better answer, for international comity, for the establishment of some kind of international rule of reason. He would much have preferred an agreement on Open Skies to the unilateral surreptitious unleashing of U-2s. And as an intermediate step toward the distant goal of world order he regularly appealed to the United Nations: in the Quemoy-Matsu crisis of 1954, the Suez crisis of 1956, the Lebanon crisis of 1958, the Congo crisis of 1960.

To describe a man of superb inner force of mind and heart, superb discipline, and transcendent loyalties is to describe a man not only effective in leadership but ethical in character. As Edward McCabe once observed, Eisenhower was "a Godfearing man. The foremost leader on this planet had a just view of his place in the scheme of things." And in these days when it has become fashionable superciliously to dismiss ethical goodness as irrelevant to government, it is salutary to remember that the President Ike admired most, George Washington, thought nothing had greater relevance: "It is substantially true, that virtue or morality is a necessary spring of popular government. . . ." And if the mind of Washington is considered insufficiently complex for our sophisticated age, one can read the same conclusion in Benjamin Franklin ("Wise and good men are, in my opinion, the strength of a state; much more so than riches or arms, which, under the management of ignorance and wickedness, often draw on destruction") and Thomas Jefferson ("The great principles of right and wrong are legible to every reader. To pursue them requires not the aid of many counselors. The whole art of government consists in the art of being honest"). Ike is in good company.

In her love for her husband, Mrs. Eisenhower saw his hand on the staircase. My own visual memory was revived recently by my son. I asked him whether he remembered the President. "Of course," he answered, "I taught him to weave gimp." Though I had forgotten the episode, immediately I recalled how eight-year-old Billy had been inseparable from his camp-learned ability to weave. Watching his interest, Ike became interested himself and demanded to be taught. And that is as good a recollection as possible of the President, blue eyes lively, willing to learn from anyone anything at all that was new, to his very end youthful. "Those whom the gods love," the poet said, "die young."

Looking out across the lush green Gettysburg fields with the hazy blue mountains in the distance, I thought often of the words of that noble aria in Handel's *Judas Maccabaeus*, so evocative of the Eisenhower years: "O Lovely Peace with Plenty Crowned." For a long while it was common to hear complaints about their dullness. The open enjoyment of money and success, the enthronement of plush solidity and comfortable complacency, the blurring of lines between art and commerce, the subterfuges of oligarchic power camouflaging old privileges, the vulgarities of American bourgeois taste inflicting narrow Puritan morality—perhaps. Perfection is never a human attainment. And if the age was more Roman than golden, we must nonetheless thank Eisenhower for his achievements, not blame him for our own faults. Genius is always an attribute not of government, but of individuals. All that any government can, or can be expected to contribute to excellence is an environment which makes it not certain, but possible. Always men will have to do the most important things for themselves. Under Ike, at least, the government did its part. A stable currency, domestic order, and not one American life lost overseas may not be so exciting as economic Russian roulette, mobs in the streets, and the bombardment of war, especially for those at the top. But good governments exist not to amuse the bored, not to provide a macho theater for the leader, but to order things so that thinkers may think, builders may build, youths may dream, children may play, and the old may rest.

The fifties were, in actual fact, a tinderbox decade. If in retrospect they appear times of calm blessed with abundance, the reason again and again was Eisenhower—the fact, as Andrew Goodpaster has said, that many terrible things that could have happened, didn't. Dwight Eisenhower's presidency gave America eight good years—I believe the best in memory. To some, other administrations may seem more enticing. But most ordinary folk who are ruled surely wish their statesmen would take to their hearts and let beat there the traditional wish with which the Chinese are said to bless the newlywed couple, "May you live in uneventful times."

ACKNOWLEDGMENTS

I owe lasting gratitude to many people for the abundance of their kindnesses, capabilities, and help on this book:

To John S. D. Eisenhower, Alfred M. Gruenther, James C. Hagerty, Mrs. C. D. Jackson, Wilton B. Persons, Jr., Mrs. J. A. Reynes, and Bernard M. Shanley for permission to quote excerpts from unpublished documents.

To Andrew J. Goodpaster and Edward A. McCabe for a reading of the manuscript in its entirety and for many valuable suggestions.

To the staffs of the Oral History Research Office of Columbia University and the libraries of the University of California, Berkeley (The Earl Warren Oral History Project), Princeton University (The Papers of John Foster Dulles and the John Foster Dulles Oral History Collection), Yale University, Harvard University, and the State University of New York at Purchase; the staffs of the Library of Congress, the Senate Judiciary Committee, the New York Public Library and the Greenwich Library, all for efficient access to sources; and to John E. Wickman and the staff of the Dwight D. Eisenhower Library in Abilene, Kansas—with particular mention of James Leyerzapf—for skilled and tireless and responsive year-in, year-out service.

To Knox Burger for his high professional excellence as agent from start to finish, and to Oscar Collier of Prentice-Hall for his uncommon sensitivity and insight as the book's editor.

And to Ruth Berger for a superb job of typing draft after draft of the manuscript.

At the heart of the book lies the contribution of a host of men and women who generously revealed information and opinion through interviews—frequently multiple interviews, some extending over a period of years—or documents or both: Eva Adams, Sherman Adams, H. Meade Alcorn, Jr., Robert B. Anderson, Phillip E. Areeda, Edward L. Beach, Elmer F. Bennett, Richard Bissell, Herbert Brownell, Jr., Percival Brundage, Arthur F. Burns, W. Howard Chase, Edwin N. Clark, Lucius D. Clay, Jacqueline Cochran, Miles Copeland, Charles D. Cremeans, John Charles Daly, Cartha DeLoach, James H. Douglas, Mamie Doud Eisenhower, Milton S. Eisenhower, Thomas S. Gates, Andrew J. Goodpaster, Gordon Gray, Alfred M. Gruenther, Homer H. Gruenther, James C. Hagerty, Leonard W. Hall, Bryce N. Harlow, Karl Harr, Gabriel Hauge, Stephen Hess, Leo Hoegh, William J. Hopkins, John N. Irwin II, Roy James, George B. Kistiakowsky, Lyman Lemnitzer, Orme Lewis, Henry Cabot Lodge, Edward A. McCabe, Kevin McCann, H. Roemer McPhee, Robert E. Merriam, L. Arthur Minnich, Mary Jane Monroe, Robert Montgomery, Gerald D. Morgan, Hugh Morrow, Floyd Odlum, Theodore W. Parker, Thomas A. Parrott, Bradley H. Patterson, Jr., Maxwell M. Rabb, Carl Raether, Nelson A. Rockefeller, Ted Rogers, William P. Rogers, Kermit Roosevelt, Raymond J. Saulnier, Robert L. Schulz, Herbert Scoville, Jr., Bernard M. Shanley, Gerard C. Smith, Maurice Stans, Thomas E. Stephens, Ted Stevens, Walter Tkach, Charls Walker, Abbott Washburn, Lawrence D. Weiler, Ann C. Whitman, and those who remain anonymous.

My "thanks to all at once and to each one."

And special thanks, finally, to my two older sons, William Bragg Ewald III and Charles Ross Ewald, who gave many hours and many improvements to successive drafts of the manuscript; to my youngest son, Thomas Hart Benton Ewald, who asked many demanding questions; and above all to my wife, Mary, who more than anyone else from the outset has shared in the shaping of this book.

William Bragg Ewald, Jr.
Greenwich, Connecticut
January 1, 1981

INDEX

INDEX

INDEX

INDEX

INDEX

INDEX

INDEX

INDEX

Thomas, Charles, 162
Thornton, Dan, 176
Thye, Edward, 141
Tito, (Josip Broz), 209
Tkach, Walter, 326
Tohamy, Hassan el, 194
Tower, John, 254
Trade, international, 129-30
Trice, Mark, 134
Trieste, 209
True Believer, The (Hoffer), 169
Trujillo, Rafael Leonidas, 272, 273
Truman, Harry S, 21-24, 31-39, 58,
    98, 139, 153, 154, 169, 177, 185,
    192, 203, 205, 224, 228, 235,
    240, 244, 269, 271, 284, 286,
    292, 302, 308, 313, 320
Truman-Acheson foreign policy, 230
Tudeh Party (Iran), 268
Twining, Nathan, 246, 269

United Nations, 172, 322

Vanderbilt, Arthur T., 80
Vaughan, Sam, 239
Vietminh, 106
Vinson, Carl, 247
Vinson, Fred, 79, 192
Voorhis, Jerry, 308

Waging Peace (Eisenhower), 31, 37, 177,
    202, 203, 205, 211, 239, 278,
    287, 316
Walker, Charls, 326
Wallace, Henry, 177
Wallace, Walter, 297
Wallis, W. Allen, 166
War, Peace and Change (Dulles), 212
Warren, Earl, 13, 77-86 *passim*, 179
Washburn, Abbott, 326

Washington, George, 137, 139, 175,
    318, 319, 320, 322
Watergate, 13, 313
Watergate hearings, 140
Watkins, Arthur, 141, 292
Weaver, Helen, 147
Weeks, Sinclair, 66, 69, 87
Weiler, Lawrence D., 326
Weinberg, Sidney, 261
Welch, Joseph N., 134, 135, 141
Weldon, Felix de, 171
Welker, Herman, 66, 134
Wherry, Kenneth, 23
White, E.B., 22
White, Theodore, 87, 167, 168, 306
White, Thomas, 246, 248
White House and Staff, 1-5
Whitman, Ann C., 6, 14, 88, 89, 93,
    94, 102, 147, 169, 176, 233, 237,
    238, 239, 240, 258, 259, 261,
    262, 272, 311, 312, 313, 326
Whitney, Jock, 41, 45, 231, 257, 260
Wickman, John E., 325
Willis, Charles F., 124, 135
Wills, Gary, 16
Wilson, Charles, 121, 133, 163, 192,
    198, 230-31, 234, 244
Wilson, Edmund, 178
Wisner, Frank, 266
Wolkinson, Herman, 139
Woodruff, Bob, 39, 315
Woods, Rose Mary, 264, 313
World Council of Churches, 1954
    Conference, 149

Yalta, 26
Young, Philip, 166
Younger, Cole, 39-40

Zahedi, Fazlollah, 268-69
Zwicker, Ralph, 126, 127